Palgrave Studies in Fashion and the Body

Series Editors
Jane Tynan
Department of Art and Culture, History and Antiquity
Faculty of Humanities
Vrije Universiteit Amsterdam
Amsterdam, The Netherlands

Suzannah Biernoff
Department of History of Art
Birkbeck, University of London
London, UK

Palgrave Studies in Fashion and the Body publishes research that offers a fresh perspective on the contemporary and historical significance of fashion as a bodily practice and cultural industry. A vibrant and growing field, fashion studies touches on disciplines such as art, film, history, design, sociology, literature, politics, geography and anthropology. The series explores modes of representation that fashion has taken historically, but also considers the cultural contexts for new directions, at a time when the fashioned body is increasingly implicated in the negotiation of individual and collective identities. By following new circuits of production and consumption the series highlights the range of social and political forces shaping fashion practices today. Looking to recent developments in new materialisms, medical humanities, disability studies, the posthuman, intermediality, decolonial and pluriversal perspectives, books in the series consider fashion's role in anticipating new cultural transformations.

Roberto Filippello • Ilya Parkins
Editors

Fashion and Feeling

The Affective Politics of Dress

Editors
Roberto Filippello
Community, Culture and
Global Studies
University of British Columbia
Okanagan
Kelowna, BC, Canada

Ilya Parkins
Community, Culture and
Global Studies
University of British Columbia
Okanagan
Kelowna, BC, Canada

Palgrave Studies in Fashion and the Body
ISBN 978-3-031-19099-5   ISBN 978-3-031-19100-8   (eBook)
https://doi.org/10.1007/978-3-031-19100-8

© The Editor(s) (if applicable) and The Author(s), under exclusive licence to Springer Nature Switzerland AG 2023
This work is subject to copyright. All rights are solely and exclusively licensed by the Publisher, whether the whole or part of the material is concerned, specifically the rights of translation, reprinting, reuse of illustrations, recitation, broadcasting, reproduction on microfilms or in any other physical way, and transmission or information storage and retrieval, electronic adaptation, computer software, or by similar or dissimilar methodology now known or hereafter developed.
The use of general descriptive names, registered names, trademarks, service marks, etc. in this publication does not imply, even in the absence of a specific statement, that such names are exempt from the relevant protective laws and regulations and therefore free for general use.
The publisher, the authors, and the editors are safe to assume that the advice and information in this book are believed to be true and accurate at the date of publication. Neither the publisher nor the authors or the editors give a warranty, expressed or implied, with respect to the material contained herein or for any errors or omissions that may have been made. The publisher remains neutral with regard to jurisdictional claims in published maps and institutional affiliations.

Cover illustration: CactuSoup/Getty Images

This Palgrave Macmillan imprint is published by the registered company Springer Nature Switzerland AG.
The registered company address is: Gewerbestrasse 11, 6330 Cham, Switzerland

Contents

1 **Introduction** 1
Roberto Filippello and Ilya Parkins

Part I Feeling Wardrobe Histories 25

2 **Closet Feelings** 27
Christina H. Moon

3 **Militarized Comfort: How to Feel Naked While Wearing Clothes** 41
Sunny Xiang

4 **Costume Design and Emotional Communication in 1940s British Cinema** 63
Bethan Bide

5 **Can Fashion Feel?** 83
Thuy Linh Nguyen Tu and Jessamyn Hatcher

v

Part II Reparative Fashion — 97

6 Designing Clothes for and from Love: Disability Justice and Fashion Hacking — 99
Ben Barry and Philippa Nesbitt

7 Beading Is Medicine: Beading as Therapeutic and Decolonial Practice — 121
Presley Mills and Justine Woods

8 All that Cloth Can Carry (on a Queer Body) — 137
Timo Rissanen

9 Looking Like a Woman, Feeling Like a Woman, Sensing the Self: Affective and Emotional Dimensions of Dress Therapy — 153
Renate Stauss

Part III Stasis and Transformation in Fashion — 177

10 Dirty Pretty Things: Stains, Ambivalence and the Traces of Feeling — 179
Ellen Sampson

11 Making Peace Sensational: Design for the Nobel Prizes — 195
Elizabeth M. Sheehan

12 Glamour Magick, Affective Witchcraft, and Occult Fashion-abilities — 211
Otto Von Busch

13 Fashion Studies at a Turning Point — 229
Lucia Ruggerone

Part IV Affective Embodiment in Media   249

14 Melancholy Fashion Moods in Aotearoa New Zealand   251
    Harriette Richards

15 On Boredom and Contemporary Fashion Photography   271
    Eugenie Shinkle

16 Hair Dressing: Fetish, School Uniforms and *Shōjo* in
    Cocoon, Entwined   285
    Masafumi Monden

17 "What's Getting Us Through": *Grazia* UK as Affective
    Intimate Public During the Coronavirus Pandemic   305
    Rosie Findlay

18 Afterword   327
    Elspeth H. Brown

Index   333

Notes on Contributors

Ben Barry is a queer, disabled fashion educator, designer and researcher. As Dean of Fashion at Parsons School of Design, he is devoted to intervening into the fashion system to shift power and design a future where worldviews and bodies that are currently stigmatized are instead valued and desired. Ben's teaching and research centres on the intersectional fashion experiences of disabled, fat, trans and queer people and engages them in the design of clothing, fashion media and fashion systems. He holds a PhD from Cambridge University.

Bethan Bide is Lecturer in Design and Cultural Theory at the University of Leeds. Her research focuses on the use of material fashion objects and considers the role of fashion in museums; the development of fashion cities; and the relationship between materiality, memory and fashion as biography. In 2017 Bethan received her PhD, entitled 'Austerity Fashion 1945–1951: Rebuilding London Fashion Cultures After the Second World War', from Royal Holloway, University of London. Prior to this, Bethan worked as a researcher and producer of comedy programmes for BBC Radio 4.

Elspeth H. Brown is Professor of History and Associate VP Research at the University of Toronto, Mississauga, where her research concerns modern queer and trans history, the history and theory of photography, the history of US capitalism and queer archives. She is the author of *Work! A Queer History of Modeling* (2019) and co-editor of 'Queering Photography', a special issue of *Photography and Culture* (2014) and *Feeling Photography*

(2014), among other publications. She is the Director of the Critical Digital Humanities Initiative and the Digital Humanities Network, U of T. She is the Director of the LGBTQ Oral History Digital Collaboratory, an SSHRC-funded multi-year public humanities collaboration with community and university partners. From 2014 to 2021, she served on the Board of The ArQuives: Canada's LGBQT2+ Archive, most recently as co-president.

Roberto Filippello is a Killam Postdoctoral Fellow at the University of British Columbia. His work, situated at the intersection of critical fashion studies, queer studies and visual culture, looks at how LGBTQ+ people across various historical and geopolitical contexts have been using fashion to voice their political consciousness and forge affective communities. His scholarly writing has been published in many journals, including *Criticism*, *Third Text*, *Fashion Theory* and *Australian Feminist Studies*.

Rosie Findlay is Lecturer in Media Studies at City University of London. Her research focuses on fashion media and communication and the ways in which material and experiential interface in fashion and dress. She had published studies on fashion blogging, Instagram influencers, niche magazines and digital branding in journals such as *Feminist Theory*; *Australian Feminist Studies*; *Communication, Culture and Critique*; *Cultural Studies Review* and *Fashion Theory*. Rosie is author of *Personal Style Blogs: Appearances That Fascinate* (2017), co-editor of *Insights on Fashion Journalism* (2022) and Open Space and Reviews Editor of *International Journal of Fashion Studies*.

Jessamyn Hatcher teaches at New York University. Her work has appeared in publications including *Women's Studies Quarterly* and *The New Yorker*.

Presley Mills is an illustrator, designer and creative scholar. She has always been a chaotic maker taking on many different forms of art and craft. She inherited this creative curiosity from her grandma who never let something go to waste without trying to transform it. Her grandma taught her to sew and do embroidery as a child, and Presley has been incorporating those into her work ever since. Presley learnt how to properly bead from Justine at the first Beading Circle. Beading has been a way for her to reclaim her Indigenous identity and build community. Presley is a descendant of the Lizotte and Tourangeau families who were located in Fort Vermillion. Presley was born and raised in Calgary, Alberta, and is a member of the Métis Nation of Alberta.

Masafumi Monden is Lecturer in Japanese Studies at the University of Sydney. He teaches and writes on modern Japanese cultural history, fashion, art and popular culture, gender studies, Japanese language and international relations focusing on Australia's ties with Asia. He is working on two book-length projects: a co-authored book on Japanese *shōjo* culture and its cross-cultural influences, and a sole-authored book project that looks at the cultural history of male modelling in Japan as a means to engage with visual and consumer culture, the interlinked history of race, ageing, technology, fashion and consumption, and the dissemination of bodily aesthetics and gender ideals within the modern Japanese imagination. His new project deals with the cultural history of Australia and Japan.

Christina H. Moon is an anthropologist and an associate professor at Parsons the New School of Design in New York. She wrote *Labor and Creativity in New York's Global Fashion Industry* (2020) and co-edited *Fashion and Beauty in the Time of Asia* (2019), with publications in *Vestoj* (2021) and *Critique* (2022). She is a fellow of the India China Institute, Fashion Praxis Working Group at Parsons, and Graduate Institute for Design, Ethnography & Social Thought at The New School.

Philippa Nesbitt is a PhD student in Communication and Culture at Toronto Metropolitan University. Her research explores the representations and experiences of multiply-marginalized people within the contemporary global fashion industry and evaluates fashion as a tool for social change. She approaches her work with a passion for social justice, advocacy and representation, engaging in the advancement of intersectional disability justice while recognizing her own embodiment limits her ability to understand the lived experiences of others.

Ilya Parkins is Associate Professor of Gender and Women's Studies at the University of British Columbia, Okanagan campus. She is the author of *Poiret, Schiaparelli and Dior: Fashion, Femininity and Modernity* (2012) and co-editor of *Cultures of Femininity in Modern Fashion* (2011) and *Fashion: New Feminist Essays* (2020) and fashion-themed special issues of *Journal of Modern Periodical Studies* and *Australian Feminist Studies*. Her work on fashion and gender/sexuality has been published in a range of journals including *Time and Society, Fashion Theory, French Cultural Studies* and *Feminist Review*.

Harriette Richards is Lecturer in Fashion Enterprise in the School of Fashion and Textiles at RMIT University, Melbourne. Previously, she was a research associate in the School of Culture and Communication at the University of Melbourne working on the ARC Future Fellowship project 'Modernism, Cosmopolitanism and Consumer Culture' (2018–2022) with Professor Natalya Lusty. She is co-founder of the Critical Fashion Studies research group and is working on projects investigating modern slavery and transparency in the Australian fashion industry and ethical and sustainable fashion innovation. Her work has been published in a range of journals including, most recently, *Australian Feminist Studies, Cultural Studies and Gender, Work & Organization* and in the edited collection *Rethinking Fashion Globalization* (2021). In 2021, she co-edited, with Natalya Lusty and Rimi Khan, a special issue on 'Fashion Futures' for *Continuum: Journal of Media and Cultural Studies.*

Timo Rissanen is an artist and a researcher with work ranging from fashion and sustainability to queer materialities and extinction. He has co-authored two books on fashion and sustainability. He is Associate Professor of Fashion and Textiles in the School of Design, Faculty of Design, Architecture and Building at the University of Technology Sydney.

Lucia Ruggerone teaches sociology in the School of Social Studies at Robert Gordon University, Aberdeen, UK, and is a research fellow at Modacult at the Universita Cattolica, Milan, Italy. She has a background in phenomenological sociology and has published in this area as well as in studies of material culture, fashion and the body. She is working on the application of affect theories to fashion studies.

Ellen Sampson is an artist and material culture researcher who uses film, photography, writing and performance to explore the sensory and emotional entanglements between bodies and garments, both in museums and archives and in everyday life. She is a senior research fellow at Northumbria University School of Design and was previously a fellow at the Metropolitan Museum of Art. Her book *Worn: Footwear, Attachment and the Affects of Wear* was published in 2020.

Elizabeth M. Sheehan is Associate Professor of English at Ohio State University. She is the author of *Modernism à la Mode: Fashion and the Ends of Literature* (2018) and the co-editor of *Cultures of Femininity in Modern Fashion* (2011). Her projects include an edited collection of essays on fashion and literature for Cambridge University Press and a monograph on the fabrication of peace in the mid-twentieth century.

Eugenie Shinkle is a photographer and writer based in London, UK. She is co-editor of the online photobook platform C4 Journal and is Reader in Photography at the University of Westminster.

Renate Stauss is Assistant Professor of Fashion Studies at The American University of Paris in the Department of Communication, Media and Culture. As Lecturer in Fashion Theory and Cultural and Critical Studies, she has been working at several universities in London and Berlin since 2003: Central Saint Martins, Goldsmiths College and the Berlin University of the Arts, where she remains an associate lecturer. She was part of the faculty at the Royal College of Art in London in the Department of Critical Studies for ten years. Renate completed her PhD on *Dress as Therapy: Working with Dress on the Self in Therapeutic Settings* at the University of the Arts London. The focus of her teaching and scholarship lies on the sociology and politics of fashion and dress. Renate has published in the areas of fashion studies, fashion theory and pedagogy. Her research interests include fashion and protest, the perception and potential of fashion, the emergence of fashion theory and fashion education—how we learn and teach fashion. She is the co-founder of The Multilogues on Fashion Education, and *Fashion Is a Great Teacher*—The fashion education podcast and platform.

Thuy Linh Nguyen Tu is Professor of Social and Cultural Analysis at NYU. She is the author, most recently, of *Experiments in Skin: Race and Beauty in the Shadows of Vietnam* (2021), winner of the PROSE Hawkins Prize.

Otto von Busch is Associate Professor of Integrated Design at Parsons School of Design. In his research he explores how the powers of fashion can be bent to achieve a positive personal and social condition with which the Everyperson is free to grow to their full potential. He has for the last twenty years examined fashion beyond consumerism, aesthetic decrees and arbitrary authority and worked towards establishing fashion practice as a shared capability, biosocial energy, a process of mutual flirting and a play of embodied attentions. His latest publications include *The Psychopolitics of Fashion: Conflict and Courage Under the Current State of Fashion* (2020), *The Dharma of Fashion: A Buddhist Approach to Our Life with Clothes* (2020), *Silhouettes of the Soul: Meditations on Fashion, Religion and Subjectivity* (2022, co-edited with Jeanine Viau) and *Making Trouble: Design and Material Activism* (2022).

Justine Woods is a garment artist, creative scholar, educator and PhD student at Toronto Metropolitan University (formally Ryerson University). She first learned how to sew at the age of six from her mother Lori-Lee Woods and instantly fell in love with anything 'stitching-related'. As a teenager, Justine taught herself how to bead as a creative way to connect deeper with her Indigeneity. Justine is grateful to various community members and kin who she has had the pleasure to learn from over the years and who have informed her skillset as a beadworker today. Justine identifies as an Aabitaawikwe and is a descendant of the St Onge and Berger-Beaudoin families. Her Ancestors come from Drummond Island (in what is now known as Michigan) and were relocated, along with their community, to Penetanguishene, Ontario, in 1828. She was born and raised in Tiny, Ontario, and is a member of the Georgian Bay Métis Community.

Sunny Xiang is Associate Professor of English and Affiliate Professor of Ethnicity, Race and Migration at Yale University. She is a scholar and teacher of transpacific studies with a special interest in cultural genealogies of militarism and imperialism. Her first book, *Tonal Intelligence: The Aesthetics of Asian Inscrutability During the Long Cold War*, was published in 2020. Her research examines US militarization in Asia and the Pacific in relation to atomic-age fashions.

List of Figures

Fig. 4.1	*Hue and Cry* scene still showing Rhona (far right) in bus queue, 1947. Studiocanal Films Ltd/Ronald Grant/Mary Evans	70
Fig. 4.2	Passport to Pimlico, 1949. Studiocanal Films Ltd/Ronald Grant/Mary Evans	74
Fig. 6.1	CX's Instagram post featuring an image of their process in the workshops with poetry and captions reflecting on their relationship to clothing	106
Fig. 6.2	CX's Instagram post showing fabric for the hacking workshop featuring a reflection on their inspiration and experience	107
Fig. 6.3	CX posing next to their wheelchair in the garment they created during the workshop	108
Fig. 7.1	*Jawira* fringe earrings beaded by Paxsi (size 10 Czech seed beads) (Paxsi, who made these earrings, shared: "I first created the jawira earrings in spring 2020 in reflection of how light flows and moves. One morning, I awoke to see a crack of light dancing on my lace curtain; the window was slightly open and the curtain was gently swaying with the warm breeze. This design—which I have named jawira after the Aymara word for river—have come to mean many things to me over the years. Everyone seems to perceive them in a different way, which is something I love about them. To me, they represent the relationship between water and light as we experience them in our realm of spacetime, akapacha, as well as the duality of alaxpacha (the realm/spacetime above us) and ukhupacha (the realm/spacetime below us) and how they are reflected in each other")	128
Fig. 7.2	Katie's beaded earring collection	129

Fig. 8.1	Cross-stitch of Munchique wood-wren *(Henicorhina negreti)* by the author, *Precarious Birds*, 2019. (Courtesy of the author)	143
Fig. 8.2	Quilts from the *NAMES Project* on display in Washington DC, USA. National Institutes of Health, public domain	145
Fig. 8.3	*Rest in Porn*, triptych of cross-stitched portraits by the author, 2018–2020. (Courtesy of the author)	148
Fig. 10.1	*A Stain and a dress*, digital photograph, Ellen Sampson (2022)	180
Fig. 10.2	*A Stain on a dress*, digital photograph, Ellen Sampson (2022)	182
Fig. 10.3	*A Stained dress*, digital photograph, Ellen Sampson (2022)	185
Fig. 10.4	*A Stained dress*, digital photograph, Ellen Sampson (2022)	188
Fig. 10.5	*Stain*, digital photograph, Ellen Sampson (2022)	192
Fig. 12.1	Gabriela Herstik (2022), photo by Alexandra Herstik	219
Fig. 12.2	Gabriela Herstik (2020), photo by Alexandra Herstik	223
Fig. 14.1	*Jimmy D, Unfinished Sympathy Dress, 'Portrait of a Reputation' SS19*	260
Fig. 14.2	*Lela Jacobs, A-E-I-O-U-Y 2019/2020*	262

CHAPTER 1

Introduction

Roberto Filippello and Ilya Parkins

This book comes out of our long-held interest in the emotional and relational potential of fashion. Over the past few years we have each been exploring how clothes can *move* us in the two-fold sense of moving us emotionally and moving us to act collectively in the social realm. Our interest in affect, feeling, and emotion has been guided by our investment in the imagining of alternative forms of life, in the intellectual and creative practices of worldmaking, in the complexities and ambivalences of being in community, as well as in our fraught relationships with normativity and social belonging within academia and the world at large. In other words, our fascination with feeling is a queer one. After all, as Lauren Berlant observed, "feminists and queers are especially interested in affect because desire is unruly and induces intensities of attachment outside of calculation, and if this is what makes us powerful and threatening and fun then affect theory should be valued as a resource" (2017: 14). It is our shared queer-feminist attunement to feeling that provided the groundwork for this book and nurtured our collaboration.

R. Filippello (✉) • I. Parkins
Community, Culture and Global Studies, University of British Columbia, Okanagan, Kelowna, BC, Canada
e-mail: roberto.filippello@ubc.ca; ilya.parkins@ubc.ca

© The Author(s), under exclusive license to Springer Nature Switzerland AG 2023
R. Filippello, I. Parkins (eds.), *Fashion and Feeling*, Palgrave Studies in Fashion and the Body,
https://doi.org/10.1007/978-3-031-19100-8_1

In response to much of the influential scholarly literature on fashion, which has long praised fashion's ability to give expression and freedom to the self (with the consequence that the facile rhetorics of individualistic self-amelioration and freedom on which neoliberal subjectivity rests are reinforced), we wanted to question ocularcentric epistemologies and offer nuanced reflections on the embodied reparative opportunities offered by clothing. Can fashion, understood and "read" through affect, be used to address traumas, grief, loss, and even catastrophes such as ecological collapse and settler colonialism? These are some of the questions that might emerge from conceptualizing fashion in affective and communal terms. *Fashion and Feeling: The Affective Politics of Dress* tackles how fashion, dress, and clothing can be both individually and collectively operationalized through their affectivity. We believe that a critical analysis grounded in affect permits us to investigate not only how bodily sensations can come to matter, but also how specific affects can be revealing of a particular "structure of feeling" (Williams 1977)—a concept which describes how a set of social changes in a precise historical situation can manifest itself in the attitudes of a given group of people, formally registering as (shifts in) manners, language, dress, or style—and finally, how we might come to feel a sense of belonging based on our sharedness in the sensitivity expressed in the clothes (or their representations). If clothes can be seen as mediating individual and collective attachments to different experiences, ideas, or ideologies in the social order, then our wardrobes are repertoires of feelings that function as historical sites of publicity and commonality which connect subjects to historical formations.

More specifically, the questions that ended up inspiring this volume are the following: What does fashion look and feel like in an age dominated by amplified anxiety, isolation, depression, and precarity? How are feelings woven into clothing and mobilized through fashion practices in ways that might sustain living with a sense of ongoing crisis? Can fashion tie us to others in our collective "dramas of adjustment" (Berlant 2011, 3)? And does it have the potential to help us imagine new lifeworlds which might be reinvigorating? In other words, how is fashion engaging with the "bad," the "good," and the ambivalent feelings associated with our personal and collective histories, with our troubled political present, and with our imagined future? In a prolonged state of emergency in which securitization processes and regimes of austerity threaten to foreclose our prospects of self- and collective actualization, new forms of solidarity and care are emerging to nurture shared attachments to modes of living that are yet to be materialized. We wonder whether, amidst such contrasting forces, dress might offer a somatic experience that simultaneously grounds our sense of self and connects us to others. Enlivened by affect theorist Jonathan Flatley's statement (inspired by Walter Benjamin) that "insofar as fashion initiates us into a melancholic historical practice and a nonhomogenous experience of temporality, it can potentially provide us with a kind of revolutionary education" (2008, 75), we want to invest fashion with the hope and capacity to unfold new aesthetic horizons and political possibilities while inducing reflection on the historical and present entanglements of fashion and the feeling body. This volume will explore the complex nexus of fashion and the feeling body from a variety of critical perspectives across fashion studies, anthropology, sociology, design practice, and media studies.

In this introduction, as a way to delineate the larger contexts from which fashion theorists have been drawing for their reflection on feeling, and to introduce key concepts for readers who might be unfamiliar with affect studies, we are going to provide an essential, if not exhaustive, overview of various theoretical understandings of affect that have emerged in the last two decades across different scholarly fields; we will then lay out the existing literature on affect and feeling within fashion studies; and finally, we will outline the structure and content of the book.

On Terminology: "Affect," "Feeling," "Emotion"

Communication scholar Eric Shouse has outlined a persuasive tripartite model wherein "feeling" is understood as a personal or biographical state, "emotion" as a social state, and "affect" as a pre-subjective state (2005). However, while we recognize the descriptive functionality of distinguishing between the terms affect, feeling, and emotion, we do not rigidly subscribe to it. Indeed, this very distinction is highly contentious in cultural studies.[1] Feminist theorist Elspeth Probyn, for instance, writes that "a basic distinction is that emotion refers to cultural and social expression, whereas affects are of a biological and physiological nature" (2005, 11). Teresa Brennan, instead, writes that "the things that one feels are affects. The things that one feels *with* are feelings" (2004, 23, our emphasis),

---

[1] See Massumi (2002), Hemmings (2005), Gorton (2007), Blackman and Venn (2010), Gregg and Seigworth (2010), Pedwell and Whitehead (2012), Blackman (2012), and Pedwell (2014).

suggesting that affects are inchoate and unnamable sensations which can become feelings once we are able to interpret and express them; "feelings" are then defined as "sensations that have found the right match in words" (5). These are just two examples of how scholars have attempted exhaustive definitions of affect, feeling, and emotion—definitions which, however, have never been unanimously established or generally agreed upon, largely due to the different theoretical backgrounds and research objects of affect studies scholars.

Some theorists have even declared that such distinctions are unhelpful and have argued in favor of more malleable and elastic understandings of these terms. Feminist theorist Sara Ahmed argues that affects are inevitably imbricated in the social realm (2004a, b); therefore, it is analytically reasonable but pragmatically unhelpful to set a distinction between, for instance, affect and emotions, according to which affects would be our pre-conscious bodily states and emotions would be the social categories through which we come to understand them: affects and/or emotions, for Ahmed, are in any case transactional and circulatory. In a different vein, but arriving at a similar conclusion, cultural theorist Sianne Ngai uses the terms affect, feeling, and emotion interchangeably; she writes: "the difference between emotion and affect is still intended to solve the same [...] problem it was coined in psychoanalytic practice to solve: that of distinguishing first-person from third-person feeling, and, by extension, feeling that is contained by an identity from feeling that is not" (2005, 11). Queer theorist Ann Cvetkovich advocates a use of such terms "in a generic sense," but in this strategic non-specificity she prefers the term feeling for it maintains "the ambiguity between feelings as embodied sensations and feelings as psychic or cognitive experiences" (2012, 4).

We share Ahmed's, Ngai's, and Cvetkovich's various frustrations with rigid terminological and conceptual boundaries, and instead of joining in the debate over what differentiates an affect from a feeling, we find it more useful to use the terms, as several cultural critics do, more flexibly. In the title of this book, we have decided to maintain both "feeling" and "affective," with the wish to traverse nominal boundaries and leave interpretive freedom to our authors. "Feeling" is, however, foregrounded in the title inasmuch as it is not only a more relatable and capacious term, but also, in common parlance and understanding, it seems to adequately mediate between the psychic and the social, the individual and the collective. After all, this is how we conceive of fashion: connecting the singular to the plural, the mind and the body, identities to social formations in multiple ways.

Using "feeling" as an umbrella term (in all its meanings: affect, intensity, touch, hapticity, sensation, emotion, vibration, attunement, attachment, or gut reaction), this volume explores the capacity of fashion to represent, challenge, and reconfigure modes of lived, felt, and embodied experience both in the past and in the present. The contributors employ and redeploy the rubrics of feeling, affect, and emotion in whatever way best fits their research objects and individual preferences.

In addressing feeling, the book is particularly attentive to lived material experience, namely the multiple ways in which the different axes of identity come to shape subjects' experiences of fashion and clothing as well as their desires and aspirations. While there might be some basic "affects" that are linked, generally speaking, to corresponding facial responses (e.g., joy as expressed through smile, shame through eyes down, and surprise through eyebrows up), nonetheless emotional expressions are managed in a variety of ways according to factors including sociocultural norms, habits, class, and so on. This clarification is crucial, for the contributors often tap into their own or their collaborators' respective experiences and personal attachments to cultural objects as an entryway into the relationship between fashion and feeling. Moreover, affective registers can be differently performed in accordance with one's own ethnicity, race, class, gender, and sexuality[2]: these facets of subjectivity are vectors for the articulation of particular ways of navigating and expressing emotions coded to historical subjects.[3]

In other words, as the following chapters, which indirectly constitute a critique of universalist and ahistorical views of feeling/affect, will lay bare, feelings are historically and socially situated. Structures of feelings can often reveal shifts in collective perception and engagement with the historical present, but they are always peculiar to a specific geographical and cultural context and are experienced differently based on social histories

---

[2] See José Esteban Muñoz's work on "affective difference" and on the role of affect in "racial performativity," as well as his critique of whiteness as a "flat" "national affect" (2000, 2006, 2020). For a recent, compelling account of the racial and sexual politics of affects that are not widely acknowledged as feelings, see Yao (2021).

[3] Such an understanding of feeling as historically situated and socialized has recently come to inform, whether explicitly or implicitly, much contemporary fashion scholarship: scholarship that looks, for instance, at the ways in which Black communities have understood self-fashioning as a practice of collective resistance in the face of oppression (moore 2018; Ford 2015; Miller 2009) or at the political impetus of sartorial ingenuity within the African diaspora (Square 2020).

and individual positionings (examples could be the last great recession of 2008–2009 which intensified a widely shared sense of precarity and hopelessness—in this case, Cvetkovich would say that feelings are political (2012)—but the impacts on people varied due to a multitude of factors; or the COVID-19 emergency which most heavily impacted economically disadvantaged and/or minoritized subjects, not to mention entire populations who did not have access to medical infrastructures, despite feelings of anxiety and dread being shared on a global scale). The chapters will, thus, emphasize the cultural, social, and political situatedness of "feeling" (the term preferred in this book), as opposed to how affect, in much literature on the subject, has been addressed as eschewing processes of signification and visualization.

In spite of the terminological and epistemic conundrum posed by the overlaps, contradictions, and ambiguities of the terms discussed above, contemporary fashion scholarship has been informed primarily by affect theory—and hence resorts to "affect" more frequently—in its investigation of the feeling body in relation to clothes and fashion. In the next section of this introduction we will outline two key genealogical trajectories of affect theory, leaving it to the reader to imagine how they could be taken further, or how they could be applied to and/or reworked for the study of fashion in localized contexts and histories.

Affect Theories

"Affect" (from the Latin *affectus*: emotion, passion) describes somatic forces and intensities that circulate between body and mind and that are sensorily mobilized in response to stimuli. The first formulation of affect in philosophy is by Baruch Spinoza, for whom affect is an "affection [in other words an impingement upon] the body, and at the same time the idea of the affection" (Massumi 1995, 92). In his *Ethics*, Spinoza writes that affect "is the modification or variation produced in the body (including the mind) by an interaction with another body which increases or diminishes the body's power of activity" (2002 [1677]: 278). In other words, for Spinoza affects are intersubjective alterations of the body-mind that can tell us a great deal about our encounters with other bodies, whether human or non-human.

Often, affects impinge upon our bodies abruptly: for this reason, they are considered pre-cognitive and pre-linguistic, because only afterward are we able to make sense of them. For Gilles Deleuze and Félix Guattari, taking cues from Spinoza, affects are passages from one bodily state to another and reflect the vitalist power of our being in constant change. They define affect as "an ability to affect and be affected. It is a prepersonal intensity corresponding to the passage from one experiential state of the body to another and implying an augmentation or diminution in that body's capacity to act" ([1980] 1987, xvi). Building on Deleuze and Guattari and breaking with post-structuralist discourse theory, Massumi (2002) elaborates a vitalist account of affect: he theorizes affects as nonconscious and dynamic bodily intensities that precede and are independent from language and emotion, and thereby resist structures of meaning. He situates affect, intended as immanent force, within an area of indeterminacy between thought and action. Emerging prior to and outside of cognition, these intensities are "incipient action and expression" (1995, 91): they have the capacity to "move" bodies in multiple ways. A rethinking of the body as both an actual and virtual realm of potential ensues. Thus, affect, for Massumi, offers a way out of the boundaries of signification and representation set by cultural theory.

It was indeed Deleuze's Spinozian articulation of affect as intensity and force, in the form that was primarily circulated by Massumi, that would be widely embraced in cultural studies. In the mid-1990s, in fact, there was a certain consensus in the humanities that post-structuralism had proved unable to fully account for human experience, especially for what concerned phenomena preceding, or exceeding, the level of signification. Thus, theories of affect spread in reaction to the alleged inability of post-structuralism to tackle the role of the body in the formation of human subjectivity due to its insistence on social structures, instead of interpersonal relationships, as formative of the subject (Hemmings 2005, 548). As critical theorist Rei Terada pointed out, post-structuralism felt "truly glacial" in declaring the "death of the subject" and in its disregard for affect and emotion (2003, 4).

This was also a time of war, terrorism and counterterrorism, the rise of nationalism, the ascendance of populism as a political force as well as austerity policies, all of which posed new challenges for cultural theorists, who began to shift their attention toward the affective dimension of collective life as a means to grapple with the bleakness of the present. Sociologist Patricia Ticineto Clough has defined this "affective turn" in the humanities and social sciences as an expression of "a new configuration of bodies, technology, and matter instigating a shift in thought in critical theory brought on by transformations in the economic, political, and cultural realms" (2007, 1–2). Affect theory, thus, developed as an approach to culture, society, politics, and aesthetics that focuses on affects, that is, non-linguistic, or pre-linguistic, resonances manifesting below the threshold of cognition. It situates affect at the center of human experience and sets out to circumvent dichotomous reasoning (mind/body, positive/negative, good/bad, etc.) as well as the epistemological boundaries posed by post-structuralism by accounting for those dynamic movements and intensities that shape our experiences and social relations prior to our conscious understanding.

The employment of affect in academic inquiry contributed to an understanding of the body as constantly dynamic, an ever-evolving relational assemblage of forces operating across both our mind and our *soma*, henceforth disrupting the Cartesian mind/body dualism (an achievement that owes a great deal to feminist theory and to "new materialism"). The renewed interest in the perceptual and non-verbal aspects of collective experience allowed for a rethinking of bodies as "always entangled processes" (Blackman and Venn 2010, 10) which are co-enacted; understood as such, the body is never singular or bounded, but instead it is porous, dynamic, and constantly in-relation. It ensues that if our bodies are not self-contained, and if relationality is the very ontological presupposition of our (co-) existence, affects can be transmitted, and their transmission between and across bodies helps shape moods and atmospheres (Brennan 2004). As Lauren Berlant cogently put it, "since affect is about *affectus*, about being affected and affecting, and therefore about relationality and reciprocity as such, affect theory is inevitably concerned with the analysis of collective atmospheres" (Berlant and Greenwald 2012, 88). In attending to the atmospheres that we navigate in and/or imagine ourselves moving through (Berlant 2015, 274), affect theory is "a training in paying attention" to our relations to social belonging, to the ambiguities of our attachments and projects—in other words, to "the force of the unsaids in collective life" (Berlant et al. 2017, 13–14).

Alongside the Deleuzian lineage of affect studies which has prevailed in the fields of social and political theory,[4] a different, albeit often overlapping, strand of affect theory has developed among queer theorists who have embraced affect as a magnifying lens for tackling issues of intimacy,

---

[4] See the work of Brian Massumi (2002, 2015), Nigel Thrift (2007, 2010), Erin Manning (2006), Jane Bennett (2010), William Connolly (2011), and John Protevi (2009), among others.

emotional life, and inequality, in particular within LGBTQ+ lives.[5] Eve Kosofsky Sedgwick led this queer turn to affect by invoking the textural quality of our embodied experience of the world. In her words: "texture seems like a promising level of attention for shifting the emphasis away from the fixation on epistemology by asking new questions about phenomenology and affect" (2003, 17). A keen scholar of the affective nuances, ambiguities, and contradictions of our relationships with cultural objects, Sedgwick presciently advocated a return to the ontological, intersubjective dimension of our being-together-in-the-world; in Sedgwick's understanding, affect is about pleasure and curiosity, and it is the key for connecting us together as a community of human beings. Vis-à-vis the essentialist (and, one might say, masculinist) emphasis on knowledge and truth that had held sway in continental philosophy until the early 1990s, attending to affect would lead us to unpredictable attachments and ways of living that are at odds with the linear nature of the drives posited by psychoanalysis as well as with the boundaries of social meaning implied by post-structural criticism.

In her theoretical "reparation" through affect, Sedgwick was largely informed by the work of psychologist Silvan Tomkins, who, beginning in the mid-1950s, had systematized an "affect system" common to all human beings. Tomkins had broken down affect into a topography of different *affects*: inspired by the evolutionary perspective in Darwin's work (1872), he identified nine discrete human affects that are linked to corresponding facial expressions. This theory of universal, basic, neurobiological affects maintains that although we all share autonomic bodily responses which affects can activate, nevertheless through our social and cultural education we come to associate these affects with different objects and situations. Thus, in Tomkins' theory, the universal systematicity of affective response coexists with the constructedness and variability of emotional experience.[6]

Sedgwick's reading of Tomkins was aimed at revamping the psychologist's work on affect so as to enable a better understanding of embodiment in queer identity formation and relationality. Sedgwick and Adam Frank explained how Tomkins' understanding of affect "is indifferent to the

---

[5] While these orientations are the most "popular" within cultural studies, they are not the only ones, for other lineages of affect have emerged from fields as varied as neuroaesthetics and the philosophy of science. As affect scholar Billy Holzberg accurately puts it, "it might be more productive to think of the different conceptualizations of affect not so much as incommensurable epistemologies but as simultaneous ontologies" (2018, 20).

[6] For a thorough account of Tomkins' affect theory, see also Frank and Wilson (2020).

means-end difference" (1995b, 7), hence it is resistant to Freudian heterosexist teleologies.[7] For Freud the drives are the main source of human motivation: in his view, the libidinal drives, albeit initially undifferentiated and unfocused (a "polymorphism" which is, however, reduced to the Oedipal poles of mother and father, male and female, thus being *de facto* constrained by an essentialist and heteronormative binarism), ultimately lead to heterosexuality (with homosexuality being a deviation from their trajectory); in Tomkins' view, instead, our primary motivation system is constituted by the affects, and "any affects may have any 'object'" (Sedgwick and Frank 1995a, 503). In other words, affects are "free radical[s]" (Sedgwick 2003, 62): they can attach to limitless objects (hence making our own attachments unpredictable), and it is precisely their being free and versatile that makes them an important source of learning about ourselves and the world around us. According to Sedgwick and Frank, in unsettling the centrality of the drives, or instincts, Tomkins dismantled the Freudian relation of enjoyment and excitement with heterosexuality and its repression, thereby opening a new stimulating line of inquiry that is useful for grappling with the relation of affects and queer embodiment. However, while for Tomkins and Sedgwick there are some basic and more or less universally shared "automatic" affects (an assumption that today would be rather easy to dismantle from a neurodiversity and disability studies-informed vantage point), they concede that people's experiences of such affects may vary on the basis of their socialization processes, habits, historical context, social and cultural settings.

Going beyond Tomkins, within gender and sexuality studies, affect has been investigated as an interface for the somatic, the aesthetic, the social, and the political: affect theorists working from a queer perspective have set out, in different ways, to trace how affective forces can shape, or be shaped by, social and political ones, and to scrutinize the role occupied by specific feelings in culture and society. Berlant's reflection on affect, for instance, was inscribed within her broader project of an autopsy of aesthetic modes of embodied relationality and atmospheres as a strategy for deciphering the cultural and the political in present times.[8] Through literary and film analyses she investigated how affective subjects are created and how subjectivity reflects, and is molded by, "genres" of sociality that are in place in contemporary culture and that organize our lives. Aesthetic genres—

[7] For a fervent critique of Tomkins' affect theory and Sedgwick's interpretation of it, see Leys (2011), Papoulias and Callard (2010), and Hemmings (2005).
[8] On "ordinary affects," see also Stewart (2007).

which are also, always, affective—not only reflect but, most importantly, shape "intimate publics" (2008, 3): by triggering desires and fantasies in their readers/viewers, genres operate in the formation of affective subjects who establish, or feel they are part of, communities. An intimate public is a shared space of mutuality and recognition in which shared attachments to a particular cultural object, idea, or even norm instigate a sense of connection, reciprocity, and belonging. Aesthetic objects (e.g., books, magazines, songs, clothes, etc.) can open up "affect worlds" for us: namely, the possibility that there might be an emotional world out there—a concrete one, made of real people—in which alternative modes of being, fantasies, desires, and qualities are validated.

The relation between felt, lived experiences and public cultures is a crucial concern in queer affect theory. Indeed, Ann Cvetkovich (2003) traced a history of how accounts of trauma can be transformed through creative practices to produce the conditions for the creation of alternative (in the case of her writing, lesbian) cultures. Negative feelings are reconceptualized as occasions for the formation of affective and political collectivities: by destigmatizing the negativity attached to feelings of depression, rage, vulnerability, and "feeling bad," their potential in the formation of publics united by shared affective experiences can unfold (2012). Put differently, "bad feelings" need to be acknowledged, analyzed, and creatively utilized for the purpose of materializing forms of sociality grounded in embodied sensorial experience. By parsing specific feelings, new and multiple cultural histories can be written.

Similarly, queer feelings of disorientation, estrangement, out-of-placeness, and discomfort deriving from "inhabiting norms differently" (Ahmed 2004b, 155) and experienced as a failure in the reproduction of normative life scripts can reveal to us the possibility of new and queer attachments to different objects and bodies. Under this light, the study of feelings or emotions becomes pivotal for grasping histories of injustice and inequality as well as our creative responses to them. In Ahmed's "economic model of emotion" (2004a), emotions do not reside in an object or a person but they exist as a result of their circulation through bodies and/or objects; they are constitutively social and relational. In such an "affective economy," emotions "do things": they involve subjects and objects and align individuals and community through their attachment (119). In other words, emotions are not personal: they do not exist within the subject; rather, they are the result of a relation between bodies: they "stick" to objects whose circulation binds people together.[9]

---

[9] For a critique of Ahmed's model, see Wetherell (2012) and Gorton (2007).

As these queer reflections on affect show, affect theory has moved outside of the box of "I," calling for new discourses on non-identitarian communities and modes of being together, that is, the envisioning of new possible assemblages beyond critical theory's fixation on the subject. The affective turn did not seek out the epistemological dissolution of the subject, but rather it questioned, unsettled, and expanded the discourses on subjectivity. It signaled a shift in focus toward collectivized communities, and its challenge was to foreground how the affective, aesthetic, and political experiences of the "singular" are always embedded in the "plural" and vice versa. This volume aims to achieve something similar: to untether fashion discourse from the strict boundaries of the subject and to shift it toward interpersonal and communal engagements rooted in the affective experience of clothes.

We have laid out two main strands of affect theory—emerging, respectively, from social theory and queer theory—because we believe those are potentially the most useful for thinking about the relationship between fashion and feeling. In our survey we have often mentioned "objects," leaving it to the reader to make possible connections with clothes and find resonances in the system of fashion. It should be noted, however, that fashion scholars who have recently employed the idiom of affect, or feeling, in their work, have primarily done so by resorting to the Deleuzian-Massumian genealogy and, to a lesser degree, (especially among sociologists and ethnographers) to the writings on affect and labor that emerged within autonomist Marxism.[10] The work on affect stemming from gender

[10] A widely used theorization of affect derives from Marxist, autonomist scholars who utilize the concept as a way to rethink the new forms that labor has acquired and the relations it has entailed in post-Fordist societies. With this aim in mind, Michael Hard and Toni Negri have coined "affective labor" (Hardt 1999; Hardt and Negri 2005) as that form of labor "that produces or manipulates affects such as feelings of ease, well-being, satisfaction, excitement or passion" (2005, 108). Based on an expansive and flexible understanding of affect, Hardt describes how in the transition from an industrial to a service economy, affective labor has become a pivotal "sector" in the economy itself, and, inevitably, affect has been "commodified" in the global markets, in the sense that the workings of affect produce "value" and, in so doing, affect lends itself to be consumed or traded without ultimately being acknowledged. On similar premises, Maurizio Lazzarato has famously theorized "immaterial labor" (2006) to designate a kind of labor that does not necessarily produce a material product; this is particularly evident in the creative and digital industries in which workers' affective activities are commodified in intangible ways: that is, individuals, through their affective work, produce something that acquires value within the capitalist economy and the processes in which it is engulfed; however, it does not cohere into a final practical good, which means their work often remains invisible. For an analysis of the relationship between labor and value in the "affect economy," see Negri (1999).

and queer studies, instead, has gained less traction, which is precisely why we have made more space for it in our introduction: in the hope that more fashion scholars will put it to use in their intellectual endeavors.

Feeling Clothes, Enclothing Feelings

While the relationship between fashion and feeling had not been directly addressed in fashion studies until recently, an interest in this nexus can be detected in the canonical literature that was, more or less explicitly, concerned with clothes and embodiment (e.g., Wilson 1985; Warwick and Cavallaro 1998; Entwistle 2000; Bruno 2010). Peter Stallybrass, for instance, movingly drew attention to how "clothes have a life of their own: they both are material presences and they encode other material and immaterial presences" (1993, 46). Clothes, especially those that belonged to our loved ones, enfold our memories and haunt us affectively; but they also offer us opportunities to "inhabit" (in a virtual yet felt way) those loved ones by "re-living" their clothes. In this re-inhabitation, loss and mourning might become more bearable. Fashion theorist Karen de Perthuis, following in the steps of Stallybrass, takes this idea further by arguing that clothes "are infinitely more, and other" and they can become themselves embodiments of feelings like love and sorrow. She writes: "instead of inanimate, ghostly and empty, they [clothes] are poetic, vital and alive; the dress, the jacket, the jumper, a body remembered. Maybe, even (why not?), its soul" (2016, 68).

Our personal histories are inevitably entangled with memories of clothes, and the affects (or effects) they had on us. In tracing a history of Marx's attachment to his coat in the context of mid-to-late-nineteenth century class struggles, Stallybrass wrote that "happiness was often measured in the buying of new clothes or the redemption of things from the pawnshop" (1998, 195). Due to their being handed over, worn, and consumed, clothes are laden with affect: their wrinkles and creases are affective traces of the material life of clothes and their wearers. In the concluding passage of his essay, Stallybrass rhetorically asks: "Why are prisoners stripped out of their clothes, if not to strip them of themselves?" (1998, 203) This emphasizes how the human sense of self, safety, dignity, and bodily presence in the world is reliant on clothes. The violent act of stripping off people's clothes and/or forcing specific kinds of clothing on them throughout the histories of colonialism, for instance, testifies to how clothes are enmeshed with all kinds of feelings that shape our somatic biographies as well as the ways in which we relate to other bodies over time and across generations. In this sense, since clothes function as carriers of memories, they can be said to have an affective life of their own that is also psychic and, of course, social; in other words, there is an aliveness to clothes that renders them agentive in the way they both physically and psychically affect our bodies.[11]

In the wake of both the "affective turn" and the expansion of transdisciplinary scholarship on fashion in the early 2000s, attention increasingly turned to the relationship between feeling and the clothed body. Drawing inspiration from the epistemological challenge to rationality posed by contemporary studies of affect, fashion scholars have begun, albeit timidly, to probe how fashion and dress function affectively and intersubjectively as "energies" and "forces," beyond subject-centered accounts of personal styling and individual creativity. The imbrication of fashion with feeling in the formation of our social identities has been cogently emphasized by Ben Highmore, who has argued that feelings are historical and material agents that drive fashion's process of "worlding," "articulat[ing] modes of identity and forms of dis-identification" (2016, 145–146). Such worldmaking potential is enabled by the affective capaciousness of clothes since they intimately connect our physical and "social skin" (Von Busch and Hwang 2018).

Moreover, the idiom of feeling, or, interchangeably, affect, has been used as a magnifying lens through which to critically illustrate the material labor and global exploitation of garment workers (Moon 2016, 2020) as well as the "immaterial" work of models in the fashion industry (Wissinger 2015, 2007a, b); as an analytic for thinking about the model's body as socially articulated through forms of labor producing public stagings of sexuality that pander to the gendered and racialized scripts of consumer capitalism (while also, potentially, functioning as "site[s] of body politics for black models, gay men, trans women, and other cultural producers

---

[11] On the "material reality of dress" and the "psychic intimacy between subject and garment," see Parkins (2008).

whose sexuality, race, or gender placed them in a nonnormative, or queer, relation to the modelling industry's reigning norms [...]") (Brown 2019); to historically track the "mood work" of fashion discourse in venues as varied as modernist literature (Sheehan 2018) and periodicals (Parkins 2014) as well as digital media (Pham 2011, 2015; Parkins 2021, 2022); to investigate how fashion images can affect viewers' perception and move them toward personal (both corporeal and financial) investments (Featherstone 2010) and to subscribe to specific forms of life (Shinkle 2011, 2013), at times prompting collective identification and community formation (Filippello 2018, 2020, 2022).

Owing a great deal to Iris Marion Young's feminist phenomenology, feeling has been central in the development of phenomenological approaches for assessing the embodied experience of the dressed body (Findlay 2016). The sensory, haptic, kinesthetic capacities (Robinson 2019, 2022; Negrin 2012) as well as the atmospheric dimension of clothed bodies in everyday life (Chong Kwan 2020) have all been addressed in recent fashion scholarship. Affect has also been employed as a valuable lens through which to interpret posthuman fashion shows and designs (Seely 2012; Smelik 2022); as an interactionist approach for showing how fashion mediates interpersonal bodily gestures and behaviors (von Busch 2021); as a pragmatic method for assessing ordinary people's bodily responses to clothes in consumption practices (Smelik and van Tienhoven 2021) and in museum contexts (Van Godtsenhoven 2021); and as a curatorial methodology for materializing political subjectivities (Tedesco 2021).

More broadly, a changing paradigm in the study of the clothed body has been compellingly invoked by Lucia Ruggerone in order to exceed the boundaries of semiotic and structural explanations, thereby focusing on how dressing practices in everyday life can function as affective "ways of becoming" (2017), ultimately leaving on both bodies and clothes the emotional traces of their mutual enfoldment (Sampson 2020). As Otto von Busch writes, "we don't *know* fashion as much as we *feel* fashion" (2021, 151). In other words, and in line with Ellen Sampson's arts-based research into the affects of clothing, we begin to learn more about clothes and our relationship with them once we consider how they *touch us back*: this kind of "affective return" (Bruno 2010)—which conjures Spinoza's formulation of *affectus* as the simultaneous capacity to affect and to be affected—functions as a haptic source that triggers desires and fantasies.

Despite such multiple, diverse, and scattered contributions, the potentialities of "feeling" for the study of fashion are still largely neglected. This edited volume seeks to tease out possible avenues of investigation of the clothed body and its representations through the lens of feeling. We wager that an affective epistemology of fashion should account for the particular ways in which subjects, based on personal and collective bodily "archives," come to experience, to attach value and meanings to, and to *use* clothing to carve out moments and spaces of intimacy and belonging. Fashion itself can be used to spark sensory awareness and conjure up memories, thereby (re)activating feelings for the purposes of sensorial and/or social engagement, offering insights into our personal stories and larger cultural histories. Seen this way, fashion and feeling interfold in gauging the "mood," or "weather," of our time. This book is animated by the belief that no univocal methodology is adept at teasing out how fashion "feels" and produces social and political imaginings.

Fashion and Feeling is especially concerned with what the engagement of fashion through an affective, embodied approach can reveal about both our relationship with clothes and the forms (social, cultural, and political) that such an encounter can take across space and time. In line with this aim, our contributors were encouraged to experiment with and develop, together with their collaborators or participants, creative frameworks of analysis that might possibly exceed conventional disciplinary parameters. Object analysis informed by new materialisms, wardrobe studies and autoethnography, artistic-based approaches such as stitching as knowing, therapeutic practices, and storytelling all attest to the richness of fashion seen through a feeling optic. A fluid and creative methodology is coherent with the ethos of this book, with the variety of backgrounds of its contributors, and, most importantly, with the inchoate and yet contagious nature of feeling. Ultimately, our goal for this book is to illuminate the centrality of feeling in creative fashion practices, fashion media discourses, and fashion labor so that future analyses of fashion will more closely account for that elusive yet felt dimension which goes beyond descriptive language.

STRUCTURE OF THE BOOK

The volume opens with a section on "Feeling Wardrobe Histories," to highlight the ways that fashion's feelings are tied to the past—to both intimate memories and socio-cultural events—as much as reflecting, in Berlant's terms, "contemporary historicity" (2011, 5). In alternating between personal narration and, respectively, military and film history, this assemblage of essays mirrors fashion's join between individual and social—and underscores its relevance for historical modes of thinking. Christina Moon's "Closet Feelings" examines the role of the closet (and the clothing it houses) in the safekeeping of diasporic memory. In this poetic chapter, Moon evokes specific memories and the feelings—of longing, melancholia, invisibility—that they crystallize. Personalizing "fashion history," she gestures toward the simultaneously intimate and epochal significance of dress. In "Militarized Comfort: How to Feel Naked While Wearing Clothes," Sunny Xiang offers a similarly precise account of the construction of race in a radically different register. Working from a voluminous military and popular cultural archive, Xiang traces the pursuit of the somatic feeling of comfort through US military dress and shows how the development of comfortable clothing relied on racialized, imperialist imaginaries that played out in the Pacific theatre during the war, but also shaped American sportswear more generally after the war. Bethan Bide, in "Costume Design and Emotional Communication in 1940s Cinema," also analyzes the considered mobilization of feeling following World War Two—in this case, through the rhetoric of clothing pictured in British film. As Bide's examples illustrate, film production worked in concert with broader discourses to affectively orient subjects to a new postwar reality, using dress as a visual language to engender particular forms of feeling in audiences. Rounding out this section, Thuy Linh Tu and Jessamyn Hatcher ask, "Can Fashion Feel?" Decentering the human subject in favor of an empathic examination of garments as sensate objects, Tu and Hatcher reflect on encounters with garments, suggesting that the materiality of dress encodes histories of feeling. Taken together, the chapters in this section thus orient readers to both how fashion's affective qualities are institutionally mobilized in particular socio-historical contexts, as well as the capacity of dress to exceed prescribed forms of feeling.

The following section, "Reparative Fashion," similarly highlights the potential of dress and its production to provoke feelings that surpass, refuse, heal from, or stand altogether apart from dominant modes of thinking and feeling. Ben Barry and Philippa Nesbitt's "Designing Clothes For and From Love: Disability Justice and Fashion Hacking," for instance, describes a fashion hacking workshop with disabled participants. The authors show how the particularities of working with clothing generate love, a feeling that is both radically disruptive of everyday ableism and enables forms of creative activism and worldmaking. In "Beading Is Medicine: Beading as a Therapeutic and Decolonial Practice," Presley Mills and Justine Woods conversationally reflect on the reparative work done by a gathering of Indigenous beaders. As they explain, the beading circle facilitates healing—as shown by Barry and Nesbitt, the process surrounding the production of dress and accessories has as much affective resonance as the products. Timo Rissanen's "All That Cloth Can Carry (On a Queer Body)" also explores process, in this case the often-solitary process of textile production. He returns us to the objects and their encoding of feeling, suggesting that the process generates works imbued with grief and trauma, which themselves have a reparative function. Lest we get caught up in the counter-hegemonic possibility of dress and fashion as therapeutic instruments, however, the section closes with Renate Stauss's "Looking Like a Woman, Feeling Like a Woman, Sensing the Self: Affective and Emotional Dimensions of Dress Therapy." Describing instances of the deliberate use of fashion for therapeutic purposes by mental health professionals, Stauss reminds us how effectively the affective resonance of dress can facilitate ideological conformity, masked as helpful intervention.

The third section, "Stasis and Transformation in Fashion," brings together a diverse selection of chapters that emphasize how fashion trades in both liveness and the inorganic, generating a range of uncanny, nearly indescribable affects. Ellen Sampson's "Dirty Pretty Things: Stains, Ambivalence and the Traces of Feeling" mobilizes psychoanalytic theory to explore the ambivalent feelings generated by stains on clothing. Offering a forensic reading of one stained garment and the complex affective responses it generates, Sampson highlights fashion's ability to index subjective complexity. And in Elizabeth Sheehan's "Making Peace Sensational: Designs for the Nobel Prizes," the author traces the *significative* complexity of dress. In a close analysis of a Swedish design school's annual exhibition of student-designed evening gowns thematizing the Nobel Prizes, Sheehan focuses on the 2021 dresses. She shows how the garments are used pedagogically to instantiate in viewers a particular—multifold, ambivalent—set of feelings about the contemporary world and the possibility of peace. Sampson and Sheehan both drive home fashion's ability to generate multiple affects, underscoring the liveliness of feeling in a singular subject or garment. Otto Von Busch picks up on this liveliness in "Glamour Magick, Affective Witchcraft, and Occult Fashion-abilities," which offers a reading of intersections of fashion, glamour, magic, and witchcraft. He illuminates the ways that fashion has been marked by allusions to magic, and how its transformative energies have been explicitly harnessed in contemporary witchcraft. Lastly, Lucia Ruggerone takes a theoretical tack to explore fashion's lively and agentic capacities in "Fashion

Studies at a Turning Point." Seeking to overcome the emphasis on representation and visuality in fashion research, Ruggerone outlines a new direction for fashion studies, one that begins from the processual, becoming qualities of embodied affect.

The book's final section, "Affective Embodiment in Media," though, returns to the question of representation with a set of essays that, in connecting representations to cultural moods and commonly circulating affects, challenges the unproductive binary between feeling subjects and cultural images. Harriette Richards's "Melancholy Fashion in Aotearoa New Zealand," for example, diagnoses the melancholy atmosphere that pervades the work and advertising strategies of fashion designers from Aotearoa New Zealand. In connecting these to the colonial history of the nation-state, Richards points to some of the ways in which lived affective experiences translate in fashion, including its photographic representation. In "On Boredom and Contemporary Fashion Photography," Eugenie Shinkle also considers fashion photography as a node of meaning with a dynamic relation to the socio-historical present in which it emerges. In this case, the cultural prominence of boredom that emerges as a response to neoliberalism translates obliquely into fashion's representational field, and fashion is shown to be as effective at communicating resistance to fashion as it is at upholding it. Masafumi Monden's study of a popular Japanese manga series, in "Hair Dressing: Fetish, School Uniforms and *Shōjo* in 'Cocoon Entwined,'" explores the works' representation of girls' hair and school uniforms to attune readers to new uses of adornment as a memory object. In this close reading, Monden connects the lively, agentic qualities of dress with their mnemonic capacity, making links across analytical modes relating to fashion. Finally, Rosie Findlay's "What's Getting Us Through: *Grazia UK* as Affective Intimate Public During the Coronavirus Pandemic" examines the affects circulating in *Grazia UK*'s Covid-19 coverage early in the pandemic. Eschewing the tendency to glorify or vilify women's fashion-related periodicals, Findlay theorizes the magazine's ambiguity: *Grazia* briefly opened, via feelings, onto a critique of neoliberal capitalism, only to foreclose its own insights as moods shifted.

REFERENCES

Ahmed, Sara. 2004a. Affective Economies. *Social Text* 79 (22): 117–139.

———. 2004b. *The Cultural Politics of Emotion*. Edinburgh: Edinburgh University Press.

Bennett, Jane. 2010. *A Political Ecology of Things*. Durham, NC: Duke University Press.
Berlant, Lauren. 2008. *The Female Complaint: The Unfinished Business of Sentimentality in American Culture*. Durham, NC: Duke University Press.
———. 2011. *Cruel Optimism*. Durham, NC: Duke University Press.
———. 2015. A Momentary Anesthesia of the Heart. *International Journal of Politics, Culture, and Society* 28: 273–281.
Berlant, Lauren, and Jordan Greenwald. 2012. Affect in the End Times: A Conversation with Lauren Berlant. *Qui Parle* 20 (2): 71–89.
Berlant, Lauren, Libe G. Zarranz, and Evelyne Ledoux-Beaugrand. 2017. Affective Assemblages: Entanglements and Ruptures—An Interview with Lauren Berlant. *Atlantis* 38 (2): 12–17.
Blackman, Lisa. 2012. *Immaterial Bodies: Affect, Embodiment, Mediation*. London: SAGE.
Blackman, Lisa, and Couze Venn. 2010. Affect. *Body & Society* 16 (1): 7–28.
Brennan, Teresa. 2004. *The Transmission of Affect*. Ithaca, NY: Cornell University Press.
Brown, Elspeth H. 2019. *Work! A Queer History of Modeling*. Durham, NC: Duke University Press.
Bruno, Giuliana. 2010. Pleats of Matter, Folds of the Soul. In *Afterimages of Gilles Deleuze's Film Philosophy*, ed. David N. Rodowick. Minneapolis, MN: University of Minnesota Press.
Chong Kwan, Sara. 2020. The Ambient Gaze: Sensory Atmosphere and the Dressed Body. In *Revisiting the Gaze: The Fashioned Body and the Politics of Looking*, ed. Morna Laing and Jacki Willson, 55–75. London: Bloomsbury.
Clough, Patricia Ticineto, and Jean Halley, eds. 2007. *The Affective Turn: Theorizing the Social*. Durham, NC: Duke University Press.
Connolly, William J. 2011. *A World of Becoming*. Durham, NC: Duke University Press.
Cvetkovich, Ann. 2003. *An Archive of Feelings: Trauma, Sexuality and Lesbian Public Culture*. Durham, NC: Duke University Press.
———. 2012. *Depression: A Public Feeling*. Durham, NC: Duke University Press.
De Perthuis, Karen. 2016. Darning Mark's Jumper: Wearing Love and Sorrow. *Cultural Studies Review* 22 (1): 59–77.
Deleuze, Gilles, and Félix Guattari. [1980] 1987. *A Thousand Plateaus: Capitalism and Schizophrenia (Vol. 2)*. Translated by Brian Massumi. Minneapolis, MN: University of Minnesota Press.
Entwistle, Joanne. 2000. *The Fashioned Body: Fashion, Dress and Modern Social Theory*. London: Polity.
Featherstone, Mike. 2010. Body, Image and Affect in Consumer Culture. *Body & Society* 16 (1): 193–221.

Filippello, Roberto. 2018. Thinking Fashion Photographs through Queer Affect Theory. *International Journal of Fashion Studies* 5 (1): 129–145.
———. 2020. Eccentric Feelings: Little Girls' Pleasures on the Feminist Fashion Set. *Australian Feminist Studies* 35 (105): 217–238.
———. 2022. Fashion Statements in a Site of Conflict. *Fashion Theory*. Online first.
Findlay, Rosie. 2016. 'Such Stuff as Dreams are Made On': Encountering Clothes, Imagining Selves. *Cultural Studies Review* 22 (1): 78–94.
Flatley, Jonathan. 2008. *Affective Mapping: Melancholia and the Politics of Modernism*. Cambridge, MA: Harvard University Press.
Ford, Tanisha C. 2015. *Liberated Threads: Black Women, Style, and the Global Politics of Soul*. Chapel Hill, NC: The University of North Carolina Press.
Frank, Adam, and Elizabeth A. Wilson. 2020. *A Silvan Tomkins Handbook: Foundations for Affect Theory*. Minneapolis, MN: University of Minnesota Press.
Gorton, Kristyn. 2007. Theorizing Emotion and Affect: Feminist Engagements. *Feminist Theory* 8 (3): 333–348.
Gregg, Melissa, and Gregory J. Seigworth, eds. 2010. *The Affect Theory Reader*. Durham, NC: Duke University Press.
Hardt, Michael. 1999. Affective Labor. *Boundary 2* 26 (2): 89–100.
Hardt, Michael, and Antonio Negri. 2005. *Multitude: War and Democracy in the Age of Empire*. New York: Penguin.
Hemmings, Clare. 2005. Invoking Affect: Cultural theory and the ontological turn. *Cultural Studies* 19 (5): 548–567.
Highmore, Ben. 2016. Formations of Feelings, Constellations of Things. *Cultural Studies Review* 22 (1): 144–167.
Holzberg, Billy. 2018. The Multiple Lives of Affect: A Case Study of Commercial Surrogacy. *Body & Society* 24 (4): 32–57.
Lazzarato, Maurizio. 2006. In *Immaterial labour. Radical Thought in Italy: A Potential Politics*, ed. Paolo Virno and Michael Hardt, 132–147. Hardt Minneapolis, MN: University of Minnesota Press.
Leys, Ruth. 2011. The Turn to Affect: A Critique. *Critical Inquiry* 37 (3): 434–472.
Manning, Erin. 2006. *Politics of Touch: Sense, Movement, Sovereignty*. Minneapolis, MN: University of Minnesota Press.
Massumi, Brian. 1995. The Autonomy of Affect. *Cultural Critique* 31: 83–109.
———. 2002. *Parables for the Virtual: Movement, Affect, Sensation*. Durham, NC: Duke University Press.
———. 2015. *Politics of Affect*. Hoboken, NJ: Wiley.
Miller, Monica L. 2009. *Slaves to Fashion: Black Dandyism and the Styling of Black Diasporic Identity*. Durham, NC: Duke University Press.
Moon, Christina H. 2016. Ethnographic Entanglements: Memory and Narrative in the Global Fashion Industry. In *Fashion Studies: Research Methods, Sites and Practices*, ed. Heike Jenss, 66–82. London: Bloomsbury.

Moon, Cristina H. 2020. *Labor and Creativity in New York's Global Fashion Industry*. London and New York: Routledge.
moore, madison. 2018. *Fabulous: The Rise of the Beautiful Eccentric*. New Haven, CT: Yale University Press.
Muñoz, José E. 2000. Feeling Brown: Ethnicity and Affect in Ricardo Bracho's The Sweetest Hangover (and Other STDs). *Theatre Journal* 52 (1): 67–79.
———. 2006. Feeling Brown, Feeling Down: Latina Affect, the Performativity of Race, and the Depressive Position. *Signs* 31 (3): 675–688.
———. 2020. *The Sense of Brown*. Edited by Chambers-Letson, Joshua and Tavia Nyong'o. Durham, NC: Duke University Press.
Negri, Antonio. 1999. Value and Affect. *Boundary 2* 26 (2): 77–88.
Negrin, Lewellyn. 2012. Fashion as an Embodied Art Form. In *Carnal Knowledge towards a 'New Materialism' through the Arts*, ed. Barbara Bolt and Estelle Barrett, 141–154. London: I. B. Tauris.
Ngai, Sianne. 2005. *Ugly Feelings*. Cambridge, MA: Harvard University Press.
Papoulias, Constantina, and Felicity Callard. 2010. Biology's Gift: Interrogating the Turn to Affect. *Body & Society* 16 (1): 29–56.
Parkins, Ilya. 2008. Building a Feminist Theory of Fashion: Karen Barad's Agential Realism. *Australian Feminist Studies* 23 (58): 501–515.
———. 2014. Texturing Visibility: Opaque Femininities and Feminist Modernist Studies. *Feminist Review* 107: 57–74.
———. 2021. 'You'll Never Regret Going Bold': The Moods of Wedding Apparel on *A Practical Wedding*. *Fashion Theory* 25 (6): 799–817.
———. 2022. Feminist Sentimentalism? Ambivalent Feeling in Inclusive Digital Wedding Media. *Cultural Studies*. Online first.
Pedwell, Carolyn. 2014. *Affective Relations: The Transnational Politics of Empathy*. London: Palgrave Macmillan.
Pedwell, Caroline, and Anne Whitehead. 2012. Affecting Feminism: Questions of Feeling in Feminist Theory. *Feminist Theory* 12 (2): 115–129.
Pham, Minh-Ha T. 2011. Blog Ambition: Fashion, Feelings, and the Political Economy of the Digital Raced Body. *Camera Obscura* 26 (1): 1–37.
———. 2015. *Asians Wear Clothes on the Internet: Race, Gender, and the Work of Personal Style Blogging*. Durham, NC: Duke University Press.
Probyn, Elspeth. 2005. *Blush: Faces of Shame*. Minneapolis, MN: University of Minnesota Press.
Protevi, John. 2009. *Political Affect: Connecting the Social and the Somatic*. Minneapolis, MN: University of Minnesota Press.
Robinson, Todd. 2019. Attaining Poise: A Movement-based Lens Exploring Embodiment in Fashion. *Fashion Theory* 23 (3): 441–458.
———. 2022. Body Styles: Redirecting Ethics and the Question of Embodied Empathy in Fashion Design. *Fashion Practice*. Online first.
Ruggerone, Lucia. 2017. The Feeling of Being Dressed: Affect Studies and the Clothed Body. *Fashion Theory* 21 (5): 573–593.

Sampson, Ellen. 2020. *Worn: Footwear, Attachment and the Affects of Wear*. London: Bloomsbury.
Sedgwick, Eve Kosofsky. 2003. *Touching Feeling: Affect, Pedagogy, Performativity*. Durham, NC: Duke University Press.
Sedgwick, Eve Kosofsky, and Adam Frank. 1995a. Shame in the Cybernetic Fold: Reading Silvan Tomkins. *Critical Inquiry* 21 (2): 496–522.
———. 1995b. *Shame and Its Sisters: A Silvan Tomkins Reader*. Durham, NC: Duke University Press.
Seely, Stephen D. 2012. How Do You Dress a Body Without Organs? Affective Fashion and Nonhuman Becoming. *Women's Studies Quarterly* 41 (1/2): 247–265.
Sheehan, Elizabeth. 2018. *Modernism à la Mode*. Ithaca, NY: Cornell University Press.
Shinkle, Eugenie. 2011. Playing for the Camera: Huizinga's *Homo Ludens*, Technology, and the Playful Body in Fashion Photography. In *Images in Time: Flashing Forward, Backward, in Front, and Behind Photography in Fashion, Advertising and the Press*, ed. Aesa Sigurjónsdóttir, Michael A. Langkjær, and Jo Turney, 165–182. Bath: Wunderkammer Press.
———. 2013. Uneasy Bodies: Affect, Embodied Perception, and Contemporary Fashion Photography. In *Carnal Aesthetics: Transgressive Imagery and Feminist Politics*, ed. Marta Zarzycka and Bettina Papenburg, 73–88. London: I.B. Tauris.
Shouse, Eric. 2005. Feeling, Emotion, Affect. *M/C Journal* 8 (6) https://journal.media-culture.org.au/index.php/mcjournal/article/view/2443.
Smelik, Anneke. 2022. Fractal Folds: The Posthuman Fashion of Iris van Herpen. *Fashion Theory* 26 (1): 5–26.
Smelik, Anneke, and Maaike A. van Tienhoven. 2021. The Affect of Fashion: An Exploration of Affective Method. *Critical Studies in Fashion & Beauty* 12 (2): 163–183.
Spinoza, Baruch. [1677] 2002. *Complete Works*. Translated by Samuel Shirley. Indianapolis, IN: Hackett Publishing.
Square, Jonathan M. 2020. How Enslaved People Helped Shape Fashion History. *Guernica*, 14 December, https://www.guernicamag.com/how-enslaved-people-helped-shape-fashion-history/.
Stallybrass, Peter. 1993. Worn Worlds: Clothes, Mourning, and the Life of Things. *Yale Review* 81 (2): 35–50.
———. 1998. Marx's Coat. In *Border Fetishisms: Material Objects in Unstable Spaces*, ed. Patricia Spyer, 183–207. London: Psychology Press.
Stengers, Isabelle, Brian Massumi, and Erin Manning. 2008. History through the Middle: Between Macro and Mesopolitics—An Interview with Isabelle Stengers. *Inflexions* 3. http://www.inflexions.org/n3_stengershtml.html.
Stewart, Kathleen. 2007. *Ordinary Affects*. Durham, NC: Duke University Press.

Tedesco, Delacey. 2021. Curating Political Subjects: Fashion Curation as Affective Methodology. *GeoHumanities* 7 (1). Online first.
Terada, Rei. 2003. *Feeling in Theory: Emotion after the 'Death of the Subject'*. Cambridge, MA: Harvard University Press.
Thrift, Nigel. 2007. *Non-Representational Theory: Space, Politics, Affect*. London: Routledge.
———. 2010. Understanding the Material Practices of Glamour. In *The Affect Theory Reader*, ed. Melissa Gregg and Gregory J. Seigworth, 289–308. Durham, NC: Duke University Press.
Tomkins, Silvan. 1963. *Affect, Imagery, Consciousness*. Vol. 4 vols. New York: Springer.
Van Godtsenhoven, Karen. 2021. Affect, Haptics, and Heterotopia in Fashion Curation. In *The Routledge Companion to Fashion Studies*, ed. Eugenia Paulicelli, Veronica Manlow, and Elizabeth Wissinger, 69–82. London: Routledge.
Von Busch, Otto. 2021. Bullying and Barren Fashion: An Affective Perspective on the Psychopolitics of Dress. In *The Routledge Companion to Fashion Studies*, ed. Eugenia Paulicelli, Veronica Manlow, and Elizabeth Wissinger, 151–158. London: Routledge.
Von Busch, Otto, and Daye Hwang. 2018. *Feeling Fashion: The Embodied Gamble of Our Social Skin*. New York: Selfpassage.
Warwick, Alexandra, and Dani Cavallaro. 1998. *Fashioning the Frame: Boundaries, Dress, and the Body*. London: Bloomsbury.
Wetherell, Margaret. 2012. *Affect and Emotion: A New Social Understanding*. London: SAGE.
Williams, Raymond. 1977. *Marxism and Literature*. Oxford: Oxford University Press.
Wilson, Elizabeth. 1985. *Adorned in Dreams: Fashion and Modernity*. Los Angeles: University of California Press.
Wissinger, Elizabeth. 2007a. Always on Display: Affective Production in the Modeling Industry. In *The Affective Turn: Theorizing the Social*, ed. Patricia T. Clough and Jean Halley, 231–260. Durham, NC: Duke University Press.
———. 2007b. Modelling a Way of Life: Immaterial and Affective Labour in the Fashion Modelling Industry. *Ephemera: Theory and Politics in Organization* 7 (1): 250–269.
———. 2015. *This Year's Model: Fashion, Media, and the Making of Glamour*. New York: NYU Press.
Yao, Xine. 2021. *Disaffected: The Cultural Politics of Unfeeling in Nineteenth-Century America*. Durham, NC: Duke University Press.
Young, Iris. 1980. Throwing Like a Girl: A Phenomenology of Feminine Body Comportment, Motility and Spatiality. *Human Studies* 3 (2): 137–156.

PART I

Feeling Wardrobe Histories

CHAPTER 2

Closet Feelings

Christina H. Moon

Closet, cabinet, c*amerino, camerata,* studio, *studiolo,* wardrobe, dressing room. According to the *Encyclopedia of Interior Design,* the closet was historically a small room, an architectural and interior space next to the bedchamber, gallery, or library, thought of as an office or study (Banham and Shrimpton 1997). The closet was a personal space, an intimately sized room tucked away in the innermost reaches of a house, inaccessible to the public. In the Middle Ages, it was a room for private business, safeguarding of valuables, learning and meditation, or displaying treasured objects including books, miniature paintings, antiquities, coins, or statues. Etymologically, closets were also called wardrobes—or *warderobe,* which entered the English language from Old French in the beginning of the fourteenth century (Curry 2015). Though the king's wardrobe from 1200 followed the monarch on his travels, full of treasures and money, it eventually became known as an item of furniture, as a place for keeping clothes and other valuables.

This piece was first inspired by Shannon Mattern's "Closet Archive" in *Places Journal* (July 2017).

C. H. Moon (✉)
Parsons The New School, New York, NY, USA
e-mail: moonc@newschool.edu

© The Author(s), under exclusive license to Springer Nature
Switzerland AG 2023
R. Filippello, I. Parkins (eds.), *Fashion and Feeling,* Palgrave Studies in Fashion and the Body,
https://doi.org/10.1007/978-3-031-19100-8_2

In Renaissance Italy, medieval closets could be found as cherished sanctuaries for the richest of men, common in affluent Italian houses from the early fifteenth century onwards. The Palazzo Medici on the Via Larga in Florence had three of them (Banham and Shrimpton 1997). These spaces were meant for secrecy, privacy, and a place for solitude. Rich with collections of all kinds, the ceilings of these rooms were built lowered to emphasize their intimate size. Closets were the most lavish and opulent rooms of the house, with richly decorated objects of meaning. One could find theological manuscripts, medical treatises, Greek texts, the libraries of classical and contemporary writings. The walls displayed pictorial intarsia, inlaid woodwork, allegorical scenes, and portraits of powerful men. A room, a closet, a cabinet in a palace or country house was the most private, withdrawn, and treasured of spaces.

By the sixteenth century, the closets of Europe began to take on a more public dimension to hold and display curiosities from the New World (Koeppe 2002; Zytaruk 2011). There was a European desire for encyclopedic knowledge, and these rooms often featured cabinets and collections, the most influential formed by university professors as a teaching resource for the natural sciences. They soon became fashionable aspects of interior design and architecture, acquired by monarchs and princes who wanted to display their cultivated pretentions, using closets and cabinets as means for learning and as repositories to convey their encyclopedias of knowledge, aesthetically impressive and dramatic in visual effect. These are the European origins of the practice of collecting, popularized among monarchs, princes, merchants, and amateur collectors who wanted to display new curiosities of the world. The objects of a closet collection, or "cabinet of curiosity," could be small, as a series of shelves, a cupboard, displays in a nook. Curiosities could be displayed in large rooms, galleries of art and marvels…the *Kunst-* or *Wunderkammer*, the proto-museum. The objects inside also mattered—their shape, rarity, how they were collected, shuffled, curated, included or excluded, sorted or kept. Paintings, fragments of ruins and classical sculpture, antique coins, precious stones, shells, and exotic objects. Things from plundered distant lands, objects of perceived historical and mythological significance. Even Pliny the Elder in AD 24 described collections of semi-precious stones, the bones of giants, the weapons of fabled heroes. The closet could hold relics of saints, ostrich eggs, inscriptions, the archeological fragments that could tell the history, mythology, and origins of oneself and a place.

With time, the closet and wardrobe increasingly transformed into a dressing room, attached to the bedroom of house. A dressing room, among women, became a place between mistress and maid, a retreat from patriarchal surveillance, a space of female camaraderie, for shared secrets, intimacy, a place for solitude (Iarocci 2008). By the eighteenth century, it was a room to store clothes, and by the early nineteenth century modernist ideas of space and function shaped by gender and class began to impact its design (Edwards 2014). The growth of clothing consumption throughout the twentieth century occurred in tandem with the rise of white-collar occupations and the emergence of wholesale, bespoke, and ready-to-wear clothing industries. These changes, along with modernism and its ideas of rational order, planning, and function, became central to new notions of progress. Compactedness—as organization and efficiency—was the key idea in the architectural design of living spaces in the first half of the century. So too the notions of the busy, industrious, productive man who saves time, along with the systematic classification of processes and the logical organization of domestic space. All the concerns of the day—private anxieties over changing gender relations, education, the economy, employment—were tidied up, ordered, stored, and disciplined. A modern solution for efficiency, storage, and the efforts of saving time and space, the closet is symbolic of the architectural and interior histories of closets in middle-class homes.

* * *

In the entry on "Wardrobe" in Lee O-Young's *Things Korean* (1999), I read that the Korean wardrobe is a *jangnong*, a large chest that does not hang clothes but holds them in place in a pile, folded and stacked on top of each other in many, many layers. When we look down inside the wardrobe, Lee writes, we are looking down into the depths of a well. "When we step back and observe those clothes piled on top of each other, we are reminded of the earth's geological strata. We might equate the deepest layer, way at the bottom, with the earth's core, and the top of the stack with the earth's surface." When we keep our clothes in the Korean wardrobe, our most precious valuables kept within its layers, "the Korean wife or mother looking for something valuable can resemble some prospector digging away shovel by shovel, or the pearly diver pushing down, down, and around among the coral reefs. Whether it be a worn-out piece of clothing or some yellowing family photo, each item uncovered during the search receives a special greeting in the mother's smile, or her sigh." It is the excavation of ancient tombs, Lee tells us. It is an archaeological site.

The deep dive of the pearl diver, holding her breath as she reaches the ocean bottom. "In the depths of the wardrobe are things lost to time, forgotten in life's forced march, naturally receiving a special welcome when they surface again and beckon us to stay a bit and remember." Lee has our eyes follow the shelves with all the layers of clothes among them, telling us to sense a "regular rhythm" found among the clothes. Lee concludes, "The Korean wardrobe is a composition of a simple rhythm weaving colors and textures into a mosaic of life. Though its contents are not locked up as if in a safe, they are protected from prying hands by the wardrobe's ever revolving depths. Never locked, in its fathomless depths it nevertheless safeguards its more precious things, as does the heart of the Korean mother" (90).

Wardrobes, which are the proto-museums of the self, as a certain archive, as places where we categorize or organize what makes up not only our histories, but our thoughts and emotions. Places to keep precious things, valued things, secret things, inner things. Cabinets within cabinets with drawers and secret compartments. The clothes which are stacked on the shelves. Collections and collections and micro collections that archive the self. Throughout are the hidden things, the secret things, the things that are intimate. The feelings that emerge when private. And my *jang-nong*, the kind that is full of the geological strata of emotion, sitting deep as a pearl at the bottom of the ocean. There, in those fathomless depths, I can find the smile, or sigh, the heart of my mother, my father, their unknown country. I can swallow the feelings I have for things I never did understand.

* * *

When I am still, I bring myself back into the closet archive of memory. As a child, it begins in the basement of my parents' home in suburban New Jersey. Down a long flight of stairs, linoleum tiles with metal nosing, a simple long wooden banister that leads into darkness. At the bottom is a door on the right side of the basement, the air breathing a certain kind of coldness. There is a spare old refrigerator filled with herbal elixirs, panting bad smells of boiled plants and deer antlers and dried jujube berries. Then there is the small closet, stuffed full of moldy counterfeit bags, what I now think must have been a quick, impulsive business idea from my mother. Looking to make a little side money, these bags were brought back from her unusual trip to Korea—the first visit she made there in a long while, since she left Seoul in her early twenties—to attend her mother's funeral. The basement with a long buzzing overhead fluorescent light above a long table. There are squared wooden rods scattered everywhere in this basement, crowded in bins, stacked, and lined up on the table. Balanced on top of these rods is the cheap metal jewelry that would be painted by my mother, often brightly spotted and stained with many different colors of touch-ups and spray paint. Flat sheets of mylar are strewn across the table, eventually rolled up into piping bags and filled with epoxy paint. My mother is under the lights, hunched over in silence, squeezing the mylar cones of paint. Their tips cut off, she oozes out colors in a controlled manner. She is filling all the small and compartmentalized spaces of a whole world, found in the designs of earrings, bangles, necklaces, belt buckles.

In the back of that basement workroom, there is a wood-lined closet where I spent much of my time as a child. It is tucked away in the furthermost reaches of the house. To get there, one needs to get past long roads of suburban split-level homes that are lined up picture-perfect next to a golf course, ending in American Dream cul-de-sacs. It is a middle-class northern New Jersey suburb of neighbors who own lawncare businesses, mattress businesses, a car dealership. Where the Albanian neighbor owns a restaurant in the city. Where the Persian Jewish neighbors own a shop in the Diamond District. Where the young white professional families with fancy jobs in advertising have moved in across and down the street. They'd all come here for the excellent schools, the freshly cut grass backyards, two-car automatic-door garages, with a ShopRite and Main Street, a synagogue and Catholic church, all just a mile away.

The wood in this closet is warm, honeyed, brown. It smells of cedar and moth balls and mildew. It is my place to be, to turn the light on or to keep the light off, to climb onto its top shelf to lay myself down and hide from the world. To spend some time there, some many hours, no one would ever know that I was even there. No one would ever be looking for me either. If my mother was home, then she was working on painting the jewelry. But mostly, as time went on, the parents were not home. They were out working, hustling, trying to keep up with this illusion of success. They had money then had no money at all, in cycles that happened over and over again. The electric bill hadn't been paid in months, the lights had been turned off for good. These parents of mine were a young couple struggling with each other and struggling with the whole world. The families they left behind had passed on without goodbyes or sentiment. These parents were not parents, but young adults—small children homesick and full of grief. They were, individually, in their own closets of aloneness. They often disappeared and were nowhere to be found.

In this basement closet, from the top shelf, I looked down for many hours upon the hanging bodies of the old clothes in this closet—what were to me the former and continued selves of my parents. Molded and mildewed, silently hanging, these shapes of garment bodies were the many, many mothers and fathers of mine. Here, I wasn't alone, but rather with many versions of their past selves. Here were their lives—the ones they had before me, before I was an idea, before I was even born. A red suede dress, a moth-eaten wool suit. I imagined my parents as youthful and vivacious people, dancing and laughing and telling jokes. I felt I could smell their perfume, their cologne. As a child, spending time in this closet, I imagined the lives they lived in these once worn clothes.

At the entrance of the basement closet are the rafters that hide mom's cash. I have, through time, witnessed her put her money in there, standing up on a chair, reaching her hand in and pushing her green cash further into the dark recesses of that ceiling. Only once had I seen her take it out, and in bundles…when she moved out of my childhood home for good. Inside the closet, the feeling of beauty is the one I see from the door, opened to the basement room. It is this scene before me: a mother working quickly and silently among the noxious smell of paint and turpentine so strong it can pass you out. There she is, squeezing plastic cones with her hands, oozing out the deep jewel-toned colors of ruby red, cerulean blue, forest green, onto earrings, rings, belt buckles. She is making riches, treasures, out of cheap, worthless baubles. From this closet, the feeling of beauty is watching a pretty mother with two hands make something out of nothing, beautiful.

There was also an old trunk—the only thing my mother brought here to this country along with a gold ring her friends had made for her. This trunk I loved to open—its inside guts an overflowing pink silk organza *hanbok* with painted flowers across the high-waisted dress. There was a bottom drawer too, part of an old piece of furniture, full of scattered old photos of my young mother before she was a mother, my father, sometimes captured as a couple together, but at times with friends, roommates, before they even knew each other. There aren't any photos of them as children—the photos only begin in northern New Jersey, in their young adulthood of their 20s and 30s. The war was over and life began again. This drawer was also full of important official papers, stamped letters, passports, documents with emblems and seals.

There is also the closet of my great aunt—another closet archive from memory—the only family relative I had or knew. The closet in her tiny studio apartment on West 3rd street in New York had been stuffed shut for four decades, only to be opened by me after she had passed away. Inside her closet I find shoes, purses, letters, and books. There are creams, jewelry-making tools, stamps, chemistry journals, toothbrushes, sunglasses, scarves. I find two photo albums of people I have never met, seen, or known. In the photos, they are staring intensely back at me. My mother shows me one photo of my grandfather as a child. This child in the photo is staring back at me with the face of my own son.

These closets are the archives I belong to. They are the ones that accommodate all my affections and sympathies, the ones that tighten the chest, well the eyes, disrupt and soothe my mood, make me ask who my parents are and where they have gone. This closet archive of memory is a place I return to in writing, reaching for the most difficult to express. It's the stuff twenty layers deep down in the *jangnong*, deep down and barely visible, where I can find myself calm again. To be in this basement closet is to write, and to be with the people I have lost and miss. It is a chance to be with every detail I wish I knew and find consolation in that difficult feeling of not knowing anything at all. This closet archive is the one of solitude, a place to confirm that I even exist. The clothes that hang in there, the pictures of those faces staring back at me in the album, the border-crossing documents found in the bottom drawer, the very few objects that remain from former lives and selves—my imagination makes up the biographies of those I can't ever truly know.

This closet archive is a portal to many worlds, many times, many dimensions, as layers and as spirals, time travel, a place without time too. Its made-up wardrobe stories express the complicated emotions, thoughts, and histories that connect me to other lives and histories. A storehouse, a repository of unexplained objects, these things that mediate between me and another life, other worlds, generations, past lives. Stories and sentiments which hide in the pockets of clothes. This closet sews silhouettes of the self, understands clothing as passports, carries bags of belonging, embroiders lost and broken languages, dwells in the pleats of time. What emotional, social, sensory, psychic landscapes emerge from the closet archive, from a wardrobe that tells us of the innermost reaches of lived experience of life? Inside this closet archive, one becomes a ragpicker, picking the scraps of fabric that tell us the relevance of these lives.

* * *

If the closet and wardrobe is an archive of stories, like the ones John Berger (1982) tells me about, then I wonder if these hanging garments are the eyewitness accounts of the persons who once wore them. Or maybe the clothing is the story of encounter, of what had already happened in time. In my closets, the clothes—like film—have always been anticipatory. One thinks, what will one wear, imagine, dream about? How do the clothes conjure beauty into being along with new potential, a new feeling or identity? Before I ever thought of being a professor, an academic, a scholar, a writer, I dreamt first of what I would look like, or what I could wear. Like Maeve Leakey, the archaeologist, I first imagined myself with short-cropped hair, a white button-down, beige slacks, and brown loafers. I imagined gold jewelry on my ears, gold bangles on my wrist. I imagined my office filled with old wooden furniture in an old building, tucked away in a hidden part of the museum. I imagined myself at the university, captivating an audience while standing at a podium in a lecture hall, and then in the next scene, out in the field driving a Jeep, hiking for days to then dig the earth. Sand and dirt caked on my face, I'd find the artifacts of human life, piecing together pottery shards, looking for old bones and coins, looking closely at objects of antiquity, seeing ancient art. The first imagination of being anything at all was to distance myself, put miles between the imagination and the girl behind the cash register. I imagined a person with a "position," a "title," cultivated with an education, far from the work of the hardware store, dry cleaners, sewing factory, bodega, wholesale trinket import shop, liquor store, flower shop, gas station—worlds that made up the adult world of work of my parents and their friends. Before there was any desire to study, any genuine curiosity to pursue "knowledge," there was first clothing as film, as an anticipatory story. Clothes that could *bear into being* a clothed future body with a position, title, status, prestige, a printed official certificate, a pedigree. A future that could only be imagined, first and always, by what I could wear…what would be the wardrobe.

But now I find myself in this closet archive of memory, rummaging around for wardrobe stories using a different kind of archaeology. The clothes are not filmic; they hang there like still photographs. The clothes are not animated. Without breath or movement, the stories they tell are more ambiguous. In this closet, I search for the young selves of my mother and father, their past histories, ideas, their innermost intimate feelings and thoughts. I search for the inner urgency, fear, curiosity, naivete, the brashness that provoked them to leave one place for another. I look to understand this young girl, this young boy. I see my mother in her home, a large compound in Seoul with a stone front gate and an inner outdoor courtyard. When she returned to the US from her mother's funeral, she carried with her a roof tile from this childhood home and four small baby turtles held in a container within her purse that went to live on forever. I envision my father as a young child, confused, lying in the dirt in front of his house which he has tumbled out of, his first memory in life. He can see from the ground up the grass thatched roof to his house with a dirt floor, somewhere in the outskirts of Taejeon. When I drive by my suburban childhood home, I wonder: what happened to that basement closet? And what happened to the homes my parents once lived in and left behind? What happened to the landscape they looked out upon every day when they were children? What happened to their mothers and fathers, their aunts and uncles, their siblings, their cousins and friends? There are no descriptions or stories, but they say it was difficult what they saw and lived through. That they survived something. That they left a certain landscape in exchange for the wide aisles of a modern American grocery store.

Wardrobe stories, from the closet archive of memory, emerge in the fog of dementia. An eighty-five-year-old memory that collapses time and dwells in the mind of a six-year-old. It is 1942 all over again. My father is using a mashed-up collage of the colonial language, his repressed mother tongue, the accent of a tough, industrial northern New Jersey. He can't remember my husband's name, but he can remember the anthems he sang at six years old. He remembers how to march in line and salute the sun. This six-year-old boy in an eighty-five-year-old man is marching around my living room, telling me how cold his hands are on this walk to school. "Because the emperor and the cruel teacher say my school uniform pockets had to be sewn closed!" Small hands are disciplined, frozen; he said he only wanted to keep them warm. Then there are unknown stories of a favorite sibling and an uncle, what they looked like and even wore, and the story of having to dig the ditches to bury them when they were children during the war. Children who dig ditches for the dead. There are memories of soldiers raiding the village homes and the clean white clothes of missionaries handing out cups of rice. There is the *hanbok* of my youthful beauty queen mother, with her manicured hands digging around in bins in search of nails and screws at the hardware store. Wardrobe stories that clutch trunks and suitcases as archives. To study the shape of pockets, their structure and form, but more meaningfully for me, to understand why they were sewn closed. How to pry them open, to warm and comfort these small six-year-old hands, wrinkled in their eighty-five years, it's no longer the cold winter of empire.

In my everyday world of living, there are few stories that lead to any origin story at all. So, in this closet archive of feelings, I release them in the old clothing, the old relics and artifacts in this basement closet, in my mother's trunk, the bottom drawer of documents and photos. I make up stories, I make fiction, to bring new things into this closet archive—film images of the war, books on the architecture of the grass thatched huts my father once called home, genealogies and family histories of the American missionaries who helped them to survive, a book of photos by Chris Marker (2008) of women from the 1960s who resemble my aunts, folk music by Kim Jung Mi in the years my parents left, the pictorial memoir and funerary photos from Martina Deuchler (2019), an anthropologist returning many years later to the village of her dead first husband, the photographs of Choi Min-Shik and Kim Ki-Chan, Instagram posts of a young modern *mudang* wailing, dinners out with burnt meat and intestine stew for my brother. When there are no stories, no archives, no emotions, just a blank history of silences and suffering, then you reach for everything, anything you can collect and collage together. You fill this closet archive with stories that are resemblances, mimetic, magical fictions. You make analogies and seek similitude. You fill this closet with things that move you, bring you to tears, bring about the bittersweet feeling of entangled sadness and happiness. You wonder about this melancholia; it always remains, but it's a wonder that you are here just breathing and alive. After all, your parents buried their loved ones. Your uncle stripped naked on the back porch of your suburban New Jersey childhood home to show you how many bullets entered in one part of his body, how many exited out his flesh. He made you touch the healed wounds which were smoothed over with another round of whiskey. You remember how beautiful his voice still was, his body still standing, numbed, naked, and drunk. His body is gone but he is singing there nonetheless.

In this closet archive, I hang out in there with all the other pieces of clothing. Like drying laundry, I air out my feelings of diasporic longing in memories and pieces of writing. I read literature in search of my condition, the racial melancholia that comes with the melancholic corpus. What I read is the outcome of guilt, the denial of guilt, the blending of omnipotence and shame, this history of sorrow. I read that it's the "not understanding" or not knowing, of not hearing the stories that act as witness. It is the result of the daily encounters with this feeling of "oversight," the invisibility which is naturalized over time as absence, "the internalization of discipline and rejection, and the installation of a scripted context of perception" (Cheng 2000, 17). I want to say to this world: I don't see myself in any fashion history other than this one, the one of the wardrobe, this closet archive. It is the primitive labyrinth to my emotions and reactions, where each rotting, mildewed thing tells the story of belonging, survival, and loss all over again, the loss of language, the children who bury their dead, the leaving it behind. I read about the illuminated ruins in Walter Benjamin's texts (1968) in search of my parents, their neighbors' families, who tell me that these false histories are written by the victors when all those others, the vast masses who once lived, have disappeared. They only appear as flashes and telling signs, blinking and flickering their message—"we were once here"—on the fiery asphalt, in the reflection of the rain puddle. I think not of "the gaze," but only of Benjamin's Tiergarten, Berlin childhood, those hidden magical places he'd find in the park, the real world he felt existing inside the large glass cube of a miniature working mine, or inside a snow globe (Benjamin 1978). My fashion history is not what they tell me, but rather the clothes rotting away in this closet, this junk, these deteriorating artifacts, buried in the layers of clothing. They are the hidden stories within a sewn-up pocket, a saved pair of shoes. They have the potential to tell stories when no stories are shared.

The closet archive to overcome the disquiet, the contradictory sensations that tear one apart. In her mother's dialect, Elena Ferrante (2016) tells us of *frantummàglia*, a jumble of fragments, these feelings that make her mother dizzy, who says it leaves the taste of iron in her mouth. Ferrante tells me it's a crowded head, the muddying water of the brain, a feeling that provokes a mother to do mysterious things. It is a reaction to the suffering, the source of the suffering, yet not traceable to any singular origin. For Ferrante, it made her mother have fits of weeping, it woke her in the middle of the night, made her talk to herself, drove her out of the house. It made her leave the stove pot on, burning the sauce inside. For my mother, it was the aimless driving to nowhere, the staring out of the windshield into an unknown distance, a daughter in the backseat always wondering where they were going. She is picking the dry skin off her lips, so nervous she cannot speak. The suffering which makes this witty and vulgar and opinionated woman speechless, her voice faint and weak; there are fits of crying for her sister on the phone. When this world appears to her, all myths of the self are discovered to be false, all sense of trust and security are gone, the world is fully foreign again—her family does not exist, there is no help to be found. This aimless stare out into nothing, her mind is somewhere else. The car has run out of gas again, and I will get out and walk to go find some for her so that we can start the car again.

At my age, I now resemble my mother's presence—her body, the style of her hair, the dry picking of her lips—it expands in me, as does this *frantummàglia* of suffering. It is a secretly inherited emotion of unarticulated feeling. It is, beyond anything else, what makes us mother and daughter—our solidarity. It is that which destroys time or chronology. It is the *maum*, the spirit-heart, the mind-heart of belonging (Cha 1982).

Let me recover us in the boxes of oily hair curlers, the rotting pink organza, the sewn-up pockets of a school uniform. Let me hold the cardboard shoes from childhood, shoes that moved with that beloved body from place to place, through an occupation, through war, from Seoul, Tokyo, Paris, New York. Those shoes were kept in a closet for nearly eighty years, through all our many celebrations at Hop Kee in Chinatown. I'm trying to make a story of belonging out of this exiled ambiguity.

REFERENCES

Banham, Joanna, and Leanda Shrimpton. 1997. *Encyclopedia of Interior Design.* Vol. 2. London: Fitzroy Dearborn.
Benjamin, Walter. 1968. Thesis on the Philosophy of History. In *Illuminations: Essays and Reflections*, ed. Hannah Arendt, 253–264. New York: Schocken Books.
———. 1978. In *Reflections: Essays, Aphorisms, Autobiographical Writings*, ed. Peter Demetz and Leon Wieseltier. New York: Schocken Books.
Berger, John. 1982. Stories. In *Another Way of Telling*, 279–286. New York: Pantheon Books.
Cha, Theresa Hak Kyung. 1982. *Dictee*. Berkeley: University of California Press.
Cheng, Ann Anlin. 2000. *The Melancholy of Race*. Oxford: Oxford University Press.
Curry, Anne. 2015. Wardrobe. In *The Oxford Companion to British History*, ed. John Cannon and Robert Crowcroft, 2nd ed. Oxford: Oxford University Press.
Deuchler, Martina. 2019. *Pictorial Memoir: Korea Fifty Years Ago*. Seoul: Seoul Selection.
Edwards, Clive. 2014. Multum in Parvo: 'A Place for Everything and Everything in Its Place.' Modernism, Spacesaving Bedroom Furniture and the Compactom Wardrobe. *Journal of Design History* 27 (1): 17–37.

Ferrante, Elena. 2016. La Frantumaglia. In *Frantumaglia*, 98–101. New York: Europa Editions.
Iarocci, Louisa. 2008. Dressing Rooms: Women, Fashion, and the Department Store. In *The Places and Spaces of Fashion, 1800–2007*, ed. John Potvin, 169–185. London: Taylor & Francis Group.
Koeppe, Wolfram. 2002. Collecting for the Kunstkammer. In *Heilbrunn Timeline of Art History*. New York: The Metropolitan Museum of Art.
Lee, O-Young. 1999. *Things Korean*. Boston: Tuttle Publishing.
Marker, Chris. 2008. *Coreenes*. Seoul: Noonbit Publishing.
Zytaruk, Maria. 2011. Cabinets of Curiosities and the Organization of Knowledge. *University of Toronto Quarterly* 80 (1): 1–23.

CHAPTER 3

Militarized Comfort: How to Feel Naked While Wearing Clothes

Sunny Xiang

In the opening scene of the 1943 WWII film *Guadalcanal Diary*, a spirited gang of U.S. Marines sprawl on the deck of their transport. It is "a peaceful, lazy day of rest," the narrator says, "somewhere in the South Pacific." The men read, smoke, sing, doze, and sunbathe. They speak longingly of the funnies, the Dodgers, and women. Yet despite the absence of such amenities, there is no shortage of smiling, touching, and loving. In the face of possible death, the Marines are suave and carefree—"as contented as if seated on their front porches." The narrator declares: "What a way to travel to war!"

In traveling to war, the Marines in *Guadalcanal Diary* seem at peace. Their casual insouciance matches the mood propagated by the U.S. military's public relations team. Photos taken by the Naval Aviation Photographic Unit depict soldiers holding cigarettes and sodas rather than guns. Of the 15,000 photographs credited to this unit, most are from the Pacific theater (Bachner 2004, 7, 8), perhaps because glittering beaches

S. Xiang (✉)
Yale University, New Haven, CT, USA
e-mail: sunny.xiang@yale.edu

© The Author(s), under exclusive license to Springer Nature Switzerland AG 2023
R. Filippello, I. Parkins (eds.), *Fashion and Feeling*, Palgrave Studies in Fashion and the Body,
https://doi.org/10.1007/978-3-031-19100-8_3

and lush jungles set an idyllic scene for fraternizing fun and recreational downtime. Laura Wexler would call such photos "domestic," insofar as their display of "the routine decency of daily life" does the propagandistic work of "lin[ing] up these particular men with American destiny." Destiny not only makes victory foreordained; it also recodes "imperial aggression" as "a peace that keeps the peace" (2000, 32–33). The ideological content of "peace" becomes even more potent in post-WWII filmic depictions of U.S. troops in the Pacific. Such films extend the aura of victory toward a new war—the Cold War—by celebrating American bounty and mobility as a more lustrous alternative to life under communism. Whether a prestige drama like *From Here to Eternity* (1953), a slapstick comedy like *Mister Roberts* (1955), or a heartwarming musical like *South Pacific* (1958), the WWII films of the 1950s–1960s express both "wartime nostalgia for exotic islands" *and* anticipatory desire for "fast travel and tourism back to Polynesia's paradise" (Geiger 2007, 230). Teresia Teaiwa has used the portmanteau "militourism" to describe this imbrication of war and recreation (1999). In a militouristic framing, the U.S. soldier-tourist, as a personification of benevolent conquest, functions as a "masculine bestower of the gift of modernity," while the islands of the Pacific are anthropomorphized as "receptive, feminized tropics waiting to be acted upon and transformed" (Gonzalez 2013, 26–27).

I begin with these "domestic" and "militouristic" images of American military men lounging in the tropics because they visualize how clothing mediates the relation between a white body and an exotic environment. In popular portrayals of the war in the Pacific, which became a Hollywood sensation during the Cold War, one repeatedly finds an overt thematization of individual comfort over and against regimented uniformity. The captain who fastidiously monitors haircuts, shirttails, and all matters of dress—for instance, in *The Caine Mutiny* (1954) and *Mister Roberts*—is openly lampooned. In *South Pacific*, lieutenant Joe Cable grows into a sympathetic hero by abandoning his stuffy overdressed look for a tousled and relaxed look. Throughout such films, military personnel appear most commendably all-American when they dress down. Dressing down has no specific regulation, and in fact, no one wears it the same way. Uniforms can be open-collared, rolled up, or untucked. If they are slashed, wrinkled, sweat-stained, or mud-caked—all the better. Such diversity notwithstanding, dressing down tends to follow two related routes, one to nakedness and the other to nativeness. As shirts are removed, grass skirts and leis are donned. In both serious and comedic films, the paragon of wartime leisure is a dance in Native drag.

A democratic sensibility of "defiant comfort" is certainly an American convention, perhaps originating with Walt Whitman's unbuttoned shirt and unworried slouch (Trachtenberg 1989, 62). But in tracing the militarization of comfort, I find it useful to read the above images against the grain. In such a reading, the mishmash of wildly varied styles evidences not the inevitability of victory but the *elusiveness* of comfort for the U.S. forces serving in the Pacific. For the white male soldier, this elusive comfort comes down to a tension between clothing and nakedness. No matter how one modifies it, clothing seems hardly capable of being worn in a tropical environment. In 1945, military textile specialist Stephen Kennedy described the dilemma this way: "Perhaps the soldier would be much better off naked in the jungle, if humid heat were the only problem, but he must also be protected against mosquitoes and other insects, the sharp-cutting vegetation, and the rays of the sun" (1952, 421). By presenting naked comfort and sartorial protection as competing aims, Kennedy shows that the Southwest Pacific, though the site of several iconic military offensives, was, unexpectedly, a *textile* failure. WWII climate scientist Paul Siple's meditations on the problem of tropical clothing land on a racial hypothesis. Whereas "native peoples" in the tropics "have solved the problem in a natural way" by going naked, Siple stipulates that two key factors "prevent most people to whom this book is directed from changing to native costume": one, the sensitivity of white skin, which is "still not as well adapted to the continuous exposure as the dark-skinned races," and two, the civilizational habit of clothing, which has caused "coverage to become a deep-seated necessity" (1949, 393). According to Siple's formulation, naked Natives might as well be a part of the tropical environment; the civilized white race, on the other hand, can only survive by staving off this environment through clothing.

The Cold War's rose-colored glasses lend the WWII battles in the Pacific a romantic tinge. This romantic view, however, draws on prewar representations of love and adventure in the South Seas rather than actual wartime experiences. In fact, two of the era's most popular films, *Mister Roberts* and *South Pacific*, are set in fanciful Polynesian paradises, even though the books from which they are adapted actually take place in the Melanesian islands of New Guinea and the Solomons. The varieties of dressing down that we find in romantic depictions of war ultimately tell us more about the militarization of civilian life during the Cold War than about the conditions of combat during WWII. A shirtless Marine in a Cold War film may seem happy and nonchalant, but such a style would likely have been intolerable in the Pacific theater. Yet, as I will show, the dress of WWII combat and the dress of Cold War daily life are fundamentally inseparable, for both predicate comfort on the intermediary function of clothing for a white body in an environment viewed as hostile. Studying the sartorial innovations provoked by tropical warfare will thus deepen our understanding of how, in the post-WWII years, a "casual, comfortable look" came to be "a distinctively American concept in fashion," particularly in sportswear and leisure wear (Blaszczyk 2006, 486).

The story of what I'm calling militarized comfort begins during WWII, when U.S. military planners found themselves scrambling to equip soldiers for a newly global war with "operations in varied climates and types of terrain" (Pitkin 1944, 1). This unprecedentedly climatological dimension of warfare led to the rapid expansion of the Office of the Quartermaster General (OQMG), the military unit responsible for clothing and equipment. It also brought new forms of expertise into the military establishment. University researchers, industry specialists, and military strategists together contemplated how best to dress the American soldier for "extreme climates" such as the arctic, tropics, and desert. The emergence of a climatological awareness in the context of military preparedness resulted in the frequent conflation of war and weather, such that the enemy and the environment were often construed as mutually reinforcing adversaries. While each extreme climate introduced its own challenges, this essay focuses on the Pacific theater, for the sartorial complications here proved to be particularly influential for post-WWII conceptions of comfort. As a lifestyle specific to mainstream American culture, comfort refers not only to physiological states, but also to ideological visions of abundance and well-being in the face of imminent apocalypse. Especially prescient is how WWII anxieties about extreme heat came to intersect with Cold War anxieties about thermonuclear warfare. In examining the twinned threats of environmental and toxicological exposure during WWII, I show how the technologies and vocabularies of comfort that emerged from the agonistic context of Pacific combat came to inform Cold War conceptions of the good life, despite an apparent paradigm shift from the white masculine soldiering body to the white feminine consuming body.

In the filmic representations of war as leisure that I discussed above, the U.S. military stages its own retreat: "war," in the form of combat, appears to be nearby but lies just outside the frame. Similarly, we can view comfort wear as a domesticated vision of American militarism that crops "war" out. Even though the *military* may not be visible or legible in the casual, sporty, feminine styles that were touted as distinctively "American," *militarism* is nonetheless present as an imperial ideology that prioritizes the comfort of a vulnerable yet high-performing white body. Cold War clothing described as "comfortable" often showcased the "protective" and "repellent" properties of synthetic fabrics. In protecting the body and repelling the environment—in bringing the military science of comfort into everyday wear—technologically advanced fabrics appeared to offer a solution to the wartime problem of needing to be both naked and clothed. Frequently metaphorized as a "second skin," fabrics such as nylon and Lycra promised to provide coverage, security, and support without sacrificing freedom. While synthetics revolutionized fashion writ large during the mid-twentieth century, a Pacific frame for tracking militarized comfort allows us to discern a continuity between WWII clothing designed for the extreme climate of the Pacific and Cold War clothing designed for the seemingly distinct thermal stresses of tropical vacations and nuclear war. Through this frame, it becomes possible to view comfort as an affectively ambivalent period style that combined effortless ease with heightened security and nationalist hubris with imperial anxiety. In environments of extreme heat, the comfortably clothed body audaciously declared victory—even as the American empire lumbered forward toward the tropical quagmire that would come to be known as "Vietnam."

Wartime Comfort

The technological refinement of comfort, whether in the metropolitan center or across distant outposts, has long been a colonial operation that centers the delicacy of the white civilized body. For example, Joan DeJean periodizes France's "age of comfort" based on its strength as a colonial power. Between 1670–1765, the Parisian metropole saw an influx of loose kimono gowns, diaphanous Indian cotton, plush Turkish sofas, and various other exotic goods that signified a life of leisure (DeJean 2009). In this scenario, the cult of domesticity, precisely in its appropriation of the exotic, patrols the boundaries of civilization itself, safeguarding whiteness from primitivism through what Anne McClintock calls "imperial commodity racism" (1995, 31). Away from the metropole, colonial comfort often becomes more of an infrastructural problem. Johan Lagae traces the mid-twentieth-century European craze for the ergonomic butterfly chair to efforts to "secure physiological comfort for the white colonizer's body" in the wilds of Central Africa. Mobile and lightweight modernist chairs, Lagae shows, are an inheritance of mid-nineteenth-century "campaign furniture" used by the Belgian military (2017, 17, 18–19). Jiat-Hwee Chang, meanwhile, has explored the "tropicalization" of architecture, which, in the British context, began with the standardization and sanitization of military barracks across the empire's Asian and African colonies. The creation of these "sanitized enclaves" served to "optimize the health and well-being of the British soldiers amidst larger landscapes of contamination where the local population dwelled in conditions of biopolitical neglect" (2016, 52, 53). These examples of colonial furniture and architecture help situate comfort in relation to what scholars call "climate determinism." Yuriko Furuhata writes, "the challenges posed by harsh and unfamiliar climate conditions prompted European settlers" to develop "strategies of acclimatization" that were "framed in the climatically determinist discourse of culture and race" (2022, 15). In the cases of Belgian campaign furniture and British military barracks, we can see that the colonial logic of climate determinism was also militaristic, for claims to territorial sovereignty were accompanied by projects to defend the white body from inimical nature—notably, a nature that is primal and hot.[1]

Most inspiring for my thoughts on the militaristic genealogy of American comfort is Thuy Linh Nguyen Tu's 2021 monograph *Experiments in Skin*. In this study, Tu examines how the U.S. military came to view white skin as uniquely vulnerable during the American war in Vietnam. The skincare products spawned by the U.S. military's race-based science experiments, Tu demonstrates, not only protected American soldiers from tropical acne in the jungles of Vietnam but also revolutionized the global cosmeceuticals industry in subsequent years. Tu uses the brilliant phrase "the science of soldiering bodies" to describe how military scientists attempted to fashion white skin into an armor that could withstand the environmental hardships of jungle warfare (2021, 11). Similar speculations about white vulnerability ran rampant during WWII. In military intelligence as well as in popular culture, the Native ally, the Asian enemy, and the African American soldier were all assumed to have greater dexterity in the jungle due to their hardier and more savage constitution. If the soldiering of skin into a kind of armor exemplifies militarized *strength*

---

[1] On the racialization of arctic climates, which likewise presume that "temperate-normativity" is required for civilizational flourishing, see Smith, "'Exceeding Beringia.'"

in the fires of battle, my inquiry into how clothing came to function as a kind of skin centers on militarized *comfort*, a quality that extends the battlefield into the climatological surround. As a physiological support system for whiteness, militarized comfort describes a range of sartorial technologies designed to preserve the colonial body—technologies that had the broader effect of securing human against environment, white against other, and culture against nature.

During WWII, the need for skin to perform like reinforced armor and the need for clothing to feel like unhampered skin presented a conundrum that was intensely felt by infantrymen yet largely overlooked by military planners. Indeed, the war in the Pacific was a crucible for the militarization of comfort, not because comfort received special consideration here but because it was consistently neglected. The relative inattention to comfort in tropical combat scenarios reflects an early bias in Quartermaster research. Whether because American military men grew up on a diet of South Sea romance narratives or because they intuitively viewed tropical beaches as sites of leisure, OQMG researchers initially defaulted to treating arctic conditions as the more urgent problem.[2] The U.S. military had begun testing experimental materials in the territory of Alaska as early as 1935. In 1941, a climate research lab was formally organized by Antarctic specialist Paul Siple, with the construction of cold weather clothing as the overwhelming objective. By contrast, even though the U.S. military has had a substantial presence in the Pacific and the Caribbean since the early twentieth century, it had never purposefully developed clothing for tropical regions.[3] In the early years of WWII, combatants stationed in the jungles of the Pacific, unlike those in the mountains of Europe or the deserts of North Africa, did not receive climate-specific ensembles. Only after General Douglas MacArthur issued an urgent request for 150,000 sets of specialized jungle gear in July 1942 did concerted testing for tropical combat uniforms and equipment finally commence (Pitkin 1944, 206).

Boots, helmets, netting, packs, hammocks, medical kits, and rain wear are among the items that the OQMG created for or adapted to the tropics. The development of such items took place in the Panama Canal Zone, the

---

[2] On the influence of South Sea films, see Lindstrom and White (1990); Brawley and Dixon (2012).
[3] The khaki uniforms worn in the Philippine-American war were based on the British colonial uniforms from the East Indian campaigns. After the war, these khaki uniforms were shipped to Hawaiʻi (Sanow and Bruun 1983a, 1983b).

conditions of which were deemed analogous to the Pacific theater. Here, an oil geologist named Cresson H. Kearny set up a "jungle equipment shop" (Pitkin 1944, 201). Adapting ideas from *Wheat and Soldiers*, a Japanese text on Chinese infiltration tactics (Kearny 1996, 9), Kearny worked with an experimental jungle platoon to implement "some unorthodox views on the possibilities of jungle equipment" (Pitkin 1944, 200). The "specialization" of clothing to service specific climate zones coexisted with a push for "standardization," a term that referred to both the "simplification" of uniform designs and the "universalization" of uniforms across regions. Threading the needle between standardization and specialization proved anathema to comfort in the Pacific. One reason is that researchers often developed "standard" clothing with arctic and temperate climates in mind. For example, in 1942, the Southwest Pacific command received a clothing shipment of which almost everything, including underwear, was made of wool (Kleber and Birdsell 1966, 242). The competing values of specialization and standardization came to a head with the herringbone twill (HBT) uniform, which was general issue to all Army personnel. Derived from the coveralls used by enlisted mechanics, chauffeurs, and machinists since the 1930s, the HBT uniform was intended for summer fatigue duty—that is, unarmed, non-combat labors. In the Pacific theater, however, Army and Marines wore the HBT uniform as a combat uniform due to the lack of a better alternative. During the war years, the OQMG, the Chemical Warfare Service (CWS), the Army Ground Forces, and various academic and industry experts subjected the HBT uniform to numerous alterations. Pursuing standardization alongside specialization called for an "all-purpose" approach to uniform design. In the Pacific theater, however, "so many military characteristics—from gas protection to reversibility, camouflage, and simplicity of design—had been advanced that the problem of developing one type of garment suitable for all troops became exceedingly complicated" (Risch and Pitkin 1946, 70).

Early discussions about the tropical combat uniform over-focused on camouflage. Ironically, these endeavors to visualize the harmony between soldier and environment coexisted with the U.S. military's violently antagonistic relation to its surroundings. Unlike troops from other nations who "fit themselves around and in the jungle," Judith Bennett writes, the Americans obliterated the environment in trying to "make bases appear more like a home" (2009, 27). Camouflage also "diverted attention from the many other characteristics that are important in clothing worn by combatants in rain and hot temperatures" (Stanton 1991, 88). Josephine

Bresnahan identifies inadequate clothing as a core cause of "combat fatigue." In the Solomons, "heat and humidity made fungal conditions almost impossible to heal," and "the soldiers' clothing was never dry." To quote one combatant, "The only clothes you have are those you are wearing, and they soon disintegrate from sweat and general wear" (Bresnahan 1999, 120, 102). Clothing, in short, intensified the sensory immediacy of an unexpectedly belligerent environment. Writing about New Guinea, Col. George de Graaf remarks, the "country was as much an enemy as was Tojo" (quoted in Brawley and Dixon 2012, 52). The Allied troops invented numerous phrases with discrepant affective valences to name the maladies arising from the tropical environment: "Guadalcanal neurosis," "Going Troppo," "Jungle Happy," and "Pineapple crazy" (Brawley and Dixon 2012, 48–9). Even in James Michener's romanticized account of the Pacific, troops suffer "the heebie-jeebies," "screaming meemies," "rock-jolly," "island-happy," "G.I. Fever," and "purple moo-moo" (Michener 2014, 131). Such phrases lend descriptive color to earlier accounts of "tropical neurasthenia," a discourse of white discomfort in the inhospitable tropics that invariably linked race to degeneration and disease (Anderson 2006).[4]

But while infantrymen viewed insects, swamps, foliage, thorns, rain, and environmentally induced psychosomatic ailments as the most immediate menaces to comfort, military researchers tended to be more preoccupied with potential Japanese chemical warfare attacks. For much of the war, the terrifying possibility of poison gases drove the most significant design decisions and presented the most recalcitrant design dilemmas. The Panama Canal Zone, where the Quartermaster Corps created clothing and equipment for the Pacific theater, was also a key site for testing protective gear through the simulation of gas attacks. In addition to conducting tests in actual tropical sites, the CWS replicated tropical conditions in climate-controlled chambers across the United States (Rall and Pechura 1993). Tropical climates were used as a norm for testing exposure to mustard gas and lewisite because heat and humidity made skin more sensitive and reactive. Researchers reasoned that "if protective devices, such as

---

[4] Efforts to resolve white discomfort often entailed experiments in dress. For example, in the early twentieth century, U.S. Army personnel stationed in the Philippines conducted various experiments on how skin pigmentation affects heat absorption, with one test involving dark- versus light-pelted monkeys and another involving orange versus white (Anderson 2006, 83-84). In the 1920s, American troops in the Philippines wore a wool-flannel bellyband to ease "stomach cramps and other tropical troubles" (Kearny 1996, 8).

clothing, prove to be adequate in these [tropical] tests they will also be adequate under more temperate conditions" (Taylor et. al. 1943). The extensive human subject tests that the military conducted in the name of developing protective clothing have led scholars to call WWII "the unfought chemical war." Especially scandalous has been the recruitment of African American, Japanese American, Puerto Rican, and white American military men (with the latter being the control group) to test out theories of racially differentiated resistance levels through prolonged exposure to toxic chemicals. Susan L. Smith hypothesizes that these military experiments served to "save white American lives": if the darker men "proved less susceptible to mustard gas than white men, then they could be used in the front lines." In other words, "protective clothing" was intended to protect only white American soldiers (2008, 519). Such clothing, I would add, served to protect whiteness itself. The experiments that enabled the production of both tropical combat clothing and anti-gas protective clothing reflect a belief that white people are more civilized and that white skin is more delicate. During the Vietnam War, the idea of using dark skins on the front lines as a shield for white skin would take a literal turn, as dermatologists attempted to create a "white corporeal armature" that could "replicate the strength of black skin for 'fragile' white bodies" (Tu 2021, 59).

The development of protective clothing through chemical exposure offers a fruitful vantage point for examining the science of comfort, insofar as efforts to defend against gas warfare came up against more immediate forms of physical irritation and environmental distress. The CWS may have taken tropical conditions as baseline for testing anti-gas clothing, but the styles of dress that emerged from these tests were by and large untenable in the actual tropics. For example, one CWS prescription that faced rebuke in the Pacific was "double-layer protection," which, in the European theater, included "antigas impregnated underwear and socks, hood, combat uniform, gloves, and leggings." When Col. William A. Copthorne protested that such clothing surely could not be worn in the Southwest Pacific, the CWS merely reiterated the War Department's desire for a "worldwide protective policy" and instructed the area commander to "weigh the risk of gas warfare against the efficiency of the soldier" (Kleber and Birdsell 1966, 167, 242).

The conflicting demands of tropical warfare and gas warfare proved to be especially vexing in the case of the HBT uniform. The CW's anti-gas recommendations of inner flaps, wrist closures, collar tabs, and gussets may seem fairly modest. But in sealing the body from potentially lethal gas vapors, these modifications also blocked off air flow, something that was essential in hot and humid climates. Researchers found that removing flaps—as well as pockets and fabric layers of all kinds—would significantly reduce the oppressive discomfort of Army and Air Force of uniforms (Robinson 1949, 347–8). This finding was strongly backed by combatants, who called the flaps "a waste of time and cloth." One man reports: "The first thing the soldier does is to cut all those things out … and curse those who put them in" (Risch and Pitkin 1946, 68–69). Perhaps the most contested protective measure was the HBT uniform's one-piece design. By completely covering the body, such a design provided maximal protection from both toxic chemicals and other environmental hazards. For the wearer, though, this full-body suit was experienced as a kind of sweltering entrapment. The design meant that "men had practically to undress to relieve themselves," a problem exacerbated by the fact that tropical conditions made "bowel disorders inescapable" (Pitkin 1944, 220; Moran 2017). Although the body-length zipper could in theory supply additional ventilation when left open, such an arrangement also had the adverse effect of "expos[ing] men's whole bodies to the bites of chiggers and mosquitoes, which carried such diseases as malaria, dengue fever and scrub typhus" (Pitkin 1944, 220). In response to such complaints, the Army spent two years investigating different drop seats but never arrived at a design that the CWS deemed gas-proof. Late in the war, complaints about the HBT uniform finally prompted a more purposeful investigation into tropical combat clothing. Although infantrymen eventually transitioned to a two-piece HBT suit, the much-maligned herringbone material itself was worn throughout the war.

As a particularly dire prognosis of the white body's vulnerability, efforts to defend against gas warfare dramatize the failure of clothing to secure both protection *and* comfort. The threat of chemical exposure compounded existing concerns about environmental exposure. Both kinds of exposure reveal that while clothing and equipment made for an elaborate armor, it was much more comfortable to be naked. Unfortunately, "conventional customs make it undesirable to strip the body completely, even when desirable from a physiological standpoint." The "clothing problem" for the tropical zone must therefore "compromise between providing the ideal of no clothing and furnishing a satisfactory covering to meet purely psychological and physical needs" (Siple 1949, 390, 393).

Comfort, as a physiological state that required both "no clothing" and "a satisfactory covering," came to be understood predominantly in terms of "thermal balance" or "energy balance." To quote a 1969 Army study: "This concept of balance between body and environment is modified by the intervention of clothing, which from one point of view is a part of the environment, but from another point of view can be regarded as an extension and modification of the body itself" (Fourt and Hollies 1969, 1). Despite this deceptively neutral language of "balance," the need for comfort in climates designated as "extreme" presupposes an adversarial relationship between a soldier and their surroundings. Hence, clothing appears to betray the wearer when it functions as a part of the environment. In the examples above, "protective features" in the name of total coverage—buttoning up collars; closing off cuffs and trouser legs; adding flaps, straps, and layers—forced soldiers to do battle with the very clothing designed to shield them. The collusion between clothing and the environment offers one definition of *discomfort*. Comfort, on this score, describes clothing that casts its loyalties with the wearer, functioning as "a quasi-physiological system, an extension of the body which interacts with the body" (Fourt and Hollies 1969, 37). Comfortable clothing helps "balance" the body, ideally by reconciling total protection with unencumbered mobility. Implied in the achievement of balance with the body, however, is conquest of the environment.

Post-WWII Comfort

Having thus far explored comfort through the frontline soldier, I want to now ponder how this ideal of a high-performing, balance-seeking thermostatic subject contributed to the hegemonic norming of comfort in the post-WWII years.[5] It is important to stress that at issue here is not so much a *shift* from military to civilian contexts but an *expansion* of militarism into an imperial lifestyle.

To begin tracing this transformation of militarized comfort into an everyday norm, we might glance at two reports on *Wartime Technological Developments* created by the U.S. Subcommittee on War Mobilization of the Committee on Military Affairs. Appearing in May and September of

---

[5] Nicole Starosielski describes a "thermostatic subject" as one who "was supposed to desire stasis and continuity, avoid fluctuation, and operate as part of an automatic control system" (Starosielski 2021, 33).

1945, these reports enumerate 2310 inventions developed by military and industry personnel to meet wartime demands: synthetic insecticides, prefabricated housing materials, anti-reflective eyeglasses, methods for quick-freezing cooked foods, interference reduction techniques in radio, a new textile fiber made of cow's milk, and a fountain pen that could write on wet paper. Such "technological and scientific advances," subcommittee chairman Harley Kilgore writes, "have shortened the war, reduced its toll in lives, and have kept down its huge financial costs" (*Wartime Technological Developments* 1945, ix). But the Kilgore report, as the compendium was known, is ultimately less concerned with what these technological advances have meant for the war cause than with what they augur for a postwar moment. In documenting wartime developments, the report "opens out possibilities for entirely new peacetime industries, new uses of materials, new benefits for mankind, an expanding economy of production and use of the good things of life, and *a higher standard of living for all Americans*" (*Wartime Technological Developments, Supplement* 1945, vii, emphasis mine). The Kilgore report helps elucidate the evolving meaning of this uniquely American phrase "standard of living." When it was first formulated through Fordist-inspired measurements of living standards, the concept of "standard of living" referred to the "absolute minimum necessary for workers to survive." By contrast, in the Kilgore report, we find "standard of living" to mean the "shared material habits" that evidence "the unity of the American people" (de Grazia 2005, 101). Produced at a transitional moment in U.S. empire building, the Kilgore report uses comfort to register the ambiguity between standard as a *minimum* and standard as a *norm*. What is more, the report's projection of Cold War commodity culture from the perspective of WWII dramatizes the paradoxical merger between wartime technologies that enabled survival and postwar adaptations that ensured ease.

There is nothing in the Kilgore report that explicitly links military uniforms to postwar fashion. However, the report's framing of a comfortable way of life as the most crucial payoff of wartime technological advancements seems especially relevant in the context of clothing. As scholars have shown, military outfits such as jumpsuits, cargo pants, blazers, t-shirts, and ponchos and military innovations such as layers, zippers, cravats, and camouflage have become civilian staples, to the extent that the militaristic origins of these styles are now hardly legible. Through such examples, we can see that military forms of dress have infused civilian fashions with not (only) discipline and constraint but *comfort*.[6] To quote Nick Sullivan, "war and its aftermath provided almost all the impetus" for shifting fashion trends "from the fundamentally formal to the fundamentally casual." Indeed, for Sullivan, military uniforms are responsible for "the whole concept of dressing down" (2000, 225). Sullivan's claim pertains to military dress across different periods and contexts, but he makes a point to single out "the casual demeanor" and "purpose-built" uniforms of American troops serving during WWII as an explanation for "the dominance of American style in fashion in the postwar period" (225).

There are numerous ways to connect the dots between combat and comfort. Whereas Sullivan, Paul Fussell, and Rachel S. Gross have discussed the influence of army attire on men's fashions, usually in winter or outdoors contexts, my interest in the simultaneous militarization and tropicalization of post-WWII casual wear leads me to analyze women's clothing.[7] To pick up on the preceding discussion of thermal balance and environmental mastery, I will focus here on "The American Look," a movement spearheaded by Lord & Taylor executive Dorothy Shaver and headlined by sportswear and leisure wear designers such as Clare Potter, Vera Maxwell, Tina Leser, Carolyn Schnurer, Bonnie Cashin, and Claire McCardell. Shaver's attempts to spotlight American fashion date to the 1930s, but the zeitgeist for "The American Look" came in WWII. In *American Ingenuity*, Richard Martin proposes that the "women of genius who invented clothes for modern living" during the war "liberated American fashion from the thralldom of Parisian design" (1998, 9, 12). Whereas "traditional Paris-based fashion was authoritarian and imposed on women," Martin writes, "American fashion addressed a democracy" (13).

Homegrown styles emerged in the throes of WWII, partly because the American fashion industry was cut off from European designs and Third World materials. While such wartime shortages no doubt affected the period's fashion trends, one could lend equal weight to the impact of wartime technologies, which, as the Kilgore report shows, were often developed with civilian applications in mind. In 1942, Cashin, Maxwell, McCardell, Helen Cookman, and Yetta Schminsky helped stimulate postwar sales by

---

[6] For a compelling analysis of how military uniforms and civilian fashion are linked through the disciplinary regime of a regulative state, see Craik (2005).

[7] Paul Achter has explored how a military aesthetic entered everyday fashion through a "feminine, campy, and a pastiche of military design elements" (2019, 275).

debuting clothes made of military-grade "laboratory fabrics" not yet available to consumers (*Women's Wear Daily* 1942, 1). In the immediate postwar years, researchers drew on uniform tests conducted by the Army and Air Force to compensate for "the lack of customer experience and the lack of wearer reaction to fabrics made with the new fibers" (Boulton and Corry 1952, 670). As the consumer displaced the soldier as the primary standard-bearer of comfort, young white women became common test subjects in comfort assessments. Such assessments continued to prioritize comfort as thermal balance and environmental mastery. Studies on "civilian clothing worn at conditions that actually exist in the summertime"—as opposed to clothing of the armed services worn in "extremes of environmental conditions"—also employed familiar metrics, such as the body's adjustments to different environments and responses to different activity levels (Werden et al. 1959, 641, 640). These metrics show that the key selling points of American casual wear not only relied on military technologies developed in WWII labs but also retained a militaristic attitude toward the surrounding environment. Clothes that promised "comfort performance" and "safe endurance" through the unique properties of their fibers did not make direct reference to military sartorial styles (Fourt and Hollies 1969, iii, 32), yet they nonetheless resurrected a militarized and racialized encounter by advocating "balance" with the vulnerable body and "resistance" against rain, radiation, abrasion, soil, and other putatively hostile forces. So, while upper- and middle-class white women may not have been combatants in the conventional sense, the clothes that accompanied their new pursuit of leisure and travel—the clothes that liberated them from home and hearth—were premised on an *embattled* relation to their surroundings. Comfort, in this Cold War context, reflects a belief that "our clothing is armor not against bullets but against life itself" (Sullivan 2000, 226).

The relation between comfort and movement—in the sense of both travel and physical activity—is crucial to underscore. Military advancements in fiber science were, from the start, particularly interested in water repellency, porosity, and air flow—properties to enhance comfort in extreme heat. In one WWII fashion show, "All-American fabrics" were celebrated as serving "every possible occasion," yet, notably, the "emphasis in the showing [was] on cruise and resort apparel" (*Women's Wear Daily* 1940, 15). The increasingly tropical coding of sport and leisure after WWII speaks to the new accessibility of the Pacific through both air travel and cultural productions. Perhaps it's no coincidence that most of the casual wear designers mentioned thus far are known for incorporating Asian and Pacific themes into their quintessentially "American" styles. For example, Tina Leser, whose star rose during WWII with a shop in Honolulu, used "Native" fabrics and designs in creating "play clothes" and "resort clothes." Leser's fame allowed her access to Celanese rayon, which transformed her "primitive" beach designs into a collection of lingerie that was "forward-looking" like "solar energy, helicopters, and glass-wall houses" (*Women's Wear Daily* 1946, 18). In the late 1940s, Leser and fellow Orientalist Carolyn Schnurer participated in Monsanto's promotion of a "smooth and smiling" wrinkle-resistant fabric finish called "Resloom." These promotions advertised "resort clothes," but "Resloom" owes its origins to studies measuring crease retention in military uniforms (*Women's Wear Daily* 1948, 22; *Vogue* 1947a, C3; Boulton and Corry 1952, 676). Another example of militarized comfort is the post-WWII mainstreaming of the "aloha shirt," which was popularized not only by military personnel stationed in Hawai'i but also by the wider availability of "newer, easy care fabrics" (Morgado 2003, 80). As mainland sportswear companies such as Ralph Lauren, Tommy Hilfiger, and Nautica began producing the aloha shirt, they relied on modern-day synthetic blends instead of cotton broadcloth, Japanese *yukata* cloth, *kabe* crepe, challis, silk, and rayon (Arthur 2006, 17).

Although synthetic fibers tend to be associated with WWII, they were actually used relatively sparingly in military clothing.[8] It is thanks to extensive testing of new fibers *after* WWII that the Vietnam War came to be "the first war in which the U.S. Army made widespread use of nylon, other advanced synthetic fabrics, and plastics in clothing and equipment" (Stanton 1989, 2). In the intervening years, women's beach fashions appeared to solve the lingering military problem of needing to be clothed yet wanting to feel naked. The new synthetic materials used for these fashions were said to function as a "second skin," providing coverage without constraint. A 1947 *Vogue* article calls the maillot "a sheath-like second skin" whose "amphibious, quick-to-dry materials" are "as flexible as your own muscles" (Vogue 1947b, 3). In 1948, a Miami apparel store depicted the "Naked Look" against a backdrop of palm trees, with "second skin" strapless bras and pedal pushers facilitating an "uncovered," "carefree," and "torpid" way of life (Drayton 1948, SII4). Unlike the uncomfortable

---

[8] The highly sought fiber nylon was largely allocated to the Air Force; when used at all by the OQMG, nylon came from rejected parachute material (Risch and Pitkin 1946, 29).

"protective" gear of WWII, second-skin fabrics combined the uninhibited ease of nakedness with the armored resilience of clothing. With the capacity to repel, protect, and balance, this form of synthetic nakedness—also a form of reinforced whiteness—was advertised as being invincible to environmental hazards rather than perilously susceptible to them.

Elsewhere, I have discussed second-skin fabrics in relation to a Cold War regime of American nuclearism (Xiang 2022). Here, I want to show how second-skin clothing allows us to trace a genealogy of comfort from the unfought chemical war to the unfought nuclear war. The tropical backstory for developing protective anti-gas clothing during WWII anticipates the more overt tropical imaginary of Cold War comfort, a style of dress that would repurpose the sartorial values of WWII to fit the nuclear age. As fears of chemical warfare on the battlefield evolved into concerns about atomic warfare in middle America, race science continued to drive military defense—specifically, the defense of the vulnerable white body. With the expansion of the U.S. military imperium across the Pacific, the very islands that the Americans "liberated" came to serve as sacrificial sites for weapons testing. Most infamously, the Marshall Islands "hosted" 67 nuclear tests, with the inaugural test on Bikini Atoll in 1946 inspiring the swimsuit that would become a mainstay of American leisure wear (Teaiwa 1994). Because nuclear bombs only directly affected "test subjects," the Cold War nuclear war, like the WWII chemical war, is remembered as "unfought." But the cultural diffusion of nuclear anxiety means that not only active combatants but ordinary citizens, too, were viewed as in need of "protective clothing." To cite a 1969 Natick study: "The hazards of war, expecially [sic] of the thermal pulse from nuclear weapons, or from napalm, are greater than ever, and seem likely to involve civilians also" (Fourt and Hollies 1969, 196). This quotation provides clues to a new orientation in the science of comfort. In contrast to WWII researchers' preoccupation with extreme cold, Cold War concerns shifted the bias to extreme heat. The interest in "extreme high temperature hazards" included but was not limited to tropical conditions: "The radiation characteristics of clothing are important in relation to sunlight, or to radiant heat as in fire fighting, or to the thermal pulses of nuclear weapons" (Fourt and Hollies 1969, 4, 66).

In a way, second-skin clothing of the 1960s attempted to resolve the contradiction between the anxious pursuit of all-over coverage (in anticipation of civilizational demise through nuclear apocalypse) and the confident display of naked comfort (in embarking on colonial adventures of tropical travel). Second-skin suits of this era began shifting away from a "natural" aesthetic and embracing the "frankly futuristic" qualities of synthetic fabrics (Lenček and Bosker 1989, 62). This fashionable futurism squared the existing rituals of modern life (such as beaches and pools) with sensational prognoses of nuclear war and space travel. One of the "seashine healthsuits" advertised in a 1968 *Harper's Bazaar* article features a gigantic collar of transparent plastic, and another is made of shiny black vinyl with an all-over hood. In the following years, this plasticky look would become even more dramatic, so that the term "second skin" referred less to human skin as an anatomical organ than to the smooth, shiny, and sculptural quality of synthetic textiles. The vaguely eugenicist exhibition of hygienic bareness (a "pared down" look) seems indistinguishable from the militaristic design of an all-enveloping vinyl coat (a "sleeked in" look) (*Harper's Bazaar* 1969). Through such fashions, the civilizational fear of nuclear annihilation and the colonial pastime of tropical travel came into simultaneous focus.

The bared look and the covered look converged in a new way with the advent of "space age" designs that used synthetic materials to reimagine the relation between the modern body and intergalactic environments. It is noteworthy that the most enthusiastic space age designers—such as Rudi Gernreich and Pierre Cardin—specialized in both swim wear and space wear. Ruben Torres, though less famous, represents the fullest synthesis of these trends. Torres's space-age lingerie, which was sponsored by the chemical company and former munitions manufacturer DuPont, used the new fiber Lycra to create "a square bra, a bull's-eye panty, and a vest-like garment called a 'subsweater.'" To advertise DuPont Lycra, Torres's 1965 collection of "Moon-shot Under-fashions" played up the "concept of dressing from the skin out" (DuPont Company Textile Fibers Product Information photographs). Fluid, sleek, and androgynous, Torres's designs suggest both radical vulnerability and unbound possibility.

Ordinary Comfort

During the 1950s and 1960s, the textile failures of the Southwest Pacific (usually the Solomon Islands and New Guinea) combined with the enduring cultural legacy of Polynesian paradises (usually Hawai'i and Tahiti) to give "comfort" its vernacular meanings. In contrast to cold-climate military clothing—which has left its fashion imprint on winter apparel, hunting apparel, and other forms of "heavy duty" apparel that one intuitively perceives as militaristic—the battle conditions of extreme heat brought the science of dress into the more general domain of ordinary comfort. I opened this essay with WWII films set in the Pacific because such films show how the tropical gloss of militarism converted R & R from a structured component of active duty into a Cold War ideal for modern living. The recasting of tropical war as tropical vacation explains why *South Pacific* gave rise to such sensational fashion trends, from halter tops to midriff skirts to a summertime "Bubble-Cap" with plastic soap suds (*Women's Wear Daily* 1949, 3). But, as I have stressed, militarized comfort does not need war to be visible as such. In taking the militarization of the Pacific as a motivating context for studying the popularity of all-American comfort wear, I have tried to locate "war" in regimes of feeling—that is, in racialized interpretations of thermo-sensory environments that center the vulnerability of the white body. Such interpretations sacrifice other kinds of bodies and experiences, invalidate other forms of thermal knowledge, and sever other relations to the environment. Under the guise of science, this cultural discourse of hegemonic comfort turn the intimate needs of the white body into a universal "standard of living."

References

Achter, Paul. 2019. 'Military Chic' and the Rhetorical Production of the Uniformed Body. *Western Journal of Communication* 83 (3): 265–285.

Anderson, Warwick. 2006. *Colonial Pathologies: American Tropical Medicine, Race, and Hygiene in the Philippines*. Durham, NC: Duke University Press.

Arthur, Linda B. 2006. The Aloha Shirt and Ethnicity in Hawai'i. *Textile* 4 (1): 8–35.

Bachner, Evan. 2004. *At Ease: Navy Men of World War II*. New York: Harry N. Abrams.

Bennett, Judith. 2009. *Natives and Exotics: World War II and Environment in the Southern Pacific*. Honolulu: University of Hawaii Press.

Blaszczyk, Regina. 2006. Styling Synthetics: DuPont's Marketing of Fabrics and Fashions in Postwar America. *The Business History Review* 80 (3): 485–528.

Boulton, J., and William A. Corry. 1952. Studies of Summer Weight Tropical Worsted Fabrics Made with Polyester Fibers and Blends of Polyester Fibers. *Journal of the Textile Institute Proceedings* 43 (8): 670–680.

Brawley, Sean, and Chris Dixon. 2012. *Hollywood's South Seas and the Pacific War: Searching for Dorothy Lamour*. New York: Palgrave.

Bresnahan, Josephine. 1999. *Dangers in Paradise: The Battle Against Combat Fatigue in the Pacific War*. PhD diss.: Harvard University.

Chang, Jiat-Hwee. 2016. *A Genealogy of Tropical Architecture: Colonial Networks, Nature and Technoscience*. New York: Routledge.

Craik, Jennifer. 2005. *Uniforms Exposed: From Conformity to Transgression*. Oxford: Berg.

DeJean, Joan. 2009. *The Age of Comfort: When Paris Discovered Casual – And the Modern Home Began*. New York: Bloomsbury.

Drayton, Edward. 1948, January 30. Sophistication for Sun-Spots. *Women's Wear Daily*, SII4.

Fourt, Lyman Edwin, and Norman R.S. Hollies. 1969. *The Comfort and Function of Clothing*. Natick, MA: U.S. Army Natick Laboratories.

Furuhata, Yuriko. 2022. *Climatic Media: Transpacific Experiments in Atmospheric Control*. Durham, NC: Duke University Press.

Fussell, Paul. 2002. *Uniforms: Why We Are What We Wear*. Boston: Houghton Mifflin.

Geiger, Jeffrey A. 2007. *Facing the Pacific: Polynesia and the U.S. Imperial Imagination*. University of Hawai'i Press.

Gonzalez, Vernadette. 2013. *Securing Paradise: Tourism and Militarism in Hawai'i and the Philippines*. Durham: Duke University Press.

de Grazia, Victoria. 2005. *Irresistible Empire: America's Advance Through Twentieth-Century Europe*. Cambridge, MA: The Belknap Press of Harvard University Press.

Gross, Rachel S. 2019. Layering for a Cold War: The M-1943 Combat System, Military Testing, and Clothing as Technology. *Technology and Culture* 60 (2): 378–408.

Harper's Bazaar. 1968, May. Sea-shine Healthsuits, pp. 136–137.

———. 1969, December. Light Turns to Color Emerging From Dark, pp. 142–147.

Kearny, Cresson. 1996. *Jungle Snafus…and Remedies*. Cave Junction, OR: Oregon Institute of Science and Medicine.

Kennedy, Stephen. 1952. Fiber Blends in Military Textiles. *Journal of the Textile Institute Proceedings* 43 (8): 681–698.

Kleber, Brooks, and Dale Birdsell. 1966. *The Chemical Warfare Service: Chemicals in Combat*. Washington, DC: Office of the Chief of Military History United States Army.

Lagae, Johan. 2017. Nomadic Furniture in the 'Heart of Darkness': Colonial and Postcolonial Trajectories of Modern Design Artifacts to and from Tropical Africa. In *The Politics of Furniture*, ed. Fredie Floré and Cammie McAtee, 15–32. New York: Routledge.

Lenček, Lena, and Gideon Bosker. 1989. *Making Waves: Swimsuits and the Undressing of America*. San Francisco: Chronicle Books.

Lindstrom, Lamont, and Geoffrey White. 1990. *Island Encounters: Black and White Memories of the Pacific War*. Washington, DC: Smithsonian Institution Press.

Martin, Richard. 1998. *American Ingenuity: Sportswear, 1930s–1970s*. New York: The Metropolitan Museum of Art.

McClintock, Anne. 1995. *Imperial Leather: Race, Gender, and Sexuality in the Colonial Contest*. New York: Routledge.

Michener, James. 2014. *Tales of the South Pacific*. New York: Dial Press.

Moran, Jim. 2017. *U.S. Marine Corps Uniforms and Equipment in World War II*. Yorkshire-Philadelphia: Frontline Books.

Morgado, Marcia A. 2003. From Kitsch to Chic: The Transformation of Hawaiian Shirt Aesthetics. *Clothing and Textiles Research Journal* 21 (2): 75–88.

Pitkin, Thomas M. 1944. *Quartermaster Equipment for Special Forces*. Washington, DC: Office of the Quartermaster General.

Rall, David P., and Constance M. Pechura. 1993. *Veterans at Risk: The Health Effects of Mustard Gs and Lewisite*. Washington, DC: National Academies Press.

Risch, Erna, and Thomas M. Pitkin. 1946. *Clothing the Soldier of World War II*. Washington, DC: Office of the Quartermaster General.

Robinson, Sid. 1949. Tropics. In *Physiology of Heat Regulation and the Science of Clothing*, ed. L.H. Newburgh, 338–351. Philadelphia: W.B. Saunders.

Sanow, Gilbert A., and Michael C. Bruun. 1983a. Uniforms for America's Tropical Empire: The Evolution of the Khaki Coat for U.S. Army Enlisted Men, 1898–1913, Part I. *Military Collector & Historian* (Summer): 50–59.

———. 1983b. Uniforms for America's Tropical Empire: The Evolution of the Khaki Coat for U.S. Army Enlisted Men, 1898–1913, Part II. *Military Collector and Historian* (Fall): 98–103.

Siple, Paul. 1949. Clothing and Climate. In *Physiology of Heat Regulation and the Science of Clothing*, ed. L.H. Newburgh, 389–442. Philadelphia: W.B. Saunders.

Smith, Susan. 2008. Mustard Gas and American Race-Based Human Experimentation in World War II. *Race, Pharmaceuticals, and Medical Technology* 36 (Fall): 517–522.

Smith, Jen Rose. 2021. 'Exceeding Beringia': Upending Universal Human Events and Wayward Transits in Arctic Spaces. *Society and Space* 39 (1): 158–175.

Stanton, Shelby. 1989. *U.S. Army Uniforms of the Vietnam War*. Mechanicsburg, PA: Stackpole Books.

———. 1991. *U.S. Army Uniforms of World War II*. Mechanicsburg, PA: Stackpole Books.

Starosielski, Nicole. 2021. *Media Hot and Cold*. Durham, NC: Duke University Press.

Sullivan, Nick. 2000. "Army Dreamers." In *Uniform: Order and disorder*, edited by Charta Bonami, Francesco, Maria Luisa Frisa, and Stefano Tonchi, 224–8.

Taylor, William H., Jr. et. al. 1943. *Chamber Tests With Human Subjects.* Washington, D.C.: Naval Research Laboratory.

Teaiwa, Teresia. 1994. bikinis and other s/pacific n/oceans. *The Contemporary Pacific* 6: 87–109.

———. 1999. Reading Paul Gauguin's Noa Noa with Epeli Hauʻofa's Kisses in the Nederends: Militourism, Feminism, and the 'Polynesian' Body. In *Inside Out: Literature, Cultural Politics, and Identity in the New Pacific*, ed. Vilsoni Hereniko and Rob Wilson, 249–263. Lanham, MD: Rowman and Littlefield.

Trachtenberg, Alan. 1989. *Reading American Photographs Images as History Mathew Brady to Walker Evans.* New York: Hill and Wang.

Tu, Thuy Linh Nguyen. 2021. *Experiments in Skin: Race and Beauty in the Shadows of Vietnam.* Durham: Duke University Press.

Vogue. 1947a, December 1. Monsanto Advertisement, p. 3.

———. 1947b, June 1. Maillot…Suit of the Year, p. 115.

Wartime Technological Developments. A Study Made for the Subcommittee on War Mobilization of the Committee on Military Affairs, 79th Congress, 1st Session, Senate Subcommittee Monograph No. 1, May 1945.

Wartime Technological Developments, Supplement for 1944. A Study Made for the Subcommittee on War Mobilization, 79th Congress, 1st session, Senate Subcommittee Monograph No. 2, September 1945.

Werden, J.E., M.K. Fahnestock, and R.L. Galbraith. 1959. Thermal Comfort of Clothing of Varying Fiber Content. *Textile Research Journal* 29: 640–651.

Wexler, Laura. 2000. *Tender Violence: Domestic Visions in an Age of U.S. Imperialism.* Chapel Hill: University of North Carolina Press.

Women's Wear Daily. 1940, September 11. Celanese Corp. To Stress 'American', p. 15.

———. 1942, October 1. Designers To Show Postwar Fashions, p. 1.

———. 1946, October 3. Use 'Modern Living' Theme for Knit Lingerie, p. 18.

———. 1948, May 5. Fabrics Included In Travel Show, p. 22.

———. 1949, April 27. 'Shampoo' Bubble-Cap, p. 3.

Xiang, Sunny. 2022. Bikinis and Other Atomic Incidents: The Synthetic Life of the Nuclear Pacific. *Radical History Review* 142: 37–56.

CHAPTER 4

Costume Design and Emotional Communication in 1940s British Cinema

Bethan Bide

Film costume is often thought of as surface. It is celebrated as the glitter that gives glamour to the tinsel of the silver screen or read as visual signifiers of character. However, enlarged on-screen films present audiences with a hyper-real version of the materiality of clothes—whether familiar through their similarity to audiences' own clothes or alien in their extravagance or historical setting—and this material experience acts as a powerful form of emotional communication. This chapter asks what we can learn about the relationship between film costume, affect, and the historical study of emotions by engaging with how the materiality of clothes is represented and used on-screen.

This chapter explores how clothes were depicted on-screen in the late 1940s in a selection of films produced by Ealing Studios and investigates how these were used by costume designers and cinematographers in order to communicate material experiences to British cinema audiences in the turbulent aftermath of the Second World War. By studying the

B. Bide (✉)
University of Leeds, Leeds, UK
e-mail: B.Bide@leeds.ac.uk

© The Author(s), under exclusive license to Springer Nature Switzerland AG 2023
R. Filippello, I. Parkins (eds.), *Fashion and Feeling*, Palgrave Studies in Fashion and the Body,
https://doi.org/10.1007/978-3-031-19100-8_4

construction, materials and wear evidenced in the presentation of clothes on screen, and by contextualising these visual representations of materiality within the broader historical context of post-war Britain, this chapter suggests that costumes were designed to evoke complex and often contradictory sets of emotions within cinema audiences. Specifically, it considers how audience members might have understood the moral, gender and class connotations of fashion in film through their own experiences of making, buying and wearing clothes and how, in turn, these films shaped the way audiences interpreted their own bodily relationships towards the clothes they wore. Through this, it argues that film costume can further our understanding of the British public's changing emotional relationship to clothes during a period when conflict and global geopolitics disrupted every aspect of life, offering an insight into how mid-century audiences understood their place within contemporary British society and their relationship to the nation and its governance.

But uncovering how historic audiences felt about the multi-layered sensory consumption of clothes on-screen is easier said than done due to a lack of evidence about audience responses and active spectatorship before the age of mass digital consumption (Uhlirova 2013a, 138; Khan 2012). In the place of recorded evidence, scholars have been left to speculate on how the visual presentation of garments as symbols of characters' feelings could trigger emotional responses in audiences, drawing on psychoanalytical theory to explore the individual, voyeuristic experience of watching a film at the expense of understanding the social nature of cinematic experience (Swann 1987, 8; Bruzzi 2011, 178). Thinking phenomenologically about the visual experience of cinema offers an opportunity to access the emotions of costume in a different way. Recognising that film is a site of double embodiment between the film maker and spectator, costume becomes a lens through which we can understand 'what it means to be both an embodied visible subject and an embodied visible object' (Sobchack 1992, 260). Instead of 'reading' on-screen clothes in order to understand their symbolic agency, this chapter suggests that focusing on their materiality provides insight into how these fictional fashions conveyed very real shared material and bodily understandings between film makers and audience. This is achieved by exploring clothes on-screen as both visual and material sources, and by situating the consumption of film costume as an embodied visual and material practice for the cinematic audience. Additionally, by focusing on the way audience members consumed cultural values and narratives through the presentation of clothes on-screen, it serves as a response to calls to consider the relationship between film and fashion consumption more broadly than simply the act of 'women shopping' for things they have seen in films (Warner 2012, 122–124).

The approach taken in this chapter further develops existing work that considers how the spectacle of clothes on-screen affects the audience (Uhlirova 2013b, 19–26). It particularly draws on Giuliana Bruno's writing, which calls for us to think differently about materiality (Bruno 2014). Bruno is interested in how materiality manifests on the surface of different media and how the physicality of material objects can be translated into other mediums, such as photography and film. If, as Bruno discusses, 'materiality is not a question of materials but, fundamentally, of activating material relations', it follows that the contemporary ready-to-wear clothes shown on-screen in Ealing Studios productions provide a connection to the lost materiality of those garments, and through this, clues to the embodied and imaginative responses that 1940s audiences had to these costumes (Bruno 2014, 8).

Understanding that clothes on-screen have a materiality is significant for their potential use as sources for exploring the relationship between historic fashions and feelings as a result of both the intimate, bodily relationship we have with the materiality of clothes and the way fashion can be used to communicate and negotiate individual and collective identity (Crane 2000). The growing field of emotional history is increasingly interested in the relationship between emotions and material objects (Plamper 2009). Historians of emotion have particularly noted the close, bodily relationship women have with garments and textiles (Dolan and Holloway 2016) and the potential of using these objects to tell narratives that give their makers and wearers historical agency (Fisk 2019). But emotional histories are not just about individuals and this is not a chapter about contemporary readings of emotions in historic films since emotions are culturally and socially situated and so emotional experiences from the past cannot transcend time and space to be perfectly translated in the present (Tarlow 2012, 179). Instead, this chapter looks to clothes on-screen to uncover clues about the structures of feeling operating in post-war Britain (Williams 1977). As Sara Ahmed (2004) notes, emotions are used to produce and maintain power structures and so exploring the histories of embodied experiences can help us understand how societies and cultures have changed and the processes and motivations behind these changes (Barclay 2020, 11).

Since the material culture of our environment can shape individual and collective feeling, it seems likely that the heightened sensory awareness of colours, sounds and light that occur in the darkness of the cinema provides a particularly effective space for the practice of emotions (Anderson 2009). Further, the popularity of cinema as a mass-entertainment medium in late 1940s Britain indicates it likely had a significant role as part of a cultural process by which the population learned appropriate emotional responses. Although the significance of the cinema as a historic space where emotions are practiced has not been explored in depth, it is well established that language and visual culture shape emotions (Rosenwein 2002). Research into the history of emotions broadly refutes the idea that humans have a set of innate emotional behaviours (Boddice 2018, 111–120). Due to the impossibility of emoting outside of a cultural framework, the field instead focuses on the practices that signal the connected processes of expression and emotion (Boddice 2018, 120). Using Pierre Bourdieu's definition of practice to connect society and the physical body, Monique Scheer has suggested that 'emotions themselves can be viewed as practical engagement' (Scheer 2012, 193). Scheer further draws on Bourdieu's idea of habitus to argue that cultural education is connected to the way that emotions are produced (Scheer 2012). Understanding emotions as something people actively do, rather than something that happens to them, this chapter uses Scheer's definition of emotional practice to suggest that the presentation of clothes on-screen provides an extremely interesting source through which to consider how cinema audiences understood and used clothes in the practice of feeling.

Ealing Studios and the Changing Relationship Between Audiences and Film Fashions in Post-war British Cinema

Cinema played a particularly important role in the visual culture of postwar Britain due to its huge popularity. 1946, a year commonly remembered in historical accounts for fuel shortages and the introduction of bread rationing, marked the peak of British cinema attendance, with audience numbers reaching 1635 million (Williams 1998, 194). Moreover, films made in Britain for a British audience were more prominent than they had been since the 1920s as a result of government quotas to ensure a minimum percentage of films exhibited were British (Swann 1987,

84–85). One of the success stories that emerged from these circumstances was Ealing Studios.

The studios had been in operation since 1931 and became well-respected for their innovative documentaries during the Second World War, but it was in the immediate post-war years that the studio produced a series of comedy films that made their international reputation. This chapter explores two of these films. The first, *Hue and Cry*, was a comedy released in 1947 and told the story of a gang of semi-feral working-class London children who managed to foil a high-level criminal organisation. Following the success of *Hue and Cry*, Ealing focused on making more comedy films that celebrated the particular quirks of life in post-war Britain (Murphy 2003, 209). *Passport to Pimlico*, the second film discussed in this chapter, was subsequently released in 1949. It tells the story of a London neighbourhood so sick of rationing and austerity that it declared independence from Britain.

These films focused on reflecting an 'authentic' view of contemporary British life, drawing on the lessons Ealing's cameramen learned while making wartime documentaries in order to create films that, according to the studio's head Michael Balcon, projected 'Britain and the British Character' (Barr 1998, 7). 1940s reviews of Ealing Studios productions demonstrate that the 'realistic' depiction of everyday life was key to their appeal (Picturegoer 1947, 12). Although the appeal of film fashions is often considered to lie in the opportunities they offer for fantastical escapism, British cinema audiences began to reject outlandish Hollywood costumes in the late 1930s, preferring instead to see clothes that were closer to their lived experiences (Roberts 2022). This trend gathered further momentum in the 1940s due to the differences between British and American experiences of wartime shortages and restrictions on clothing consumption.

The choice of clothes and the way they were depicted on-screen provided an important way of communicating a shared sense of social realism to audiences, and the wardrobe department took great pains to ensure the clothes on-screen were representative of what was available to buy, conducting in-depth research in both shops and street markets (Surowiec 2012, 115). The majority of contemporary costumes for female characters were items of ready-to-wear sourced from London shops. Ealing's costume designer, Anthony Mendleson, would supply a costume list to the Board of Trade and receive a corresponding supply of clothing coupons in order to purchase these garments (Surowiec 2012, 114). This made sourcing last-minute additions or replacement costumes problematic—particularly during 1947 when factories were closed due to the winter fuel crisis and supplies were severely disrupted—and actors were encouraged to treat their costumes with care because the clothes were embedded in these austerity consumption processes (Surowiec 2012, 113–115).

Costumes for use on-stage or screen are generally considered as separate and different to the creations of fashion designers, but this method of sourcing clothes blurs this distinction between the materialities of clothes on- and off-screen (Stutesman 2011, 20). Many London audience members were familiar with the materiality of the clothes they saw on-screen because they frequented the same shops and owned garments by the same brands featured in the films. Yet the close-up shots of these garments on large cinema screens would have also confronted them with a strangely hyper-real view of these familiar clothes, prompting them to look again. The uncanny nature of this shared understanding between audiences and clothes on-screen made the costumes particularly effective tools for evoking sensory memories and emotions in audience members. However, these garments would also have signified different feelings to different people according to their socio-economic, cultural and geographical backgrounds (Barclay 2020, 3). This chapter thus considers the complexities of how the on-screen materiality of a garment's weight, smell and marks of wear might have been understood by 1940s audiences in multiple ways and reflects on how this ability of clothes on-screen to simultaneously elicit multiple and sometimes contradictory emotions enables them to provide insight into the way people used fashion as a tool to negotiate their experiences of a deeply changed environment and society. In particular, it highlights how these on-screen clothes provided space to mourn what was lost and what people feared they were going to lose in the changes brought by post-war modernity.

Hue and Cry: Negotiating the Morality of Desire and Consumption at a Time of Austerity

The Second World War changed the physical and social landscapes of Britain. It loosened social hierarchies and widened opportunities (Porter 2000, 418). This had implications for the way people understood and interpreted how others dressed, since clothes are coded with cultural understandings of class, respectability and social hierarchies. By extension, the consumption of clothes on-screen provided a means by which the

British public could practice and navigate these changes through what Erin Sullivan describes as 'emotional improvisation', a process by which individuals adjust their emotional responses to their surrounding environment so that those responses more closely correspond with prevailing linguistic and visual representations of emotions (Sullivan 2016, 9).

Ealing's post-war films play with audience assumptions and perceptions of respectability in dress to explore the boundaries of Britain's new social freedoms and the changing meaning of class at this time. On its surface, *Hue and Cry* (1947) uses the materiality of worn clothing to express an optimistic view of the power of the British public to topple unfair and corrupt social hierarchies by working cooperatively together. The film tells the story of a group of working-class London youths who discover that criminal networks have been sending coded messages using the pages of a children's comic. In spite of widespread police corruption and incompetence, the children eventually manage to foil the criminal gang in a hopeful narrative of honesty and integrity triumphing over the vested interests of a powerful social elite.

The scale of the struggle faced by the children in order to bring down a criminal network entrenched within London's social and cultural establishment is reinforced through the materiality of their clothes. The child-heroes of the film wear distinctly shabby attire. They appear dressed in the working-class uniform of hand-me-down suit jackets and ties, displaying various rips in their ill-fitting clothes. These outfits provide a clear visual distinction with those of the criminal elements in the film, who are not only neatly dressed in newer clothes, but are fashionable in a way that seems out-of-place and notably ostentatious amid the rubble and bomb damage of post-war London. The character of Rhona, a member of the criminal gang, most clearly exemplifies this visual distinction. As is evident in Fig. 4.1 (picturing Rhona waiting in a bus queue with some of the children), Rhona is the model of contemporary high fashion. From her crisp turban to her well-heeled shoes, Rhona embodies an aesthetic that nods unpatriotically towards the latest Parisian trends. The jarringly clear visual distinction between Rhona and the other figures in this street scene raises questions as to how Rhona is able to get her hands on these fashions at a time of ongoing rationing and shortages, implying that such a look could only be obtained through the proceeds of criminal greed.

Beyond stylistic references, however, it is the material differences between how the criminals and the children wear their clothes that really cast suspicion on these characters and their self-interested motivations. In

Fig. 4.1 *Hue and Cry* scene still showing Rhona (far right) in bus queue, 1947. Studiocanal Films Ltd/Ronald Grant/Mary Evans

contrast to the children she stands with, Rhona's clothes look jarringly new. This is less to do with their style, and more the result of visual clues that indicate the difference between new and well-worn garments. For example, the shoulders of Rhona's jacket are smooth, whereas the children's are dented where the shoulder padding has broken down and shifted as a result of a long period of wear. Similarly, the children's jackets show puckering on the quarters below the lapels, a product of shrinkage during washing that would be familiar to members of the audience at this time. Furthermore, Rhona's shiny open-toed heels contrast with the scuffed and stretched leather of the children's shoes, and her fine, sheer stockings stand out against the folds of their coarse wool socks.

The visual clues as to how the costumes in *Hue and Cry* had been worn, washed and used drew on the audience's shared understanding of what happens to clothes when they are embodied. This challenged the audience to reconsider their own cultural assumptions that associated being well-dressed and being respectable. The materiality of the worn costumes worked against the underlying prejudices many Londoners felt about the clothes of the working classes, the shabbiness of which they interpreted as signs of vulgar and inferior tastes.[1] Conversely, *Hue and Cry* used dirty and heavily worn clothes to signify the eminently respectable characteristics of integrity and hard work. The central protagonist, a boy named Joe Kirby, is frequently shot in close-ups that clearly show the dark dirt marks around his cuffs. This dirt is gathered from his laborious work at Covent Garden Market as well as from the time he spends hanging out with the gang on dusty bomb sites, and it roots him as a productive contributor to the landscape he lives in.

In appealing to the audience's material understanding of what it was like to wear and care for clothes at a time of austerity, the film subverts prevailing cultural narratives about which members of society were most likely to make up the criminal class. This provided an opportunity for the audience to engage in processes of emotional improvisation by adjusting their conditioned responses to more closely correspond with an emerging and idealised vision of post-war Britain as a social-democracy where class played a diminished role in determining opportunities. The film's concern with criminality is a particularly fruitful site for this type of emotional improvisation due to the extensive media coverage in 1946 of a perceived crime wave and large numbers of petty burglaries (Hennessy 1992, 445). *Hue and Cry*'s dirty clothing explicitly challenges the moral panic contained in the newspaper reports that blamed this crime wave on the real gangs of youths who played on bombsites—the result, according to newspaper columnist Molly Panter Downes, of wartime family breakdowns and lack of disciplining father figures (Kynaston 2008, 113). However, rather than pointing fingers at these semi-feral children, the film harnesses these stereotypes within the story, playing off the understood material meanings of worn clothing to expose the hypocrisy of British society's tendency to turn a blind eye to the criminal behaviour of certain types of people simply because they look respectable. The association between worn clothing, honesty and integrity is emphasised by the way *Hue and Cry*'s young characters get noticeably shabbier as the film progresses. Joe Kirby's journey

---

[1] These prejudices are apparent in contemporary diaries, typically commenting on working-class dress as 'unmistakably vulgar in colour and design'. Diary for 12 November 1948. Mass Observation, Diarist 5474.

from daydreaming youth to action hero is not marked by a transformation into a well-dressed young man, but can be traced in the deteriorating materiality of his crudely home-made jumper. Joe's visibly aged jumper, with a baggy, stretched neckline and darned holes, physically unravels in a series of ever longer loose threads as he solves the crime.

In contrast, the use of neat, new clothes to indicate an association between fashionable excess, self-interest and morally dubious behaviour in *Hue and Cry* echoes state narratives about post-war austerity, which associated material self-sacrifice with patriotism and concern for the greater good. In choosing this portrayal of clothes on-screen the cinematographers and producers seem to be supporting the emotional regimes of post-war Britain. Emotional regimes can be understood as the practices by which a 'set of normative emotions' are used to support the authority and power of organisations or groups, such as the government and the church, and through this act to underpin stable societies (Reddy 2001, 129). Close-ups of luxurious pieces of clothing in *Hue and Cry* invite the audience to test themselves according to the morality of post-war emotional regimes by contrasting materially attractive objects against the unappealing costumes of the youthful street gang. When the criminals attempt a hit on Riches (an aptly named fictional department store on Oxford Circus), the children foil their plans against the backdrop of a fashion display that is stocked full of expensive evening dresses. The way the dresses are lit conveys a tactile sense of the luxury of these garments, accentuating the drape, weight and sheen of expensive fabrics against the clean marble floors of the store. As the camera closes in on one particularly dramatic full-length dress in silk satin, the visual pleasure of the shot is disrupted by a mouse escaping from underneath its voluminous skirt, swiftly followed by a grubby child's hand and a threadbare jacket sleeve. The lack of regard this scruffy child shows for the luxury of the dress's fabric as he roughly pushes it aside chides audience members who were distracted from the higher order business of the film's plot by the visual pleasures of material goods and reminds them of their social responsibility to sacrifice pleasurable consumption for the sake of national priorities at a time of austerity.

However, the materiality of clothing in *Hue and Cry* also highlights the complexity of the British public's relationship with the way they were encouraged to feel about ongoing shortages and sacrifices, and particularly the narrative that austerity regulations meant an equality of material sacrifice. On the one hand, the film clearly exemplifies a continuation of wartime emotional regimes celebrating patriotic material self-sacrifice for a greater good. On the other, it highlights the inescapable lure of material consumption and growing cracks in the mythology about fair shares for all under a Labour government, using contrasts between worn and unworn clothing to evoke a raw sense of the material unfairness of persistent class inequalities, which ran counter to the narrative of social reform and a new, fairer, post-war Britain (Hennessy 1992, 129). The ingrained and ever-present debris from bomb damaged buildings on the children's clothes also highlights the persistence of wartime trauma and the depth of these emotions. This particular type of dry dirt, formed of brick and plaster dust, seems to inescapably cling to their clothes, as if the built environment itself is resisting the modernising project of post-war social change. Through the lens of Avery Gordon's work on haunting, this simultaneously lingering and unreachable reminder of the pre-war built environment provides an insight into feelings that might be repressed under the politically sanctioned emotional regimes of the day (Gordon 2008). While these young characters may embody the hopes of a fairer and more egalitarian society, their clothes encapsulate the emotional difficulty of escaping the past.

Passport to Pimlico: Navigating Conflicted Emotions Through Out-of-Place Clothes

Hue and Cry's moral message of sartorial self-denial felt increasingly out of touch with the national mood by the time Ealing Studios came to shoot their next comedy film. By 1948, the persistent difficulties of austerity, notably ongoing rationing and the high cost of living, left many feeling weighed down by the 'constant struggle' of life in post-war Britain (Kynaston 2008, 296). The 1949 release *Passport to Pimlico* mirrors this rising public frustration and introduces a heightened moral ambiguity into the way costume is used to convey individuality and material desires, once again allowing audiences space to engage with processes of emotional navigation and improvisation through their imagined responses to the clothes on the cinema screen.

Passport to Pimlico offered cinema-goers the tantalising possibility of a return to unbridled consumption in an alternate post-austerity reality, with the opening credits humorously dedicating the film 'to the memory of' ration books—a clever solution to the fact that the government announced the ending of rationing on a number of items, including clothing, while the film was in post-production, rendering most of its rationing references immediately historical (Sellers 2015, 138). The film's plot centres around the discovery of a royal charter in a crater left by the detonation of an unexploded bomb in London's Pimlico area. This charter details that, due to historic land ownership, Pimlico is legally part of Burgundy. Seizing the opportunity to escape oppressive government regulation, the locals declare themselves independent Burgundians and enjoy the excesses of unrestricted consumption for the first time in years—at least until their supplies run out.

Unlike *Hue and Cry*, which celebrated reuse and repair, *Passport to Pimlico* finds hope through a rebellious rejection of austerity rules relating to clothes (Fig. 4.2). The consumption of clothing is one of the first signs of the new freedoms enjoyed by Pimlico residents after gaining their independence. Upon hearing the news, the grocery shop assistant Molly (played by Jane Hylton) abandons her shop counter and runs to the local

Fig. 4.2 Passport to Pimlico, 1949. Studiocanal Films Ltd/Ronald Grant/Mary Evans

dress shop to purchase a blouse that she had previously not had enough coupons to buy. The freedom symbolised in the act of purchasing an item without coupons is further explored through the use of the materiality of clothes to convey a powerful sensory experience of consumption. The presentation of the material properties of fabrics in the shop evokes sensory memories of the excitement, pleasure and promise of shopping for new clothes. The clothes Molly rifles through on the shop's rack are made of lightweight patterned cottons, silks and new synthetic materials that move easily through her fingers with a tactile promise they would be accommodatingly comfortable to wear. The materiality of these garments provides a stark contrast to Molly's work overalls, which are made of a coarse, heavy cotton, the weight of which is further emphasised by the way the sleeves are rolled up into thick, tight bunches. The fabric of the overalls is aged into a grubby shade of white, and the back is covered in dirty marks from the day's work activities. The juxtaposition of these materials on-screen uses the implied tactile experience—beyond even the look—of the lightweight shop garments to equate this coupon-free purchase with the promise of an easier and less laborious future.

The physical weight of women's clothing is important throughout *Passport to Pimlico*. Audiences familiar with contemporary fashions would have known that the lightweight qualities of the garments worn by the newly liberated Burgundians indicate that they are mass-produced items of ready-to-wear. These inexpensive clothes, which were unlined and made from cottons and synthetic fabrics, conveyed a material understanding of accessibility because they were affordable—so affordable in fact that it is only rationing that limits the film's characters from buying them. Britain's rapidly expanding medium-quality ready-to-wear industry sold the egalitarian notion that people from all walks of life should be able to access new fashion trends, and dressing characters in these clothes helped anchor the film's narrative as a relatable fantasy. By suggesting that, in a world without purchase tax or controls, British people of all classes might find pride in their ability to look stylish, Ealing Studios drew on the transformative promise of ready-to-wear as a method of indicating Britain's upward trajectory from austerity to modernity.

Elsewhere in the film, however, clothes are used to disrupt the idea that this was a purely linear trajectory of progress. Although Ealing's post-war comedy films have proved enduringly popular as nostalgic representations of a gentler past, focused on community and celebrations of small triumphs, they are also rife with clues that point to the 'underlying anxieties' of post-war Britain (Boyce 2012, 6). From frustration at continued austerity to anger at pervading social inequality—as well as broader unspoken fears of an uncertain future, which compelled characters to long for a return to wartime and its reassuring sense of solidarity—Ealing's post-war films are underscored by a sense of sadness at the impossibly large gap between their fantastical narratives and the realities of their audiences' experiences (Barr 1998, 104–106). Although film scholars have considered how Ealing's comedy output made space for mainstream films to discuss troubling social narratives—and even celebrate ambiguous morality—through plots, music and actors that conveyed a light-hearted tone, the compelling insight that their presentation of clothes offers into the conflicted nature of the post-war hopes and fears of audiences is still widely overlooked (Daubney 2006, 61).

Where Ealing's wardrobe team used contemporary ready-to-wear fashions to root films in the present, the incongruous materiality of placing old clothes in contemporary settings was used to create a sense of unease by confusing audiences' expectations of what they thought they should be seeing. While *Passport to Pimlico* provides plenty of visual clues that remind the audience that the film is set in London in 1949, the costumes on the screen often challenge and confuse this temporality. Much like the layers of London's built history that were exposed by bombs during the blitz, the presence of old, out-of-style clothes on-screen dug up and exposed a version of past that intruded, unwelcomely, on the present.

Passport to Pimlico's darker, anti-authority, sentiment is encapsulated in its use of out-of-date military dress to ridicule and undermine establishment systems and the regulations that stem from them. These military costumes are worn in strange combinations and odd settings to muddle the audience's understanding of socially accepted power structures and hierarchies by placing these material signifiers of wartime authority within consciously atypical contexts. The most powerful example of incongruous military attire comes in the form of the makeshift uniform worn by the local policeman, P.C. Spiller, after he has taken on the role of Burgundian passport control officer. Spiller trades in his official police uniform for one that looks to be improvised from parts of his daily wardrobe, combined with a shirt and a British Wolseley pattern helmet of the type worn during the North Africa campaign—presumably remnants from his military service. The audience would have understood that this desert uniform was not only utterly out of time but jarringly out-of-place in Pimlico. This ridiculous attire is also ill-fitting and sloppily worn. The way the tie has been styled to hang carelessly off-centre reveals gapes between buttonholes where the shirt is stretched by Spiller's rounded stomach, suggesting he has physically let himself go somewhat since the end of the war. Both the clothes and the way they are worn serve to utterly undercut his claim to authority. This supposed uniform, comprised of objects that were once material symbols of patriotic service, has become a joke at the expense of official authority figures, likely resonating with members of the audience left politically disengaged and cynical of authority after their experiences of conflict (Fielding 1992, 623).

The film also incorporates non-military items of wartime costume, such as the old wartime tin helmets donned by shopkeeper Arthur Pemberton and his daughter Shirley in order to explore the crater left by a recently exploded bomb, itself a wartime relic. These Zuckerman helmets would have been instantly familiar to audiences as they had been standard wartime issue for civil defence personnel such as Fire Guards and ARP wardens. Arthur's helmet is even painted with the letters 'PW', indicating his mid-ranking wartime role as a Post Warden and, with this, aiming a subtle dig at his inflated sense of self-importance. Shirley visibly struggles with the heavy materiality of her helmet throughout the scene, eventually resorting to fastening its chin strap extremely tightly in an attempt to keep it balanced on her head. Many members of the audience would likely share similar material memories of wearing such awkward and uncomfortable helmets on war service, and this may well have evoked embodied memories of the emotions they associated with civil defence duties during that frightening time. But the heavy materiality of the helmet is also juxtaposed with Shirley's lightweight civilian summer clothes, and the reflective qualities of its dull, dented metal contrasts with the shine of her newly painted nails, mixing the material memories of the past with a more modern tactile understanding of the present.

Although their overall effect is comic, the sheer number of these repeating remnants of an unpleasant past on the large cinema screen provided an inescapable provocation to the audience—reminding them of the length of time that had elapsed since the end of the war, and of the continuing distance between the unfulfilled promises made by wartime and post-war governments and the darker realities of their post-war lives (Williams 1994, 98–100). Thus the juxtaposition between the materiality of clothes from past and the present in *Passport to Pimlico* embodies both the disorientating emotional impact of rapid social change and the role of clothes on-screen as a tool to help audiences navigate their emotional responses to this.

Conclusions

The presentation of clothes as weighty, challenging and disruptive on-screen presences in *Hue and Cry* and *Passport to Pimlico* highlights their ability to evoke embodied emotional practices from cinema audiences, conjuring a spectrum of responses and linking to individual and collective memories through their material associations. Through this, these clothes provided a way for audiences to navigate the difficulties, confusion and grief of living through an extremely turbulent period in British history and a means to process the disappointment and resentment caused by a lingering suspicion that, in spite of the grand promises of social reform, little of importance had really changed in Britain's New Jerusalem.

Enlarged on a cinema screen, Ealing films presented audiences with a hyper-real version of the familiar realities of their own clothes. The documentary-inspired style of the cinematography of these films highlights the materiality of how clothes are worn in unusual detail for fiction films of the time. It draws attention to marks of wear in the form of pulled threads and worn patches that might otherwise seem insignificant, and exaggerates the violence of ripped seams. 'Reading' the details of these film costumes and considering how they communicated with audiences through a shared language of material experience demonstrates that the presentation of clothes on-screen did more than just support the narrative told by the script. Unlike many Hollywood films from the era, the Ealing comedies of the 1940s did not offer an escape from austerity through fantasy or historical costumes. Instead, they held a mirror to it, exaggerating and distorting aspects of post-war life in order to provoke cathartic audience responses. Through the familiar materiality of the garments used and the realism with which they were worn, these on-screen clothes provided audiences with opportunities for emotional negotiation, evoking the moral ambiguity that lurked beneath the surface of life in post-war austerity Britain.

This material presentation of clothes on-screen demonstrates how fashion played an integral role in the way the British public understood post-war social change, helping people locate themselves, their desires and their fears in a much-changed physical and cultural landscape (Bide 2021). As a result, studying the clothes in these films provides insight into the historical emotions of the 1940s and the importance of fashion as a tool for navigating and expressing these emotions. They reveal a public fearful that Britain's post-war problems went far deeper than material shortages and ongoing rationing. The compellingly realistic material mise-en-scène of clothes underpins the humour, comradery and localised community spirit of these films with an inescapable sense that Britain had paid the price for wartime victory by condemning itself to a future as an unpleasant, dirty and broken nation in which individuals found themselves confined to stifling lives with limited opportunities. But this presentation also offered audiences escape from their worst fears by allowing individuals to experience a cathartic purging of their own conflicted sentiments towards this strange time of change and tremendous loss, reminding them that there was also hope for a different future.[2]

By providing space in the darkness of the cinema for audiences to engage in these processes of emotional improvisation, these films actively used the materiality of fashion to help shift and shape the emotional regimes of post-war Britain. This reflects the politics of many at Ealing Studios, including the producer Michael Balcon, an ardent socialist who became increasingly disillusioned with the Labour Party and its post-war settlement throughout this period (Sinclair 1989, 250). Understanding the power that fashion had to resist and subvert the official government narratives and institutional propaganda that underpinned the emotional regimes of wartime Britain provides an important tool for reassessing the nostalgic lens through which the 1940s if often presented and dispel some of the historical mythologies about this period.

Film costumes play a significant role in crafting our understandings of national, cultural and class identity (Hole 2011). Acknowledging the conflicted emotions expressed and elicited by the materiality of clothes in these films therefore demands we also interrogate how these clothes have subsequently been discussed as representations of austerity moralities in Britain, finding heroism in the wearing of old worn clothes and plucky underdog spirit in clever legal loopholes around rationing. These types of narratives about the representational meaning of costume in *Passport to Pimlico* and *Hue and Cry* have validated a particular set of collective

---

[2] Catharsis here refers to the sense of pleasurable calm achieved by witnessing a tragic narrative unfold from beginning to end, allowing the audience to imagine the worst that could happen, experiencing a sense of completion as this unfolds and then a sense of relief at remembering that this is fiction (Nuttall 1996, 76).

memories about both 1940s fashion and the broader cultural mood of the period—which revolve around narratives of creative making do and the nobility of sartorial sacrifice for the greater good—at the expense of excluding divergent experiences (Misztal 2003, 10–16). The continuing popularity of the Ealing comedies and the prevailing cultural nostalgia for austerity that they feed make this a powerful narrative about the emotional cultures of post-war Britain, as exemplified by their use by the right-wing press in support of causes including the Conservative party and Brexit (Littlejohn 2020; Smith 2020).

Instead, by considering the spectrum of emotional responses that the material details of clothes might have evoked in audiences, this chapter unsettles these narratives by revealing the conflicted emotions of the immediate post-war period. These emotions speak of the contrasting experiences of the sections of British society enabled by the opportunities offered by post-war change and those frustrated by the lack of progress they perceived in reforms that were achieved through legislation, rather than bottom-up social change, leaving inequality, sexism and prejudice ingrained into British society (Morgan 2001, 108). Thus not only does close scrutiny of the materiality of clothes on film offer opportunities for the study of emotional histories, it also provides a means to resist the co-option of fashion by nostalgic and simplistic historical narratives that serve contemporary political interests.

References

Ahmed, Sara. 2004. *The Cultural Politics of Emotion*. Edinburgh: Edinburgh University Press.

Anderson, Ben. 2009. Affective Atmospheres. *Emotion, Space and Society* 2: 77–81. https://doi.org/10.1016/j.emospa.2009.08.005.

Barclay, Kate. 2020. *The History of Emotions: A Student Guide to Methods and Sources*. London: Bloomsbury.

Barr, Charles. 1998. *Ealing Studios*. Berkeley: University of California Press.

Bide, Bethan. 2021. In Their Shoes: Using Fashion Objects to Explore the Duration and Complexity of Wartime Experiences. *Critical Military Studies* 7 (4): 418–434. https://doi.org/10.1080/23337486.2020.1751492.

Boddice, Rob. 2018. *The History of Emotions*. Manchester: Manchester University Press.

Boyce, Michael. 2012. *The Lasting Influence of the War on Postwar British Film*. New York: Palgrave Macmillan.

Bruno, Giuliana. 2014. *Surface: Matters of Aesthetics, Materiality, and Media*. London: University of Chicago Press.

Bruzzi, Stella. 2011. 'It will be a magnificent obsession': Femininity, Desire, and the New Look in 1950s Hollywood Melodrama. In *Fashion in Film*, ed. Adrienne Munich, 160–180. Bloomington: Indiana University Press.

Crane, Diana. 2000. *Fashion and its Social Agendas. Class, Gender and Identity in Clothing*. Chicago: University of Chicago Press.

Daubney, Kate. 2006. Music as a Satirical Device. In *European Film Music*, ed. David Burnand and Mera Miguel, 60–73. Aldershot: Ashgate.

Dolan, Alice, and Sally Holloway. 2016. Emotional Textiles: An Introduction. *Textile* 14 (2): 152–159. https://doi.org/10.1080/14759756.2016.1139369.

Fielding, Steven. 1992. What Did 'The People' Want? The Meaning of the 1945 General Election. *The Historic Journal* 35 (3): 623–639. https://doi.org/10.1017/S0018246X00026005.

Fisk, Catriona. 2019. Looking for Maternity: Dress Collections and Embodied Knowledge. *Fashion Theory* 23 (3): 401–439. https://doi.org/10.1080/1362704X.2019.1603871.

Gordon, Avery. 2008. *Ghostly Matters: Haunting and the Sociological Imagination. New University of Minnesota Press edition*. Minneapolis: University of Minnesota Press.

Hennessy, Peter. 1992. *Never Again: Britain 1945–1951*. London: Jonathan Cape.

Hole, Kristin. 2011. Does Dress Tell the Nation's Story? Fashion, History, and the Nation in the Films of Fassbinder. In *Fashion in Film*, ed. Adrienne Munich, 281–300. Bloomington: Indiana University Press.

Khan, Nathalie. 2012. Cutting the Fashion Body: Why the Fashion Image is No Longer Still. *Fashion Theory* 16 (2): 235–250. https://doi.org/10.2752/175174112X13274987924177.

Kynaston, David. 2008. *Austerity Britain 1945–51*. London: Bloomsbury.

Littlejohn, Richard. 2020, September 25. Passport to Tunbridge Wells. *Daily Mail*.

Misztal, Barbara. 2003. *Theories of Social Remembering*. Maidenhead: Open University Press.

Morgan, Kenneth. 2001. *The People's Peace*. Oxford: Oxford University Press.

Murphy, Robert. 2003. *Realism and Tinsel: Cinema and Society in Britain 1939–48*. London: Routledge.

Nuttall, Anthony. 1996. *Why Does Tragedy Give Pleasure?* Oxford: Clarendon Press.

Picturegoer. 1947, June 7. Review: Hue and Cry. *Picturegoer*.

Plamper, Jan. 2009. Introduction: Emotional Turn? Feelings in Russian History and Culture. *Slavic Review* 68 (2): 229–237.

Porter, Roy. 2000. *London: A Social History*. London: Penguin.

Reddy, William. 2001. *The Navigation of Feeling: A Framework for the History of Emotions*. Cambridge: Cambridge University Press.

Roberts, Cheryl. 2022. *Consuming Mass Fashion in 1930s England: Design, Manufacture and Retailing for Young Working-class Women*. London: Palgrave Macmillan.

Rosenwein, Barbara. 2002. Worrying About Emotions in History. *American Historical Review* 107 (3): 821–845. https://doi.org/10.1086/ahr/107.3.821.

Scheer, Monique. 2012. Are Emotions a Kind of Practice (and Is That What Makes Them Have a History)? A Bourdieuian Approach to Understanding Emotion. *History & Theory* 51 (2): 190–220. https://doi.org/10.1111/j.1468-2303.2012.00621.x.

Sellers, Robert. 2015. *The Secret Life of Ealing Studios: Britain's Favourite Film Studio*. London: Aurum press.

Sinclair, Andrew. 1989. *War Like a Wasp: The Lost Decade of the 'Forties*. Hamish Hamilton.

Smith, Oli. 2020, July 3. SNP Humiliated. *Daily Express.*

Sobchack, Vivian. 1992. *The Address of the Eye: A Phenomenology of Film Experience*. Princeton: Princeton University Press.

Stutesman, Drake. 2011. Costume Design, Or, What Is Fashion in Film? In *Fashion in Film*, ed. Adrienne Munich, 17–39. Bloomington: Indiana University Press.

Sullivan, Erin. 2016. *Beyond Melancholy: Sadness and Selfhood in Renaissance England*. Oxford: Oxford University Press.

Surowiec, Catherine. 2012. Anthony Mendleson: Ealing's Wardrobe. In *Ealing Revisited*, ed. Mark Duguid, Lee Freeman, Keith Johnson, and Melanie Williams, 111–124. Basingstoke: Palgrave Macmillan/BFI.

Swann, Paul. 1987. *The Hollywood Feature Film in Postwar Cinema*. London: Routledge.

Tarlow, Sarah. 2012. The Archeology of Emotions and Affect. *Annual Review of Anthropology* 41 (1): 169–185. https://doi.org/10.1146/annurev-anthro-092611-145944.

Uhlirova, Marketa. 2013a. 100 Years of the Fashion Film: Frameworks and Histories. *Fashion Theory* 17 (2): 137–157. https://doi.org/10.2752/175174113X13541091797562.

———. 2013b. Introduction. In *Birds of Paradise: Costumes as Cinematic Spectacle*, ed. Marketa Uhlirova, 15–27. London: Koenig Books.

Warner, Helen. 2012. Tracing Patterns: Critical Approaches to On-screen Fashion. *Film, Fashion & Consumption* 1 (1): 121–132. https://doi.org/10.1386/ffc.1.1.121_1.

Williams, Raymond. 1977. *Marxism and Literature*. Oxford: Oxford University Press.

Williams, Kevin. 1998. *Get Me a Murder a Day! A History of Mass Communication in Britain*. London: Arnold.

Williams, Tony. 1994. The Repressed Fantastic in Passport to Pimlico. In *Re-Viewing British Cinema, 1900–1991*, ed. Wheeler Winston Dixon, 95–106. Albany: SUNY Press.

CHAPTER 5

Can Fashion Feel?

Thuy Linh Nguyen Tu and Jessamyn Hatcher

I wear an easy garment,
O'er it no toiling slave
Wept tears of hopeless anguish,
In his passage to the grave.

Upon its warp and woof shall be
No stain of tears and blood…

This fabric is too light to bear
The weight of the bondsmen's tears,
I shall not in its texture trace
The agony of years…

"Free labor" (1857), *Harper's Monthly Magazine*

In "Free labor," an antebellum poem written by the abolition and suffrage activist, Frances Ellen Watkins Harper, the speaker touts the virtues of free labor in a somewhat surprising manner—by arguing that free hands make light clothing (cited in Schuller 2017). The speaker proposes that these

T. L. N. Tu (✉) • J. Hatcher
New York University, New York, NY, USA
e-mail: tnt2000@nyu.edu; jh118@nyu.edu

© The Author(s), under exclusive license to Springer Nature Switzerland AG 2023
R. Filippello, I. Parkins (eds.), *Fashion and Feeling*, Palgrave Studies in Fashion and the Body,
https://doi.org/10.1007/978-3-031-19100-8_5

garments are, in turn, easier to wear because their fabric is unburdened by the anguish and agony of slavery. Published during the early days of the industrial revolution, the ballad asks audiences to consider the feelings of a garment maker at precisely the moment when their every existence was being effectively erased by the emergence of the commodity form. The speaker insists, to the contrary, that commodities like clothing can never be fully divorced from the work that makes them possible. These garments retain and reflect—in their very materiality, their "warp and woof [sic]"— workers' lives, losses, and longings.

Over a century later, the speaker's claim that clothing never comes to us completely empty—as mere fetish—continues to circulate. During our many years of learning, teaching, and writing together about the clothing industries, we have heard a version of this assertion in numerous different contexts. A fashion designer we once interviewed told us, with some frustration, that her supplier could not promise her consistently knitted sweaters, because a sad knitter's stitches look different from a happy knitter's stitch. A textile artist who quilts collaboratively noted in a talk we attended that each seam in the piece was like a ledger, recording the sewer's dreaming and waking life. A curator and conservator friend, while walking us through a room of eighteenth-century tapestries, whispered, "Textiles are witnesses to everything." She meant every drop of oil from a hand's touch, every bit of dust that settles, or ray of light that crosses its surface–not unlike the way our skin bears witness to the days of our lives.

Why has this idea of cloth and clothing endured? The ballad constructs the garment as a site of transit, moving affect from producer to consumer. But while the speaker invokes the pain of the "bondsman's tears," it is the wearer that the ballad tries to hail. The residue of all that agony weighs ultimately on the consumer; to avoid this burden, they must purchase the lighter cloth of "free labor." Free labor is not, of course, freedom from labor; it is work with wages. Liberation from the weight of work is possible only for the wearer.

In recent years, consumers have become more aware and agitated about the ethics of fashion production. They worry about the environmental costs and, after witnessing the spectacular collapse of Rana Plaza and the death of over a thousand workers, about the conditions of garment work. Some have called for an end to "fast fashion." Collections like *Worn Stories*, which document the memories we attach to clothing, teach us to embrace instead the slowly made and long-treasured garment by telling us what's possible when we do: we can love our clothes, and maybe they can love us, too (Spivak 2014).

These kinds of narratives about feeling tend to reify our relationship to clothing. They extend fashion's mystification by re-narrating capitalism's demands on us as little more than our own emotional attachments. The very fact that clothes can stir feelings—longing for love; connection to a family or community; memories of another time or place—has been used to sell us clothes. Advertisements tell us that we are not buying an object but a relationship and, moreover, that our loss and longings can be met through these acts of consumption. We buy clothes, in turn, to feel, if only momentarily, freedom, luxury, adventure, love, or to keep from feeling boredom, sadness, envy, and the like. Our feelings, in other words, are part of the engine of fashion's growth, and someone else's alienated labor becomes our point of connection.

Is it possible to think about fashion and feeling without continually positing, as the ballad and its inheritors do, the consumer as the centralizing agent? The claim that a maker's agony (or joy, love, fear, and more) lives in the texture of a garment—passed along to us from a nineteenth-century writer to the many sewers, stockers, designers, archivists, artists, and educators we have encountered over years of teaching and researching together—offers us an occasion to consider discourses of feeling as analytic, one that can allow us to see the materiality of clothing and the work required to make it legible as clothing, or as more than mere stuff. Here we share two different encounters with clothing, both of which begin with the provocation that a fully realized high-fashion garment is, from a certain perspective, just an undifferentiated mass. In each instance, we ask, what are the properties of this mass? Who does the work of transforming this undifferentiated mass into something else? What is the nature of this work? And what does recognizing that work do, not just for consumer desires but for workers themselves?

In asking these questions, we are less interested in determining whether clothes can feel or if we can feel through clothing. Rather, we're wondering what happens when we think about fashion not just as a commodity, or even as a thing, but, as our many interlocutors in the clothing and textile industries have suggested, as animate or lively material. How does seeing clothing as "vibrant matter," in the political theorist Jane Bennett's words, with the ability to "animate, to act, to produce effects dramatic and subtle" (2010, 6), help us to foster a connection to work and workers that doesn't prioritize the freedom of the consumer?

The encounters we describe below directed our attention to clothing's liveliness. In both instances, we came to recognize clothing as having animating characteristics and being capable of emanating feelings. The first involves disembodied clothing hanging in a warehouse and the workers who must learn to see it as lively matter in order to care for it. In this case, we ask how clothing's ability to produce effects both "dramatic and subtle" organizes warehouse work and how witnessing this work might disturb rather than facilitate consumption. The second concerns a French couture dress that carries a strong uneasy feeling. When taken seriously as data, this strong uneasy feeling leads us to the conditions under which the dress was made. In the process, we start to uncover an episode in fashion history when couture workers' feelings rendered them unable and unwilling to fully transform an undifferentiated mass of stuff into clothing or fashion, either symbolically or materially. Instead, it pressed them to transform the conditions of their labor.

The Work and Care of Biotic Clothing

For many years, we used to migrate every spring back to the fashion brand Lafayette 148's warehouse in New York City. We would walk from the N/R train stop at 59th Street, cross under the expressway, zig and zag our way through the maze of structures in the Brooklyn Army Terminal to finally arrive at its East Building. Lafayette 148 relocated its headquarters there in 2018, but its distribution center has been around much longer. Known affectionately as "Albert's warehouse," the facility stores and sends clothes made in Shantou, China, to over 100 retailers as well as thousands of online and catalog customers worldwide.

Every spring we teach a course on fashion and globalization, in which we ask students to see fashion not as an object but as a process, as a lens through which to see histories of colonialism and capitalism; configurations of race, gender, and embodiment; global patterns of labor and supply; ecological destruction and visions for more "sustainable" futures. In order to begin to de-objectify clothing, we ask students to see beyond the garment to the various practices and structures that make its existence possible. We brought our class to the warehouse to observe one such organizing structure: the coordinated movements of workers as they unloaded shipments from Shantou twice a day, and ironed, sorted, tagged, stocked, picked, packed, and reshipped clothes so that they could arrive at their final destination as early as the next day. We wanted them to see what clothing looks like from behind the walls of these built-not-to-be-seen warehouses, where it is neither produced nor consumed, and yet where, arguably, it is liveliest.

Despite its massive scale, spanning two block-sized floors, the warehouse is quiet. The staff work quickly and silently. There are few windows, but the ceilings are high, giving the feeling of airiness. Albert, the warehouse's director of operations, appreciates its height, though less for the atmospherics than for its capacity to accommodate ever higher shelves and racks. "More racks, more clothes," he tells us, though we could hardly imagine any more clothes. The entire space is filled with rows of hanging garments. Each is squeezed so tightly against the next that it's hard to tell where one ends and the other begins. If you're a picker like Xian, though, this undifferentiated mass can be known. Xian's job is to pull clothing from the racks and deliver them to the packaging area. A scanner now tells her where to find them, but before the barcodes arrived, she searched for them herself, thumbing through each piece to find the right one. During one of our earliest visits, in 2017, Albert told us that some pickers are better than others. When we asked him what are the qualities that make a good picker, he demurred, only hinting that Xian is one of them.

Xian is fast. On a typical day, she walks about five miles, back and forth, up and down the aisles, arms draped in dresses. She moves quickly and reaches for garments decisively. The scanners tell her what rows to approach, but different sizes look the same. Color variations are not always clear. Your eyes can deceive, devices can fail. To be a good picker—or really, good at most of the warehouse jobs—you have to know clothing in a different sense. You have to recognize it, first, as matter with particular characteristics and, second, to see it as constitutive of a kind of sociality. You can't assume it is an inanimate or preconstituted entity, existing outside of its relationship with you. You'd have to see it as more than an empty form, as the scholar Peter Stallybrass might say, in need of a consumer to "rematerialize" it as "objects that are touched, and loved, and worn" (1998, 187). In the warehouse, it's you, the worker, who does the materializing. Not by wearing clothes or loving them, but by knowing their properties and caring for them in your every day.

Here is what we mean. When you enter the warehouse, there is always a faint smell of rice in the air. In a small corner of the space, there is a makeshift kitchen with a large rice cooker. Rice is provided every day to the staff. "The smell reminds me of home," we hear Xian say. Eating together is important. At the factory in Shantou where Lafayette 148 produces its clothes, a whole floor is reserved for workers to eat. There are signs written in Chinese throughout the space. Most are informational. One, near the kitchen counter, says *Happy New Year*, leftover from a month ago, Albert says.

We tend to think of the warehouse as what French theorist Marc Augé called a "non-place" (Auge, 1995). These are spaces, like the airport or train station, where most people simply whizz through, if they enter at all. Of course, workers in these non-places don't dash; they spend hours each day, week after week, making it possible for others to move. Albert's warehouse is a transit hub but is not simply transitory. Like those other non-places, it too is abuzz with life. There is, in fact, evidence of sociality everywhere, and not just among the staff. A tall green plant stands near the warehouse kitchen. Someone has been tending to it; despite the lack of light, it thrives.

At its most basic level, the work carried out here is a kind of care work. Every worker handles the garments—from the ones unpacking the shipping boxes, to those ironing the blouse and hanging the dress, to pickers and packers—with great deliberation, attention, and care. Each interaction tells workers something about the clothes' material composition. Like the sewers and pattern-makers who understand the properties of clothing (how fabric folds and falls), warehouse workers learn the qualities that make a garment difficult or easy to wrinkle, tear, warp, and even rot. Each bit of knowledge is directed toward its maintenance. Recently, for instance, Lafayette 148 began adding shoes to its collections. Where the company's designers saw a sandal, Albert and his team saw flesh and skin. To fight further decomposition, Albert enclosed a dark, windowless corner of the warehouse and filled it with cool conditioned air. He made a kind of meat locker for the shoes, so the leather won't crack.

Clothing is rarely seen as biotic material; however, fur, leather, and other luxury fabrics were once living flesh. They retain these properties. Shoes must be kept at cooler temperatures, much like the way we refrigerate our meats. Fur produces unpleasant odors if not properly housed. Theirs is the work of preservation. And like other conservators, warehouse workers understand that even the most durable goods can deteriorate. They know that the touch of a hand, with its invisible oils, or the exposure to air can, over time, wear down a thread. So they tend to it, the way they might their plant. Because here clothing is seen not as dead and durable, but fragile and in need of care. Albert worries constantly, in fact, that the clothes might get "ruined." It's not just the material decomposition he fears, it's the erosion of economic value too. If he can't get clothes to retailers and buyers fast enough, they won't sell. "If we're late, they might not accept it at all. We can't sell them. They're ruined," he says. Because our markets are glutted with clothes, after a few weeks, sometimes days, they are discounted or removed from the shelves altogether. There is a reason we use common food terms like "leftovers" to describe overstocked clothing sold at discounted stores. Like those organic substances, clothes too can spoil.

Over the last decade, Albert has done everything he can to ensure that Lafayette 148's clothes do not spoil. The company now flies their clothes across the Pacific, rather than using the far slower shipping method. They maintain their own trucks to pick up deliveries from the airport. They have invented new shipping crates. These metal boxes, which are built in Shantou and discarded in Brooklyn, allow 3000 pieces of clothing per box to hang. It's hard to overstate this innovation. Hung clothing doesn't wrinkle, which means less time ironing, less damage overall.

To suggest that these workers are careful stewards of clothing is not to say that they love them or have any particular feelings toward them at all. It is to suggest that at the same time that workers act upon the garments—preserving their use value and coaxing from them more exchange value—clothes can affect work and workers too. The clothes help to organize the space of the warehouse and shape the movements of the workers: they make demands, in other words, that must be met. This is the social life of warehousing. Actors come in many forms. Albert once told us, for instance, that their sweaters used to misbehave. These garments arrive at the warehouse folded and wrapped in plastic. Every time a picker reached for one, several more slipped to the ground. Albert had to manufacture shelves that tilt ever-so-slightly upward to keep them from falling down. Still, workers approach them carefully. Gravity is relentless, and the sweaters don't like to be contained.

If we began to see clothing through the lens of the warehouse, we would begin to recognize it as unstable matter, as an object that can also spoil. As a thing that can, in Bennett's words, "produce effects." As a commodity whose life and value are shaped through the worker's knowledge and care. We might begin to recognize the creativity of workers and even think differently about our own consumption as well.

Our students often feel disoriented by this quiet and cavernous space. The fashion historian Elizabeth Wilson once wrote, "There is something eerie about a museum of costume." The "deserted galleries seem haunted," and the "living observer moves, with a sense of mounting panic, through the world of the dead" (Wilson 1985, 1). There is a similar stillness in the halls of the warehouse, where clothing hangs in racks. But this is no "world of the dead." And when viscerally confronted with clothes as perishable commodities, our students feel their consumer desires flag. They can't believe these indistinguishable objects are worth the price that they come to fetch. They draw parallels to meat lockers, slaughter houses, and other spaces for the storage of the partially alive—places that have turned off consumers since the time of Upton Sinclair. There is a crumbling of commodity fetishism playing out before their eyes. What if we embrace that feeling of disturbance that these clothes can make us feel?

An Uneasy Dress

For a number of years, Jessamyn has been studying a collection of dresses that were manufactured by the French couture house Callot Soeurs between the 1890s and the 1920s. The dresses were owned and worn by an American woman named Hortense Mitchell Acton and are still housed in the villa in Florence, Italy, where Acton lived. The first time Jessamyn saw the dress numbered LG 81 at Villa La Pietra, she was struck by the feeling that there was something wrong with it. It's not that she didn't like it, although in her opinion it is an ugly dress. Made from *crème-de-menthe* colored figured silk overlaying a salmon silk sheath, it has black lace batwing sleeves, passementerie tassels encrusted in rhinestones and pearls, and beads that dangle heavily from each shoulder. The silhouette has a drop waist but also a panniered skirt. It wasn't a matter of taste that she found disarming, but rather a strong, uneasy feeling that seemed to be emanating from the dress itself.

What room is there for feelings as an analytic? In this case, a feeling that something is wrong? We both have been trained to distill and interpret a range of symbolic content: language, images, text, spaces, objects, social interactions, even some sounds, and some gestures. But so much of the evidence in Hortense Mitchell Acton's Callot Soeurs dresses also comes in the form of biotic material—stains or smells—or in the case of LG 81, an uneasy feeling in the viewer, and chaotic-looking and haphazard construction. How can we learn to read these things?

When we do fieldwork together in Florence, Alabama, on the afterlife of a town that used to be the "t-shirt capital of the world," Jessamyn knows to bring along the soft brown wool shawl Thuy likes, because no matter how hot it is, there will be moments when Thuy will be "psychically cold," as she puts it. Like the workers in Albert's Warehouse, we are learning to register these moments seriously as something to be paid attention to—as data, in other words—even as we understand that doing so strays from the empirical mode of knowledge production privileged by much of academia.

During one of Jessamyn's research trips to Florence, Costanza Perrone, a conservator at Villa La Pietra, was putting LG 81 on a mannequin when she called Jessamyn over. It's a joke between Costanza and Jessamyn that Jessamyn doesn't like this dress. Costanza pointed to the back seam. The selvages were partly exposed, partly folded in, and then sewn together, leaving a seam that is crooked and puckered. Exposing a selvage can be a couture technique. A conservator once told us that sometimes couturiers reveal a selvage to emphasize the beauty and costliness of a piece of fabric. "But not in the way that you are describing," she added. In contemporary mass-produced clothing, the selvage is often used as a structural part of the garment to save time and fabric. The seam up the back of LG 81 looked more like this, but stranger. Like it was a rush job or that there was not enough fabric to make a seam allowance. As Costanza worked the dress onto the mannequin, it became clear that the back seam was not the only anomaly in the construction of LG 81. The armholes are far too deep. Costanza had to pin the dress in a complicated way to make it drape plausibly.

One of the idiosyncrasies of working with Hortense Mitchell Acton's dresses is that the collection has not been dated. But one day, we received an email from a curator writing to say that she had found a sketch of LG 81 in the archives of the Brooklyn Museum, likely the work of a fashion illustrator who had seen the dress at the Parisian fashion show. The date on the sketch was summer 1914 (Brooklyn Museum, 1914).

The summer of 1914 was when the First World War began. The Paris fashion shows were slated for August 15, 1914, twelve days after France entered the war. The Callot staff expected that the city would be invaded within a few days, and that the couture house would have to close. The plan "was to throw everything out and put up the shutters," as one worker at Callot put it. Yet, when the clients and the reporters presented themselves at the annual show, Callot was among the firms that stayed open, although they had not yet finished the clothes. And so a set of questions were raised for us: Was this one of the dresses the Callot manufactured at the outbreak of the First World War? Could a dress made in wartime carry or provoke an uneasy feeling? Is this carrying or provocation perhaps not as entirely mysterious as it sounds, if the feeling is produced in part by the strange, haphazard construction, and manic design? Could these be the material signs of what we came to identify as an impaired ability, a flagging desire, or even a refusal on the part of the people who made the dress to continue to conduct business as usual, namely to continue the often brutal process of turning stuff into fashion?

Certainly, at least one of those reporters noticed at Callot a flagging desire, edging toward a refusal, to continue to suppress their own feelings—or to alienate woman from herself, to revise the old Marxian adage—so that the commodity could continue to be produced. In an unsigned article that appeared in October 1914, a reporter for the *New York Times* described the scene at Callot as they experienced it on August 15, 1914, like this:

> The house of Callot off the Boulevard Hausmann presented the saddest and the least autocratic presentation in the month of August I ever believe it could have accomplished. When a well-known woman buyer entered the rooms wearing a white muslin gown which each of us envied on that heated day, the premiere vendeuse said to me: "How can she wear that white frock when all our ladies and the poor women are in black?" Any argument that all white was not only excellent mourning and in excellent taste on a hot, humid day left the venduese sadly shaking her head and saying, "It's inhuman, it's unfeeling." And when the mannequin slid in on her high-heeled brocade slippers—those well-known slippers of the House of Callot and that well-known walk—wearing a decolletée gown which was bought by one of the American buyers, the venduese again said: "How can anyone be so unfeeling as to buy a gown of gayety?" The only ray of interest she showed the whole afternoon was listening to the argument that the dollars spent by a neutral country would help keep alive many sewing girls.

One of the things that strike us about this encounter is how, although everyone is depicted as doing what they always do (the models are modeling, the shoppers are shopping, the saleswomen are selling, the reporters are reporting), it is only the customers who seem to be doing it in the same spirit they always do—in the spirit of capitalism, we might call it, to invoke Max Weber. The buyers are variously envying, arguing, excelling at taste, and buying. But the staff at Callot are sad, the saddest they could be. It is "an awful time, when our hearts are elsewhere," they told the reporter. As this sadness seeped into the *salle de vente*, a sadness that also starts to sound a lot like rage to us, a fact that makes itself known as a feeling seemed to emerge in real time in those rooms. It's a fact and a feeling only ever imperfectly suppressed in the first place: that for the clients, if not for the reporter, the dresses are more important than the people who make and sell them.

As this feeling-that-is-a-fact emerges, the saleswoman is increasingly engulfed by emotions that render her unable or unwilling to maintain her part in the familiar and routine choreography that helps materialize fashion as a desirable commodity in the showroom. The vendeuse's job is to lubricate the relationship between the client and the clothing, as anyone who has ever worked in retail knows. This lubricity depends on the saleswoman's affective labor, including the suppression of any feelings she might have that could cause friction between the client and the clothes as the client moves toward a purchase. But the vendeuse can't do it. She is too angry and too sad. Her anger is directed at the client by expressing outrage at the client's choice of dresses–in other words, right where it counts. It is intolerable to the saleswoman that these frocks—this white muslin gown, this "gown of gayety"—could be set above the lives of the people who make them and their compatriots in the context of war.

To varying degrees, we know what it is like to be sad, angry, frightened, and exhausted, and still be asked to complete a task that requires concentration, skill, and the suppression of your feelings. We also probably know something about what it is like to try to work in a room with other distressed people: the comfort a shared experience can offer, but also how shared feelings amplify in a room. Of course, good feelings can work like this, too. How difficult is it, then, to feel, which is to say to know, that a strangely fabricated dress like LG 81 could be the product of tired, shaken hands? That a seam of a couture dress really is like a ledger, recording a sewer's dreaming and waking life? The vendeuse's inability/refusal to perform her prescribed role altered the smooth operations of the showroom, and thus the process of commodification. It's possible that sewers during the war experienced similar inabilities/refusals that altered the very materiality of the dresses they manufactured.

We have at least two clues: one that comes from the reporter, and one that comes from the workers themselves. The *New York Times* article we have been detailing is titled "Coats at Callot's Are Short," callously enough given the wartime context ("Coats at Callot's Are Short" 59). Fashion reporters must report the fashion. And so the reporter, too, moves from a description of the people to a description of the clothes. "And

What of Callot's Gowns?" the writer asks. The gowns are "experimental," the reporter says. "They look it," they add. Imagining how the clothes are constructed, the reporter issues a "shrewd guess" that "many of [the Callot] gowns are put together out of a heap of good material which they find lying around loose, and looping it here, and catching it there, send it into the rooms on a fetching mannequin …"

When this writer describes Callot's clothes in this way, it's hard not to feel as if we were reading a description of LG 81 itself, which looks exactly like a heap of good material found lying around loose, looped and caught and erratically sewn together. Likewise, when we read in the same article that the wartime injunction at Callot was that "only those models can be copied when it is possible to buy more of the material," how can we not think of LG 81, a dress where there seems to be barely enough fabric to complete it? At the same time, we know this may be fanciful on our part. The writer seems to be speaking generally of Callot designs, even if their thoughts are prompted by the clothes they have seen on the runway in August 1914. And of course we don't (we can't) know for sure when or by whom this dress was designed or made or under what conditions. But what if, as the war deluged them, Callot workers, like the saleswoman, simply could not complete tasks that required their concentration, skill, and the suppression of their own feelings? What if they could not sew a dress without their distress leaving its imprint, any more than the saleswoman could complete a sale without leaving hers? The reporter's assessment of the dresses is that they look "experimental." Maybe one translation of "experimental," in this case, is that these dresses were redolent with distress, incompletely or unsuccessfully materialized as fashion, and it showed.

A second clue furthers these speculations. It comes in the form of a postwar interview that we first encountered in the scholarship of Maude Bass-Krueger, originally conducted by Madeleine Colin with a woman named Alice Brisset, who had labored as a second assistant in a couture house during the war. In her recollections, Brisset emphasized the feelings shared among her co-workers that suffused the atelier where they sewed. In particular, she described the degree to which the garment workers' working days and working nights were structured around collectively helping one another bear both unbearable work and unbearable feelings about the war and their own working conditions in the context of war. "[The] work hours were endless," Brisset recalled. "The premiere, or head seamstress, would burst into the atelier, saying, 'Ladies, you must work tonight, the client wants her dress.' ... There was never any talk of paying overtime or of being fed ... Fatigue made our nerves taut, and, on top of that, anxiety had filled our hearts." Bass-Krueger elaborates: "Brisset emphasized that the all-female environment of the ateliers created a sense of solidarity but also heightened the women's emotions. The women confided their fears to each other while they sewed" (Bass-Krueger and Kurkdjian, 2019, 464).

Brisset makes it clear that the wartime atelier was saturated with the workers' shared feelings. How much of a stretch is it to recognize that the hand that sews is connected to the anxiety-filled heart? And then to entertain at least the glimmer of possibility that garments sewn by these hands might retain the residue of these strong and collective feelings? Of course, the heart is not only connected to the hand; it's also connected to a desire to make life more livable. For Alice Brisset, who went on to become the secretary general of the *Fédération d'Habillement* (Clothing Union), the unbearable feelings of anxiety and fear that she and her co-workers experienced sewing in the wartime ateliers did not only manifest in distressed dresses. In the case of these wartime sewers, the accreting suppression of their own feelings, bodies, and lives in service of clients became insupportable and galvanized as labor activism. In March 1917, Brisset and her comrades led a strike that resulted in a shorter work week and a pay increase for couture workers. Linking fashion and feeling not to the burnishing of commodities but rather to an incitement to social change, Brisset recounted: "All this misery, all this anxiety, this fear accumulated, and the strike exploded like a clap of thunder" (Ibid., 464).

Conclusion

Reflecting on the two examples of clothing in this essay, we are struck by what they allow us to wonder and imagine differently. We have long lived in a world where every *thing* can become a commodity. Even writing a sentence like the previous one feels a bit exhausting, so well do we know the operations of commodity fetishism and descriptions of its operations. There also can be a kind of sinking feeling that commodity fetishism has so thoroughly co-opted the relationship between things and feelings that getting anywhere near the topic of fashion and feeling is to sign on to produce, at best—and this is probably self-flattery—novel ways of fetishizing commodities. But at the same time, we are struck by the ways that trying to think about the liveliness of things in the examples of Albert's

Warehouse and LG 81 point us not deeper in the direction of the phantasmagoric vivacity of commodities or the sentiments of consumers but rather toward the lives of workers. Which is to say, toward people who remain much more hidden both in fashion's histories and fashion's present, and whose feelings and lives often seem to count much less.

The sociologist Loïc Wacquant wrote: we are "sensate, suffering, skilled, sedimented, and situated corporeal creatures" (2015, 2). We confront social structures—work and war among them—not simply as facts but as "dynamic webs of forces inscribed upon and enfolded deep within the body as perceptual grids, sensorimotor capacities, emotional proclivities, and indeed as desire itself" (3). If Wacquant is right, we might begin to understand that perhaps it is the rule rather than the exception that the sediments of garment workers' feelings are woven into the "warp and woof" of the clothes they move and make. Our job might be to get better at reading this weave. And this starts with making space for feeling as an analytic.

REFERENCES

5 Coats at Callot's Are Short. *The New York Times*, October 4.
Augé, Marc. 1995. *Non-Places: Introduction to an Anthropology of Supermodernity.* London and New York: Verso Books.
Bass-Krueger, Maude, and Sophie Kurkdjian, eds. 2019. *French Fashion, Women, and the First World War.* New York: Bard Graduate Center.
Bennett, Jane. 2010. *Vibrant Matter: A Political Ecology of Things.* Durham, NC: Duke University Press.
Brooklyn Museum. Evening Dress, Callot Soeurs, 'Surgas', 1914. *Bendel Collection, HB 006-18*, Fashion and Costume Sketch Collection, 1912–1950.
Schuller, Kyla. 2017. *The Biopolitics of Feeling Race, Sex, and Science in the Nineteenth Century.* Durham, NC: Duke University Press.
Spivak, Emily. 2014. *Worn Stories.* New York: Princeton Architectural Press.
Stallybrass, Peter. 1998. Marx's Coat. In *Border Fetishisms: Material Objects in Unstable Spaces*, ed. Patricia Spyer, 183–207. New York: Routledge.
Wacquant, Loïc. 2015. For a Sociology of Flesh and Blood. *Qualitative Sociology* 38 (1): 1–11.
Wilson, Elizabeth. 1985. *Adorned in Dreams: Fashion and Modernity.* New Brunswick, NJ: Rutgers University Press.

PART II

Reparative Fashion

CHAPTER 6

Designing Clothes for and from Love: Disability Justice and Fashion Hacking

Ben Barry and Philippa Nesbitt

"Disability Justice is simply another term for love," remarked Mia Mingus (2018) during her keynote at the 2018 Disability and Intersectionality Summit at the Massachusetts Institute of Technology. Mingus is a Disabled Korean-American woman, transnational adoptee and one of the creators of the Disability Justice framework. Conceived by Mingus along with Patty Berne, Stacey Milbern, Leroy F. Moore Jr., Sebastian Margaret and Eli Clare in 2015, Disability Justice is "a movement building framework" that centres the wholeness, desirability and affirmation of multiply marginalized D/disabled people (Lamm 2015). The framework responded to gaps in the Disability Rights Movement that focused on whiteness, maleness, heteronormativity and mobility as the default disability experience (Kafai 2021). Disability Justice was created to honour the intersectional experiences of queer, trans and gender nonconforming disabled people

B. Barry (✉) • P. Nesbitt
Parsons The New School, Toronto Metropolitan University,
Toronto, ON, Canada
e-mail: barryb@newschool.edu; philippa.nesbitt@torontomu.ca

and to cultivate community with them. At the core of this activism is love, because, as Mingus (2018) explains, "if we can't love each other and ourselves, then what good is any of our work to get free?"

In this chapter, we explore how the practice of fashion design can centre Disability Justice and, subsequently, enact love. We share our experiences from working on the ongoing project, *Cripping Masculinity*. Through three phases—wardrobe interviews, fashion hacking workshops and a fashion show—this project examines how D/disabled, D/deaf and Mad-identified men and masculine non-binary people experience their intersectional gender identities through dress and fashion. Our project follows the work of Disability Justice activists by proudly using the word "crip" as a reclamation of language that was originally used to oppress disability to instead affirm it. We draw upon activists and scholars who suggest that cripping has a similar meaning to queering: "cripping is a troubling, a door opening to invite us toward challenging what is normal and what we assume is defective" (Kafai 2021, 188). Crip therefore holds space for the creativity that disability generates by disrupting normalcy, while recognizing that this wisdom is developed from living in an ableist and sanist society (Hamraie and Fritsch 2019).

This chapter centres our fashion hacking workshops and highlights the forms of love that were generated in and through them. Fashion hacking is a methodology in which people intervene in designed fashion outputs—including media, clothing and shows—by altering them to inscribe their histories and bodies. At the centre of this methodology is politics: the physical act of un-making and re-making existing artefacts enables people who have been excluded by the fashion industry and society to insert themselves into these systems on their own terms and through their own design. Moreover, fashion hacking fosters community and skills that can be mobilized to affirm intersectional identities and resist oppressive discourses beyond the workshop spaces (Barry and Drak 2019). In our fashion hacking workshops, project participants deconstructed and recreated one of their existing garments in collaboration with fashion researchers to provide better access for their bodyminds and aesthetically express their intersectional gender identities. We originally aimed to foster love by creating a garment that honoured participants' intersectional bodyminds. However, we discovered that the very process of recreating each garment, in addition to the final garments themselves, fostered love.

Fashion provides a material interface between the physical body and the social world. As Joanne Entwistle (2015) explains, fashion is an embodied practice influenced by social and cultural forces. It can be a means to express individuality or affirm identity; it can provide connection with other people and communities; and it can display adherence or resistance to expectations of normativity. A connective force between body and world, fashion becomes an important vehicle for practicing love. By reclaiming fashion from the logics of the capitalist fashion industry, we move towards liberation that values the needs, desires and beauty of multiply marginalized disabled bodyminds. This chapter maps out paths that others might follow to cultivate love through fashion design and, in particular, through fashion hacking.

To examine how love was cultivated in our workshops, we first explore our understanding of love outside of non-disabled supremacy, whiteness and cis-heteropatriarchy. We then analyse how our process of fashion hacking enacted love by heeding the wisdom and manifesting the principles of Disability Justice. In particular, we practised love by centring collective access, sharing knowledge, holding intersectional disabled stories, and grounding self-reflection and accountability.

Cripping Love

We ground our understanding of love in the concept of "crip-centric liberated zones" (Kafai 2021, 43). Coined by Patty Berne, co-founder of the Disability Justice performance project Sins Invalid, these are spaces and encounters that cultivate the feelings that come from experiencing Disability Justice. Crip-centric liberated zones can be realized when disabled people are together in workshops, or alone in their bedrooms, but at the centre of the encounters, disabled people's multiple identities are recognized and desired. Shayda Kafai (2021, 43) explains that these zones are grounded in the practice of love:

> A crip-centric liberated zone is a multidirectional community love practice. It is a place of our own creation where we, the disabled, queer of color many, can exist and thrive liberated from the oppressions that relegate our daily lives. When directed inwards, the love practice of a crip-centric liberated zone gifts us with strategies for re-centering and decolonizing our bodyminds. When directed outwards, the zone politically transforms the places we inhabit—even temporarily—into hubs of communal bodymind witnessing.

As Kafai explains, a crip-centric liberated zone works to help heal and free disabled people from the multiple systemic oppressions that are both internalized and experienced within the world-at-large. The spaces allow multiply marginalized disabled people to experience themselves in ways that challenge dominant narratives of trauma, tragedy and overcoming that are associated with disability, and instead centre joy and beauty (Kafai 2021).

By holding space for the intersectional experiences of disabled people, crip-centric liberated zones foster what Mingus (2018) calls "liberatory access." Mingus (2018) explains that liberatory access expands functional access by ensuring disabled people can fully engage in encounters as disabled people, and as queer people, trans people and people of colour. For Berne at Sins Invalid, all performances consider access for diverse disabilities as well as gender and sexual identities, embodiments, and class backgrounds. They offer American Sign Language, gender neutral washrooms, seating for audience members who might need extra space and tickets priced on a sliding scale (Kafai 2021). As Mingus (2018, np) explains, "Access for the sake of access or inclusion is not necessarily liberatory, but access done in the service of love … is liberatory and has the power to transform." Being in the service of love is about making and holding space for the complexities of power and oppression in disabled communities, providing expansive access and working to prevent the causes of inaccessibility from repeating themselves.

Both Mingus and Berne offer understandings of love that break open non-disabled conceptualizations. Their crip perspectives connect to the expansiveness of love offered by Black, Indigenous and queer scholars and activists. In *All About Love*, bell hooks (2000) uses love as a verb because she understands it as a "transformative force" (xix). She argues that the enactment of love deepens and expands the actions of activist communities and, as such, love is critical for advancing social justice. Kim Tallbear (2020) describes intimacy as a component of love and offers a framework beyond colonial heterosexual relations. According to asexual polyamorists in her community, intimacy is understood as being "in good relation" with another; it is expressed through, for example, listening, reassuring and sharing resources. TallBear (2020, np) explains that they "don't necessarily have to have what we consider genital sex … as part of their intimacy, it doesn't mean that they don't fall in love." Lauren Berlant (2001) understands love as a queer concept that can be used to "open up the intimate to the political" (437–438). In this context, the concept of love expands from being a relational feeling to a political force that has the power to question, intervene into and transform dominant systems and discourses.

These understandings move love beyond white, ableist heteropatriarchal frameworks that are often confined to romance and sex (Kafai 2021). Instead, love is expansively celebrated as a feeling and practice of honouring the complexity of our intersectional identities, of deeply being with and sharing with one another, and of working towards social justice. By heeding these worldviews, this chapter crips dominant notions of love by celebrating the glorious ways that it is generated and felt within crip community through fashion hacking and Disability Justice.

LOVE THROUGH FASHION HACKING

In the following section, we explore how fashion hacking nourishes the feeling and practice of love by manifesting the principles of Disability Justice. The analysis examines our encounters with four participants during workshops that took place between January and August 2021. We explore: CX, a white, trans masculine, disabled artist in their late 40s; Logan, an East Asian, disabled trans man who is a student in his early 20s; Pree, a South Asian, trans masculine, disabled artist in their late 20s; and MG, a South Asian, trans masculine, mad social worker in their early 30s. We describe four ways in which love was expressed and experienced.

Centring Collective Access

A key principle of Disability Justice is to centre the leadership of those most impacted by ableism. This principle insists on foregrounding the voices and leadership of multiply marginalized disabled people who experience intersectional able-bodied supremacy. In *Skin, Tooth and Bone: The Basis of Movement is Our People*, Sins Invalid explain how this principle is understood: "We are lifting up, listening to, reading, following, and highlighting the perspectives of those who are most impacted by the systems we fight against. By centring the leadership of those who are most impacted, we keep ourselves grounded in real-world problems and find creative strategies for resistance" (Sins Invalid 2019, 23). Our fashion hacking workshops centred the leadership of participants in the design process. In contrast, Aimi Hamraie and Kelly Fritsch (2019) explain that disabled people are often treated as clients or users during the design process, and design is often understood as a tool for solving the perceived problem of disability. Our workshops aimed to move away from this transactional co-design model to interdependent collaboration: research participants became collaborators, as the collective sharing of knowledge, skills and experiences developed expansive interdependent relationships. Our participants led us through a rearrangement of lived, material conditions and developed ways of sharing fashion and knowledge beyond isolated products and individual gain. These interdependent practices were ones of kinship, of trust and of hope; they were practices of access intimacy and love.

We had originally planned to host our fashion hacking workshops as in-person events over a weekend, but due to the COVID-19 pandemic, we moved them to a virtual format of video calls, phone and direct messaging. The online format of our revised workshops allowed for an unexpected flexibility, moving away from the strict timeline of the originally planned in-person event towards the malleability of crip time. Louise Hickman and David Serlin (2018) explain that a key component of developing a crip methodology is an engagement with the shifting temporal registers of crip subjectivity, foregrounding access and situating knowledge in a way that is dynamic and unfolding rather than linear; in other words, a way that centres crip time. Developed in Disability Justice communities, crip time reimagines expectations of temporality by recognizing that existing expectations of time and productivity are based in ableist and sanist systems (Kafer, 2013). Kafer explains, "Rather than bend disabled bodies and minds to meet the clock, crip time bends the clock to meet disabled bodies and minds" (27). Foregrounding crip time honours sustainability, another key principle of Disability Justice. Sustainability in this context is a collective and individual regulation of pace that allows each person to sustain themselves over the long-term. Disabled bodyminds are valued as teachers and as guides away from the urgency of capitalism and towards transformative slowness to create an "unstoppable wave of justice and liberation" (Sins Invalid 2019, 10).

For many of our participants, crip time is a reality of survival in a world with ableist barriers. It is also a way of respecting the changing capacity of each bodymind, even when the constraints of capitalism work against it. In our fashion hacking workshops, the participants set the pace of the project. Through their leadership, we came to understand and depend on slowness and flexibility, learning how to forefront each of our changing capacities and lean into crip time. *Cripping Masculinity* designer-researcher

Jonathan explained, "Our participants have demolished all of those [capitalist] boundaries, coming into this not with an attitude of, 'yes, there's only so much that I can do,' but an attitude of 'there's only so much that I can do with the time and energy that society expects of me.'" With this crip attitude, researchers and participants kept in touch with each other about changing access needs and personal capacity, and were able to take breaks, reschedule or redistribute labour. Participants also challenged themselves to accept slowness through their own approaches to the workshops. For example, MG opted to hand-embroider a bee onto a garment, a process they described as encouraging them to slow down and feel connected to their body. The workshops moved away from spaces of labour and productivity towards spaces of love and nourishment. *Cripping Masculinity* designer-researcher Alexis explained, "Every time I left there, my cup felt full. I think fashion has taught a lot of these conduits for other forms of relationship-building. They're just tangential, because they're all connected. Fashion isn't just isolated or a product, it's these processes. I've learned a lot of that from [participants] Pree and MG." This suspension from the structures of capitalism and academia also allowed our us as designer-researchers to understand our own bodyminds differently. We were able to develop new habits and practices within the framework of crip time that nurtured us and that we would carry into our own academic and creative practices.

The porosity of the virtual workshops also led to a more accessible and sustainable space that fostered learning and care. For example, Pree found that they were able to actively participate in the virtual meetings while at the same time attending to pressing daily tasks like cooking or using the space for rest. Pree remarked, "I feel like that lack of rigidness has been what's made this process a bit more accessible, pleasant and different." CX and Logan found that the slowness and flexibility of the project made learning about fashion design more accessible. CX said, "I like there being a process for me to build trust. The sewing had to come slowly, and I definitely didn't get it right off the bat. It took me maybe a couple of months before it started feeling more comfortable for me. It's a neat, abstract process, because I don't always remember things in a linear way. But sewing isn't exactly like that. It's forgiving." Leah Piepzna-Samarasinha Lakshmi (2021) highlights that many disabled people are confined to their homes, and so they turn to their computers and phones to participate in community. Shifting the project to a virtual space provided an unforeseen level of access, where participants were given electronic entry to engage in our project, while also attending to their own personal needs.

With the guidance of our participants, we learned to utilize alternative ways of communicating that encouraged access and promoted relationships. By using Instagram direct messages (DMs) for communication between video calls, we were able to have conversations that felt personal and mimicked the feeling of a real-time interaction. MG expressed that emails felt cumbersome and formal, while DMs felt more intimate and allowed for conversations to occur naturally while they worked on their garment. They snapped and shared photos with Alexis in real time, and developed a space of friendly conversation in tandem with their learning [Figs. 6.1, 6.2 and 6.3]. This also allowed participants to keep in touch with us outside of scheduled video meetups, while working at a pace that felt comfortable for their bodyminds.

These alternative ways of communicating gave rise to deep, ongoing interpersonal relationships of support, friendship and disabled mutual aid. Lakshmi Piepzna-Samarasinha (2021) explains, "With disabled mutual aid, the stuff we do to help each other doesn't look like a big deal or fall

Fig. 6.1 CX's Instagram post featuring an image of their process in the workshops with poetry and captions reflecting on their relationship to clothing

Fig. 6.2 CX's Instagram post showing fabric for the hacking workshop featuring a reflection on their inspiration and experience

into 'dramatic rescue of the cripples' tropes. They're preventative. They're casual and loving. They're about disabled noticing and caring." Our relationships with participants started as conversations about the project, but turned into ways of noticing and caring for one another. This included casual wellness check-ins, as well as aid that felt more low-key, such as sending each other funny memes and TikToks unrelated to the project. Some collaborators and designer-researchers have continued to support one another in fashion hacking through Instagram, while others have maintained deep friendships, communicating on the phone or through social media, and even sending handmade gifts and letters to one another by mail.

Sharing Knowledge and Resources

Love in our fashion hacking workshops looked like knowledge sharing and the development of creative interdependency (Chandler and Ignagni 2018). Building on the concept of access intimacy (Mingus 2011), creative interdependency is not about an insistence on collaboration, but

Fig. 6.3 CX posing next to their wheelchair in the garment they created during the workshop

instead about accommodations that give rise to the possibility of creating "independently *or* collaboratively" (Chandler and Ignagni 2018, 260). Designer-researcher Alexis explained, "When we're making something together it's that care and attention. That's how these relationships hold us."

As researchers and designers, we shared knowledge and skills that we garnered through our privileged access to formal education and training. These were skills that would support participants in the workshops, as well as provide them with the opportunity to rework clothing beyond the workshops. Mailing the garment back and forth between one another, the participants directed the design process and applied their own new and existing skills to alter, adjust and recreate their garments. When they met a challenge or reached their personal capacity, they could send them back to the designer-researchers and direct them on how they would like it finished. Participant CX explained that the workshops gave them a new understanding of interdependence through creative interdependence. CX is an artist, and art for them had previously been experienced as something independent. However, the hacking workshops developed an interdependent creative practice, where CX could execute their vision for their garment, but look to *Cripping Masculinity* designer-researcher Jonathan for the technical design support, such as measurements and adjustments that would make their piece more wearable. This creative interdependence looked to the leadership of the participants, centring access and love.

For CX, the hacking workshops provided them with the skills, confidence and understanding of altering clothing as a new avenue for access: access to customized garments and access to new forms of creativity. Sewing became a form of liberation from ableism, homophobia, transphobia and economic constraints created by capitalism. CX explained:

> I've reinvented myself as an artist through imagining myself sewing. Because I'm low income I don't really have access to purchasing art supplies, and I love painting, I love creating things. But sewing is just beautiful because I have tons of clothes, and it means that I'm not running out of creativity. I just imagine sewing now for years on end. Even just bringing it with me, carrying a little bag of sewing gear wherever I'm at, so if I'm dealing with stress, I can just start sewing. It's this brave tool for me to ignite my own inner fire and just feel well.

Developing confidence and skills in designing clothing was echoed by participant Logan, who slowly came to value his own creativity and growth during the workshops. He said:

> The sewing was a bit of a challenge for me, and I actually really appreciate it. It was frustrating at the beginning, but I really appreciate the result, what

I've learned, and how it came out. It gave me a sense of pride in myself for doing something creative, because I don't actually see myself as a creative person a lot of the time.

By sharing knowledge, skills and experiences, creative interdependence gave rise to love and kinship as threads sewn into each garment.

The participants also used the workshops as an opportunity to share their experience and new skills with their existing virtual community on social media. CX continues to share photos, videos, quotations and poetry on Instagram to create a wider conversation around the value of clothing and fashion for identity, empowerment and disabled embodiment, while Pree shares TikTok videos and Instagram reels showing the creative ways they use sewing and textiles to connect with friends and family or to ground their bodyminds in times of stress or burnout. In doing so, our participants have taken the experiences and skills they garnered from the fashion hacking workshops beyond these spaces, sharing them with a wider community in new, creative ways. In sharing outside of the workshops, our collaborators centre community and explore crip fashion as a tool for liberatory access (Mingus 2017), free from the expectations of capitalism.

Holding Intersectional Disabled Stories

Our workshops illuminated the ways that interdependence, love and the embodiment of Disability Justice exist well beyond interhuman relationships. Clothing was created as a part of this interdependence: we are not isolated from our clothing; it supports us in holding our bodies, carrying us through the world and sharing our identities (Barry et al. 2021). The fashion hacking workshops were an opportunity to honour the intersections of each participants' identity—their histories, life experiences and internal selves (Sins Invalid 2019, 23)—by redesigning clothes to meet the needs of their bodyminds alongside the many layers of their intersectional identities. The way each participant envisioned their hacked garment and how it would carry them through the world differed greatly, but what was consistent across them was a desire to honour their particular embodiment through the shapes, textiles and embellishments of the item and create clothing that would celebrate and hold them as they moved through the world. Clothing became a tool of interdependence and an embodiment of love.

Joanne Entwistle (2000) explains, "Clothing marks the boundary between self and other, individual and society" (327). In order to "fit in" with the normative sociocultural expectations, clothing that is suitable must fit within existing aesthetic ideals and act as a tool to conform to bodily standards and expectations of beauty (Entwistle 2000; Klepp and Rysst 2016), standards grounded in white supremacy, cis-heteropatriarchy and ableism. Tobin Siebers (2010) conceptualizes disability aesthetics as an aesthetic orientation where disability can be provocative by challenging and expanding hegemonic frameworks of beauty. Disability Justice, too, calls for a disruption of normative standards of beauty and the body by disentangling beauty from its oppressive history and reimagining it as intersectional and liberatory (Kafai 2021). Our workshops used fashion to desire and value disabled bodies. By hacking their clothing, CX and Logan both discovered the way clothing could support and carry them through challenging conversations about disability, crip fashion, beauty and other axes of their identity. Logan found his new clothing to support him in sharing parts of his identity in new ways. He explained, "I want people to notice my disability. Obviously I don't want it to be the first thing they notice, but I want to be able to talk about my shirt that I made, or talk about my fashion, in a way that relates to my disability." In contrast to Logan, CX has discovered fashion as a support system to divert conversations away from their body and identity. They explained, "I would rather people talk about the flowers that I have sewn onto my dress than make a comment about my body. With fashion, I'm creating boundaries with myself and others about how I can use myself and my body to get what I need. I find it super empowering." These experiences illustrate the way that interdependent relationships can develop beyond human relationships through clothing, but serve as support in similar ways. For CX and Logan, their clothing became an embodiment of love and a part of their community by carrying them through difficult spaces and offering new tools of support in their lives.

Embodying love through clothing also meant honouring kinship and community through used clothing. Many of the participants we interviewed during the first phase of *Cripping Masculinity* explained that they were often drawn to used clothing for the way it connected them to the history of their communities. This was especially true for CX, who spent their youth houseless. Throughout their life, much of their wardrobe was given to them by community members who supported and uplifted them as they navigated houselessness, changes in their gender identity and the development of their disability. CX honoured this experience by hacking a dress they received from a friend, changing the fit and attaching recycled fabric and scraps from other garments they no longer wore. They explain that the dress holds a deep connection:

> This dress that a friend of mine gave me just came with so much love ... We might cry because they're giving up something that they once really loved but they're not going to be able to wear again because our bodies change, and so they want someone like me to cherish it and love it. There's something sentimental about that, especially when not all of us have family in the same way. I think I'm part of a queer chosen family network that is ever-growing, ever-changing.

As a result, CX's hacked garments represent their connection to those they referred to as their "ancestors": other queer, trans, disabled people that helped them survive in a hostile world. By honouring their community through their garment, CX has discovered a new way of valuing themselves through their personal history, and they embody this kinship when wearing the dress.

Moreover, CX used their dress to elaborate their gender identity in ways that intersect with their relationship to their bodymind. They explained:

> After ten years of trying to pass as a guy, I realised I do pass, but it's more important to me to be authentic to my gender. I identify as transmasculine, but also as a femme. So, for me, wearing bright lipstick and a dress, I feel so well in my body. It changes my whole persona. The workshops challenged me to invite that into my realm, and to offer me space to be a model and to be femme. To be a femme guy, that's cool, too, to just honour that and to have fun with it. And to learn how to make my own clothes, I think that's also something that inspires me.

By referring to themself as "a model," CX shows how participants were able to celebrate crip beauty in a way that challenges the way in which beauty is most often represented in mainstream fashion. Participants were able to dismantle beauty as an ableist, white supremacist, capitalist and transphobic framework, and instead realize their whole selves through their custom garments and new-found community of support. Beauty and fashion became a crip cultural practice (Chandler 2019) that centred their own lived and embodied experiences.

For other participants, embodying love meant honouring and celebrating their physical selves. For Logan, this meant making distinctive changes to his garment that would celebrate his gender identity, but also allow him to get dressed independently, something that was previously challenging. This was done by changing the clear buttons on a dress shirt to ones in a colour that stood out against the colour of the shirt. Initially an aesthetic choice to better embody his masculinity, this change allowed Logan to reimagine his own bodily capacity as he buttoned his shirt alone for the first time. He explained, "Being able to do them up independently really gave me some confidence to be able to put it on and wear it more often. I think that realisation that this was something that was inaccessible to me before was really empowering." While this change has allowed Logan to experience greater independence in his life, the crip value of interdependence becomes embedded in the garment as a new tool for support. His new buttons guide him through the process of getting dressed, while the masculine changes to the shirt carry him through the world in a way that better expresses his gender embodiment.

Pree had previously accepted that they could not access clothing that was comfortable and affordable, and their choices were limited to low-quality garments, uncomfortable fabrics and dull colours. As a fat and low-income person, Pree was limited to fast fashion retailers such as ASOS and H & M, both of which carry extended sizing options at a price that was accessible to them. However, most of these garments were often only available in greys and blacks, and made of materials like polyester, which didn't work well with Pree's body temperature and propensity to sweat. Moreover, Pree's anxiety around germs, heightened by the pandemic, meant they needed to wash their clothing frequently and the polyester wouldn't hold up. To combat this, Alexis found a bolt of baby blue hemp cotton that was breathable, durable and colourful. Clothing made of this type of material tends to be prohibitively expensive and thus inaccessible; however, Alexis had access to resources that would allow them to share the fabric with Pree. As they used this fabric to create a new sweatsuit, the bolt of cotton became an outfit that celebrated the intersections of Pree's personal embodiment in a way they had never seen reflected in fashion before. Pree explained, "I felt kind of excited about clothes again. I was like, whoa, this is actually really cool. I really wanted it to be something that's so special, and functional, and wearable, and washable, and cool." The new sweatsuit honoured the physical functioning of their bodymind and helped to convey their relationship to their gender through its colour. It has become a go-to outfit that carries their bodymind with greater confidence and comfort as they move through the world, and has allowed them to recognize their own relationship to beauty through fashion.

Through our workshops, we aimed to recognize each person as coming from intersectional experiences of race, class, sexuality, disability and more, finding ways of embracing with love the nuances and perspectives each person offered (Sins Invalid 2019, 23). These spaces and garments disrupted normative expectations of beauty by centring crip beauty as a "politicized, disabled, queer of color beauty politic" (Kafai 2021, 161). Through these garments, collaborators had the opportunity to see their whole selves within a space of fashion that had previously erased them and collectively reimagine what beauty can be.

Self-reflection and Accountability

Dominant narratives of disability are rife with failure and shame, and disabled people are often asked to share their trauma in exchange for validation (Kafer, 2013). However, we wanted to create a space for the experiences of pain and alienation to exist in tandem with experiences of joy and pleasure. The crip experience would not be seen as "either/or," but "both/and" (Barry et al. 2021). Through the process of creating clothes, space was also held for collaborators to discuss and work against experiences of racism, transphobia, ableism, sizeism and more. The workshops became encounters grounded in intergenerational knowledge sharing, and spaces where groups of people came together to make things and at the same time find space to learn from one another and talk about life. Within the fashion hacking workshops, participants and designer-researchers built trust and developed conversations about their experiences in everyday life. These were conversations of vulnerability and shared experience, but also conversations that shifted away from the heaviness of moving through the world as a multiply marginalized person. Love in these conversations was about holding intersectional disabled stories of pain and alienation alongside those of pleasure and joy.

These conversations that enmeshed positive and negative experiences were shared throughout the workshops. For example, when Logan and CX reflected on the importance of clothing in relation to the way they convey their disabilities in everyday life, their framing was different: Logan experienced clothing as a tool to elaborate their disability while CX experienced it as a tool of distraction. Their opposing views generated new understandings in each other that accounted for vast differences in personal embodiment and experiences, and viewed crip fashion from different standpoints. In another instance, designer-researcher Jonathan noted that Pree had begun to use the word "fun" to describe fashion as they moved through towards the end of the workshop, a word they had not previously used when speaking about clothing. This conversation prompted Pree to reflect on their own relationship to fashion and new-found embrace of fashion's playfulness, while at the same time calling upon Jonathan to recognize that "fun" fashion was prohibitive for someone of Pree's economic status and body size. The power of this conversation was twofold: Jonathan opened Pree's eyes to the way their relationship to fashion had positively shifted, while Pree redirected Jonathan to think about the multifaceted layers embedded in their relationship to fashion.

To hold intersectional disabled experiences with love, we were required to check in with our own positions in the world. Speaking on the challenges of practising justice within disabled communities, Mingus (2018) explains, "The moment we acknowledge intersectionality, it also means we must acknowledge and face ourselves … I want us to do our work so that when people whose oppression benefits us, share their truths or their questions, we can meet them in those conversations." The Disability Justice framework reminds us that self-inquiry and self-reflection is a practice of love that moves us towards collective liberation (Kafai 2021). In order to connect with our inner selves and cultivate an awareness of our own positionality, we as designer-researchers engaged in reflexivity exercises that would interrogate our personal values, beliefs and assumptions. By looking inwards and challenging our own experiences and biases, we unlock the potential to hold love in spaces of Disability Justice, and hold love for our own bodyminds.

We approached accountability in the project with strategies developed by educators working in the Bay Area Transformative Justice Collective (2014). Recognizing that harm may occur even within spaces of Disability Justice, we developed our own accountability pods (Mingus 2016) that set out to deepen relationships through dialogue and intervene in harm with broader networks of support. While each fashion hacking workshop consisted of two participants and two designer-researchers, the accountability pods brought in other members of the *Cripping Masculinity* team, as well as friends and community members outside of the project that the collaborators looked to in their own personal networks to ensure wide systems of trust, support and accountability were in place. *Cripping Masculinity* team members who did not participate in the workshops were positioned on standby for participants and designer-researchers to speak to if harm occurred, or as a sounding board to debrief on experiences, challenges and triumphs. Participants were also invited to engage with a member of their own community outside of the project in a similar way, and if they chose to do so, the community member would be offered funds from the project to carry out their work. Pod members provided recognition that some participants may have people in their lives to speak to about harm or celebrate success, while also accounting for those who may not (Mingus 2016).

Overall, the pods provided networks of accountability should harm occur during the workshops and provided everyone involved with a sense of ease in knowing their voices and experiences would be met with love and trust. Alexis, Jonathan and CX consistently turned to other *Cripping Masculinity* team members to expand upon their workshop experiences, while Pree and MG took the opportunity to meet with those outside of the team for debriefing. Although we are grateful that the pods have thus far not been necessary for instances of harm, they provided excellent networks that could help those involved in the workshops talk through the complex emotions and experiences that may have developed in these spaces.

Fashion Hacking as Multidirectional Community Love Practice

Our fashion hacking workshops provide a map to designing clothing for and from love. With the intention of cultivating crip-centric liberated zones, love was enacted "as multidirectional community love practice" (Kafai 2021, 43). The workshops enacted love for participants, but also for us as designer-researchers. By developing each component of the fashion hacking process based on the needs and desires of participants, we developed ways of designing clothing outside of the goals and temporalities of the fashion industry and instead aligned with those of Disability Justice. Together, as designer-researchers and participants, we developed fashion design processes that were slow and flexible, made space for complex conversations about power and fostered meaningful relationships. Most importantly, we held space to appreciate parts of our bodyminds that the fashion industry and society-at-large has told us to hide and dismiss. It was through these workshops that designer-researchers and participants began to appreciate, value and claim the beauty of our individual D/disabled and mad identities.

In this way, fashion hacking not only enacts love but exchanges it. Participants and designer-researchers left the workshops nourished with an abundance of love, and we were prepared to share it in the pursuit of liberation towards Disability Justice. As Mingus (2018) writes, "I would argue that our work for liberation is simply a practice of love—one of the deepest and most profound there is." Hacking clothing therefore offers us the confidence and community to pull apart systems that oppress, and to re-make them by collaboratively re-stitching with the multiple threads of love.

Acknowledgement and Addendum This research is funded by an Insight Grant from the Social Sciences and Humanities Research Council of Canada. We are grateful to the participants who collaborated in the *Cripping Masculinity* project by sharing their experiences, wisdom and creativity. While this chapter was written by us—Ben and Philippa—the project is a collaborative effort and many ideas in this chapter emerged through our collective dialogue. We thank our fashion hacking research team, Alexis De Villa, Jonathan Dumitra, Madison Hollamon, Kristina McMullin and Alex Peifer. In particular, Alexis and Jonathan facilitated the workshops that we shared, and the relationships they fostered were invaluable to this chapter. We recognize our analysis is limited by our positionalities and engagement in the hacking process, and we plan to expand upon it in future publications that are co-authored with additional team members.

References

Barry, Ben, and Daniel Drak. 2019. Intersectional Interventions into Queer and Trans Liberation: Youth Resistance Against Right-Wing Populism Through Fashion Hacking. *Fashion Theory* 23 (6): 679–709.
Barry, Ben, Alexis De Villa, Jonathan Dumitra, Kristina McMullin, and Philippa Nesbitt. 2021. Crip Community Can Save Fashion: How Disabled People Generate Alternative Fashion Practices. Paper presented at The Responsible Fashion Series, Antwerp.
Bay Area Transformative Justice Collective. 2014. Accessed 22 April 2022. https://batjc.wordpress.com.
Berlant, Lauren. 2001. Love, A Queer Feeling. In *Homosexuality & Psychoanalysis*, ed. Tim Dean and Christopher Lane, 432–451. University of Chicago Press.
Chandler, Eliza. 2019. Introduction: Cripping the Arts in Canada. *The Canadian Journal of Disability Studies* 8 (1): 1–14.

Chandler, Eliza, and Esther Ignagni. 2018. Strange Beauty: Aesthetic Possibilities for Desiring Disability into the Future. In *Interdisciplinary Approaches to Disability*, ed. Katie Ellis, Rosemarie Garland-Thomson, Mike Kent, and Rachel Robertson, 255–266. London: Routledge.

Entwistle, Joanne. 2000. Fashion and the Fleshy Body. *Fashion Theory* 4 (3): 323–347.

———. 2015. *The Fashioned Body: Fashion, Dress and Modern Social Theory*. 2nd ed. Cambridge: Polity Press.

Hamraie, Aimie, and Kelly Fritsch. 2019. Crip Technoscience Manifesto. *Catalyst: Feminism, Theory and Technoscience* 5 (1): 1–34.

Hickman, Louise, and David Serlin. 2018. Toward a Crip Methodology for Critical Disability Studies. In *Interdisciplinary Approaches to Disability*, ed. Katie Ellis, Rosemarie Garland Thomson, Mike Kent, and Rachel Robertson, 131–142. London: Routledge.

hooks, bell. 2000. *All About Love: New Visions*. New York: Harper Collins.

Kafai, Shayda. 2021. *Crip Kinship: The Disability Justice and Art Activism of Sins Invalid*. Vancouver: Arsenal Pulp Press.

Kafer, Alison. 2013. *Feminist, Queer, Crip*. Bloomington: Indiana University Press.

Klepp, I.G., and M. Rysst. 2016. Deviant Bodies and Suitable Clothes. *Fashion Theory* 21 (1): 79–99. https://doi.org/10.1080/1362704x.2016.1138658.

Lakshmi Piepzna-Samarasinha, Leah. 2021. How Disabled Mutual Aid Is Different Than Abled Mutual Aid. Disability Visibility Project. Accessed 30 March 2022. https://disabilityvisibilityproject.com/2021/10/03/how-disabled-mutual-aid-is-different-than-abled-mutual-aid/.

Lamm, Nomy. 2015. This Is Disability Justice. The Body Is Not an Apology. Accessed 28 April 2022. https://thebodyisnotanapology.com/magazine/this-is-disability-justice.

Mingus, Mia. 2011. Access Intimacy: The Missing Link. Leaving Evidence. Accessed 14 April 2022. https://leavingevidence.wordpress.com/2011/05/05/access-intimacy-the-missing-link.

———. 2016. Pods and Pod Mapping Worksheet. Bay Area Transformative Justice Collective. Accessed 25 April 2022. https://batjc.wordpress.com/resources/pods-and-pod-mapping-worksheet.

———. 2017. Access Intimacy, Interdependence and Disability Justice. Presented at the 2017 Paul K. Langmore Lecture on Disability Studies, San Francisco State University, CA.

———. 2018. 'Disability Justice' is Simply Another Term for Love. Keynote presented at the 2018 Disability Intersectionality Summit, Cambridge, MA.

Siebers, Tobin. 2010. *Disability Aesthetics*. Ann Arbor: University of Michigan Press.

Sins Invalid. 2019. *Skin, Tooth and Bone: The Basis of Movement is Our People*. 2nd ed. Berkeley, CA.

TallBear, Kim. 2020. Dr. Kim TallBear on Reviving Kinship and Sexual Abundance. *For The Wild* (Podcast), February 5. https://forthewild.world/listen/kim-tallbear-on-reviving-kinship-and-sexual-abundance-157.

CHAPTER 7

Beading Is Medicine: Beading as Therapeutic and Decolonial Practice

Presley Mills and Justine Woods

Justine Woods and Presley Mills met each other in the first-ever *Beading Circle* hosted by Woods at Toronto Metropolitan University (formerly Ryerson University) in the winter of 2019. Held within one of the Fashion department's classrooms, Indigenous students, staff, faculty, and non-Indigenous allies of all beadwork levels gathered with a shared passion and interest to learn how to bead, start a new project, or work on in-progress beadwork. Gathered around a table made from desks, the first teaching Woods shared with the group was to only bead while in a positive and calm mindset as the beads take in our energy and, with each stitch, become embedded with our intentions. Over the remaining two hours, knowledge was shared, stories were told, tea was sipped, beads were stitched, and community was fostered.

In March of 2020, the *Beading Circle* moved online to accommodate the physical distancing and isolation measures that were put into effect due to Covid-19. Woods decided to open the virtual space to community

P. Mills • J. Woods (✉)
Toronto Metropolitan University, Toronto, ON, Canada
e-mail: justine.woods@ryerson.ca

© The Author(s), under exclusive license to Springer Nature Switzerland AG 2023
R. Filippello, I. Parkins (eds.), *Fashion and Feeling*, Palgrave Studies in Fashion and the Body,
https://doi.org/10.1007/978-3-031-19100-8_7

members from all across Turtle Island, prioritizing a safe space for the Indigenous community to connect, build kinship, and bead together during times of isolation and uncertainty. According to Lana Ray (2016), beadwork and beading circles "strengthen relationships and community knowledge" (364). The relationships built within the *Beading Circle* inspired Woods and Mills to explore the concept of beading as medicine. This phrase frequently appears in Indigenous communities because of the lessons inherent to the practice. To engage in a closer investigation of the phrase "Beading is Medicine" and how it relates to fashion and feeling, beadwork itself became the method of inquiry.

Indigenous beadwork was born out of colonization, as glass seed beads are a post-settler contact trade good. Ancestor artists mastered beadwork, adopting this practice as their own through distinct creativity and unique technical skills. Indigenous beadwork developed into an art form foregrounded by ethics of reciprocity and ceremony through gift giving and cultural adornment. The practice of beadwork within an Indigenous context asserts and mobilizes cultural sovereignty in relation to the land, to Indigenous bodies, and within and between community.

The introduction of the Indian Act in 1876 directly impacted the cultural production of Indigenous beadwork (Prete 2019). A federal law written by the Canadian government, the Indian Act targeted Indigenous sovereignty and self-determination by obtaining legal control over Indigenous bodies and prohibiting multiple cultural and ceremonial practices. Amendments to the Indian Act in 1884 and 1895 made it illegal for Indigenous peoples to engage in gift giving, a common practice involved within ceremony which often included beadwork (Prete 2019). An amendment in 1914 made it illegal for Indigenous peoples to wear regalia off-reserve without legal permission from an Indian Agent. This amendment directly impacted beadwork as an expression of Indigenous body sovereignty, as the majority of regalia components such as moccasins, leggings, jewelry, headbands, and barrettes include beadwork. During this time, many beadwork pieces were seized, and the new creation of beadwork was limited and/or surveyed (Prete 2019).

The ongoing practice of beadwork is an act of resistance against the colonial domination and assimilation of Indigenous bodies and Indigenous knowledge. Practiced by many Indigenous peoples across a diverse array of nations, beadwork has survived colonial attempts of cultural genocide and continues to pass knowledge through time and space from one generation to the next. As stated by Tiffany Dionne Prete (2019), "while in the face of such oppression, we took the colonizer's beads, made the beads a part of our culture and created beautiful art with it" (40–41). As a decolonial practice, beadwork mobilizes Indigenous knowledge transmission and facilitates space where Indigenous bodies can re-member (Smith 2012) themselves and each other through embodied gestures of love and care.

Centering Prete's (2019) research paradigm of beadworking, Woods and Mills hosted three small virtual beading circles with four beadwork artists from the *Beading Circle* as collaborators on this project. Enacting a beading circle as a qualitative community-based participatory research method not only prioritizes the values and ethics held within an Indigenous research methodology but also mobilizes Indigenous knowledge-based and art-based resurgence. As Prete (2019) writes:

> Beadworking is rooted in the historically and geographically located epistemologies, ontologies, and axiologies of Indigenous Peoples. While it recognizes that variations exist between groups of Indigenous Peoples, beadworking is founded in the historical, political and cultural commonalities that exist amongst Indigenous Peoples. (30)

Additionally, according to Lana Ray (2016), "because Indigenous knowledges are spiritual and relation-based systems, engaging in an activity such as beading that evokes a collective and spiritual consciousness allows us to access and contribute to these systems" (364).

The beading circles Woods and Mills hosted were informal, intimate, and familiar as each of the individuals involved already knew each other from the *Beading Circle*. Each artist was invited to bring a beadwork project they were working on to virtually visit and bead alongside one another for a period of two hours. Each circle began by checking in on everyone's energy and well-being as tea was poured, needles were threaded, and beads were gathered. Each community member shared about their week's triumphs and/or tribulations and acknowledged each other's presence as not only a fellow beadworker but as a fellow friend—*kin*.

With each circle, our bodies, minds, and spirits felt more connected to one another as kin, fostering a space grounded in mutual respect where conversations organically explored questions such as: Amidst ongoing settler colonialism, how can beadwork restore and repair your relationship to community, identity, and ancestral lands? How does beading impact you emotionally? How does practicing beadwork contribute to individual and collective efforts of decolonization?

The four beadwork artists invited to join us were Kristine, Paxsi, Katie, and Craig. Kristine is Latvian and Anishinaabe from Nipissing First Nation. Kristine first learned how to bead at Toronto Metropolitan University's 2018 PowWow and later joined the *Beading Circle* in 2019. As an Urban Indigenous graduate student, being a part of a space such as the *Beading Circle* has helped her to reconnect to her Indigenous identity and build kinship with other members of the Indigenous community in Tkaronto (Toronto).

Paxsi is a queer, disabled Aymara and Welsh-Irish multidisciplinary artist based in amiskwaciywaskahikan (Edmonton). They taught themselves how to bead and have refined their skills by learning alongside community. The aesthetics and meanings found within their work are deeply inspired by art, textiles, colors, prints, and creation stories from within Aymara culture.

Katie is Yerington Paiute and Washoe from California. She first learned how to bead from her grandparents, who were vendors on the PowWow trail. She would often help her grandparents with loom work to make chokers and bracelets. After her grandparents passed away, she gradually stopped beading. When she was an undergraduate student, she joined an Indigenous women's beading circle at her university, which reignited her passion for the practice.

Craig is an Anishinaabe multidisciplinary artist from Kitigan Zibi based in Tiohtiá:ke (Montreal). He works in moving images, poetry, music, sound composition, and beadwork. His beadwork practice engages with various methods and techniques of beading, resulting in innovative, sculptural forms. Craig carries a passion for contributing to cultural preservation and revitalization for and by Indigenous peoples.

After the three beading circles, Woods and Mills came together to review the dialogue and stories shared. Story and knowledge are deeply interrelated within Indigenous thought and Indigenous research as "data [is] more than things; they are living connections animated through the exchange of story" (Kovach 2021, 156). In honor of Indigenous and decolonizing methods of research such as storytelling (Archibald 2008; Smith 2012; Kovach 2009, 2021), the discussion to follow features a transcribed version of an oral conversation that took place between Mills and Woods in the fall of 2021. The conversation happened virtually with Woods in Toronto on the traditional territories of the Haudenosaunee,

Anishinaabe, and Mississaugas of the Credit, and Presley in Calgary on the traditional territories of the Niitsitapi (Blackfoot Confederacy) and the people of the Treaty 7 region.

A Common Denominator: Beadwork

Justine: First of all, there is a common denominator of *we're all in this space, and we're all beading*. We're all doing the same thing, and we're all doing something that we absolutely love. The relationship we all have to beadwork is very similar but also very diverse at the same time because we come from different geographical locations and different nations that carry different stories and different lived experiences. But it's the common denominator of the beads themselves that brings us all together.

Presley: Something that has stood out to me is how folks came to the circle and feel comfortable sharing how their day went—good or bad. So often, we are forced to put on a strong front of "I'm fine," but when we are a part of the circle, everyone can be honest.

Justine: It is really beautiful to be in a space where you can just feel your emotions, let go and be present with yourself and others. Also, acknowledging all this out loud. There is something powerful about being able to sit back and say, "You know what ... I didn't have a good day." I think this is important and something that I don't do often, but I would like to do more of. Beading circles open up the possibility for that. We saw it in the circles we held together, and I see it all the time in the *Beading Circle*.

Presley: With the smaller group, it was an ideal situation to have the time for everyone to think and share. We engaged with some hard questions and folks dove in fearlessly, which was really wonderful. Especially having our first circle on Orange Shirt Day when everyone was feeling a lot of emotions. Talking about it with others who felt the same way was therapeutic. It was nice to hear other perspectives that validated those feelings.[1]

---

[1] September 30th is Orange Shirt Day in what we now know as Canada. The day was "designed to commemorate the residential school experience, to witness and honour the healing journey of the survivors and their families, and to commit to the ongoing process of reconciliation" (*The Story of Orange Shirt Day* n.d.). The date was chosen in reference to the time of year that Indigenous children were taken away from their homes to attend residential school. In May 2021, the remains of 215 Indigenous children were discovered buried in unmarked graves at a former Kamloops Indian Residential School. The ongoing search has uncovered hundreds more children buried at other residential school sites across the country. To acknowledge the murder of thousands of Indigenous children, the government of Canada declared Orange Shirt Day 2021 as the first National Day for Truth and Reconciliation.

Justine: Absolutely. Thinking back, I remember the day for me was very difficult. There was a part of me that thought maybe we should postpone the circle because it was Orange Shirt Day and the first National Day of Truth and Reconciliation. I then realized that this is one of the most important days to have a beading circle. Being in that space and being able to open up and have conversations alongside others while doing beadwork was very therapeutic. I remember that afterwards the feeling of anxiety and heavy grief I was carrying was cared for.

Presley: On that day, I was grieving my dog's passing as well, so I found it very helpful to have conversations that focused on our love of beading and allowing space to process and grieve on such a painful day.

Justine: Beading together provided us with the opportunity to think through the complexities of that day critically and with care. There is something especially powerful about holding space for these kinds of conversations to happen and being able to be in conversation with other folks from other Indigenous nations all across Turtle Island. I recently was re-reading Leanne Simpson's book *As We Have Always Done* (2017), and she talks about settlers' desire to keep Indigenous nations away from each other. When we come together and engage in Indigenous internationalism, it is a threat to ongoing colonialism in what we now refer to as Canada.

Presley: Also, how our "silence benefits white supremacy."[2] Having a space to be in conversation together is radical. That was something that came up often in our conversations: the importance of community and having a space to be together is beneficial in so many different ways. Community was mentioned the most.

Justine: Community and storytelling are tied to the transmission of knowledge and the mobilization of Indigenous brilliance. This was one of the first things I reflected on and made a note of after our first circle:

---

[2] The statement "silence benefits white supremacy" is in reference to the book *White Fragility* (2018) by Robin DiAngelo. The concept of white fragility explains how white people are protected and insulated from race-based stress. When placed in a situation that confronts race, it challenges their expectation of comfort, and white fragility is a state in which they become defensive. These defensive moves include displays of emotions like anger, fear, and guilt, and behaviors such as arguing, leaving, or becoming silent. These actions return the white racial equilibrium, reduce their racial stress, and, in turn, reinforce values that maintain white supremacy.

7 BEADING IS MEDICINE: BEADING AS THERAPEUTIC AND DECOLONIAL...

beading holds culture, beading holds stories, and beading carves out spaces of community care.

Presley: During our circles, multiple different modes of storytelling were shared. For example, Paxsi talked about fringe earrings with stories built into them (see Fig. 7.1). We also talked about Navajo blankets and Kristine's Latvian culture's similar use of storytelling through beadwork and how the knowledge these objects hold is then passed on to whomever the item is gifted to.

Justine: I really loved when Paxsi and Katie decided to do an earring tour and how, with each pair of earrings, they would tell a story about who made them, when they were made, how long they have had them, what memory is tied to them, and how they received the earrings (see Fig. 7.2). There is something really beautiful about the reciprocity that's inherent to Indigenous knowledge sharing, especially knowledge that is gifted through beadwork.

Presley: This makes me think of when we asked the circle if the practice of beadwork had ever improved someone's negative feelings, and everyone responded that is not how it works. Instead, they shared how wearing, for example, a pair of fringe earrings gives their body a *boost*. I found this so fascinating—how a tiny handmade object has such a deep spiritual effect on our bodies because of the energy that was put into making it.

Justine: This question made a lot of us realize that beadwork is more so a practice that helps us not necessarily to escape our negative emotions but to process them. Beading facilitates a space where we can actively communicate with ourselves. I think working through emotions in the way that beading helps us to do so is radical as it helps us redefine how to engage with our emotions and thoughts. It helps us to slow down and really *feel*.

Presley: It's honoring what you're actually experiencing because the beads force you to slow down. Those who have done beadwork know it is impossible to speed through the practice without making mistakes. Making mistakes is a way the beads communicate with you to take a break or stop for a while. The beads themselves are telling you what is best for your mind and body.

I made a note when Katie specifically said—*beading is therapy*.

Justine: There is no better way to say it. Beading is therapeutic through repetition and also by engaging in humility. Beadwork helps us to prioritize the well-being of not just our mind and our spirit but also our body. Our body can suffer from beading for three or four hours straight, and

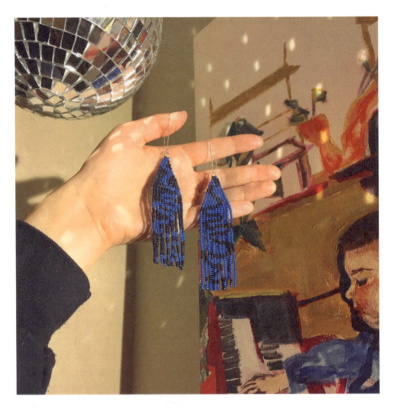

Fig. 7.1 *Jawira* fringe earrings beaded by Paxsi (size 10 Czech seed beads) (Paxsi, who made these earrings, shared: "I first created the jawira earrings in spring 2020 in reflection of how light flows and moves. One morning, I awoke to see a crack of light dancing on my lace curtain; the window was slightly open and the curtain was gently swaying with the warm breeze. This design—which I have named jawira after the Aymara word for river—have come to mean many things to me over the years. Everyone seems to perceive them in a different way, which is something I love about them. To me, they represent the relationship between water and light as we experience them in our realm of spacetime, akapacha, as well as the duality of alaxpacha (the realm/spacetime above us) and ukhupacha (the realm/spacetime below us) and how they are reflected in each other")

Fig. 7.2 Katie's beaded earring collection

when I start to feel the tension, I know it's time to take a break, do some stretches, and move around. Beadwork has taught me how to prioritize the health and well-being of my physical body to ensure I can do this practice for a really long time and eventually pass these skills down to my children and grandchildren one day.

Presley: That reminds me of how Katie's grandparents introduced her and other members of her family to beadwork when she was young. It was a family affair where each member of the family was assigned a task. I loved how different generations of her family worked together to support the grandparents' business by doing beadwork. We know why there are not many stories of grandparents passing the practice down to their children or grandchildren, and so I found it really comforting to hear Katie's story.

Justine: I often think about the Indian Act and how for close to 100 years Indigenous peoples were not allowed to engage in cultural practices under the law, including forms of creative expression such as beadwork. Even though beadwork and other cultural art forms continued to be done silently, this is one of the main reasons why, for the majority of us, beadwork was not passed down through our families.

Presley: Thinking back to what Craig told us about how he had just come from teaching a beading workshop at a high school. He talked about how 50 years ago, that would never have happened—he would have been arrested for it. We have progressed to a point where we are able to share this art form with other people and pass it along so others can become artists and the community can grow even more.

Beading Decolonial Space into Existence

Presley: The writings of scholars such as Simpson (2017), Tuck and Yang (2012) and Smith (2012) have offered us various understandings of decolonization as it relates to Indigenous sovereignty, resurgence, education, and social understandings. From these offerings, we have learned that decolonization is *for* Indigenous peoples first and foremost. In recent years it has become an important topic of discussion, especially in relation to "Indigenizing" academic Institutions (Gaudry and Lorenz 2018). Paxsi mentioned how decolonization has become performative and that there is no such thing as reconciliation, especially when tangible actions needed to actually engage in the act of decolonization are removed. It just becomes a big band-aid.

Justine: Absolutely. This is what Tuck and Yang discuss in their article "Decolonization is Not a Metaphor" (2012) when referring to *settler innocence*. When decolonization is situated as a metaphor, it prioritizes settler futurities over Indigenous futurities, and that is the epitome of the problem. We don't want to maintain settler futurities; we want to re-center Indigenous futurities.

Presley: This is why it is important to understand what decolonization *really* means. It is a responsibility. For me personally, it is important to acknowledge this with respect to my positionality. As someone who is white-presenting and has family that made an effort to assimilate into settler society after attending residential school, I have to take accountability for the huge negative impact settler colonialism had and still has on Indigenous peoples, communities, and nations. The only way we can make actual change in our everyday lives is by taking actions in our everyday lives that challenge colonialism (Corntassel et al. 2018). And when I say this, I don't mean just wearing an orange shirt one day out of the year. As you said, there is a difference between a gesture and actual tangible action.[3]

Justine: Beading circles and beadwork are tangible forms of decolonization. Beadwork is as much action as it is aesthetic. It re-centers Indigenous futures and knowledge and creates decolonial space through practice. At the same time, it is interesting to acknowledge the origins of beads and how beads are a post-settler contact trade good. Understanding the relationship between glass beads and Indigenous peoples critically acknowledges beadwork as an established art form within the complex histories of colonization.

Presley: It also acknowledges how Indigenous culture is forever evolving, dismantling the dead Indian trope.[4] When we were introduced to something new, like beads, we embraced them and found ways to create beauty through making. Even before settlers were in so-called Canada, there were interconnecting trade relationships and trade routes happening. For example, how did seashells get to the prairies? There were trade routes long before Western contact. It's not that different from today, where we are sharing different cultural practices and traditions with each other on a reciprocal and consensual basis of respect.

Justine: Also, the amount of innovation too. Our ancestors were incredibly intelligent and talented.

Presley: It is interesting how beads came to Turtle Island through colonization, became a part of Indigenous culture through trade, were banned through the Indian Act, and were later appropriated to be sold in

---

[3] Jeff Corntassel et al. (2018) emphasize the need for Indigenous individuals, communities, and nations to adopt and engage in everyday acts of decolonization and resurgence. This could include learning and speaking an Indigenous language, harvesting and eating traditional foods, or participating in cultural art forms. As Corntassel et al. shared with us, "focusing on everydayness helps make visible the often unseen or unacknowledged actions that embody Indigenous nationhood" (17). By engaging in forms of decolonization and resurgence in our everyday lives, "our ancestors along with future generations will recognize us as Indigenous to the land" and "our homelands will recognize us as being Indigenous to that place" (Corntassel 2012, 99).

[4] The dead Indian trope is a term referencing the imaginary "noble savage" depicted throughout Western pop culture. According to King (2012), these characters are stereotypes and clichés conjured with a jumble of Indigenous signifiers to create Native characters that are frozen in an imaginary past (59).

gift shops and fast fashion stores. Our beading practices became flattened to a point where their significance was removed. This is why reclamation is so important, because it allows for stolen aesthetics to be placed back into the culture's rightful ownership again.

Justine: I've been thinking a lot about the resurgence of craft—the intimate relationship between form and function and pushing tradition to new levels. These concepts go back to the point you mentioned earlier, about how Indigenous cultures are continually evolving: how Indigenous individuals, communities, and nations continue to innovate, expand on tradition, and seek new ways to express ourselves and our Indigeneity that is informed by the past but is also cultivating an alternative future.

Presley: You mentioned, during one of the circles, the democratization of design and how this concept is something you like about the philosophy of the Bauhaus. I think the *Beading Circle* is literally that—you are sharing skills and making it accessible to a lot of people.

Justine: Definitely. If we think about the reciprocity of knowledge sharing grounded in Indigenous pedagogical frameworks, there is a big contrast to Western pedagogy, which takes a top-down approach. Collective forms of reciprocal learning foster such beautiful spaces that generate relational knowledge. Additionally, how collective modes of learning and teaching dismantle hierarchy within the pedagogical space. This is something that beading circles naturally do because everyone is asking each other questions or sharing skills or trading knowledge within the space. We are gifting knowledge and receiving knowledge at the same time. We're all teachers, but we're also all students. This decolonizes the learning space where everyone in the room feels empowered to gift knowledge but then also receives knowledge. It facilitates the feeling that *I am worthy, my thoughts and the knowledge that I hold are valid, and I am capable of being a part of this collective space.*

Presley: Not having a hierarchical system allows people to establish unique forms of kinship with like-minded people who also love the same things they do—beadwork. The unique kinship held within the beadwork community is grounded in mutual respect and relationality fostered through a shared restorative practice such as beadwork.

Justine: Coming full circle, the common denominator is beadwork.

Beadwork as a *Fashion* Practice?

Presley: During a conversation that happened in our second circle, we all agreed that Indigenous beadwork is a fashion practice, but it is not really considered a *Fashion* (capital F) practice as it is not a part of the dominant fashion system in a way that it receives mainstream attention. We can see similarities here in relation to the long ongoing discourse between art and craft. I appreciated the conversation we had about how craft is deemed to be a lower status practice and how we distinguish between art, craft, and design. I also thought it was ironic that when Craig contributed to the conversation, he acknowledged, "yes, I make art," whereas the rest of us were unsure about where our work fits within the discourse of art versus craft. This was a great example of how colonial gender binaries are tied to these discussions. Craig is lucky not to have the preset in his mind that his work might not be considered art. The rest of us in the circle (who are women and non-binary identifying) have been taught by society to question our beadwork's value and authenticity as an art practice.

Paxsi mentioned how basket weaving is traditionally performed by women in Aymara culture and knitting is performed by men: a practice that within a Western context would be considered a *woman's* practice because Western society has conditioned us to categorize art and craft alongside gender binaries. Continual work needs to be done to dismantle these binary categorizations by acknowledging the nuances that exist outside of the Eurocentric perspective of gender found within non-Western cultures and tied to various art/craft forms.

Justine: We must also remember that these binary categories have been made by those who have historically held power: cis-het European men.[5] Resisting and refusing categorization is an anti-colonial gesture. Thinking alongside my own practice, I don't feel the need to put a binary label on my work because the focus of the work should not be what category it fits into, it should be on the meaning the work holds and the impact the work gifts to the world.

---

[5] Foucault's theory of categorization proposes that what we determine to be acceptable and to be the *truth* is informed by dominant historical epistemic assumptions. These assumptions linearly and subjectively inform systems of thought and behavior within society determined by those in power (Foucault 1994). I would like to acknowledge one of my past professors, Professor A. Glaze, who first introduced me to Foucault's writings on classification, knowledge, and power.

Presley: I really love that. Categorization is limiting for anyone who is creative.

Justine: Thinking back to the question "is beadwork a *Fashion* practice?" I would argue that it is, as much as it is a craft practice and an art practice. However, I don't think it is meant to fit within the dominant mainstream Eurocentric fashion system. Beadwork arises from its own distinct knowledge base informed by Indigenous episteme and therefore does not fit within Eurocentric fashion frameworks. Instead, beadwork fits within the Indigenous fashion system, a community-oriented fashion framework foregrounded by relationality, slow-making processes and ethics of reciprocity, mutual respect, consent, and care. By considering beadwork as a fashion practice within the Indigenous fashion system, we are offering a new way for beadwork to exist in the world on its own terms. Or maybe it is more appropriately acknowledged as a re-membering (Smith 2012) of beadwork as a fashion practice. If we look at examples of historical beaded garments, it is evident that our ancestors have always considered beadwork within their own fashion contexts.

Beading as Medicine During the Covid-19 Pandemic

Presley: There's just one more thing we haven't talked about—the pandemic. It consistently came up in our circle conversations since it has been such a traumatic time. Especially early in the pandemic, the *Beading Circle* was a space that helped folks process everything going on.

Justine: It really was. It turned into a virtual space that helped a lot of folks process their emotions and their anxiety when there was so much uncertainty. It was a space where folks could grieve for those who sadly lost someone close to them. During lockdown and isolation, the *Beading Circle* provided a space for individuals to feel connected to community. This was something everyone was looking for due to the collective loss and grief of not being able to connect with each other in person. With community and kinship so integral to our lives, moving the circle online was the best decision.

Presley: I think during those early traumatic times, having a sense of consistency by beading alongside others and listening to one another was really comforting. To exist with other humans, even if it was through a screen, is something to look forward to. Even hearing a little bit about what was happening in another city versus your own contributed to building community bridges.

Justine: Katie mentioned this when we were talking about the pandemic, how the *Beading Circle* turned into this transnational space because we were sharing knowledge from multiple geographical locations all across Turtle Island. Being able to hear what was going on in other places and learning about the different ways folks were coping (like making bread or knitting or watching Netflix). The circle facilitated a sense of connection that a lot of us were really longing for and are still longing for. By moving the *Beading Circle* online within the digital sphere, our community is now made up of members from all across Turtle Island. We have broken down colonial borders. Going back to what I said previously about the settler desire to keep Indigenous folks separated from each other, we are actively refusing this through the practice of beadwork. I think about how hard Indigenous communities have been hit throughout the course of the pandemic and how we have continued to build community and kinship regardless of the challenges we have faced. I feel so proud of how strong we are as Indigenous peoples. How resilient we are and how much love we have for one another. A kind of love and strength that transgresses colonial borders and transcends into an alternative world. It overwhelms me with emotion and happiness. And it wouldn't be possible without every single person who makes up that space. It's not just one of us, two of us, or three of us; it is every single body that joins our circles regardless of if they only join once, if they join twice, or if they attend regularly. Their presence contributes to our collective space, and they will always be a part of that space.

REFERENCES

Archibald, Jo-Ann. 2008. *Indigenous Storywork: Educating the Heart, Mind, Body, and Spirit*. Vancouver: UBC Press.
Corntassel, Jeff. 2012. Re-envisioning Resurgence: Indigenous Pathways to Decolonization and Sustainable Self-determination. *Decolonization: Indigeneity, Education & Society* 1 (1): 86–101. https://jps.library.utoronto.ca/index.php/des/article/view/18627.
Corntassel, Jeff, Alfred Taiaiake, Noelani Goodyear-Ka'ōpua, Aikau Hokulani, Noenoe K. Silva, and Devi Mucina. 2018. Introduction. In *Everyday Acts of Resurgence: People, Places, Practices*, 16–18. Daykeeper Press.
DiAngelo, Robin J. 2018. *White Fragility: Why It's So Hard for White People to Talk About Racism*. Boston: Beacon Press.
Foucault, Michel. 1994. *The Order of Things: An Archaeology of the Human Sciences*. New York: Vintage Books.

Gaudry, Adam, and Danielle Lorenz. 2018. Indigenization as Inclusion, Reconciliation, and Decolonization: Navigating the Different Visions for Indigenizing the Canadian Academy. *AlterNative: An International Journal of Indigenous Peoples* 14 (3): 218–227.

King, Thomas. 2012. *The Inconvenient Indian: A Curious Account of Native People in North America*. Toronto: Doubleday Canada.

Kovach, Margaret. 2021. *Indigenous methodologies: Characteristics, Conversations, and Contexts*. 2nd ed. Toronto: University of Toronto Press.

Orange Shirt Day. n.d. *The Story of Orange Shirt Day*. https://www.orangeshirtday.org/about-us.html. Accessed 20 Dec 2021.

Prete, Tiffany D. 2019. Beadworking as an Indigenous Research Paradigm. *Art/Research International: A Transdisciplinary Journal* 4 (1): 28–57. https://doi.org/10.18432/ari29419.

Ray, Lana. 2016. "Beading Becomes a Part of Your Life": Transforming the Academy Through the Use of Beading as a Method of Inquiry. *International Review of Qualitative Research* 9 (3): 363–378. https://doi.org/10.1525/irqr.2016.9.3.363.

Simpson, Leanne B. 2017. *As We Have Always Done: Indigenous Freedom Through Radical Resistance*. Minneapolis: University of Minnesota Press.

Smith, Linda T. 2012. *Decolonizing Methodologies: Research and Indigenous Peoples*. 2nd ed. London: Zed Books.

Tuck, Eve, and Yang, K. Wayne. 2012. Decolonization is Not a Metaphor. *Decolonization: Indigeneity, Education & Society* 1 (1): 1–40. https://jps.library.utoronto.ca/index.php/des/article/view/1863.

CHAPTER 8

All that Cloth Can Carry (on a Queer Body)

Timo Rissanen

ACKNOWLEDGEMENT OF COUNTRY

I begin by acknowledging the Gadigal People of the Eora Nation upon whose ancestral lands I live and work, and where this text was written. I pay my respect to the Elders both past and present, acknowledging them as the traditional custodians of knowledge for these lands.

GUIDANCE FOR THE READER

This chapter does not make grand universal claims. Rather, it suggests that in some instances, the deliberate stitching of cloth that is turned into a garment and worn has implications for the vitality of the stitched cloth, the garment made from it and the person wearing the garment. Universalism in fashion discourse is problematic due to its capacity to erase and mask locally and culturally specific ideas. This chapter acknowledges that it is important to view perspectives in their proper geographic and cultural contexts. Many of the ideas presented in this chapter are locally,

T. Rissanen (✉)
University of Technology Sydney, Ultimo, NSW, Australia
e-mail: Timo.Rissanen@uts.edu.au

© The Author(s), under exclusive license to Springer Nature Switzerland AG 2023
R. Filippello, I. Parkins (eds.), *Fashion and Feeling*, Palgrave Studies in Fashion and the Body,
https://doi.org/10.1007/978-3-031-19100-8_8

that is geographically and culturally, specific. This chapter is written on Gadigal land, in so-called Sydney, by a queer immigrant settler from Finland. The reader is best placed to determine the ways in which the ideas presented in this chapter play out in their location and context.

INTRODUCTION

Some cloth and clothing exist as repositories for grief, for example arising from witnessing ecological collapse and extinction, a devastating pandemic, personal loss. This chapter explores queer materialities in fashion: what can cloth carry? Through examples, including the author's cross-stitched poems and portraits, this chapter examines the transference of loss, of grief, into cloth. Grief is a potent facet of being alive: stitching loss amplifies the vitality of cloth. Altering the cloth surface by stitching grief into it effects a transformative change in both the stitcher and the cloth. Thousands of stitches traversing the two faces of a cloth become a repository of memory and emotion, an honouring of loss. Does the stitched cloth then become sacred? And conversely, when does a sacred cloth become a rag?

The chapter explores the material knowledge of the stitcher, of the wearer and of the viewer: what can cloth carry when we know it to contain the grief of the stitcher? While many of the works discussed here remain as textiles, this chapter also examines instances when such cloths are fashioned into garments or otherwise placed on a body, and when the surface of a garment is altered with stitches of sorrow. What happens when the stitched surface is placed on a living body and it is viewed by both the wearer and others? Can cloth carry the grief of the wearer or the viewer in the way it carries the grief of the stitcher? While this chapter focuses on grief, trauma and loss, it acknowledges that vitality and aliveness include other experiences and emotions, such as joy and wonder. A queer experience of the world is nonetheless a never-ending negotiation of loss by way of not fitting in. Queer people experience discrimination on a spectrum ranging from throwaway comments to violence and loss of life. To be queer and alive is to be strong and resilient, in part because of the constant embodied negotiation of loss, both historical and current.

This chapter approaches fashion as expressed through physical garments made from cloth, while acknowledging that a garment upon completion is not always 'fashion'. The textiles that garments are made of are of particular interest here, specifically textiles that have been embroidered by hand. Several textiles discussed in the chapter are not made into garments. They nonetheless reveal critical insights about stitching grief into cloth, hence their inclusion. The physical action of pushing a threaded needle through cloth over and over to embellish the surface of the cloth is not a neutral act. At any and every moment the stitcher has thoughts and experiences emotions. This chapter asserts that a transference of emotion may occur from the stitcher to the cloth. If that cloth is made into a garment that is worn, the experience of the wearer carrying the embedded emotion is regarded here as a significant act.

In a chapter titled 'In praise of hands', Henri Focillon writes: "The hand is not the mind's docile slave. It searches and experiments for its master's benefit; it has all sorts of adventures; it tries its chance" (1989/1934, 180). This echoes my experience of stitching, and it colours my reading of other stitchers' processes. To stitch is to think, a way to process thoughts: one reflects while stitching, one has eureka moments while stitching, one arrives at difficult questions while stitching. In the book *In Praise of Hands*, Octavio Paz states, "Since it is a thing made by human hands, the craft object preserves the fingerprints — be they real or metaphorical — of the artisan who fashioned it. These imprints are not the signature of the artist; they are not a name. Nor are they a trademark. Rather, they are ... the scarcely visible, faded scar commemorating the original brotherhood of men and their separation" (1974, 21). Outdated gendering aside, the authors of both texts underline an earlier argument: to stitch is not a neutral act.

Mauri and Aliveness in Fashion

This chapter takes cues from two authors, Amie Berghan and Otto Von Busch, who discuss fashion and vitality or life force from two different yet complementary perspectives. Berghan (2020) discusses mauri, the Maori term for life force, in fashion supply chains. According to Berghan, mauri is the "vitality or lifeforce, that weaves the physical and spiritual worlds together" (8). Mauri exists in both living beings and entities often considered "non-living" in modern western contexts, such as soil and water, and, argues Berghan, textiles and garments. Berghan posits that the primary reason for fashion's waste is not "human greed and entitlement, but [it arises] as a reaction to the mauri of the garments" (4). Berghan's powerful argument guides the discussion of textiles here.

Berghan speculates that the throwaway culture in fashion is due in part to a subconscious sensing of the mauri-depleting nature of fast fashion garments. We discard them relatively quickly because we innately know they are not good for us, that they diminish our life force. While Berghan primarily focuses on toxic textile manufacturing and dyeing processes, the idea could expand to the conditions in which the garments are manufactured, where expert machinists handle the cloth at the machine. Examples of stitched cloths and garments later in the chapter demonstrate the transference of the stitcher's emotions and trauma into cloth through stitching; a similar transference of the garment worker's experience into the garments is possible.[1] Given that we wear garments directly on our bodies for much of the day and often while we sleep, we ought to be more curious about the conditions in which the garments are made, and the wellbeing of the people making them. Human hands have touched everything we wear: through our clothes we are connected to people we will likely never meet. Yet this connection holds power and promise. Each day we have myriad reasons for getting dressed in the clothes that we wear, and every day one of those reasons could be to honour and celebrate the individuals who with their expert hands at the sewing machine brought the garments into existence.

In building on the work of biologist Andreas Weber to develop a thesis of vitality in fashion, Von Busch asserts: "A vitalist perspective in fashion starts the sustainability journey by affirming how fashion contributes to a sense of aliveness. Sustainable practice is not merely to keep living but to enhance life and desire" (2021, 15). Vitality or aliveness is not limited to 'positive' qualities/experiences such as joy: grief and trauma are as much functions of aliveness. Not feeling anything would be more akin to death or stasis, the opposite of aliveness. Von Busch (2021, 27) explicitly promotes three changes of perspective in fashion, one of which is a shift "from fashionable goods to how the vitality of fashion cultivates *fashion-abilities*, that is, capabilities to engage, embrace and modulate the aliveness of fashion". In the context of stitching grief, these fashion-abilities can be

---

[1] I was recently asked about the relationship between labour conditions and prayer in regard to Muslim prayer mats (Saed 2021). The journalist noted that some prayer mats are manufactured in questionable labour conditions, with problematic materials such as polyester, going "against the religious principles they aim to embody". I opined that "if there's trauma and abuse in the factory, that [trauma] gets transferred into the product".

understood to include both the skill to intentionally stitch while reflecting on grief and the capacity to read the layered meanings in the stitched cloth. Aliveness is a concept that helps us understand the state of fashion today: the absence or deficit of aliveness in fashion is arguably catastrophic in scale in various parts of the fashion system, from fibre production to garment manufacture, to consumption patterns, to body image issues and so forth. Examinations of fashion supply chains by fashion brands and various measurement tools are often mechanistic and reductive, with narrow measures. Admittedly, 'aliveness' or 'mauri' would present challenges for assessment; however, it is worth noting that mauri is now being embedded into other systems. For example, the Mauri Model Decision-Making Framework (MMDMF) integrates mauri with systems thinking, and the tool has been successfully employed in New Zealand to arrive at decisions about water use that impact a wide range of communities and stakeholders (Morgan et al. 2021). In a similar vein, embedding notions of aliveness in western systems seems plausible, and aliveness could be examined systematically within fashion and textiles. As Morgan et al. (2021, 205) note, the MMDMF has been adapted to other cultural contexts, such as forest management with local communities in Papua. Its potential in fashion and textiles ought to be investigated further, guided by Berghan. For example, while specific measures such as the greenhouse gas emissions of a fibre's production phase or the toxicity of a dye chemical are vital, they tell nothing about the health of the overall system. There is an urgent opportunity to connect ideas of life force or mauri with the now established work of planetary boundaries (Rockström et al., 2009) in fashion and textiles as a frame for a more detailed and specific work.

Stitching Queer Grief and Trauma

There are long histories of hand-stitching used to process grief and trauma. The examples here include scholarly accounts of hand-stitch by practitioner-researchers, as well as accounts of historical and ongoing examples. The common thread through the examples is that they embody an explicit statement about the emotional state of the stitcher. I will discuss relevant examples of my own stitched work in the chapter, situating them in this larger arc and community of practice. The stitched cloths and their stitchers discussed throughout this chapter are in various ways queer. During a panel titled *Are You Still a Slave?* (The New School 2014), bell hooks defined queer as "not being about who you're having sex with (that can be a dimension of it); but queer as being about the self that is at odds with everything around it and has to invent and create and find a place to speak and to thrive and to live". Whether it is a queer design academic stitching about avian extinctions because the overwhelming loss of extinction compels them, or a patient at a psychiatric hospital driven to embroider fragments of an autobiography onto their patient uniform in protest of their predicament, these are inherently queer acts and artefacts at odds with their surroundings.

In discussing the curation of an exhibition of "conflict textiles" titled *Stitched Voices*, in Aberystwyth, Andrä et al. argue that "needlework and its curation introduce forms of knowledge and ways of knowing that have the potential to unsettle prevalent approaches to and understanding of war and militarized violence" (2020, 342). As a cross-stitch artist with a long career in fashion education focusing on sustainability and social justice, I speculate that needlework can equally expand our understanding of other traumatic phenomena, including climate change and biodiversity loss. I do this in *Precarious Birds*, a collaboration with design scholar Zoë Sadokierski focusing on avian extinctions (Sadokierski and Rissanen 2022). Conversations about extinction and loss with scientists inform the poetry I cross-stitch in the project; the emotional qualities of the conversations transfer to the stitched cloth. The stitching imbues the cloth with a particular aliveness coloured by grief. Andrä et al. discuss conflict textiles as "object witnesses" (2020, 344–345), with the capacity to speak in documentary, visual and sensory registers. While the textile objects of *Precarious Birds* are not conflict textiles in the same sense as those in *Stitched Voices*, they are object witnesses in the irreversible loss of bird species in a conflict of survival brought about by one species, ours (Fig. 8.1).

Eileen Harrisson, one of the artists in *Stitched Voices*, processes her personal experiences of the Troubles in Belfast during the 1970s and 1980s through stitching. While stitching, she considers the viewer with the intention that they can similarly process their experiences of the same events when encountering her work titled *Continuum*. For Harrisson, "stitching acts as a metaphor for both damage and healing" (2020, 419). On the one hand, the needle pierces the cloth, while on the other, the stitches collectively make the cloth whole again, not unlike the stitches made by a surgeon. The analogy with surgery is not uncommon among embroidery artists. My own artist statement for several years has included some version of the phrase: "I stitch myself back together again, and again."

Fig. 8.1 Cross-stitch of Munchique wood-wren *(Henicorhina negreti)* by the author, *Precarious Birds*, 2019. (Courtesy of the author)

The *Common Threads Project* conceived by Rachel Cohen, a clinical psychologist, works with victims of gender-based violence. An account of a pilot project in Ecuador (Cohen 2013) describes how a series of workshops create a space in which participants can stitch *arpilleras*, a Chilean tradition of narrative textiles. *Arpillera* is Spanish for burlap, perhaps echoing the ordinariness of the tradition. Stitching *arpilleras* is a way for the participants to express and process trauma that may sometimes be too painful to express verbally: "survivors of violence may find it helpful to engage in nonverbal approaches to respond to what has happened to them, and for healing from its effects" (Cohen 2013: 157). Cohen notes that many cultures have traditions of narrative textiles, and that locally specific traditional cultural practices must be considered by clinicians when designing interventions such as the workshops in *Common Threads*. In discussing touch and textiles, Pajaczkowska argues that when we conceive of textiles as language-like, as in the narrative textiles produced in Common Threads, "the textile is no longer conceived as inert matter but as an active material system ... imbued with meaning" (2010, 139). 'Active and alive' easily describes all textiles and garments discussed in this chapter, regardless of the 'completion' date of their stitching. The aliveness, a life force, persists through time.

Convalescing soldiers returning from the First World War were sometimes assigned embroidery and other forms of needlework while in hospital healing from the traumas of war, in Australia and New Zealand (Davidson 2004) and in the United States and the UK (McBrinn 2021, 110). Although these examples are now in the more distant past than those created within the Common Threads project, healing an unspeakable trauma by stitching unites both the stitchers and us, the viewers, across time. Both my grandfathers fought in the Second World War, and we were taught from a young age not to ask them questions about the war. Sometimes hints of the horrors were whispered among adults. Sometimes when I stitch, I think of my late grandfathers and of the generation of soldiers before them who stitched to heal, and I wish them all, and us, peace.[2]

In a more recent and personal context, Berlo (2020, 162) describes the grief after her husband abruptly left, in relation to her encounter with the Bayeux Embroidery[3]: "My academic work was stalled. I cried in my office, panicked that I did not have the strength to face my students. I couldn't eat, or think. But I could pick up a needle and thread and sew." She expands: "The streaming light illuminated my embroidery hoop and – ever so slightly – thawed my frozen heart" (163). McBrinn (2021, 26–7) writes about Rock Hudson's needlework, first noted in the press in the 1970s and again after his death from AIDS in 1985. Apparently, Hudson stitched in his final weeks in hospital. While this was fodder for the tabloid press as Hudson's homosexuality became public, I cannot help wondering what comfort or joy stitching might have brought to Hudson in the face of impending death from AIDS. Stitching, while often solitary, never feels

---

[2] This chapter is being finished during the Russian invasion of Ukraine in the northern spring of 2022.
[3] Often referred to as the Bayeux Tapestry, the cloth is embroidered, not woven.

lonely; there is peace in the solitude. And while many quilts created as part of the *NAMES Project*, perhaps better known as the *AIDS Memorial Quilt*, are put together through several means, some are stitched, sometimes by groups of people. When I witness quilts from the *NAMES Project*, I look for hand-stitches, and upon encountering them, I think of the stitcher in the company of the person that the quilt memorialises, with gratitude (Fig. 8.2).

A well-known embroidery sampler by Elizabeth Parker at the Victoria & Albert Museum dating to circa 1830 is essentially one long paragraph of stitched text outlining Parker's experiences and concerns. Embroidery samplers have centuries of history as tools to develop skill and mastery in embroidery. Parker's sampler is unusual in that it is entirely text, and written in a highly personal, confessional tone when she was still a teenager. Parker discusses at length her suicidal thoughts (the Victoria & Albert Museum notes that thankfully she lived to an old age) and reading the

Fig. 8.2 Quilts from the *NAMES Project* on display in Washington DC, USA. National Institutes of Health, public domain

sampler, questions arise about Parker's motivation while stitching. She may have stitched with another viewer in mind, or the sampler may have been a way for her to process her traumatic experiences, or both. Based on my experience as a stitcher I estimate the piece to have taken Parker more than 200 hours to stitch. Its survival is testament to others, including museum curators and conservators, recognising the inherent value in Parker's stitching. It possesses an undeniable aliveness almost two centuries after Parker's efforts, and while we live in a world vastly different from hers, we can identify and empathise with her concerns. In *The Subversive Stitch*, Roszika Parker (2010, 89) describes an earlier, unsigned sampler that is similarly unusual for its personal tone. Aliveness is stitched into cloth and is again recognised by strangers centuries later.

The examples discussed so far exist as textiles, without contact with the body except perhaps a stroke of a hand. An embroidered jacket in the Prinzhorn Collection in Heidelberg, Germany, offers us a glimpse of stitched trauma on the body. On first encounter the jacket is harrowing. Agnes Richter was a patient at a mental health facility in Germany from 1893 until her death in 1918 (Röske 2014). During her institutionalisation Richter stitched autobiographical text on the jacket extensively. Not all of it is legible; however, among other things it contains the phrase "I plunge headlong into disaster". It is clear from sweat stains and other signs of wear that Richter regularly wore the garment. Bryan-Wilson notes how cloth can "traverse the line between public and private as it travels with us on our bodies as we shift from the domestic realm to the street" (2017, 34). The act of stitching the words, just as in Parker's sampler, externalises Richter's thoughts and emotions and as such already offers some release. I speculate that the act of wearing the garment has the capacity to further amplify healing. The trauma becomes a conquered trophy worn by the subject. As with Parker's sampler, along the way a curator or a conservator recognised the potency, the aliveness, stitched into an otherwise mundane jacket so that we can bear witness to Richter's turmoil more than a century later. Furthermore, American fibre artist Michael Sylvan Robinson is heavily influenced by Richter's jacket in their textile activist practice (Calahan and Zachary 2022); the aliveness of her stitches exudes power that inspires activist needlework today, and hopefully far into the future.

Stitching Queer Loss

I examine all of the stitched works discussed here as a gay man who cross-stitches, in a world that often treats a man who stitches as unusual, as queer. Yet for me, while stitching is sacred, it is also an everyday, mundane activity. McBrinn's (2021) expansive and loving account of queer men who stitch is affirming. I began an ongoing series of cross-stitched poems in 2016 with #communication. It is an embroidery sampler of short phrases cross-stitched daily over 100 days and posted on social media. They are responses and reactions to written communications (text messages, chats, online comments) that are today very immediate, sometimes public and often ambiguous in their meaning. The daily stitching was a radical act of slowing down, at a time when there was, as there still is, a sense of urgency around all communications. Working on #communication was an alternative experience of time in my then home of New York, a city that often claimed its inhabitants as chronically insufficient no matter how little we slept and how many hours we worked. Over the 100 days, the piece took approximately 120 hours to complete. The stitched frame circling the piece was a response to the June 12th, 2016, mass shooting at the Pulse nightclub in Orlando, Florida, which occurred on day 90 of the project. The violence of the Pulse shooting was overwhelming. The dance floor of a gay club had always been a safe place for me, and reading about such a space being violated, with unbearable loss of queer life, was distressing. Stitching, at times while sobbing and shaking, helped process the grief and anger. Today those stitches hold the anger, as much as they hold the memory of the dead.

Whispers is a poem that loosely recounts my experience of leaving the Lutheran Church in Finland at the age of 19, in reaction to deeply homophobic comments made by senior leaders within the church at the time. Reading old diary entries helped revisit the emotions more than two decades later. The poem builds on the common experience that many LGBTQIA+ people have of constructing their chosen families, to build a community around oneself to whom one doesn't need to constantly explain oneself, to have a family that keeps one safe. I stitched the poem three times during 2017, including a Dutch version for *DW B*, a Belgian literary magazine (Rissanen 2018). Each experience of approximately 40 hours of stitching was equally emotive. While the stitched cloth holds a deep loss—the church had until my late teens been a safe place—it also holds a deep love of my queer family.

In 2013 I exhibited the first phase of an embroidered series, *Rest in Porn*, in response to the suicides of three prominent gay porn actors in 2012 and 2013: Dror Barak (porn name Roman Ragazzi), Peter Kozma (Arpad Miklos) and Wilfried Chevalier (Wilfried Knight). I created the work because I was aghast at the callous and dismissive reaction of some people online to the suicides, due to the men having been sex workers. With this work I wanted to restore their humanity while being unapologetic about their line of work. In 2018–2020 I cross-stitched a triptych of portraits of the actors, an object witness to honour them. For much of the 170 hours of stitching I reflected on the suicides of the men, and to me the stitched cloth is now sacred, arguably no different from a religious, sacred textile. Posting about the work on social media as it progressed became another space for healing: several people who read the posts knew Kozma and Barak personally. Learning more about them was an unexpected joy of the project. I still hope to learn more about the third, Chevalier. The triptych is now in a private collection, where the current custodian tells its story to those encountering it newly, and I dare to hope the collective healing continues (Fig. 8.3).

Placing stitched textiles on a body can occur directly or through an intermediate step of making a garment from the textile and placing that on a body. Depending on context, either approach may or may not occur within fashion. Here, the primary interest is two-fold: first, the contact

Fig. 8.3 *Rest in Porn*, triptych of cross-stitched portraits by the author, 2018–2020. (Courtesy of the author)

made between the stitched cloth and the living body, whether of the stitcher or another person, and second, the experience of the viewer of the cloth situated on a body. Reading the stitched textile, whether in garment form or as cloth, on the body is risky. This risk is something that fashion and textile artists and designers, curators and scholars ought to pay attention to. Through stitching, the cloth is embedded with experience and emotion, in many cases trauma, yet this may not be obvious to a viewer, especially if they have not been informed of the nature and motivation of the stitched work. The risk is that the stitched cloth is read primarily visually and interpreted as merely another garment. This in turns risks it being seen as somewhat disposable: perhaps of some value now but not in the not-so-distant future. That risk was highlighted recently in the highly emotive social media debate about the trend for garments made from quilts. Mary Fons (2022) argues that making garments from quilts dishonours the labour of the quilt makers. Yet Fons does not sufficiently discuss the various contexts in which quilt clothes are worn. The reverence that many wearers of quilt clothes have for quilt makers must be acknowledged, even as there are valid criticisms to be made about the economic logics driving the trend.

In writing this chapter I took the sampler #communication off its frame and placed it on my body six years after the Pulse massacre. While the stitched cloth was on me, I read the names of the 49 LGBTQIA+ people killed at the nightclub in 2016. The purpose of this exercise was to have an embodied experience of the grief I felt six years earlier while stitching the frame. I did not know any of the victims; yet it was impossible for me to read the 49 names without my voice breaking, without the grief and anger overtaking my body. I also took the poem *Whispers* off its frame to place it on my body. Once carrying the poem, I read it out loud. I concentrated on the feeling of the words on my skin as they came out of my mouth. While the loss is there, the overwhelming love in the cloth envelops me. These are cloths electric with aliveness.

Materiality in fashion, in part through globalisation and the economic perspective of fashion often imposed on it, is often universalised. Both the place in which clothes are made and the hands that made them, are abstracted from fashion's materiality. At best we may know the primary place of garment construction through one line in a label, 'Made in'. This masks the material provenance, the complexity of garment manufacture and the makers. I argue that we must be determined in our effort to reinstate a sense of place and a sense of the maker in the materiality of fashion, to understand its vitality in endless locally specific contexts. For example, cotton is grown in Australia in highly extractive monoculture settings, but it is also grown on farms through regenerative farming practices, with care for earth and all her inhabitants. The poverty of aliveness in the dominant system must not mask aliveness in the fringes. For vitality to emerge where it is missing and to flourish where it already exists in fashion's materiality, we must be intentional in holding space for and breathing life into it.

Conclusion: Stitches to Come

This chapter has examined a series of hand-stitched textile objects through a lens of aliveness, a life force. The examples focus on loss and trauma, explicitly recognising that stitching is a practice of healing for the stitcher. For some viewers, experiencing these textiles may also be a healing experience; they certainly are to me. This work strives to better understand how such healing practices may be intentionally amplified in textiles and fashion. Further research is required by scholars and practitioners in different geographic, linguistic and cultural contexts to test these ideas. Different languages may have different words for vitality and life force, or none at all, and further work ought to consider these nuances. Rachel Cohen's *Common Threads Project* has been repeated by various communities in several continents since the pilot, pointing to stitching being a potent healing force across humanity. Similarly, versions of the AIDS quilt have emerged in North America, Europe and Australia: stitching individual and collective grief can transcend culture and language.

I am a middle-aged gay man who came out in 1991. Back then, my younger, naive self imagined that progress in human rights was an inevitable force of nature, that at some point in the future we would be more free, with more rights, with less fear. That is not uniformly the case.[4] Admittedly, in some respects there are more 'rights' in several countries where one may live a life that feels generally safe. Nonetheless, our 'rights' are fragile as ever, and in many parts of the world gay men are murdered with impunity, and gay teenagers commit suicide in larger numbers than their heterosexual counterparts. So I keep stitching myself back together as I continuously fall apart in facing the precarity of queer life, mine and

[4] As one example, during the writing of this chapter in March 2022, Florida passed the 'Parental Rights in Education' bill, widely known as the 'Don't Say Gay' bill. The bill bans discussions of gender identity and sexuality in Florida schools up to the age of nine.

others'. I have made it further along than many of my generation, and for that I am grateful, yet I despair for the generations of queer children today and in the future. I dare to dream of a world where they have an opportunity to grow into themselves, however they are, without discrimination, without bullying, with their innate vitality intact. I stitch to hold that possibility alive. One day I will stitch my last stitch, and my hope is that it exists in some temporal proximity to my last breath.

References

Andrä, Christine, Lydia Cole Berit Bliesemann de Guevara, and Danielle House. 2020. Knowing Through Needlework: curating the difficult knowledge of conflict textiles. *Critical Military Studies* 6: 341–359.

Berghan, Amie. 2020, unpublished. Fashion, Mauri, and Waste. *INDIGEN 711: Indigenous Environmental Politics.* University of Auckland.

Berlo, Janet Catherine. 2020. Suturing My Soul: In Pursuit of the *Broderie de Bayeux.* In *Stitching the Self. Identity and the Needle Arts,* ed. Johanna Amos and Lisa Binkley, 155–170. London & New York: Bloomsbury.

Bryan-Wilson, Julie. 2017. *Fray: Art and Textile Politics.* Chicago: University of Chicago Press.

Calahan, April, and Cassidy Zachary. 2022. The Art and Activism of Dress of Michael Sylvan Robinson. *Dressed: The History of Fashion* (podcast), April 26. https://www.iheart.com/podcast/105-dressed-the-history-of-fas-29000690/episode/the-art-and-activism-of-dress-96075365/ Accessed 30 April 2022.

Cohen, Rachel. 2013. Common Threads: a Recovery Programme for Survivors of Gender Based Violence. *Intervention* 11: 157–168.

Davidson, Jonathan. 2004. Threading the Needle: When Embroidery Was Used to Treat Shell-shock. *Journal of the Royal Army Medical Corps* 164: 390.

Focillon, Henri. 1989/1934. *The Life of Forms in Art.* New York: Zone Books.

Fons, Mary. 2022. *Stop Cutting Up Quilts To Make Clothes.* January 29. https://www.youtube.com/watch?v=e8w91u2ARRs. Accessed 31 Jan 2022.

Harrisson, Eileen. 2020. The Significance of Stitch as Vehicle for Visual Testimony and Metaphor for Violence and Healing. *Critical Military Studies* 6: 414–420.

McBrinn, Joseph. 2021. *Queering the Subversive Stitch. Men and the Culture of Needlework.* London & New York: Bloomsbury.

Morgan, Te Kīpa, Kēpa Brian, John Reid, Oliver Waiapu Timothy McMillan, Tanira Kingi, Te Taru White, Bill Young, Val Snow, and Seth Laurenson. 2021. Towards best-practice inclusion of cultural indicators in decision making by Indigenous peoples. *AlterNative: An International Journal of Indigenous Peoples* 17: 202–214.

Pajączkowska, Claire. 2010. Tension, Time and Tenderness: Indexical Traces of Touch in Textiles. In *Digital and Other Virtualities. New Encounters: Arts, Cultures, Concepts*, ed. Antony Bryant and Griselda Pollock, 134–148. London & New York: I B Tauris & Co Ltd.

Parker, Roszika. 2010. *The Subversive Stitch. Embroidery and the Making of the Feminine.* London & New York: I.B. Tauris.

Paz, Octavio. 1974. *In Praise of Hands. Contemporary Crafts of the World.* Greenwich: New York Graphic Society.

Rissanen, Timo. 2018. Fluisteringen. *DW B.* 1: 44–48.

Rockström, Johan, Will Steffen, Kevin Noone, F. Åsa Persson, I.I.I. Stuart Chapin, Eric Lambin, Timothy M. Lenton, Marten Scheffer, Carl Folke, Hans Joachim Schellnhuber, Björn Nykvist, Cynthia A. de Wit, Terry Hughes, Sander van der Leeuw, Henning Rodhe, Sverker Sörlin, Peter K. Snyder, Robert Kostanza, Uno Svedin, Malin Falkenmark, Louise Karlberg, Robert W. Corell, Victoria J. Fabry, James Hansen, Brian Walker, Diana Liverman, Katherine Richardson, Paul Crutzen, and Jonathan Foley. 2009. Planetary Boundaries: Exploring the Safe Operating Space for Humanity. *Ecology and Society* 14: 1–33.

Röske, Thomas. 2014. Agnes Richter's jacket. *Epidemiology and Psychiatric Sciences* 23: 227–229.

Sadokierski, Zoe, and Timo Rissanen. 2022. Drawing the Extinction Crisis. *Tracey* 16: 1–19.

Saed, Omnia. 2021. The Quest to Find a Sustainable Prayer Rug. *Vox*, December 23. https://www.vox.com/the-goods/22846699/prayer-rug-islam-sustainability. Accessed 4 Jan 2022.

The New School. 2014. *Are You Still a Slave?* Panel Talk with Bell Hooks, Marci Blackman, Shola Lynch and Janet Mock New York: The New School. May 6. https://livestream.com/thenewschool/slave/videos/50178872. Accessed 1 Dec 2021.

Von Busch, Otto. 2021. *Vistas of Vitality. Metabolisms, Circularity, Fashion-Abilities.* New York: SelfPassage.

CHAPTER 9

Looking Like a Woman, Feeling Like a Woman, Sensing the Self: Affective and Emotional Dimensions of Dress Therapy

Renate Stauss

INTRODUCTION

"All my life, [...] I suppose I knew I was a woman. But now, for the first time, I feel like a woman."
   patient, Therapy of Fashion (In Silverman and Silverman 1961, 23)

   Throughout psycho-medical history dress and fashion have been used to calm patients, make them more sociable, more compliant, to make them 'look good' and 'feel better'. The emotional and physical impacts of dress on the wearer have been employed in the institutionalized treatment of 'mentally-ill' patients, both male and female, in Western Europe and North America for over 250 years. Contrary to popular representations and the current state of research, dress played an important and varied role in madhouses, asylums and mental hospitals, from diagnostic tool and

R. Stauss (✉)
The American University of Paris, Paris, France
e-mail: rstauss@aup.edu

© The Author(s), under exclusive license to Springer Nature Switzerland AG 2023
R. Filippello, I. Parkins (eds.), *Fashion and Feeling*, Palgrave Studies in Fashion and the Body,
https://doi.org/10.1007/978-3-031-19100-8_9

occupation to coercion and cure (Stauss 2017). In these settings, dress, in the form of institutional wear, restraining garments but also ball gowns, was supposed to fulfil the institutions' reforming function. While it primarily constituted a controlling mechanism and was employed as a disciplining and normalizing 'technology' of the body and self (Foucault 1982), the role of dress was far more complex and contradictory—oscillating between control, cure, care and creative play (Stauss 2022). This becomes explicit in a small number of dress-therapeutic approaches that emerged from the 1960s.

This chapter explores the correlation between fashion and feeling in dress therapy. It draws on three dress-based psycho-medical therapeutic approaches: 'Therapy of Fashion' (1960s, US), *vêtothérapie* (1999–, France) and Sensory Stimulation Treatment (2005–, Germany). While (fashionable) dress is constructed as a therapeutic technology of the self across these therapies, they differ considerably in their conceptual underpinnings. Different notions of self, dress, gender, the body, and therapy result in distinctive therapeutic approaches, such as making and modelling fashionable dress in a make-over setting, trying on and borrowing garments in a fashion library during therapeutic sessions and wearing a diving suit as part of haptic-centred body therapy. Nonetheless, the notion of 'feeling', as a descriptor and evaluative category, runs through each of these projects. Accordingly, this chapter explores the emotional and affective discourse around dress across these settings, their purposive employment, inadvertent occurrence and enclothed creative opportunities, whilst considering some of the methodological challenges. In its analysis it draws on empirical and documentary research, on author interviews, and participants observation.

Much has been written about the affective moment, and its passing. 'We are in the moment after the moment', argues Nigel Thrift, acknowledging 'a wealth of studies' on 'specific forms of affect' (2010, 289). While his observations might hold true for social sciences, in dress and fashion studies affect and emotions have not 'become an accepted background to so much work' (290). Some pioneering work explored affect in fashion photography (Filippello 2018; Shinkle 2012), others in 'high' fashion conceptual design (Manning 2016; Seely 2013; Smelik 2014, 2016). Ruggerone's article 'The Feeling of Being Dressed' (2017) stands out as the most comprehensive and interdisciplinary analysis,[1] alongside Ellen Sampson's practice-led work on the affects of wearing (2020). The field is generally marked by a focus on representation over experience. Ruggerone calls for the 'transgression of the boundaries of semiotic, structural and sociological explanations' (2017, 573) and an abandonment of 'the mind–body dualism' which intellectualizes our relationship with clothes. Affect studies thus provide an opportunity to explore 'the body–clothes assemblage; in particular, the notion of body as a composition of forces' (573), and dress/ing as 'a process of becoming, a line of flight, the final result of which we cannot foresee' (582). Fashion might be the 'stuff of feelings', dress inherently affective, yet the research landscape still leaves much room for enquiry. This analytical gap might also be related to the ambiguous nature of the subject itself—its instability and irrationality. Like much of global Western social thought and theory, dress and fashion studies have been marked by a 'flight from ambiguity' (Levine 1985) and, I would add, a flight from feelings. Their exploration undoubtedly entails a number of epistemological and methodological challenges: How to explore fleeting fashion and feelings? How to write about fashion and feelings of other people? How to analyse the emotional and affective dimensions of dress other than our own?

THE IMPOSSIBILITY AND INDIGNITY OF WRITING ABOUT OTHER PEOPLE'S (VESTIMENTARY) FEELINGS: A METHODOLOGICAL DISCLAIMER

"Why," she asked herself, "can't I feel one thing always…?" (Woolf 1927, 708)

Probably 95 percent of embodied thought is noncognitive, yet probably 95 percent of academic thought has concentrated on the cognitive dimension of the conscious "I." (Thrift 2000, 36)

In my opinion, you [Foucault] were the first—in your books and in the practical sphere—to teach us something absolutely fundamental: the indig-

---

[1] Ruggerone's article forms part of a small, yet instrumental body of work on the physical and/or emotional experience of dress mainly since the mid-1990s, rooted in different disciplines, e.g. Wilson (1985), Craik (1994), Kaiser (1997), Dunseath (1998), Entwistle (2000), Guy et al. (2001), Clarke and Miller (2002), Woodward (2005), Johnson and Foster (2007) and Findlay (2016).

nity of speaking for others. We ridiculed representation and said it was finished, but we failed to draw the consequences of this "theoretical" conversion—to appreciate the theoretical fact that only those directly concerned can speak in a practical way on their own behalf. (Deleuze in Foucault 1972, 209)

I understand affect as a term related to but distinct from feelings and emotions. Describing 'the capacity to affect or be affected' (Massumi 2015, 91), affect 'arises in the midst of *in-between-ness*' (Seigworth and Gregg 2010, 1). While affects describe a transformative 'pre-conscious visceral perception' (Massumi in Ticineto Clough 2009, 48), feelings are personal and biographical (Shouse 2005). Emotions, as the display of feelings, suggest 'something that happens inside and tends towards outward expression' (Flatley 2008, 12). Affects are abstract, ephemeral, pre-cognitive and pre-personal. Feelings and emotions are ambiguous, context-dependent and subjective. Hence, when we talk about our experiences of being dressed, we translate pre- and extra-linguistic affects into words. We reduce emotional complexity and contradiction. We straighten the creases, the messiness. We fix what is in flux. When we talk about other people's experience of being dressed, we are essentially bound to fail.

The challenges and chances of affective methodologies have been addressed by several theorists,[2] also but less so in relation to dress studies.[3] Following on from John Law's (2004) work on the messiness of social life, hence of sociological methods, there is a movement to explore 'the messiness, ephemerality and unpredictability of social life' (Knudsen and Stage 2015, 2). The challenge lies in accepting the mess, in not cleaning up. It lies in the exploration of reflexive research methods and modes of writing, such as auto-ethnography, with its borrowing from autobiography. The value of autobiographical accounts for insights into affective and emotional dimensions of dress richly comes to life in A.L. Kennedy (1998) recounting the physio-psychological embrace of her basque, or in Hiromi Goto (1998) reflecting on the loaded pleasures of silk pajamas. It also becomes apparent in Umberto Eco's ([1976) 1998) experiential analysis of 'lumbar thought', of the way dress imposes demeanour and 'epidermic self-awareness'—a tight pair of jeans in his case. Or in Virginia Woolf's

[2] See Ahmed (2010), Knudsen and Stage (2015), Seigworth and Gregg (2010) and Clough (2009).
[3] See Filippello (2018), Ruggerone (2017), Sampson (2020), van Tienhoven and Smelik (2021).

([1925] 1953, 75) diaristic contemplations of 'frock consciousness'[4] or 'clothes sense'[5] (238)—a relational quality, between clothes sense and social presence, which she has fictionally explored in 'The New Dress', where Mabel springs into existence through the dress to then suffer tortures because of it in the social context of a party. The wealth of fictionalized dress experiences essentially extends existing academic analyses. Both autobiography and fiction illustrate the situational, irrational and transient nature of the relationship between fashion and feeling. They can inspire our writing to be less absolute, less final, but more porous and processual.

Accordingly, what follows is more a search than a secure arrival. I originally set out on this research journey with the aim of exploring the discursive construction of dress as therapy. Because most of the psychiatric patients involved are children and teenagers, I took the ethical decision to only interview medical staff, to analyse conceptual underpinnings and developments, and not evaluate experience. I brought together what was said about and done at these therapies; I observed but did not enter a conversation with patients. The statements from patients quoted here were published elsewhere, mainly in journalistic articles about the respective treatments. They have to be read with contextualizing doubt: are they overdirected or edited? Would they be repeated or revised? Regardless, for the purpose of this chapter they provide insights and patterns of practice and language. It is for the first time that I focus my analysis of this research on the affective and emotional dimensions. Both the data and my experience of it suggest these dimensions that go beyond the cognitive. Moreover, the notion of 'feeling' is a recurring theme in descriptions and evaluations of the respective dress therapies, motivating me to re-visit and re-analyse post-situ, albeit aware of the limitations of this undertaking.

'Looking, Feeling, Acting Very Much Better': Therapy of Fashion

> One conclusion was immediately apparent. [...] a large majority of patients and staff indicated they noticed some improvement [...] in the "looking better" and "feeling better" categories. (Dr Miller et al. 1960, 43)

---

[4] Monday, 27th April 1925.
[5] Wednesday, 23rd January 1935.

"Until I took this course, I knew I was a woman, but I had forgotten what it felt like to be one"
patient (In Willis 1962, 15)

Therapy of Fashion set out 'to recreate healthy feminine characteristics in a selected group of women patients' (Miller et al. 1960, 42). In 1959, staff at the women's psychiatric ward of Napa State Hospital in California contacted the Fashion Group of San Francisco,[6] 'the local branch of a national organization of key professionals in the fashion field' (42), because they were concerned about the appearance of their discharged patients, their passing in society.[7] In October that year, a pilot study entitled Therapy of Fashion—a programme of grooming, dress design and self-presentation classes—was undertaken with a group of 40 female patients in 'the chronic and the acute categories' (42).[8] Sponsored by the Mental Health Association of San Francisco (MHASF), this programme was carried out as a volunteer project by the Fashion Group. Following a professional fashion show was a series of three weekly classes where 'fashion experts advised individual patients about the type of clothes best suited to them [and...] gave demonstrations and instructions concerning correct facial make-up, hair styling, dress designing, proper foundation garments, and simple exercises to improve posture and develop poise' (42). 'With professional guidance each patient was given the opportunity to design a dress for herself', selecting fabrics and colours, which were presented, 'after a practice session in modelling' (42) in a show staged by the patients to a 400-strong audience. Therapy of Fashion was regarded as an experimental success by hospital officials and the fashion professionals involved, who evaluated the project after the show by asking participants if they thought it had helped them to 'look' and 'feel' 'very much', a 'little' or 'no better' (42).

The correlation between looking good and feeling good was central to the official assessment of the treatment—and in that order, with looking prioritized over feeling. Individual stories were singled out to illustrate the 'immediate' and 'positive' effect of the treatment. 'A patient in the acute ward felt that the fashion project was the turning point of her illness. [...]

---

[6] The term 'State Hospital' refers to state-funded psychiatric hospitals in the US.
[7] For a detailed discussion of processes of passing in Therapy of Fashion, see Stauss (2020).
[8] No further information is given concerning the diagnoses or details of participating women.

"I felt like myself again". She left the hospital not long afterwards' (Miller et al. 1960, 42). 'It is therapy; there's no question in my mind about it. It is excellent therapy', reflected Dr Miller, superintendent and medical director, 'I think this will develop into something of national scope in our state hospitals. We are tremendously enthusiastic over the results' (in Clinton 1960, 11). Indeed, Therapy of Fashion grew from a local pilot project into a national volunteer service that lasted throughout the 1960s, apparently 'introduced in 11 major United States cities and in Paris' (Thompson 1962, 835), potentially reaching thousands of women.[9] The little feedback from patients that is transmitted as direct centres on an emotional transformation, on feeling more feminine, on 'feeling like a woman', as mentioned above.

> Perhaps the most significant comment was provided by a farmer's wife who had been hospitalized for years with severe schizophrenia, and then recovered remarkably after the fashion therapy. "All my life," she said as she left the hospital to return to her home, "I suppose I knew I was a woman. But now, for the first time, I feel like a woman". (Silverman and Silverman 1961, 23)

The official aim of Therapy of Fashion, the recreation of 'healthy feminine characteristics' was naturalised, its aesthetic norms internalized so thoroughly that in their feedback (or in what was transmitted of it) patients described 'feeling like a woman' in terms of an achievement.

What emerges from the evaluations and limited documentation is a series of premises, or naturalizations of this treatment. Apart from a fundamental belief in the self as immanent in appearance, they include, firstly, the existence of a 'natural' connection between women and appearance ('every woman has an inborn desire to be beautiful', Clinton 1960, 11); consequently, and secondly, a naturalized belief in a female obligation concerning appearance management and behaviour ('You are a woman and you must look pretty', Cline 1960, 27); thirdly, these normative notions of female being and behaviour, were complemented by a belief in the rehabilitating effect of dress, especially on women. Project volunteer Jane

---

[9] The expansion can be traced to other mental institutions in Illinois, Indiana, Maryland, New York and Wisconsin. Evidence of an international proliferation, however, could not be found. Its demise by the mid-1970s was apparently related to a lack of financial resources and volunteer time. The last obtained references to the treatment at Napa date back to 1970 (Logrippo 1970), in Greater Chicago to December 1974 (Anon 1974).

Meek-Barker reflects: 'If you look good, you feel better. And that is both in make-up, hair styling and clothes. And that is particularly true of women' (author interview, 17 November 2015).[10] The correlation between looking good and feeling better, including this very expression, runs through descriptions and evaluations of Therapy of Fashion.[11] It illustrates a predominantly visual understanding of dress, and the fact that feelings connected to dress and appearance are taken to be based on visual knowledge and social comfort rather than tactile sensations or haptic comfort. This ocularcentric understanding of dress perseveres, just as '[t]he "look good: feel good" transformational logic of consumer culture is presented as within the reach of all' (Featherstone 2010, 202).

Thus, three essentializing premises constituted the ground on which Therapy of Fashion was constructed. Its starting point was a normative notion not only of gender roles but also of feminine beauty and behaviour. Contributing to the complexity and moral ambiguity of this treatment is the fact that it was staged in public in spite of the vulnerability of its participants. Journalists were present throughout, and the final patient fashion show was held in front of 400 observers (Miller et al. 1960, 42), including the press (e.g. Clinton 1960; Nelson 1960). It seems that not unlike the nineteenth-century 'lunatic balls', such humanizing reform efforts were to be publicized. In the US of the mid-twentieth century, state mental institutions had stood for the mass management of 'inmates'. Reports and articles of life in such institutions had raised public awareness of overcrowding and dehumanization.[12] A field study of a Washington mental hospital published by Erving Goffman in 1961, for example, recorded the 'personal defacement' (30) of patients stripped of their 'identity kits', made to wear 'collectivized garments' (76) and subjected to 'physical indignities' (30). In all likelihood, the participants of Therapy of Fashion were dressed in institutional garments at the beginning of the programme—worn garments in their affective and entangled nature, retaining the agency of previous users (Sampson 2020)—vestimentary 'indignities' that formed part of institutionalized treatment. At the same time, the rise of psychotropic drugs, termed the 'chemical straitjacket', had enabled an 'open-door policy' and more participatory and

---

[10] Referred to as AI hereafter. See list of interviews in References.

[11] 'Look Good Feel Better' is also the name of the global cancer cosmetotherapy programme developed in the US in 1989. See http://lookgoodfeelbetter.org.

[12] See, for example, Maisel (1946), Goffman (1961) and Kesey (1962).

'humanizing' therapeutic approaches. 'The fashion-therapy program fits logically into the modern total-push attack against mental disease and the treatment of each individual as a person rather than a patient' according to Dr Miller (in Silverman and Silverman, 80). However, as Foucault ([1961] 2001) demonstrates in relation to modern institutions, the replacement of coercive techniques with non-coercive ones under a humanizing ideology of care does not mean these new measures were less controlling, disciplining or indeed subjectifying.

Fashion, the concept at the core of this treatment, is said to constitute not only a disciplinary power, but also a creative one. Leslie Rabine (1994, 64), for example, describes the act of dressing as entailing a 'mythical moment' and the clothed body as 'symbolizing a self-produced coherent subject'. According to her: 'the pleasures of fashion include the symbolic replay of this profoundly productive moment when subjectivity emerges'. In her situated experiential account of women's pleasure in clothes, Iris Marion Young identifies three aspects: touch, bonding and fantasy (2005, 69). These affective aspects include sensuality—'the simple pleasure of losing ourselves in cloth' (70); 'threads in the bonds of sisterhood' (70)—shared intimacy and stories (71); and fantasies of transport and transformation (71)—inviting us to dream, to become again and again (72). The touch of cloth, its connective tissue, the creative fantasies and journeys it might enable, can all be imagined in Therapy of Fashion. While the participants' highly individual perceptions and possible pleasures remain unknown, the treatment might have provided emotional engagements, new lines of flight, at the same time as aiming to reform the patients. Writing in relation to asylum dress, Rebecca Wynter corroborates that dress 'could also serve as a means with which patients could undermine therapeutic intentions and even claim control of their own lives' (2011, 41). It is thus worth acknowledging the capacity of these women to make even small parts of this prescriptive treatment programme their own. To heed Young, we can speak of the touch, the affects and emotions, the bonding 'that move in the shadows', hidden from the psycho-medical light, and criticize the essentializing and disciplining fantasies 'even as we make up our own' (2005, 74).

'IF IT CAN MAKE GIRLS LIKE ME FEEL BETTER ABOUT THEMSELVES IT MUST BE A GOOD THING': *VÊTOTHÉRAPIE*

I tell them that by making themselves presentable they will feel better. It sounds simple, but it's true. Dr Michele Battista, former head psychiatrist *Espace Arthur*. (In Sage 2001, 19)

I have been very ill and haven't been to school for several months. When I first heard about this idea, I thought: "Wearing an Agnes B T-shirt is not going to make me better." I thought it was pathetic, I tried it, though, and realized it can really help girls like me who have anorexia. I was frightened of my own clothes because I had become obsessed with what I fitted into, so it was good to mess around with some new things. I looked at myself in the mirror for the first time in months. If it can make girls like me feel better about themselves it must be a good thing. Marie, 16, patient (In Groskop 2001a, 49)

Vêtothérapie grew out of a concern over the affective and emotional impact of medical uniforms on adolescent patients, especially the effect of the white coat on children. In 1999 prominent French child psychiatrist Marcel Rufo approached the Fashion Institute of Marseille to find out what staff should wear at his recently founded psychiatric unit for adolescents: *Espace Arthur*. A new approach to psychiatric treatment was to be trialled here: *soins culturels*, cultural therapies. Thus, the small clinic, which housed around a dozen day and hospitalized patients aged 12 to 20 at a time, featured a media library and spaces for occupational therapy, psychomotricity and cooking, among other activities (APHM 1999, 6). 'Culture is a therapy', argues Rufo (2007, 81)[13]: '[T]he cultural activities represent a therapy in their own right, in the same way as psychotherapy. ... one does not exclude the other' (83).

Vêtothérapie also grew out of an aesthetic understanding of culture and a cultural understanding of fashion. In this therapeutic setting, fashion is constructed as intrinsic to culture in general, and to the life culture of adolescents in particular. 'Fashion is culture', maintains Rufo (AI, 3.4.2008), 'because in France the notion of fashion is a cultural notion'. After establishing that staff would do away with medical uniforms and wear their own garments to work, the focus turned to what patients were

---

[13] French and German quotations that have not previously been published in English were translated by the author. The original statements can be obtained upon request.

wearing during their stay, their access to fashionable dress. The idea of a fashion library emerged: the *vêtothèque*. To somewhat mirror real life, this library was conceived as a biannually changing collection of garments, designed and donated by local and national designers and labels, which patients could borrow. It was also conceived as a space where group therapeutic sessions could take place. Just as the other cultural therapies, *vétothérapie* was to be 'prescribed by doctors and take place under the direction of a professional carer and with a therapist [...] whose presence reassures that it effectively constitutes a therapy not a sponsored activity intended to kill time' (Rufo 2007, 83). Another form of fashion therapy was developed: *vétothérapie*.[14] Its principles were summarized in a brief unpublished document by head nurse Roselyne Descloux et al. (2001):

> The vêtothèque offers a space of expression to the adolescents, a space of discovery, of research, from choice to appropriation, recognition, acceptance and participation—by way of a concept, which is highly present in our society: fashion.

At *Espace Arthur* fashion was discursively constructed as a therapy, and so was culture. Conveyed as a central element in teenage life, fashion was regarded as a diagnostic 'indicator' (Rufo 2003, 64), reminiscent of nineteenth-century asylum practice, and 'a remedy that facilitates words' (Battista in Revilla 2001, 17). Patients are not only to discover but also to divulge themselves through the garments. 'All their gestures are analysed', describes one of the psychologists, 'dress is a support that facilitates the dialogue with the psychologist. It is also a way for them to express their feelings and look at themselves as who they are' (Carli in Sultan 2001, 77). Supervising a vêtothérapie session, psychiatric nurse Martine (in Groskop 2001b, 62) explains:

> The sizes start at extra small, and they're really meant for children. Some of the older girls have to admit that even the tiniest clothes are too big for them, and this can be an important first step in helping them realise that they are not as 'enormous' as they think they are. The aim is to make the girls feel good in their own bodies.

---

[14] While there is an insistence on working with fashion (not dress), on changing the garments every six months, the term *vêtothérapie* (dress therapy) was chosen over *mode-thérapie* (fashion therapy) for better sound and pronunciation (AI, Battista, 2.4.2008).

The premises on which *vêtothérapie* is built differ somewhat from those of Therapy of Fashion. Here appearance is regarded as revelatory, a diagnostic tool, and garments are seen to facilitate self-reflection and therapeutic conversation. Moreover, the gendered connotation is not as explicit. While *vêtothérapie* was conceived for both girls and boys, the garments were kept apart, marked by gender and almost exclusively 'female'. Thus, a natural correlation between girls and fashion is implied by example, a greater therapeutic effect suggested. Yet, there is a shared firm belief in the therapeutic properties of fashion: looking 'good' will make you feel better, as noted by Battista above. She explains: 'The first contact you have with other people is your appearance, and how you look affects how you feel. At first, the teenagers almost always say they don't care. But gradually, they become involved, and we are able to observe them as they do' (in Sage 2001, 19). While the emotional impact of dress is foregrounded, its foundations are taken to be social and visual. Just as the white coat was feared to elicit negative emotions, so a 'good' look would get positive reactions and have a positive impact on self-perception. Underlying this approach seems to be not only an undefined standard of beauty and presentability, but also a visual understanding and obligation of self-care—both a lookism and healthism (Greco 1993). '"Taking care of oneself": the expression is self-explanatory,' maintains Rufo (2007, 88); 'it is important to make yourself look good: you don't feel as bad if you manage to like your looks'. An unspoken responsibility is handed to the patients. Silenced in this understanding of fashion is its disciplinary dimension, the obligation to take care of the self (Foucault [1984a] 1988), the duty to look good and be well, as evident in Therapy of Fashion.

Since its first conception, *vêtothérapie* has been implemented at a children's psychiatric day clinic in Fréjus in 2003 (as costume therapy: dressing up for different imaginary roles) and at Maison de Solenn in Paris, a purpose-built, state-of-the-art psychiatric unit for adolescents launched by Rufo in November 2004. Specialist educator Martine Kagan (AI, Kagan, 23.1.2009) was initially in charge of the treatment in Paris and observed that 'there are several levels of use of the *vêtothèque*': style guidance, occupation, play, self-discovery, identity work, body image work, tool for relationships and a socialising activity, albeit with therapeutic intent. Kagan always returned to the aim of style guidance. She described her role as 'leading the teenagers' to find 'their style' (AI, Kagan, 10.4.2008). In setting up *espace mode*, as it is called here, she wanted to create a pleasant 'shop atmosphere'. The *vêtothèque* is situated in a vast multi-purpose space that is window fronted, two long walls lined with mirrors. Transparency and reflection are at the core of this treatment approach, exemplified in the setting, the rooms—spatial technologies of power (Foucault [1975] 1995).

The omnipresent mirrors are far from being the neutral reflective surfaces they are often taken for. As I have argued elsewhere (Ruggerone and Stauss 2020), mirrors are subjectifying, their presence is social, and defines dress and self in visual terms. In the context of the *vêtothèque*, they also constitute forced forms of reflection, which is pervasive. One patient voiced here ambivalent feelings about the mirrors and clothes: 'After a week in hospital Delphine is already feeling better. However, like many of the girls in the first few weeks, the mirror in the "boutique" poses a problem. "I'm still nervous about the clothes," she says' (in Groskop 2001b, 62). 'One is reflected a lot here', another female patient with anorexia observes (in Rufo 2007, 24). 'Does it bother you?' Prof Rufo asks her. 'No', she says, 'anyway I don't look at myself'. To try on the garments, patients use a small adjacent storeroom. To use a mirror, they have to return to the group in the main space. Changing rooms like these can elucidate how 'emotional experiences are spatially contingent' (Colls 2004, 584).

What emerged in the interviews with staff and observations of therapeutic sessions is that the *vêtothèque*, the space, the mirrors and the garments are regarded as neutral tools. The prescriptive nature of dress remains unacknowledged. Fashionable dress in particular is inscribed with normative notions of gendered physical and aesthetic beauty, which are largely naturalized in this setting. While psycho-social effects and the highly individual ways in which patients perceive, use and resist *vêtothérapie* cannot be determined, this therapy seems to negate its own impact. While these lending garments might open up different processes of becoming, as indicated by patient Marie above, this treatment approach appears to negate the fact that dress is constructed as a gendered, socializing (thus normalizing) and disciplining technology of the fashion-able adolescent self here, that dress might not feel good.[15]

---

[15] For a more detailed account and analysis of *vêtothérapie*, see Stauss (2017).

'It Is a Feeling of Security.': Sensory Stimulation Treatment

The feedback from patients is positive during the time of wearing the suit. It is useful in getting patients to deal with their body schema and its distortions. [...] Some are very positive and say that it feels like a second skin, that they can finally feel themselves through it. Prof. Thun-Hohenstein, University Clinic Salzburg (AI, 6.9.2016)

The first days and weeks [of wearing the wetsuit] were really very exhausting. I felt an extreme sense of pressure in my head. By now, I regard wearing the suit as normal. It definitely calms me a great deal. It is a feeling of security. Julia, patient (3sat 2010: 1'50)

Just one item of clothing is used in Sensory Stimulation Treatment: a neoprene wetsuit, which is used only because it was thought to be the most effective way to simulate the sense of touch. In 2003 at the University Hospital Leipzig in Germany, Professor Martin Grunwald, psychologist and head of the haptic laboratory, was searching for a way to remap the distorted body schema of patients with anorexia nervosa. As he was looking for body-hugging materials, he considered latex and trialled a wetsuit.

The development of Sensory Stimulation Treatment was accidental, as was its focus on dress. In the context of an unrelated study, Grunwald had been running a series of haptic tests. Probands explore sunken reliefs with closed eyes to then draw what they feel with open eyes. They transform what they feel into what they see: an easy task that we all do regularly (when searching for something in a bag for example). Yet, one proband's drawings were completely unrealistic. Grunwald discovered that this proband was severely anorectic. He developed further tests which led to the hypothesis that anorexia involved a body schema disorder that could only be treated haptically (AI, 24.8.2007).[16] Even though Grunwald only happened upon this illness by chance, as he put it (ibid.), effectively as a data-driven by-product of his core research, the haptologist decided to make the eating disorder one of his fields of professional activity. He criticizes that 'too little neuro-biological research' has been undertaken with regard to anorexia nervosa, and the role of body schema, designated by him as the 'central element' (Grunwald 2008, 335). Grunwald identifies two main reasons for this 'lack': firstly, the complexity of researching an entity

[16] For a detailed written account of the development of SST, see Grunwald (2008).

which is linguistically inaccessible; and, secondly, the predominance of largely visual-centred and language-based approaches in both the research and treatment of anorexia (2008 & AI, 24 August 2007). These approaches are related to a wider psycho-medical discourse of the 'verbalization of self' as well as to underlying ocular- and logo-centric cultural parameters. His critique of the field echoes Thrift's above-mentioned criticism of the cognitive orientation of academic thought, and indeed the concern of affect studies: the existence of pre-cognitive forces.
Concerning anorexia, Grunwald (AI, 8.7.2016) elaborates:

> Cognitive behavioural therapy focuses entirely on the "restructuring" of wrong cognitive processes into right ones—a very mechanistic model, which is, however, taught at 97% of all German universities. Equally, most German hospitals only use CBT in their treatment, [which] wants to hold on to the approach that anorexia nervosa is treatable through language and cognition. While this might be the case for certain aspects of the disease, it is certainly not for the disordered body schema. If at all, this level of the disease can only be treated with physical therapy.

His description of the circulation and validation of a cognition-based 'regime of truth' (Foucault 1984b, 73), is reverberated in a study of the field that describes the 'wide acceptance' of CBT as 'the treatment of choice' (Murphy et al. 2010, 611). Grunwald wanted to develop a haptic treatment trial; however, due to lack of funding he had to improvise. He piloted the wearing of a wetsuit for one hour, three times a day, for six weeks to remap the body schema of patients and achieve more realistic physical self-perception (Grunwald and Weiss 2005, 379–80). Accompanied by body therapy and more classic treatment, Sensory Stimulation Treatment showed very promising results. Grunwald evaluated the treatment as effective in remapping and correcting a distorted body schema: 'Although this case only involved one patient, the data collected supports the belief that it is possible, with this treatment, to positively change the body schema disturbance without medication or side effects' (Grunwald 2008, 350). One of the most immediately visible results was the weight gained by the proband (349). He explained elsewhere that it is through consistent haptic stimulation and the pressure 'that this tight garment applies to the skin and joints [that] the brain learns to perceive the body more realistically' (Grunwald in Hilgemeier 2016).

The haptic suit, the therapeutically reinscribed wetsuit, has since been integrated into the treatment of eating disorders at several hospitals in Germany and Austria.[17] While there is no representative study on its effectiveness, body therapist Gabriele Riess (in Hilgemeier 2016), who has been practising Sensory Stimulation Treatment at Charité University Hospital in Berlin since 2005, evaluates: 'More than half of the patients agree to the therapy and approximately 80% of treated patients clearly felt better because of it'. In an interview, she told me: 'Judging from experience, I regard it as an important part of the treatment' (AI, Riess, 11 September 2013). Elsewhere, she explained:

> The diving suit constitutes only one element of therapy. It does not replace the therapist, the dialogue and all the other elements of inpatient treatment here. Yet, I notice that body therapy constitutes a great relief for patients, because there is someone touching them or the diving suit, which touches them and gives them a feeling of support. (Riess in mdr 2010, 4'10)

Feedback from patients is often expressed in similarly emotional terms. They speak of a sense of security and stability, based on feeling their body parts and boundaries:

> It makes a huge difference. It is much more physical. I wear the diving suit, I engage with it. I feel the individual parts of my body, beginning with my thighs, especially when I walk. Julia, patient (3sat 2010: 6:00')

> I just feel this pressure against my skin. And I can feel my limits—where I really end. And this wetsuit helps me above all to actually perceive myself as I really am. Luisa, patient (ZDF, 2020, 0:22')

> I have a long-sleeved diving suit, which I wear for a good hour every morning and evening. The therapy is really good for me, have a much better body feeling now. The suit shows the boundaries of my body and also helps the perception of my body. Kerstin, patient (Kerstin 2016)

The haptic suit, which is generally made-to-measure for each patient, is repeatedly described as a second skin (e.g. Riess in Stoll 2014). The tactile engagement with the suit seems to be a tactile entanglement which enables

---

[17] E.g. Charité University Hospital Berlin, Pfalzklinikum für Psychiatrie und Neurologie in Klingenmünster, and the University Hospital Salzburg in Austria.

a 'subject/object blurring' (Sampson 2020) for some patients. 'Generally speaking, the feedback from patients differs quite a bit', says Prof. Thun-Hohenstein, head of child and adolescent psychiatry at University Clinic Salzburg, Austria; he continues: 'some are very positive and say that it feels like a second skin, that they can finally feel themselves through it. Others, however, find it too close, too tight, too hot, it forces them to deal with something they don't want to deal with' (AI, 6.9.2016).

While the experience of Sensory Stimulation Treatment cannot be generalized, this therapeutic approach can draw attention to the affective potential of dress. It calls into question the hierarchy of the senses by challenging the ocularcentrism and lookism in relation to dress. It illustrates how accustomed we have become to considering dress mainly through our eyes, and thereby move us away from the look-good-feel-better-logic (Featherstone 2010, 207) and towards a sensing-feeling trajectory. Maybe the haptic suit is affective dress in its purest form, the launch of a different line of flight. As Gabriele Riess notes: '[I]t is an important part, which can be developed. Through dress, certainly, a lot can still be developed' (AI, 11.9.2013).

Conclusion

> And when the prisoner began to speak, they possessed an individual theory of prisons, the penal system, and justice. It is this form of discourse which ultimately matters, a discourse against power, the counter-discourse of prisoners and those we call delinquents—and not a theory *about* delinquency.
> (Foucault 1972, 209)

If the patients could have spoken freely, they probably would have told different stories of Therapy of Fashion; perhaps they would have spoken of different emotional impacts in *vêtothérapie*, and articulated different affective forces around Sensory Stimulation Treatment. This chapter explored the affective and emotional dimension of three dress therapies whilst acknowledging their methodological limits. What emerges from this research for me is an ethical ambiguity around dress therapy: a fascination and discomfort in the face of what dress can do to the self. In all their affective and emotional qualities, dress and fashion lend themselves to therapeutic use, from diagnosis to treatment. Yet at the same time they can 'fix' people, reduce them and pry them open. Fashion also fits too neatly into the late capitalist and therapy cultural logic of inner and outer self-optimization. As loaded as fashion is with normative notions of body and beauty ideals, is it possible to work with dress whilst circumventing its prescriptive and oppressive aspects? As subjective and ever shifting as dress is in its meaning, is it possible to remain open and forego judgement or diagnosis? As inherently entwined with our bodies, as intimate as clothes are, is it possible to be non-intrusive? Dress therapies illustrate the impossibility and indignity of un/dressing other people.

What emerges also are considerations of how fashion is regarded and researched in relation to the self. While the study of fashion and dress has opened to lived experience, it remains heavily invested in representation. In popular (especially digital) culture, fashion is presented as a visual trope of endless possibility, negating its materiality, its socio-cultural and environmental impact. Fashion necessitates a perception and exploration as ambiguous: as multi-sensory in its materiality, as connective in its creativity, as product and process, as verb and noun, as fluxes of becoming (Stauss 2019). In writing about affective fashion, Stephen Seely (2013, 263) argues that

> Fashion need not be seen only as that through which we make ourselves more attractive, adorn, or enhance ourselves. [...] Rather, fashion can be that "something else" that leads to our own becoming-otherwise, that actualizes the virtual capacities that we were not even aware of, that puts us in touch with what is least human in us, that opens our bodies to a virtual field of limitless creativity, intensity, sensation, and transformation.

While his inquiry focuses on high fashion (presented on idealized bodies in a conceptual yet still commercial context), Seely's exploration of its queering potential, particularly his ideas around 'becoming otherwise' are pertinent to the urgent question of what fashion can contribute to the more widely relevant and relatable discourse of dress for every day and everyone. Otto von Busch and Daye Hwang also argue for a perceptual shift to further the question of what fashion can do: 'If we shift our understanding of fashion from commodities to emotional play, could clothing be used to sense and articulate our emotions in different contexts? [...] A method to mix up the material, the cognitive, and the emotional in new ways to serve new purposes?' (2018, 104).

Dress therapy illustrates both the disciplining forces and the emotional play inherent in dress, and, in some instances, new purposes. Sensory Stimulation Treatment can open ways of thinking about the tactile impact of our garments and their affective potential: about feeling good based on sensing rather than about looking good. It can contribute to the everyday challenge of conceptualizing 'feeling good' as a transient, complex and contradictory mixture of affective, emotional, multi-sensory and social reactions. The fact that the most original dress therapy approach comes from a project unconcerned with dress per se also illustrates the need for interdisciplinary research—a coming together of unrelated fields interested in pre-cognitive, multi-sensorial and emotional experiences. Hence, more research is needed on different experiences of wearing—experiences recorded with the care and knowledge that emotional experiences are fleeting moments rather than essences, the most valuable kinds of fiction. More research is needed to begin to comprehend the affective and emotional dimensions of everyday dress and fashion, not for the purpose of delineating 'positive' and 'negative' emotions but to better understand how they are produced and experienced (Colls 2004); not for the purpose of optimization or commercialization, but to make up our own fantasies of becoming.

References

3sat. 2010. Magersucht / Anorexia Nervosa: Neuer Therapieansatz mit Neoprenanzug. [television programme]. Accessed 24 May 2014. https://www.youtube.com/watch?v=-ucDo0o8Ec0.

Ahmed, Sara. 2010. Happy Objects. In *The Affect Theory Reader*, ed. Melissa Gregg and Gregory J. Seigworth, 29–51. Durham, NC: Duke University Press.

Anon. 1962. Fashion Therapy Is Help for Women in Hospitals. *The Corpus Christi Caller-Times.* November 26, 2C.

———. 1974. Operation Snowball Aids Mentally Ill. *Suburbanite Economist.* 15 December, CSR p7.

APHM. 1999. *Espace Arthur.* Marseille: Assistance Publique Hôpitaux de Marseille.

Clarke, Alison, and Daniel Miller. 2002. Fashion and Anxiety. *Fashion Theory* 6 (2): 191–214.

Cline, Alan. 1960. Fashion Experts Provide Lift for Mental Patients. *The Kansas City Times*, 5 February: 27.

Clinton, Mary Ann. 1960. Fashion Show Is Aid to Mental Health Patients. *New Castle News.* 7 April, 11.

Colls, Rachel. 2004. 'Looking Alright, Feeling Alright': Emotions, Sizing and the Geographies of Women's Experience of Clothing Consumption. *Social and Cultural Geography* 5 (4): 583–596.

Craik, Jennifer. 1994. *The Face of Fashion*. London: Routledge.
Descloux, Roselyne, Helene Bartolomei, Sandrine Donadu, and Florence Forest. 2001. *Et si l'Habit Faisait le Moine, La Mode en Tant que Soin* [unpublished paper]. Marseille: L'Espace Arthur.
Dunseath, Kirsty, ed. 1998. *A Second Skin: Women Write About Clothes*. London: The Women's Press.
Eco, Umberto. [1976] 1998. Lumbar Thought. In *Faith in Fakes: Travels in Hyperreality*, 191–195. London: Vintage.
Entwistle, Joanne. 2000. *The Fashioned Body*. Cambridge: Polity Press.
Featherstone, Mike. 2010. Body, Image and Affect in Consumer Society. *Body & Society* 16 (1): 193–221.
Filippello, Roberto. 2018. Thinking Fashion Photographs Through Queer Affect Theory. *International Journal of Fashion Studies* 5 (1): 129–145.
Findlay, Rosie. 2016. Such Stuff as Dreams are Made On. *Cultural Studies Review* 22 (1): 78–94.
Flatley, Jonathan. 2008. *Affective Mapping: Melancholia and the Politics of Modernism*. Harvard, MA: Harvard University Press.
Foucault, Michel. 1972. Intellectuals and Power: A Conversation between Michel Foucault and Gilles Deleuze. In *Language, Counter-Memory, Practice: Selected Essays and Interviews by Michel Foucault*, ed. Donald F. Bouchard (1977), 205–217. Ithaca: Cornell University Press.
———. 1982. Technologies of the Self. In *Technologies of the Self: A Seminar with Michel Foucault*, eds. L. Martin, H. Gutman, and P. Hutton (1988), 16–49. Amherst, MAC: University of Massachusetts Press.
———. [1984a] 1988. *The Care of The Self*. Translated by Robert Hurley. New York: Vintage Books.
———. 1984b. Truth and Power. In *The Foucault Reader: An Introduction to Foucault's Thought*, ed. Paul Rabinow, 51–75. London: Penguin.
———. [1975] 1995. *Discipline and Punish: The Birth of the Prison*. Translated by Alan Sheridan. New York: Vintage Books.
———. [1961] 2001. *Madness and Civilization: A History of Insanity in the Age of Reason*. Translated by Richard Howard. London: Routledge.
Goffman, Erving. 1961. *Asylums: Essays on the Social Situation of Mental Patients and Other Inmates*. Harmondsworth: Penguin Books.
Goto, Hiromi. 1998. The Pleasure of Pajamas. In *A Second Skin: Women Write About Clothes*, ed. Kirsty Dunseath, 21–24. London: The Women's Press.
Greco, Monica. 1993. Psychosomatic Subjects and the 'Duty to Be Well': Personal Agency Within Medical Rationality. *Economy and Society* 22 (3): 357–372.
Groskop, Viv. 2001a. The Clinic where Couture is the Cure. In *Daily Express*. 1 February, 48–49.
———. 2001b. The Fashion Designers who Cure Anorexia. In *Glamour*. July, 60–63.

Grunwald, Martin. 2008. Haptic Perception in Anorexia Nervosa. In *Human Haptic Perception*, ed. Martin Grunwald, 335–351. Basel: Birkhäuser Verlag.
Grunwald, Martin, and Thomas Weiss. 2005. Inducing Sensory Stimulation in Treatment of Anorexia Nervosa. *QJM: An International Journal of Medicine* 98 (5): 379–380.
Guy, Ali, Eileen Green, and Maura Banim, eds. 2001. *Through the Wardrobe: Women's Relationships with their Clothes*. Oxford: Berg.
Hilgemeier, Iris. 2016. Kann ein Neoprenanzug Magersucht heilen? In *Ihre Gesundheitsprofis Magazin*. 3 March, Accessed 10 June 2016. http://www.igp-magazin.de/kann-ein-neoprenanzug-magersucht-heilen/.
Johnson, Donald Clay, and Helen Bradley Foster, eds. 2007. *Dress Sense: Emotional & Sensory Experiences of the Body and Clothes*. Oxford: Berg.
Kaiser, Susan B. 1997. *The Social Psychology of Clothing and Personal Adornment*. New York: Fairchild Publications.
Kennedy, A.L. 1998. The Basque. In *A Second Skin: Women Write About Clothes*, ed. Kirsty Dunseath, 17–20. London: The Women's Press.
Kerstin. 2016. Magersucht Therapie im Neoprenanzug Erfahrungsaustausch. Accessed 8 July 2016. http://www.ab-server.de/thema/57071721/magersucht-therapie-im-neoprenanzug%2D%2Derfahrungsaustausch.html.
Kesey, Ken. 1962. *One Flew Over the Cuckoo's Nest*. London: Methuen & Co.
Knudsen, Britta Timm, and Carsten Stage. 2015. Introduction: Affective Methodologies. In *Affective Methodologies*, ed. Britta Timm Knudsen and Carsten Stage, 1–19. London: Palgrave Macmillan.
Law, John. 2004. *After Method: Mess in Social Science Research*. London: Routledge.
Levine, Donald N. 1985. *The Flight from Ambiguity*. Chicago: The University of Chicago Press.
Logrippo, Ro. 1970. Anything Goes in Spring Fashions. *The Times*. (San Mateo, CA.). 14 March: 7.
Maisel, Albert Q. 1946. Bedlam 1946: Most U.S. Mental Hospitals Are a Shame and a Disgrace. *Life* 20 (18): 102–10, 112, 115–16, 118.
Manning, Erin. 2016. Dress Becomes Body: Fashioning the Force of Form. In *The Minor Gesture*, ed. M.I. Minneapolis, 86–110. University of Minnesota Press.
Massumi, Brian. 2015. *Politics of Affect*. Cambridge: Polity Press.
mdr. 2010. Hier ab vier—Mit Rat & Tat: Neuer Therapieansatz mit Neoprenanzug bei Magersucht [television programme]. Accessed 24 May 2016. https://www.youtube.com/watch?v=O2wEVHqqQLM.
Miller, Theo K., Lewis G. Carpenter, and Robert B. Buckley. 1960. Therapy of Fashion. *Mental Hospitals: Hospital Journal of the American Psychiatric Association* 11 (8): 42–43.
Murphy, Rebecca, Suzanne Straebler, Zafra Cooper, and Christopher G. Fairburn. 2010. Cognitive Behavioural Therapy for Eating Disorders. In *Psychiatric Clinics of North America* 33 (3): 611–627.

Nelson, Harry M. 1960. Fashion Shows for Insane Women. In *Sunday Gazette-Mail* (Charleston, W. VA.), July 24, 12F.
Rabine, Leslie. 1994. A Woman's Two Bodies: Fashion Magazines, Consumerism & Feminism. In *On Fashion*, eds. Benstock et al., 59–75. New Brunswick: Rutgers University Press.
Revilla, François. 2001. La Mode Entre Chez les Ados de la Timone. *Accents* February: 16–17.
Rufo, Marcel. 2003. Il Était une Fois. *Revue de Psychothérapie Psychanalytique de Groupe* 41: 63–70.
———. 2007. *La Vie en Désordre: Voyage en Adolescence.* Paris: Éditions Anne Carrière.
Ruggerone, Lucia. 2017. The Feeling of Being Dressed: Affect Studies and the Clothed Body. *Fashion Theory* 21 (5): 573–593.
Ruggerone, Lucia, and Renate Stauss. 2020. The Deceptive Mirror: The Dressed Body Beyond Reflection. *Fashion Theory* 26 (2): 211–235.
Sage, Adam. 2001. Designer Way to Treat Anorexia. In *The Times.* 29 June, 18–19.
Sampson, Ellen. 2020. *Worn: Footwear, Attachment and the Affects of Wear.* London: Bloomsbury Visual Arts.
Seely, Stephen D. 2013. How Do You Dress a Body Without Organs? Affective Fashion and Nonhuman Becoming. *Women's Studies Quarterly* 41 (1/2): 247–265.
Seigworth, Gregory J., and Melissa Gregg. 2010. Introduction: Affective Methodologies. In *The Affect Theory Reader*, ed. Gregory J. Seigworth and Melissa Gregg, 1–25. Durham: Duke University Press.
Shinkle, Eugenie. 2012. Uneasy Bodies: Affect, Embodied Perception, and Contemporary Fashion Photography. In *Carnal Aesthetics: Transgressive Imagery and Feminist Politics*, eds. Bettina Papenburg and Marta Zarzycka, 73–88. London: I.B. Tauris.
Shouse, Eric. 2005. Feeling, Emotion, Affect. *M/C Journal* 8 (6) https://journal.media-culture.org.au/index.php/mcjournal/article/view/2443.
Silverman, Milton, and Margaret Silverman. 1961. Glamour Treatment for the Mentally Ill. *The Saturday Evening Post*, 26 August: 22–23, 79–80.
Smelik, Anneke. 2014. Fashioning the Fold: Multiple Becomings. In *This Deleuzian Century: Art, Activism, Life*, ed. Rosi Braidotti and Rick Dolphijn, 38–55. Leiden: Brill.
———. 2016. Gilles Deleuze: Bodies-without-Organs in the Folds of Fashion. In *Thinking Through Fashion*, ed. Agnès Rocamora and Anneke Smelik, 165–183. London: I.B. Tauris.
Stauss, Renate. 2017. *Dress as Therapy: Working with Dress on the Self in Therapeutic Settings.* PhD Thesis, University of the Arts London, London.
———. 2019. What Fashion Is Not (Only). *Vestoj* 9: 55–76.

———. 2020. Passing as Fashionable, Feminine and Sane: 'Therapy of Fashion' and the Normalisation of Psychiatric Patients in 1960s US. *Fashion Theory* 24 (4): 601–637.

———. 2022. Dress as Therapy: Working with Dress and Fashion in Psycho-Medical Settings—Between Control, Cure, Care and Creative Play. In *Mirror Mirror: Fashion & the Psyche*, ed. M. Ankele, E. De Wyngaert, L.M. Ferreira, M.-J. Kölmel, Y.H. Lamot, and R. Stauss, 133–151. Veurne, Belgium: Hannibal Books.

Stoll, Angela. 2014. Neopren gegen Magersucht. In Neues Deutschland. 27 November, https://www.neuesdeutschland.de/artikel/953723.neopren-gegen-magersucht.html (8.7.2016).

Sultan, Mylène. 2001. La Mode au Secours des Ados en Détresse. *Le Point* 1481, 2 February, 77.

Thompson, Thelma. 1962. Fashion Therapy. *Journal of Home Economics* 54 (10): 835–836.

Thrift, Nigel. 2000. Still Life in Nearly Present Time: The Object of Nature. *Body & Society* 6 (3–4): 34–57.

———. 2010. Understanding the Material Practices of Glamour. In *The Affect Theory Reader*, ed. Gregory J. Seigworth and Melissa Gregg, 289–308. Durham: Duke University Press.

Ticineto Clough, Patricia. 2009. The New Empiricism: Affect and Sociological Method. *European Journal of Social Theory* 12 (1): 43–61.

van Tienhoven, Maaike, and Anneke Smelik. 2021. The Affect of Fashion: An Exploration of Affect Method. *Critical Studies in Fashion & Beauty* 12 (2): 163–183.

Von Busch, Otto, and Daye Hwang. 2018. *Feeling Fashion: The Embodied Gamble of Our Social Skin*. New York: SelfPassage.

Wilson, Elizabeth. 1985. *Adorned in Dreams*. London: Virago Press.

Woodward, Sophie. 2005. Looking Good: Feeling Right—Aesthetics of the Self. In *Clothing as Material Culture*, ed. Susanne Küchler and Daniel Miller, 21–39. Oxford: Berg.

Woolf, Virginia. 1927. The New Dress. *The Forum* 77 (5): 704–711.

———. [1925] 1953. *A Writer's Diary: Being Extracts from the Diary of Virginia Woolf*. Edited by Leonard Woolf. London: The Hogarth Press.

Wynter, Rebecca. 2011. 'Good in All Respects': Appearance and Dress at Staffordshire County Lunatic Asylum, 1818–54. *History of Psychiatry* 22 (1): 40–57.

Young, Iris Marion. 2005. Women Recovering Our Clothes. In *On Female Body Experience*, 63–74. Oxford: Oxford University Press.

ZDF. 2020. Magersucht: Neoprenanzug kann helfen. TV show Volle Kanne, 5 February, Accessed 10 October 2021. https://www.youtube.com/watch?v=-NAEclhUNwg.

AUTHOR INTERVIEWS

Michèle Battista, Dr, child psychiatrist, Psychatrie Infanto-juvénile, Centre Hospitalier Intercommunal Fréjus Saint-Raphaël, Fréjus, France, 2.4.2008.
Martin Grunwald, Dr, head of haptic laboratory, University of Leipzig, Germany, 24.8.2007.
Martine Kagan, *educatrice spécialisée*, *Maison de Solenn*, Hôpital Cochin, Paris, France, 10.4.2008.
———, *educatrice spécialisée*, *Maison de Solenn*, Hôpital Cochin, Paris, France, 23.1.2009.
Jean Meek-Barker, volunteer of "Therapy of Fashion", member of The Fashion Group, US, telephone, 17.11.2015.
Gabriele Riess, body therapist, Charité, University Hospital Berlin, Germany, 11.9.2013.
Marcel Rufo, Prof, child psychiatrist and head of pedo-psychiatric service, Hôpital Sainte-Marguerite, Marseille, France, 3.4.2008.
Leonhard Thun-Hohenstein, Prof Dr, head of department of child and adolescent psychiatry, University Clinic Salzburg, Austria, email, 6.9.2016.

PART III

Stasis and Transformation in Fashion

CHAPTER 10

Dirty Pretty Things: Stains, Ambivalence and the Traces of Feeling

Ellen Sampson

This chapter starts with a stain and a dress: a stain on a dress: a stained stress. The distinction between these categories may seem arbitrary, for in material terms they are of course one and the same—a fluid sheath of blue silk hanging in my wardrobe, its hem catching the dust which gathers on the floor; and yet in the process of writing this chapter these distinctions have been central, helping me to think about the ways that feeling is located in, produced by and moves between bodies and things.

There are multiple ways that one could approach the theme of fashion and feeling: the interminglings of sensation, emotion, person and garment. This chapter does so from a phenomenological and a psychoanalytic position, exploring the psychic and material entanglement of human and non-human bodies. In doing so it moves between the material and the metaphorical, between my own embodied experience and broader cultural themes to explore the ambivalence, or duality, of feeling which typifies many experiences of worn and used clothes.

E. Sampson (✉)
Northumbria University, Newcastle upon Tyne, UK
e-mail: ellen.sampson@northumbria.ac.uk

© The Author(s), under exclusive license to Springer Nature Switzerland AG 2023
R. Filippello, I. Parkins (eds.), *Fashion and Feeling*, Palgrave Studies in Fashion and the Body,
https://doi.org/10.1007/978-3-031-19100-8_10

179

Fig. 10.1 *A Stain and a dress*, digital photograph, Ellen Sampson (2022)

In their introduction to *The Affect Theory Reader* (2009) Gregg and Seigworth describe affect as "a state of in betweenness" (2010) and this chapter addresses two in-betweennesses—garments and stains. Both garments and stains are in-between things; things which we create, which we act upon, and which act upon us, entangled with and separate from the bodies they touch. Importantly they are also things which ebb and flow between the symbolic and the material so frequently that oftentimes it is hard to tell where metaphor and matter begin and end. Garments are fundamentally intermediary objects, surfaces which sit at the interface between us and the world. Their outer edges demarcate the point at which the dressed self, the body schema ends and other bodies begin. They are objects which are part of us and yet not of our body: extended and yet distinct parts of the body schema, capable of being distributed beyond the boundaries of the self. These entangled objects mediate our tactile and emotional experience and through these mediations they are changed.

Neither garment or body is ever static, but instead is in a constant state of change—adapting, stretching, tearing, healing and being reformed—so that clothes are constantly affecting and being affected: an ongoing iterative conversation between the wearer and the worn. Through these tactile and emotional entanglements, both clothing and the body become records; as Barad states, "matter feels, converses, suffers, desires, yearns and remembers" (Barad et al. 2012, 60). This chapter thinks about stains as both material outcomes of these affective experiences and as affects made material, things themselves imbued with substantial affective capacity. Things which oftentimes create ambiguous or ambivalent feelings.

Ambivalent Objects: A Stain and a Dress

This chapter starts with two in-betweennesses. A dress and a stain. It is hard sometimes for me to reconcile them as one and the same—the beauty of the garment and the ugliness of the stain.

Garments are many things to us, mediators, symbolic vessels, object of shame, fantasy and desire, and yet they are also material things—pieces of fabric which shroud the body—offering covering, comfort, status and display. Garments are simultaneously sites of fantasy and failure, surfaces where desire, internal experience and material realities meet, and at times fail to fit. These complex layers of sensation and meaning are only added to as garments are worn, as our bodies change them, and they become material memories. So, though we "feel our clothes" we do not feel just one thing about them; enclothed feelings[1] are mixed and plentiful. When one opens one's wardrobe, rifles through the pile of clothes lying on the floor, or steps into the calm of an archive, one meets entangled objects capable of retaining and producing a multiplicity of feelings. The feelings garments produce are rarely singular or discrete. In fact, I would suggest that often those feelings we experience towards the clothes we own and wear, as opposed to those we covet or desire from a distance, are ambivalent. This duality of feeling is, I think, distinct from Tomkins' (1962) more congruent affect pairings (interest-excitement, enjoyment-joy, distress-anguish, etc.) and instead more akin to Freud's and later Klein's work on Love/Hate and ambivalence.

---

[1] Borrowing from Cvetkovich (2012) I use feelings to covey the intertwined nature of both sensory and emotional experience.

Fig. 10.2 *A Stain on a dress*, digital photograph, Ellen Sampson (2022)

In psychoanalysis, ambivalence is not to be confused with uncertainty, or mixed feelings; instead, as Charles Rycroft observes, "it refers to an underlying emotional attitude in which the contradictory attitudes derive from a common source and are interdependent, whereas mixed feelings may be based on a realistic assessment of the imperfect nature of the object" (1968, 6). Despite its contradictory nature, for psychoanalytic theorists, ambivalence does not stem from dislike or even indifference but, as Adam Phillips notes, from the importance or value of the object: "we are ambivalent, in Freud's view, about anything and everything that matters to us; indeed, ambivalence is the way we recognise that someone or something has become significant to us…wherever there is an object of desire there must be ambivalence" (2015). Ambivalence is in particular at the centre of Melanie Klein's object relations theory, first in the paranoid-schizoid position where the child's understanding of and feelings towards the mother (or "caregiver," a Winnicottian term I prefer) are fragmented and split ("the good and bad breast") and later in the depressive position as the infant accepts and is able to accommodate the idea of the mother being a "complete object," both good and bad. For Klein, the ability to accommodate and accept the duality of the object (the mother) is a crucial stage in development.

Ambivalence is also central to Klein's ideas of reparation, whereby the infant fears their fantasy aggression towards the bad object has done it real/material harm and in turn experiences both guilt and a desire to repair and make it whole again so that the desire to care for and repair the object is always predicated on the (fantasy of) the capacity to do harm. Though Klein locates the onset of these fantasies and urges in early infancy, they are for her something which persists throughout our lives, so that, as Jackie Stacey writes, all "…relations of the subject to its objects are ambivalent ones, forged through processes of projection and introjection that continue into adult life" (2014, 45). This idea of ongoing ambivalence towards the fantasy object is, I think, particularly interesting when we think about clothes—things which often exist simultaneously as both objects of imagination and material things.[2] Clothes, as frequent objects of desire, have a particular capacity to create ambivalent feelings, both in the ways that they often fail to meet our expectations of them, but also in the ways that they fail to remain pristine: the ways we harm them, the ways they change through use.

The duality of ambivalence, the simultaneous feeling of love/hate, desire/shame, or pleasure/disgust, is particularly useful when thinking about damaged and dirtied garments, those which sit somewhere between their original status as commodities, practical acquisitions, or objects of desire, and objects damaged beyond repair. Stains, in particular, seem to produce ambivalence, a simultaneous cultural fixation and disgust. References to stains and staining pervade our culture, from the literary (Lady Macbeth's "Out, damn spot!"),[3] and religious (most famously the Turin shroud),[4] forensic and legal (the stain as evidence),[5] to the domestic and the environmental. Stains both denote and connote ideas of violence, mortality, pollution, proof, evidence, and simultaneously reveal the intermingling of person and thing which is the inherent outcome of being in the world. From mundane and everyday stains such as a coffee, toothpaste or menstrual blood, to the residues of violence, crime or environmental neglect, stains disrupt multiple binaries: cleanliness and dirt,[6] self and other, person and thing. The distinctions between stains, marks and patina

[2] See Sampson (2017).
[3] William Shakespeare, *Macbeth*, Act 5, scene 1, line 30.
[4] See Didi-Huberman (1984).
[5] See Matthews David (2019) and Turney (2019).
[6] see Douglas (1966).

are complex, socially constructed and value-laden.[7] This overdetermined quality means we often approach stains as metaphors or metonyms, as standing in for something else. And yet stains are also every day and mundane, they readily accumulate as we travel through the world.[8] Stains are bodily, gestural and often difficult to remove. Whilst rips and tears can sometimes be repaired, the permanence of stains (the very word a synonym for indelibility) means that they remain on, in and with the garment long past the initial causal event.

A STAIN ON A DRESS: MATTER, AMBIVALENCE AND SHAME

The blueness of this dress of course cannot help but remind one of another blue dress, one deeply imbued with shame and practices of shaming.[9] But the stain on this dress is not bodily (or not of my body at least): it is chicken fat dripped from a fork as I sat and ate. And yet shame, or at least a certain ambivalence, seeps in: the memory of wearing the dress—too much perhaps for the event, and of my gluttony, my hunger, my desire.

Stain is a loaded word, resonant with guilt and shame.[10] Yet the stain itself is oftentimes little more than an accident, a slip of the hand or failure to keep the edges of the body schema in check. As with many issues of cleanliness,[11] stained garments are often perceived as a moral as well as a practical failure. Whilst the capacity of a stained garment to induce shame or disgust is in part due to its potential abjectness, namely its disruption of the binaries of inside/outside and self/other, often it is the evidentiary nature of stains, their capacity to make visible ethical lapses, which draws judgement. Stains reveal what should be kept hidden, and in doing so they offer up the wearer/maker to be judged.[12]

---

[7] See Charpy (2013).
[8] Caroline Evans' beautiful essay "Materiality, Memory and History: Adventures in the Archive" (2014) explores stains and damage in Isabella Blow's clothing archive.
[9] As Beart writes, "the stain on the blue dress of Monica Lewinsky, which partly destroyed her life..." (2017, 283).
[10] Stain is of course an enormously loaded word so much so that stain is often used as a synonym for shame itself. See for example Jonathan Square's article on *Brooks Brothers'* historic use of enslaved labour (2021).
[11] See Kelley (2010).
[12] Beavan (2019) makes a power connection between our bodily responses to shame, blushing, and the stain itself, as she writes: "We blush, publicly stained by redness flooding our faces; we avert our eyes and bow our heads. We remember shaming episodes and (re) blush again decades later..." (2019, 51).

Fig. 10.3 *A Stained dress*, digital photograph, Ellen Sampson (2022)

Stains make visible both ethical and social missteps (e.g. grass stains on skirts and lipstick on collars) and that which should remain within the body: sweat, blood, semen, tears. Our responses to this perceived loss of control highlight the stain's valency, namely the ways in which the meaning of stained garments repeatedly shifts between the material and the metaphorical:[13] dirtiness as a moral failing in more ways than one. Though these judgements are perhaps most evident when we think of bodily or sexualised stains, we reserve particular judgement for stains which make apparent the wearer's failure to maintain the immaculate surfaces of the body schema which so often connotes the mastery of life. They disrupt the fantasy that we can move through the world unstained.

Though stains are frequently used as metaphor, they are fundamentally material—records of our interactions with and impacts on the world. The stain is intimately entwined with gesture—with the ways we move through, experience and are changed by the world. As Barbara Baert writes in her beautiful meditation on stains in art and iconography, "Intentionally or unintentionally, in various ways and places, we leave our own traces in the

---

[13] The judgements applied to stains reveal numerous biases surrounding class, bodies, gender and sexuality.

form of liquid relics. A stain of this kind is an extension of our own physical boundaries and marks our dealings with the world…" (Baert 2017, 285). This inability to move through the world unaffected (or at least affected only by choice), disrupts and challenges notion of the self as fully separate from the world which surrounds it. Stains reveal the porous nature of our interactions with the world. These marks are traces of the ways we affect and, in turn, are affected: stains are traces of feelings. Thus, stains reveal a particular vulnerability: our inability to move through the world unscathed—to resist or deflect the dirt which surrounds us and to keep what should remain inside within.

The evidentiary nature of stains—the stains as a record of action—is perhaps bought to its logical conclusion in "The Index of the Absent Wound (Monograph on a Stain)" (1984), in which Didi-Huberman makes the analogy between the stain and the photograph as an indexical record of experience.[14] This idea is seductive (the stain as a singular moment preserved in material form), and yet I would suggest that reading the stain only as an index does not address a central aspect of its capacity to affect and induce ambivalence. For stains—overdetermined, symbolically loaded and yet habitual traces of our interactions with the world—are also liminal things, neither mark nor gesture, lying somewhere in between. Stains confuse and cross categories of objects, the lines between person and thing, existing not so much as indexes but as blurrings, amalgamations and seepages. In my previous work I have explored the idea of the stain as something beyond the index:

> If for Didi-Huberman the stain is an index, then I would suggest that it is both that and more. For a stain is not simply an indent like a footprint or a thing left behind, such as the still smoking cigarette butt, it is a transposition of the material of the original: a rearrangement of matter so that one becomes part of another. (Sampson 2020, 149)

The transposition which stains materialise and embody blurs the lines between different kinds of bodies, so that in affecting one, part of the other is left behind. This transposition renders stained garments themselves ambivalent, composed of two opposing things at once. Stains are

---

[14] He writes: "One kneels before a photographic negative, as it were, enshrined in the altar and illuminated from within" (1984, 63). However, it is worth noting that Didi-Huberman ends the article by questioning whether the stain exists at all, thus challenging the idea of its indexicality.

simultaneously indices of actions performed and referents to other and potentially differently affecting stains, but also traces of the bodies with which the stained items have mingled.

> This intermingling blurs the edges of the object. This transposition is the exchange of material agencies. If one spills a drop of wine on a dress and it is absorbed, it is then unclear whether the stain is part of the dress (irreversibly absorbed by its form) or part of the wine one was pouring when the accident occurred, or both, an additional layering of agencies in an already complex object. (Sampson 2020, 149)

Thus, stained garments are ambivalent objects in two ways, both because they have the capacity to provoke ambivalent feelings and because they are two things at once—part of the stained object and yet also separate from it.

A Stained Dress: Present Pasts and Things Between Two Times

I cleaned it of course, just a little too late.
Reluctant to dampen my dress and make my clumsiness more visible still…

Stains change garments both figuratively and literally, shifting their meaning and material form. These changes afford garments additional and more complex valency, rendering them ambivalent objects in multiple ways. In being stained, the garment, already both part of the body schema and other to it, absorbs aspects of other bodies, so that the stain is an "…explicit manifestation of the intermingling of the self and the world. In staining, […] the matter of one agent is absorbed into the surface of another" (Sampson 2020, 149). These marks, as evidence of action performed, render stains things which sit between two times: immediately materially present and indexes of a past event. The stained garment is in possession of a kind of dissonant temporality: a folding in or bringing together of present and past. This present/past quality disrupts the temporality of the garment in a way which is akin to Michel Serres' description of time as like a crumpled handkerchief:

> If you take a handkerchief and spread it out in order to iron it, you can see in it certain fixed distances and proximities. If you sketch a circle in one area, you can mark out nearby points and measure far-off distances. Then take the

same handkerchief and crumple it, by putting it in your pocket. Two distant points suddenly are close, even superimposed. (Serres with Latour 1995, 60)

This present-past quality is not unique to stained garments; in fact, it could be said that all things sit between two times, and yet there is something in the loadedness of the stain—its cultural connotations and material realities of indelibility as well as the risk presented by abjection—which gives stains a particular quality, one which I would argue is other than that of creases, crumples and tears.

Often, we think about garments in the context of their futurity, of what they might allow us to do or become. Indeed, often it is the potentiality of a garment that draws us to it: the fact that through and with it we can imagine new and future selves. Through their social and material mediations, garments afford both positive and negative transformative potential.[15] As Lucia Ruggerone writes, "…the dress is something that will morph into my body and into which my body will change when I go out into the world, something that will open up or close down for me

Fig. 10.4 *A Stained dress*, digital photograph, Ellen Sampson (2022)

---

[15] See Sampson (2017), in which I briefly discuss how Bollas' (1979) idea of Transformational Objects (as distinct from Winnicott's Transitional Objects) can help us to think about the inevitable inability of garments to fulfil our desires.

possibilities of becoming, of immersing in the flow of worldly practices more or less easily..." (2016, 14). Stains do not reduce this transformative potential or alter the fact that a garment will continue to change through entropy and use.[16] However, stains subtly shift the garment's relationship to time: they change the garment from something imbued with potential to something which is intimately and indexically affixed to a single point in the past. As Baert observes, "the stain has a particular relationship with time and space. A stain is the tangible reminder of something that is past. A stain is a history, a trace, and so it also evokes the place where it originated" (2017, 273). Thus, though the garment may be in a continuous state of change (both entropy and alteration through use, laundering and repair), the stain is fixed: it is an end point which continually and intimately refers us to a bodily and embodied past.

The referential quality of the stain—its ability to return us to a specific point in time, place or body—has been widely explored in writing on clothing and memory (Bide 2017; Jenss 2015; Evans 2014; Chong Kwan et al. 2014). Often, in writing about the clothes of others, the stain's capacity to compel us to recollect takes on a benign or even comforting quality.[17] The stain acting as contact point,[18] which allows the viewer the temporary ability to retrieve what (or whom) has been lost. This idea of stain as a *contact point* is perhaps most famously explored in Peter Stallybrass' essay on the loss of his friend Allon, in which he writes: "He was there in the stains at the very bottom of the jacket, he was there in the smell of the armpits" (1993, 2). For Stallybrass, the ability of bodily traces to invoke the presence of the dead is unsettling but desired: the trace materially connects him to this lost friend and in doing so mitigates loss. However, with our own clothes, with stains which intimately and indexically return us to our own past embodied experience, stains afford a

---

[16] Indeed, staining may increase the degradation of the garment whether it continues to be worn or not.

[17] The stains of others are not always benign, the stain as evidence of assault, sexual violence and crime little our material world and popular culture. Though I don't have space to discuss the affects of violent stains here, there is a growing literature in fashion studies on the indices of violence and crime. Notably, the work of Turney (2019), Matthews David (2019), on fashion and crime and Elenowitz-Hess (2020) whose text on the McQueen A/W 1995 collection "Highland Rape" explores the affects of fake stains as non-indexical marks which imply historic violence.

[18] See Feldman (2006), in which he describes contact points as "a general category of object that results from physical contact with the body and then subsequent removal or destruction of the body" (246).

different and perhaps less conformable kind of recollection. The stain locates us in and ties us to our past selves, to aspects of identities we have altered or changed and to embodied experiences we may no longer wish to recall. The stained garment becomes a material memory that we may not wish to have. This ambivalent temporality affords stained garments another layer of ambivalence: the tension between past and present selves, between what we want to be and who we have become. Foremost, these objects reveal a tension between action performed and the future potential of the garment: a continuity which is at odds with more transformative or transformational interpretations of fashion. As such, these marks disrupt the sense that we are truly ever distinct from our past and future selves.

Capturing Stains

> *The silk jersey of the dress shimmers, cleaving to the body and falling away. The sheen of the fabric makes the stain difficult to capture; it emerges and disappears from view, appearing only when the light changes or I turn to raise my arms. In the studio I light it in different ways, trying to face it head on, asking it to face me.*

Nowhere is the doubleness or multiplicity of feelings towards garments more present than in garments we love but have dirtied or damaged through use: things which, when new, afforded considerable transformative potential, but which through use have become bodily and entangled. These objects encapsulate multiple dualities, crossing and recrossing the lines between body and self, dirt and cleanliness, now and then. As such, these objects are ambivalent in multiple ways—materially, conceptually and temporally—and in turn induce or create ambivalent feelings. To return to the psychoanalytic interpretations of ambivalence, ambivalence towards clothes is distinct from shame (although shame may be an aspect of the opposing feelings which ambivalence encapsulates); ambivalence lies instead in the paradoxes of loving and hating, pride and shame, attraction and disgust. As Freud notes (1917),[19] ambivalence is often entwined with a (sense of) loss, with mourning for the ideal or lost object which we know cannot come back. Stains confront us with the loss of the fantasy

---

[19] In *Mourning and Melancholia* Freud writes: "Ambivalence gives a pathological cast to mourning and forces it to express itself in the form of self-reproaches to the effect that the mourner himself is to blame for the loss of the loved object" (1917, 14).

garment, and with it the loss of the potentials that fantasy afforded, forcefully returning us to the material and lived realities of a life in clothes.

Conclusion

But what of my own ambivalence? I have not discarded the dress after all…

This chapter stems from practice-based research (from processes of looking at and photographing stains) (Figs. 10.1, 10.2, 10.3, 10.4, 10.5) and in doing so asking what it is to attend to imperfection, to allow oneself to be touched by it. I wish to end this chapter by returning to my own stained dress, and my own ambivalence towards it, to think about the complexities of attending to these entangled and ambivalent things, to the traces of being in the world which litter our clothes. Although my work is concerned with the affects of imperfection, I realise I am resistant to attending to my own stained garments, to confronting the bodily reality of my own clothes and the multiple opposing feelings they induce. This avoidance is perhaps in part an outcome of shame, in the marks which litter it—material evidence of my own appetites and desires spilling out into the world. The dress, so intimately entwined with my own bodiliness, its shape and size, posture and gait, evokes a discomfort akin to unexpectedly viewing one's reflection or a snapshot taken unawares, highlighting the dissonance between the fantasy of my *body image* and the material realties of my *body schema*. And yet the dress is beautiful, and made me feel the same, so that when I view it, I am torn between wanting to look and to imagine the possibilities of my dressed self and at the same time not wanting to see.

This ambivalence, this toing and froing between pleasure and shame is, I think, central in my practice of recoding imperfection—a desire to look and a simultaneous discomfort with what I see. In recoding stains, I ask myself to look at what is usually removed hidden or simply ignored, and to confront clothes not as fantasies but as material records of the oftentimes difficult or discordant meetings of bodies and things, relinquishing some part of the fantasy space that clothes so often occupy. The stains I most often approach are those of others, occasionally abject and often overdetermined, but free from my own bodily shame and perhaps somewhat neutralised by distance of time. Yet these stains, like those on my own dress, remain ambivalent, caught between meanings and times.

Despite my efforts, these stains often prove difficult to photograph (the images I make failing to capture them fully, the edges bleeding into cloth

Fig. 10.5 *Stain*, digital photograph, Ellen Sampson (2022)

and becoming diffuse). The most evocative stains, such as tears and sweat, are often the hardest in capture, visible only in certain lights so that they shimmer in and out of view. In fact, I would suggest that these stained and damaged objects shimmer[20]—that they are difficult to capture—in more ways than one. In continually evoking and invoking multiple and divergent feelings, stained garments cannot be "read' as one thing; rather, they shift in light of the context and dispositions with which we meet them.

Accommodating the divergent feelings these marks create is at times difficult, and alongside their potential abjectness, this difficulty perhaps explains my and our collective reluctance to look too closely at stains (and imperfection more generally). Yet, to return to Klein (1975), accepting of the duality of used garments and our own ambivalence towards them as well as the tensions between fantasies and futures and what has come to pass, is necessary, for "not until the object is lived as a whole can its loss be felt as a whole" (Klein 1975, 118). Accepting and engaging with the ambivalence which underscores many of our relationships to clothes, both afford us a fuller, more nuanced understanding of our embodied entanglements and allow us to begin to care of what otherwise might become

[20] In his notes on the neutral Barthes describes the shimmer as "that whose aspect, perhaps whose meaning, is subtly modified according to the angle of the subject's gaze" (2005 {1978}, 51).

fragmented or lost. Although to return to Phillips we are ambivalent "... about anything and everything that matters to us" (2015), studies of clothing, fashion and the dressed body perhaps require a particular capacity to endure, manage and attend to this ambivalence: the good and bad which is inherently part of fashion's past and present and of our lives lived in clothes.

REFERENCES

Baert, Barbara. 2017. Stains, Trace—Cloth—Symptom. *Textile* 15 (3): 270–291.
Barad, Karen, Rick Dolphijn, and Iris Van der Tuin. 2012. Matter Feels, Converses, Suffers, Desires, Yearns and Remembers: Interview with Karen Barad. In *New Materialism: Interviews & Cartographies*, 48–70. Ann Arbor, MI: Open Humanities Press.
Barthes, Roland. 2005. From the Neutral: Session of March 11, 1978. Translated by Rosalind Krauss. *October* 112: 3–22.
Beavan, Katie. 2019. (Re)writing Woman: Unshaming Shame with Cixous. *Management Learning* 50 (1): 50–73.
Bide, Bethan. 2017. Signs of Wear: Encountering Memory in the Worn Materiality of a Museum Fashion Collection. *Fashion Theory* 21: 449–476.
Bollas, Christopher. 1979. The Transformational Object. *International Journal of Psychoanalysis* 60 (1): 97–107.
Charpy, Manuel. 2013. Patina and Bourgeoisie: Appearances of the Past in Nineteenth-Century Paris. In *Surface, Finish and the Meaning of Objects*, ed. Glenn Adamson and Victoria Kelley, 45–59. Manchester: Manchester University Press.
Chong Kwan, Sara, Morna Laing, and Mario J. Roman. 2014. Fashion and Memory. *Critical Studies in Fashion & Beauty* 5 (2): 201–204.
Cvetkovich, Anne. 2012. *Depression: A Public Feeling*. Durham, NC: Duke University Press.
Didi-Huberman, George. 1984. The Index of the Absent Wound (Monograph on a Stain). *October* 29: 63–81.
Douglas, Mary. 1966. *Purity and Danger: An Analysis of Concepts of Pollution and Taboo*. London: Routledge.
Elenowitz-Hess, Caroline. 2020. Reckoning with Highland Rape: Sexuality, Violence, and Power on the Runway. *Fashion Theory* 26 (3): 399–417.
Evans, Caroline. 2014. Materiality, Memory and History: Adventures in the Archive. In *Isabella Blow: Fashion Galore!* ed. Caroline Evans, Alistair O'Neill, et al., 136–141. New York: Rizzoli.
Feldman, Jeffery. 2006. Contact Points: Museums and the Lost Body Problem. In *Sensible Objects: Colonialism, Museums and Material Practice*, ed. Elizabeth Edwards, Chris Gosden, and Ruth Phillip, 24–68. Oxford: Berg.

Freud, Sigmund. 1917. Mourning and Melancholia. In *The Standard Edition of the Complete Psychological Works of Sigmund Freud, Vol. 14*, ed. James Strachey, 243–258. London: Hogarth Press and the Institute of Psychoanalysis.
Greg, Melissa, and Gregory Seigworth. 2010. *The Affect Theory Reader*. Durham, NC: Duke University Press.
Jenss, Heike. 2015. *Fashioning Memory: Vintage Style and Youth Culture*. London: Bloomsbury.
Kelley, Victoria. 2010. *Soap and Water: Cleanliness, Dirt and the Working Classes in Victorian and Edwardian Britain*. London: I B Tauris.
Klein, Melanie. 1975. *Love, Guilt, and Reparation, and Other Works, 1921–1945*. London: Hogarth Press.
Matthews David, Alison. 2019. First Impressions: Footprints as Forensic Evidence in Crime Fact and Fiction. *Costume: The Journal of the Costume Society* 53 (1): 43–66.
Phillips, Adam. 2015. Against Self-Criticism. *London Review of Books* 37 (5), 5 March https://www.lrb.co.uk/the-paper/v37/n05/adam-phillips/against-self-criticism.
Ruggerone, Lucia. 2016. The Feeling of Being Dressed: Affect Studies and the Clothed Body. *Fashion Theory* 21 (5): 573–593.
Rycroft, Charles. 1968. *A Critical Dictionary of Psychoanalysis*. New York: Basic Books.
Sampson, Ellen. 2017. The Cleaved Garment: The Maker, The Wearer and the "Me and Not Me" of Fashion Practice. *Fashion Theory* 22 (6): 1–20.
———. 2020. *Worn: Footwear, Attachment and the Affects of Wear*. London: Bloomsbury.
Serres, Michel, and Bruno Latour. 1995. *Conversations on Science, Culture and Time*. Translated by Roxanne Lapidus. Ann Arbor, MI: University of Michigan Press.
Shakespeare, William. 1992. *Macbeth (Wordsworth Classics)*. Ware: Wordsworth Editions.
Square, Jonathan Michael. 2021. A Stain on an All-American Brand. *Vestoj*, http://vestoj.com/how-brooks-brothers-once-clothed-slaves/.
Stacey, Jackie. 2014. Wishing Away Ambivalence. *Feminist Theory* 15 (1): 39–49.
Stallybrass, Peter. 1993. Worn Worlds: Clothes, Mourning and the Life of Things. *The Yale Review* 81 (2): 35–50.
Tomkins, Silvan. 1962. *Affect Imagery Consciousness: The Positive Affects (Vol. 1)*. New York: Springer.
Turney, Jo. 2019. *Fashion Crimes: Dressing for Deviance*. London: Bloomsbury.

CHAPTER 11

Making Peace Sensational: Design for the Nobel Prizes

Elizabeth M. Sheehan

Since 2011, students at Stockholm's Beckmans College of Design have created clothing and objects inspired by each year's Nobel Prizes, which are awarded in physics, chemistry, medicine, literature, economics, and peace. Most of the garments are gowns, while the designs include lamps, bowls, and sculptures. In recent years, students at other Swedish institutions, such as the Royal Academy of Music, have created pieces inspired by the prizewinners's achievements. The students' work has been showcased by the Nobel Museum through a few temporary exhibitions under the title "Nobel Creations." As that phrase intimates, the project as a whole emphasizes that "creativity" is "what unites Nobel laureates, artists, and creators" (Nobel Prize Museum 2014).

This essay explores how this fashion design project links a constellation of feelings associated with "creativity" to the project of peace-making. Peace, after all, is a key part of the Nobel brand. Alfred Nobel founded the

E. M. Sheehan (✉)
Ohio State University, Columbus, OH, USA
e-mail: sheehan.223@osu.edu

© The Author(s), under exclusive license to Springer Nature Switzerland AG 2023
R. Filippello, I. Parkins (eds.), *Fashion and Feeling*, Palgrave Studies in Fashion and the Body,
https://Doi.org/10.1007/978-3-031-19100-8_11

institute partly to ensure that his name would not be synonymous with the manufacture of weapons, especially dynamite, which was a main source of his fortune. The Beckmans project demonstrates how fashion as a means of generating and circulating feeling adapts liberal international visions of peace-making, in which cultural production forges cross-cultural understanding, for a neoliberal era of creative capital. When linked to the Nobel, fashion renews the project of making peace central to Sweden's image, such that Sweden's reputation for good design (from furniture to welfare statehood) eclipses its profitable arms trade. Underscoring the connections between mood and *la mode*, the Nobel-Beckmans collaboration models a vision of peace as a sensational phenomenon that is creative, teachable, and sustainable. By drawing attention to peace as an affective and aesthetic category as much as a legal and political concept, this fashion design initiative enforces what Eunsong Kim and Gelare Khoshgozaran note is the widespread presumption that "culture is the experiment towards peace" (2016).

Promoting Swedish Design

The Beckmans project is part of the Swedish government's effort to promote Swedish fashion design in the twenty-first century. This effort included sponsoring a travelling museum exhibition called "Swedish Fashion: Exploring a New Identity," which was launched in 2008, and then in 2017, the Swedish government made promoting design part of its "export and investment strategy" (Swedish Institute 2020). "Swedish Fashion" featured the work of current Swedish designers and travelled internationally, including to the Museum of Contemporary Art in Tokyo in 2009–2010. The sub-title of the show signals how fashion serves as a metonym for the nation and for Swedish culture, such that a shift in the "identity" of the industry in the country remakes visions of Swedishness. That transition is away from collectivity and homogeneity associated with Sweden's welfare state; the short description of the exhibition announces that "experimental Swedish designers who display strong individuality, unfettered by traditional values, have successively come to the fore and attracted attention from the international fashion world" (Museum of Contemporary Art Tokyo 2009). Fashion, as a neoliberal industry *par excellence*, leads Sweden towards the kinds of individual creativity and experimentation that are needed to stand out on the world stage. This emphasis on individuality and the promotion of designers via elite museums carve out a space for Swedish high fashion apart from the global success of the Swedish "fast fashion" company H & M. Like the furniture conglomerate IKEA, which was founded in Sweden (but now controlled by a Dutch company), H & M is associated with the "democratization" of design and depends upon the reproducibility of Swedish style. It generates far more profits but less cultural capital than the work of individual Swedish designers. Given that the idea of individual genius is central to the Nobel Prize, it is an ideal means to draw attention to Swedish high fashion.

No matter how exclusive or innovative a designer is, fashion is perceived as deeply commercialized and market-driven. As a result, various critics have claimed that museums should not feature shows on the subject, especially exhibitions on living designers, which can be seen as "merely an advertisement" (Steele 2008, 16). Yet the idea of creative genius celebrated by "Swedish Fashion" fits quite comfortably with art museums' practices of collection and display—which celebrate the work of individual artists, often decontextualized from their material circumstances—as well as the museum's long-standing practices of taxonomizing and representing national cultures. The explosion of museum exhibitions that focused on fashion, which began in the 1990s and continued in the early twenty-first century, can thus be understood as continuous with the history of the museum, even if it represents something of a shift for the fashion industry. As Valerie Steele noted in the introduction to an issue of *Fashion Theory* dedicated to the fashion exhibition, "along with the catwalk and the retail store, the museum has become an increasingly important site for fashion" (2008, 8). The rise of the museum fashion show frames fashion designs as unique and singular rather than, in the case of the catwalk and, especially, the retail store, as reproducible.

The display of gowns at the Nobel Museum and on its website represents a unique version of the fashion exhibition in so far as it attempts to align the apparent aims of the museum, the state, and the fashion industry with those of academia, literature, and peace activism. It implicitly frames fashion as a benefit to the public good, in keeping with the Nobel Prizes' recognition of those who, according to Alfred Nobel's will, "shall have conferred the greatest benefit to mankind" (Nobel Prize 2022). This is accomplished in part through the rubric of creativity, which the exhibit description defines in terms of "the courage to think in new ways, to question established theories, and innovative combinations of insights from different fields" (Nobel Prize Museum 2014). Courage involves an affective orientation towards the world, which includes grappling with emotions like fear and hope. Feeling is thus at the heart of this project and of the Nobel more broadly. With the Prizes redefined in these terms, the seemingly individualistic, iconoclastic practice of fashion design takes its place comfortably alongside literature, physics, chemistry, medicine, economics, and peace. By featuring the designs of "young students" at Beckmans, the exhibition also redefines Sweden as not only a leading arbiter of what creations most benefit humankind, but also as itself a source or incubator of such creativity.

Despite the rhetoric of innovation, the fashion design project strikes a balance between the old and new. This is epitomized by the fact that the students are tasked with creating evening gowns, which, as Celia Marshik notes, are a "particularly *conservative* form," associated with formal social events and the ritual display of feminine bodies (2017, 33). Accordingly, in the photographs of the garments displayed on the website for Beckmans and the Nobel Museum, the gowns are worn by models who appear to have the measurements and physical appearance associated with high and mainstream fashion media. As traditional garments that mark occasions that are at once exceptional and conventional—qualities that often characterize the designs and the people who wear them as well—gowns set a predictable tone for the Nobel's celebration of extraordinary individuals whose achievements supposedly have universal benefits. Yet, as Marshik shows, there is a history of depicting evening gowns as "negative, threatening, and even animate," especially in so far as they shape the bodies and experiences of the women who wear them (2017, 27). This highlights a less salutary set of affective and political dimensions of the Nobel garments. It resonates with Walter Benjamin's claim that "every fashion stands in opposition to the organic. Every fashion couples the living body to the inorganic world. To the living, fashion defends the rights of the corpse" (1999, 79). For Benjamin, fashion's constant innovation points towards lifelessness. In an era in which the fashion industry is one of the leading producers of environmental pollutants, Benjamin's assertion takes on new meaning. Recent Nobel prizes have been awarded to activists seeking to prevent or address the effects of climate change. The Nobel design project, then, makes us feel the tensions between creativity and destruction, past and future, which are embedded in the Nobel Institute's attempts to promote peace and advance that which is a "benefit to mankind."

Sustaining Feelings

The photograph of the gown that "interpreted" the 2021 Nobel Prize in physics provides a case study in how the Beckmans creative project makes peace available as an aesthetic emotion and a design project. The Prize was awarded to three scientists, Klaus Hasselmann, Syukuro Manabe, and Giorgio Parisi, "for groundbreaking contributions to our understanding of complex systems," as the citation states. For two of the scientists, Manabe and Hasselmann, those systems specifically include models for "the Earth's climate and how humanity influences it" (Nobel Prize 2021b). The garment draws attention to humanity's impact on and endangerment by climate change. The designers, Emma Carling and Tim Bunwassana, explain their creation as follows: "We wanted to protect people from natural disasters under an umbrella in an atmosphere of fabric that symbolizes the ozone layer. Under the umbrella there is an opening where the dress, which used to be even pink, has been water damaged by natural disasters. How long will the fragile umbrella last before it wears to pieces and the water rains down on the man?" (Hulting 2021). In the photograph by Carl Bengtsson that is displayed on the websites of the Nobel Prize Museum and Beckmans College of Design, the model holds aloft an umbrella whose white fabric extends from the dress itself, creating giant loops of material that form a partial enclosure around her body. Clearly, however, that enclosure does not guarantee safety. The pink stains on the dress suggest traces of blood, linking climate change to war and violence. The twists of the garment also resemble bandages, tourniquets, and shrouds. The garment thus becomes the site where water and blood have mingled; it holds both without being able fully to stop their flow. As it stretches outward, one side of the garment with its rippling edge seems at the point of dissolving into the darkness around it. The fragility of the garment-as-shelter is emphasized by the fact that the model's outstretched hand and the billowing fabric recall the waving of a white flag: a signal for a cease-fire, an indication of surrender, as well as a call for peace. The hope for peace can be felt in the model's pose, which maintains the shelter, temporarily.

In that sense, the garment figures peace as a combination of design and desire—as depending on humans' willingness to try to hold things in place, to forestall the further destruction of a fragile creation. That situation is expressed through the aesthetics of fashion photography: if the model's raised arm suggests the act of waving a white flag, the model's steady gaze, three-quarter profile, and hand resting on her hip all belong to the idiom of fashion modelling. As the word suggests, models are meant to be imitated and replaced and to spark the desire of the viewer to don the garment themselves. That dynamic suggests that this image presents the maintenance of peace as question of a universalized human agency; the model can stand in for all of humanity as well as the earth, partially swathed in and holding aloft the ozone layer.

The designers' choice of fabric and dye—"old curtains" and "black rice," the Beckmans website tells us—implies that, if the garment figures peace as a combination of design and desire, those designs and desires must be sustainable and resilient. Carling and Bunwassana's pointed question—"how long will the fragile umbrella last…?"—recalls a rhetoric of sustainability. In addition, one way of describing what the model does is to sustain the position of the umbrella. Even in the relatively short time period of a fashion shoot, that gesture requires strength and persistence. The concept of "sustainable design" has a lot of currency in the fashion industry. It is an explicit focus of the Swedish government's recent initiatives to promote Swedish design across the globe (Swedish Institute 2020). That is unsurprising, given that the discourse of sustainability can imply that there need not be a radical change from business as usual in order to stave off the disastrous effect of climate change. It is particularly fitting, then, that the model's pose registers both as a possible gesture of surrender and one of defiance. As Stacy Alaimo puts it, albeit in a specifically U.S. context, "the discourse of sustainability" has a "tendency to render the lively world a storehouse of supplies for the elite" (2012, 558). Recent accounts of the production of "sustainable" fabrics make clear that this rhetoric can function to hold in place unsustainable practices (see, for example, Wicker et al. 2022). Discourses of sustainability enable us to imagine that what is needed is to pick amongst or to refine current practices so that they might be continued. Hence there is no need to abolish the fashion system, which sits at the heart of capitalism. What is required instead is the proper design—one that is sustainable and aesthetically appealing.

The glamour of the image of the garment also registers that tenuous distinction between, on the one hand, feelings and practices that fuel meaningful climate activism and, on the other, those that masquerade as such. The posed features and lighting on the model's face speak in the idiom of glamour, which Nigel Thrift maintains is "a form of allure [that] blurs the boundary between person and thing in order to produce greater captivation." For Thrift, that captivation is "bent to capitalist means" (2010, 290). Yet as a way to draw attention to the degradation of the ozone layer, this design ostensibly points to the need to interrupt capitalist business as usual. As Min Hyoung Song observes in *Climate Lyricism* (2022), a key challenge in addressing climate change is simply getting people to sustain attention to it, given the media's tendency to underreport it, politicians' willingness to downplay it, and the inclination to avoid the bad feelings that must be endured when contemplating it. We can understand the design then as trying to take advantage of the "captivation" that Thrift notes as well as what he describes as the power of "aesthetic pleasure" as "an affective force that is active, intelligible, and has genuine efficacy: it is both moved and moving" (2010, 292). In that sense, the model's effort to sustain the umbrella's position finds a parallel in the viewer's capacity to sustain their attention on the model and what she wears. An appreciation for creative design becomes an opening to appreciate—that is, recognize and sense—the threat of climate change. This is an invitation to sustain a particular way of feeling and sensing.

Rather than generate only bad feeling in the viewer, however, this image deploys the evening gown and glamour to circulate senses of liveliness and deathliness, beauty as well as horror. Judith Brown argues that glamour is a "magical remainder" or a "consumable and degraded version of the earlier aesthetic and affective category" of the sublime (2009, 13).[1] In so far as glamour is "consumable and degraded," it undercuts the sublime feeling that an object or force might have greater power than the human viewer. In that sense, glamour can be understood as a version of the sublime in the Anthropocene, when a perception of nature's superior force gives way to a confrontation with the overwhelming implications of humanity's effects on the climate. But whereas critics have discussed versions of an Anthropocenic sublime that dramatize how vast the problem is, this image and its glamour are human-sized (see, for example, Fressoz 2021). The orientation of model Nitia Sengnsengiyumva's body and the upward tilt of the umbrella help the viewer to feel their way into the garment's embrace, while her steady gaze makes contact with the audience in a way that seems to insist on recognition and reciprocity. The image invites viewers to sense themselves in the garment—to feel the weight of the

---

[1] Brown locates this "magical remainder" specifically in the early twentieth century, but this image makes clear that such a remainder can also be reanimated in the early decades of the twenty-first century.

umbrella in their hand and the fabric enveloping them—as well as to consider how they have, do, or will experience the effects of the degradation of ozone layer that the design depicts. This prompts viewers to understand climate change as an intimate experience and dealing with it a matter of attitude and comportment.

One could rightly say that reducing the problem of environmental degradation to an individual scale trivializes it. At the same time, we could read this design as registering what Thuy Linh Tu argues is the link between beauty culture and the management of environmental toxicity. While Tu focuses on Vietnamese women's skin-care practices as a way of grappling with the poisonous legacies of war, she asserts that they

> remind us that we too accept a certain amount of toxicity in the everyday—in the fish we eat, the milk we drink, the toys we touch, the clothes we wear, and, of course, the cosmetics we apply—reassured in our faith that the real risks lie elsewhere. They may even force us to recognize that the damage we inflict is not endlessly reparable, and that the boundaries and borders we build to secure ourselves, at great human cost, may not indeed hold. (Tu 2021, 20)

Carling and Bunwassana's design punctures the "faith" that risk is distant while rendering the question of repairs and boundaries through tears and seams in fabric. In fact, as Tu's comment reminds us, the "old curtain" and perhaps even the dye made of rice are likely sources of at least some toxicity. So it is not only that damage may not be repaired, but also that the distinction between damage and repair does not hold. We cannot feel certain that we perceive the difference.

Fashion Modelling, Climate Modelling

This ambiguity is fitting for a design that represents climate modelling. As Heather Houser explains, climate models "cross over from number into figuration, from quantification into interpretation, because they are built on scenarios and require tweaks that make them nonrealist" (2020, 36). For example, a General Circulation Model, which Syukuro Manabe helped to invent, draws on a vast range of empirical data to map and forecast the earth's atmosphere and oceans, but must involve speculation. Climate models entail "practices of 'building worlds,' inventing, and simulating" and they "make knowledge move rather than fix facts about present and future states of the climate system" (Houser, 2020, 36–37, 37). Climate modelling, then, is partly an aesthetic and affective practice.

The history of fashion modelling also bears on the photograph's function as a way to display a design inspired by climate modelling. In *The Mechanical Smile* (2013), Caroline Evans describes early twentieth-century models as embodying Fordist aesthetics and modernist visions of the mechanized body. This legacy of mechanization coexists with what Elspeth H. Brown notes is a late twentieth-century shift towards an emphasis on naturalness and spontaneity in high fashion models' poses and fashion imagery. As a sartorial rendering of a climate model, this image is at the nexus of those traditions. The pose of the model, Nitia Sengnsengiyumva, is narrowly dictated by the design; the reach of her right arm is extended by the stem of the umbrella as if they are linked parts of a mechanical system. Yet her hairstyle and the positioning of her left hand on her hip recall the more "natural" aesthetic that emerged in the 1970s, not least because that stylistic change accompanied the greater visibility of black models in high fashion (see Brown 2019, 211–270).[2] That combination of mechanical and spontaneous is in keeping with the nature of climate modelling as a seemingly mechanistic but actually creative and unpredictable project. More specifically, both fashion modelling and climate modelling are ways of mobilizing and circulating perceptions and feelings. Elizabeth Wissinger argues that models "produce affective images, by tuning into a felt sense of vitality, aliveness, or engagement that takes no particular form, but taps into affective energy that is then conveyed via the virtual human contact of the image" (2007, 258). In the case of the photograph of Sengnsengiyumva, affective circulation and vitality are both attributes and subjects of the image, since keeping the umbrella and fabric aloft forestalls destruction and collapse.

The image generates feeling and hence interest in part through its play of textures, including the contrast between the glossy shine of Sengnsengiyumva's smooth skin and the creases and tears of the fabric. As Elspeth H. Brown and Thy Phu note, drawing on Eve Kosofsky Sedgwick's writing on texture, the "dual meaning of feeling as 'tactile plus

---

[2] We can understand this image in terms of what Eugénie Shinkle contends is the move by contemporary fashion photographers including Jurgen Teller and Terry Richardson to create images of awkward bodies that, in turn, are "part of a wider trend towards the production of images which quite literally *incorporate* the viewer into the production of meaning" by provoking visceral reactions (2012, 74).

emotional'" is key to photography, which is a haptic as well as visual medium (2014, 13). This is not simply a photograph, however, but a digital image. Since most people will encounter this design as an image on a website, they may be inclined to zoom in: to try to make out the nature of the stains (or are they abrasions?) in the fabric behind Sengnsengiyumva's head or to discern the water marks along the seams. That act of zooming in will serve as a poor substitute for the ability to touch the garment: to determine the composition, texture, and quality of the fabric by taking bits of it in hand. The resolution of the online image prevents a very close look, let alone a touch; the perception of fabric gives way to pixilated blocks of colour. The viewer cannot hope to scrutinize the fabric or the model. If the three-dimensionality and texture of the image first invite the audience to feel their way into the garment's embrace and the work of sustaining its material, this yields to a sense of its flatness and banality. In trying to bring the image close, I am reminded of the virtuality of the image, the limitations of my perception, and my distance from this garment and from the scientific theories it represents. I cannot perceive, let alone interrogate, the elements that make up either the sartorial or climate model. In that sense, the image epitomizes the challenge of creating aesthetic objects that can generate feelings and actions that are capable of addressing the ecological crises it represents. Such flatness and obscurity forestall the idea that affective engagement clearly leads to needed action.[3]

This point underscores the temporal and narrative dimensions of this image. The garment and the model's outstretched hand tell a story of past violence and destruction, while the movement and suspension in the fabric generate a sense of suspense and uncertainty about the future. Wissinger contends that "a good model…is someone who has that x-factor, who has the ability to play on the energy that flows between us, to resonate with the virtual tendrils that form potential paths into our mutual futures and pasts" (2007, 244). In so far as those energies and flows carry economic value, however, that mutuality is fiction. After all, "while some bodies are exploited at the very lowest end of the fashion industry—the sweatshop workers, for example, who produce the clothes models wear—the fashion model's body is marked to collect the surplus value produced by these workers" (Wissinger 2007, 244). The Nobel designs might seem to provide an alternative to that framework, since they are unique creations

---

[3] That is not to say that affective flatness necessarily blocks any political effects. For a discussion of the queer possibilities of flat affect in fashion photography, see Filippello (2018).

fabricated by the students and displayed as works of art that are not for sale. But the fact that the garment is made of old curtains makes clear that the design cannot be disentangled from extractive systems of production. While such a choice to recycle fabric may seem sustainable, it highlights the impossibility of removing the touch and trace of bodies labouring in exploitive conditions, even if they are temporally and geographically distant.[4]

Sengnsengiyumva's Blackness also raises questions about the perception of "our mutual futures and pasts," which is suggested by this image. Sengnsengiyumva models all of the 2021 Nobel Creations featured on the Beckmans website. But it is in the gown for the Physics Prize that she appears to represent all of humanity and the earth, which can be interpreted as highlighting or obscuring the fact that Black, Indigenous, and people of colour disproportionately suffer the consequences of climate change, even as white people disproportionately cause it. The difference between whether a viewer feels that this image highlights or erases these facts—or both—depends on what Sara Ahmed might describe as the orientation of the viewer: the angle from which they encounter the image, which is shaped by histories of race, class, gender, and sexuality (see Ahmed 2006). Ahmed's approach to history as both sensible and material makes it clear why it is appropriate to use "feels" to refer to the process of reacting to and evaluating this image. Her work also attunes us to the racialized dimensions of idioms of glamour and spontaneity, since a key element of her conceptualization of feeling is that it is shaped by race as a lived experience and a material condition (see Ahmed 2004). It is important that Sengnsengiyumva is not simply performing glamour and naturalness; she specifically is giving or serving face.[5] As Nicole Fleetwood explains, that mode of performance became associated with Black actors, models, and celebrities thanks to stars like Diana Ross. Fleetwood writes, "within black vernacular and expressive cultures, to give face is a mimetic engagement with and transformation of the mythos of cinematic glamour and resonates beyond celebrity" (2015, 64). It is a way of addressing multiple audiences while negotiating how, in Ross's time (and in our own), "racial iconicity hovered in the tensions of veneration and denigration" (66).

---

[4] In making this claim, I am thinking of Poulomi Saha's insistence in *An Empire of Touch* (2019) that even "fast fashion" or "ready-made" garments bear the traces of the labourers who produce them.

[5] I am indebted to Rivky Mondal for this point.

Such tensions resonate with the question the Nobel design seems to ask about whether people will properly value or will continue to degrade the earth and ozone layer as depicted by Sengnsengiyumva and the garment she wears. The fact that Sengnsengiyumva's hair recalls 1970s styles is relevant, since it reminds us that, as Fleetwood notes, "celebrity culture and politics have historically been intertwined for black public figures" (Fleetwood 2015, 72). Images of Black men and women in "natural" styles—celebrities and otherwise—were at the heart of a global iconography of the political and cultural mobilization associated with the Black Power and Black Arts movements. That legacy helps by fuels a dynamic in which a viewer's appreciation for Sengnsengiyumva's beauty and that of the image can serve as an indication that they have the right kinds of political feelings and desires for justice, in this case with regard to climate crises and pursuing peace. At the same time, the retro dimension of Sengnsengiyumva's style allows associations between Black activism and climate activism to remain suggestive (and subjective) rather than prescriptive.

Sengnsengiyumva was represented by a Stockholm-based modelling agency that bills itself as "inclusive" and as featuring "POC" (Fye 2021). While the population of Afro-Swedes is relatively small, one effect of the global visibility of the Black Lives Matter movement has been to draw attention to Afro-Swedish politics, culture, and people. That includes the appearance of more Black models both in Sweden's mainstream white-controlled fashion industry and via venues like *Krull Magazine*, which describes itself as a "a creative digital platform and the preeminent, lifestyle publication for black culture in Stockholm, Sweden" and for which Sengnsengiyumva has modelled (Krull 2016). As in the 1970s, the employment of Black models in white-controlled projects is, in part, a belated reaction to Black-led political movements.

The racial dimensions of the disproportionate impact of the climate crisis finds parallels in the disproportionate opportunities within the fashion industry. While modelling is generally an unsustainable career path, Black models face even greater precarity. As Elizabeth Wissinger notes, they shoulder a particular affective as well as material burden in dealing with the narrower professional opportunities resulting from the industry's racist aesthetics and practices (2015, 232–242). Given that Carling and Bunwassana's design connects precarity with exposure to toxicity, Tu's work is again relevant. She argues that "the struggle over making beauty is also a struggle over making life in deeply toxified environments, borne on bodies, and grappled through bodies, the excesses and imperfections of which are already read as 'woman'" (2021, 20). But she also focuses on how Black and Vietnamese bodies have "borne" and bear such conditions to a much greater extent, including serving as a kind of living laboratory for scientists to measure and mitigate the dangers to white bodies.

The apparent stylistic influences on this design also register this sense of disproportionate precarity and toxicity. The umbrella and gown in swaths of distressed off-white fabric recall the sartorial aesthetics of Alvin Ailey's ballet *Revelations* (1960), Julie Dash's *Daughters of the Dust* (1991), and scenes from Beyonce's visual album *Lemonade* (2016) (which were influenced by Dash's film). While the moods of these works differ, they all feature encroaching waters and a sense of both renunciation and transcendence. The filming locations of *Daughters of the Dust* and scenes from *Lemonade*—the Sea Islands of South Carolina and Louisiana, respectively—invite us to read these features in terms of climate catastrophes, since those areas are particularly endangered by rising waters. In addition, all of these works are concerned with the preservation of African diasporic traditions, which are threatened by the encroachment of modernity. Those traditions are represented, in part, by Black women with off-white dresses and umbrellas who perform moments of leisure, peace, and community. Like the photograph of Sengnsengiyumva wearing Carling and Bunwassana's design, their performances and the images of them are at once highly choreographed and shot through with a sense of natural beauty. As it carries echoes of those earlier works in its creased fabric, the image of the Nobel gown invokes accumulated attempts at preservation, which have failed to forestall disaster, but cannot be given up. To observe this, however, is to repeat rather than answer the question of whether mobilizing models of Black culture and politics for a global audience is an ethical or effective means to generate the needed feeling and action to address climate crises.

To conclude, I will briefly turn to the 2021 garment inspired by the peace prize. It underscores the way that the Beckmans project encourages one to see the capacity to value good design and to sustain aesthetic emotion as part of peace-making. The 2021 Peace Prize was awarded to Maria Ressa and Dmitry Andreyevich Muratov "for their efforts to safeguard freedom of expression, which is a precondition for democracy and lasting peace" (Nobel Prize 2021a). These journalists are best known for their critical coverage of the Philippine and Russian governments, respectively, despite the dangers involved in such work. As the image on the Beckmans website shows, the design features a long-sleeved, close-fitting, black floor length gown (Hulting 2021). Over that and seemingly hanging from the model's neck, is a sculptural creation made up of thick white strips that connect with each other to create a soft, bending cage around the model's body. The designers explain that this "external structure consists of 22 forms in which each product design represents one year, calculated from 2000 to 2021. Every product design is printed with years and with figures on statistics on the number of journalists killed, civilian journalists and media assistants for each year. The statistics come from the Reporters Without Borders Press Freedom Barometer." They note, however, that "unfortunately, due to censorship and limited freedom of the press, it is impossible for all individual lives to come to light. Hence the black underdress that will reflect the dark number of journalists killed that are not included in the barometer" (Hulting 2021). The overgarment recalls 1960s mod fashion and is thus very different from the romantic style of Carling and Bunwassana's work. But both designs register traces of a violent past and uncertainty about a fragile future, and both work with the affects and aesthetics of mourning, resilience, and beauty. They link peace-making to a sustained attention to loss and violence and hence a capacity for tolerating bad feeling, which, however, is leavened by an appreciation for human strength and grace.

Earlier in this essay I noted that the Nobel Museum asserts that the winners of the Nobel Prizes and the fashion designers share the capacity for creativity, defined as "the courage to think in new ways, to question established theories, and innovative combinations of insights from different fields" (Nobel Prize Museum 2014). Yet what we see here is that the designs actually make use of fashion's tendency to renovate rather than create *de novo* as they depict the work of peace-making in terms of retrospection, continuity, and persistence. These designs make clear that the Nobel does not embrace radical innovation. Rather it celebrates shifts in existing forms and feelings. The fashion design project thus expresses how the Nobel's vision of peace-making is caught between the maintenance of the status quo and gestures towards radical alternatives to a violent past and present.

References

Ahmed, Sara. 2004. *The Cultural Politics of Emotion.* New York and Oxfordshire: Routledge.
———. 2006. *Queer Phenomenology: Orientations, Objects, Others.* Durham and London: Duke University Press.

Alaimo, Stacy. 2012. Sustainable This, Sustainable That: New Materialisms, Posthumanism, and Unknown Futures. *PMLA* 127 (3): 558–564.
Benjamin, Walter. 1999. *The Arcades Project*. Translated by Howard Eiland and Kevin McLaughlin. Cambridge, MA and London: Belknap Press of Harvard University Press.
Brown, Judith. 2009. *Glamour in Six Dimensions*. Ithaca, NY: Cornell University Press.
Brown, Elspeth H. 2019. *Work! A Queer History of Modeling*. Durham and London: Duke University Press.
Brown, Elspeth H., and Thy Phu. 2014. Introduction. In *Feeling Photography*, ed. Elspeth H. Brown and Thy Phu, 1–25. Durham and London: Duke University Press.
Evans, Caroline. 2013. *The Mechanical Smile: Modernism and the First Fashion Shows in France and America, 1900–1929*. New Haven, CT: Yale University Press.
Filippello, Roberto. 2018. Thinking Fashion Photographs through Queer Affect Theory. *International Journal of Fashion Studies* 5 (1): 129–145.
Fleetwood, Nicole R. 2015. *On Racial Icons: Blackness and the Public Imagination*. New Brunswick, NJ and London: Rutgers University Press.
Fressoz, Jean-Baptise. 2021. The Anthropocenic Sublime. In *Climate and American Literature*, ed. Michael Boyden, 288–299. Cambridge: Cambridge University Press.
Fye Management. 2021. The Story Behind Fye. Accessed 15 May 2022. https://www.fyemgmt.com/about-us.
Houser, Heather. 2020. *Infowhelm: Environmental Art and Literature in an Age of Data*. New York: Columbia University Press.
Hulting, Sofia. 2021. Nobel Creations. Accessed 15 May 2022. https://beckmans.se/en/nobel-creations-2021/.
Kim, Eunsong, and Gelare Khoshgozaran. 2016. Politics as Currency and the Souvenirs of War: Reflections on Rijin Sahakian's Statement on the Closing of Sada for Iraqi Art. *Contemptorary*, 1 April. https://contemptorary.org/politics-as-currency-and-the-souvenirs-of-war-reflections-on-rijin-sahakians-statement-on-the-closing-of-sada-for-iraqi-art/.
Krull Magazine. 2016. About. Accessed 15 May 2022. https://krullmag.com/about/.
Marshik, Celia. 2017. *At the Mercy of Their Clothes: Modernism, the Middlebrow, and British Garment Culture*. New York: Columbia University Press.
Museum of Contemporary Art Tokyo. 2009. Swedish Fashion—Exploring New Identity. Accessed 15 May 2022. https://www.mot-art-museum.jp/en/exhibitions/110/.
Nobel Prize. 2021a. The Nobel Peace Prize 2021. Accessed 15 May 2022. https://www.nobelprize.org/prizes/peace/2021/ summary/.

———. 2021b. Press Release: The Nobel Prize in Physics 2021. Accessed 15 May 2022. https://www.nobelprize.org/prizes/physics/2021/press-release/.
———. 2022 Statues of the Nobel Foundation. Accessed 28 January 2022. https://www.nobelprize.org/about/statutes-of-the-nobel-foundation/#par1.
Nobel Prize Museum. 2014. Nobel Creations—The Nobel Prize 2014. Accessed 28 January 2022. https://nobelprizemuseum.se/en/nobel-creations-the-nobel-prize-2014/.
Saha, Poulomi. 2019. *The Empire of Touch: Women's Political Labor and the Fabrication of East Bengal.* New York: Columbia University Press.
Shinkle, Eugenie. 2012. Uneasy Bodies: Affect, Embodied Perception and Contemporary Fashion Photography. In *Carnal Aesthetics: Transgressive Imagery and Feminist Politics*, ed. Marta Zarzycka and Bettina Papenburg, 73–88. London: I.B. Taurus & Company.
Song, Min Hyoung. 2022. *Climate Lyricism.* Durham and London: Duke University Press.
Steele, Valerie. 2008. Museum Quality: The Rise of the Fashion Exhibition. *Fashion Theory* 12 (1): 7–30.
Swedish Institute. 2020. Swedish Design Movement. Accessed 15 May 2022. https://si.se/en/events-projects/swedish-design-movement/.
Thrift, Nigel. 2010. Understanding the Material Practices of Glamour. In *The Affect Theory Reader*, ed. Melissa Gregg and Gregory J. Seigworth, 289–308. Durham and London: Duke University Press.
Tu, Thuy Linh. 2021. *Experiments in Skin: Race and Beauty in the Shadows of Vietnam.* Durham and London: Duke University Press.
Wicker, Alden, Emily Schmall, Suhasini Raj, and Elizabeth Paton. 2022. That Organic Cotton T-Shirt May Not Be as Organic as You Think. *The New York Times*, 13 February.
Wissinger, Elizabeth. 2007. Modelling a Way of Life: Immaterial and Affective Labour in the Fashion Modelling Industry. *Ephemera: Theory and Politics in Organization* 7 (1): 250–269.
Wissinger, Elizabeth A. 2015. *This Year's Model: Fashion, Media, and the Making of Glamour.* New York and London: New York University Press.

CHAPTER 12

Glamour Magick, Affective Witchcraft, and Occult Fashion-abilities

Otto Von Busch

When fashion designers such as Alexander McQueen and Rei Kawakubo use references to witchcraft and occultism in their collections, it is easy to interpret their works as yet another spectacle in line with a long tradition of exploiting any sphere of the exotic or foreign for *haute couture* inspiration. But Maria Grazia Chiuri, creative director of Christian Dior, in her interviews about the Tarot-inspired collection of spring 2022, called *Le Chateau du Tarot*, hints towards something more. Like the Tarot, the user of fashion seeks a richer reality, not limited to the spheres of reality that fashion scholars habitually refer to, such as advertising, semiotics, popular, or material culture. With the Tarot collection, Chiuri points towards more profound and meaningful levels of experience and, I would argue, the more magical aspects of fashion.

It is not foreign to think of fashion as a form of magic experience (Vestoj 2011). Where the Old Persian word *magush* meant "to be able, to

---

O. Von Busch (✉)
Parsons School of Design, The New School, New York, NY, USA
e-mail: vonbusco@newschool.edu

© The Author(s), under exclusive license to Springer Nature Switzerland AG 2023
R. Filippello, I. Parkins (eds.), *Fashion and Feeling*, Palgrave Studies in Fashion and the Body,
https://doi.org/10.1007/978-3-031-19100-8_12

211

have power," the Old French *magique* pushed the meaning towards "the art of influencing events and producing marvels" (Hume and Drury 2013, viii). And sure enough, we could consider fashion as a world producing marvels and influencing the aesthetic of the time, seeping into the subconscious of people. Also, the magical is a process of mind, Susan Greenwood (2000, 4) argues, merging a sensory and psychic connection with material and nonmaterial reality, which makes magic a "universal aspect of human consciousness." This is how it appears in the fairytales, too, as clothing items, especially shoes, put their wearer through metamorphosis: "shoes are magical objects that can help or hinder, reward or wound, liberate or imprison," Summer Brennan (2019, 27) argues; "they can turn a cat into a prime minister and a serving girl into a queen."

Tying together magical references and fashion is not as far-fetched as one may think. Over the last decade, witches and Tarot-readers have claimed spaces across popular fashion magazines such as *InStyle*, *Cosmopolitan*, *Teen Vogue*, and *Nylon*, where the esoteric realm now explicitly intersects with style and self-development, going beyond the old astrology-dating sections of lifestyle magazines. As a further point, in 2021, *Cosmopolitan* magazine released its Tarot-deck, "The Cosmo Tarot," by its columnist Sarah Potter, a professional witch and established practitioner of Color Magic. In it, the intentional use of hues of the rainbow is meant to conjure energies and manifest personal transformation.

Indeed, the witch is having a moment. "Film and television are filled with tales of witches and otherworldly women, visual art and literature are plumbing the depths of pagan lore, and runways are replete with occult symbolism" (Sollee 2017, 13). The crafting of emotionally powerful items is in turn nothing new, as witchcraft lives in and through old folkloristic traditions across the world, from amulets warding off danger, such as blue glass charms against the evil eye, entwining red threads in children's hair to protect them from demons that bring disease, to stitching buttons for protection, to talismans that attract what the owner seeks, from horseshoes to four-leaf clovers, from embroidering occult symbols onto garments to the crafting of robes and ceremonial attire and altar cloth (Henderson 2019; Johnson 2021).

The practices and beliefs around agency and change present in these practices differ from the magic of entertainment or the sleight of hand that is commonly implied with the everyday use of the word magic or the works of the magic showman. To differ from these kinds of entertainment, the term "magick" with a "k" is often used to signify the history of occult and practices of participation and manipulation of energies using intention and intuition. In a similar vein, magick is not the workings commonly seen in fantasy or superhero movies but can be simple, quotidian, and often invoked through practices in line with craft or design. Magick can be imbued in gardening and homegrown wands (MacLir 2015), ropes and knots (Williams 2021), cooking (Bussi 2022), and not least in the mythically profound item at the heart of both fashion and magick, an object bound by bad omens as well as luck, clairvoyance, and divination: the mirror (Mueller 2016). Most of these objects may not be magical in a sense we come to think of in tales of fantasy or myth. Still, their prime purpose is to assist the practitioner in focusing the work of visualization, summoning, and directing the will towards its aim. Amalgamating imagination, intention, and intuition, magick and witchcraft work their deeds by what they keep at hand through rituals and invocations, or what is most often just called "the Craft."

The crafts we associate with fashion design are not foreign to magical properties and imaginations. Throughout history, practices of alchemy and magic lie at the foundation of perfume, where different scents were connected to each of the planets, and "a pleasing and fragrant odour was favorable to the angels and good spirits" (Thompson 1995, 167). Similarly, rings engraved with runes and spells could help heal and protect, and jewels and crystals had their properties contributing to their use in adornment, dispersing light while staying resistant to fire. Each stone was endowed with properties of planets, elements, and moods, and as Pliny observes: "Magicians use this jet stone much in their sorceries which they practice by the means of red hot axes, for they affirm that being cast thereon it will burne and consume, if that we desire and wish shall happen accordingly" (Thompson 1995, 202).

From a sociological perspective, the witch's identity calls to a need inherent in contemporary power structures and is used to challenge normative subject positions for many contemporary young women (Ezzy and Berger 2007). But while much of the references from fashion and craft may, from a secular or sceptical perspective, primarily seem to operate on a symbolic level, there is an underlying worldview that witchcraft works with deeper layers of dressing. As will be further seen, there is a strand of fashion designers and style-conscious witches that guide us towards the metaphysical realms of dress. While in some of the cases above, these aspects primarily play out on the catwalk, this text will examine how affective and magical perspectives are applied by practitioners of contemporary witchcraft. Specifically, I will explore how practitioners of magick calling themselves "glamour witches" share a view of the world in which affect is manipulated with purpose towards specific goals, bringing fashion and appearances to bear as active forces in the world.

I will start by examining the underlying perspective of contemporary tropes of magic and witchcraft to then see how affect, in alignment with what Nigel Thrift calls "technologies of glamour," is used as means to shape their world. I will then unpack how magick comes to play a role in the "minding" of fashion, that is, how it comes to enter our inner lives and become an affective energy to manipulate. By examining the perspective of Gabriela Herstik, a self-proclaimed glamour witch, I will seek how "fashion magick" acts as a means of *affective fashion-abilities*, claiming agency for wearers that challenge the default and market-driven distribution of aesthetic means and properties.

Magick, Glamour, and the World of Appearances

That clothing can be charged by emotional energies may not be something new. Adorning the body accentuates its use as a signifier and a vehicle for desire. Myth and folklore are full of garments empowering the user with magical energies, enhancing strength or beauty, agency, or passion. Mythical heroes wear magical robes or enchanted boots, and popular teenage wizards sneak under invisibility cloaks or use protective talismans. Our popular imagination seems saturated by the otherworldly abilities of attire, in using shape-shifting materials and patterns, transforming the wearer's body, silhouette, and appearance. These tools gain the wearer new emotional sensibilities as well as capacities for action, whether it is the trope of "masculine strength" of enhancing inner and outer potency or playing with the "feminine mystique" that Betty Friedan (1963, 38) famously posits as the highest value for women as "the fulfilment of their own femininity." Garments manipulate our being; just think of the witch Morgan la Fey in Arthurian legend, who weaves an enchanted robe, designed to consume the body of King Arthur by fire. No wonder magical items of dress are controversial, or even forbidden, such as in the Bible (Ezekiel 13:20), where it is stated, "This is what the Sovereign Lord says: I am against your magic charms with which you ensnare people."

Building on Gabriel Tarde's ideas of economies as the generation, processing, and circulation of passionate interests, which in turn have their own "vibrancy," social theorist Nigel Thrift (2010) explores a particular instance of affect in unpacking the material practices and circulations of aesthetics and allure. Here, the passionate interest of intimacy is inverted towards the public realm as a form of "extimacy," to mobilize and direct affective motility. Glamour is a quality that captures our attention with a taint of passion. It calls with an embodied awareness and works in a particular spectrum of interest tied to allure. With the help of what Thrift calls "technologies of glamour," allure comes to blur the boundaries between persons and things, media, and expressions, to "produce greater captivation" that in turn makes persons appear "fractal," that is, "able to incorporate others and parts of others" (291). As Thrift suggests, glamour, in its contemporary and mediatized use, must be seen as a special form of capitalist "worlding." To unpack glamour, Thrift connects appearances with style. Thrift sees style as having an agency of itself in social relationships and in what he calls the "technologies of glamour":

> style does not consist of a list of factors that have to be ticked off, nor does it constitute a totality of meaning. *Style is a modification of being that produces captivation, in part through our own explorations of it.* Style wants us to love it and we want to be charmed by it; we want to emulate it, we want to be definite about it, we want to be absorbed by it, we want to lend ourselves to what it has become. Style, in other words, can be counted as an agent in its own right in that it defines what is at issue in the world that we can engage with. (Thrift 2010, 297)

Thrift furthermore connects this type of glamour as a mode of aesthetic capitalism or a way in which "capitalism makes its mark on the aesthetic sphere" (Thrift 2010, 296). Indeed, as Elizabeth Wissinger (2015) notes, the fashion world both conjures and exploits various forms of glamour labour through seduction, captivation, and commodification. According to Elspeth Brown (2017, 291), glamour "connotes a certain type of optical allure that suggests both beauty and sex appeal [...] a visual experience, one associated with the dark arts of deception." As consumers, we want to be "absorbed" by it, not unlike the burning robes of la Fey.

Elizabeth Wilson's (2007) perspective on glamour is slightly different from that suggested by Thrift, more explicitly tied to the overlaps with magick and witchcraft. Building on her previous work on fashion and magic (Wilson 2004), Wilson emphasizes glamour as a mystical and esoteric element, apparent in fashion's recurring love of gothic themes and the dress practices of the dandies, such as Beau Brummel and Oscar Wilde.

In contrast to Thrift's capitalist worlding of glamour, according to Wilson "glamour is not about consumption in the consumer society, although the word has come to be continually misused to suggest that it is. Nor is it simply about luxury" (Wilson 2007, 105). To Wilson, celebrity is the opposite of glamour; it is desacralization of the allure of appearances: celebrity is profane, while glamour is sublime. However, we must see how both Wilson and Thrift wrote these texts at the early advent of social media. Today's careful curation of attention and affect makes intimacy and extimacy overlap, and professionalized influencing techniques allow a broader palette of options and shades of exposure and allure. Celebrity does not necessarily mean a flattening of emotive energies and depth but instead allows influencers more options to curate allure and captivating forms of affective mystique. Celebrity and glamour solicit different affects; they work with different energies. But energies they are, and this is what aligns them well with the worlds inhabited through witchcraft and magick.

The Energies of Life

Seeing glamour as an affective energy shares many common traits in contemporary witchcraft and magick. As a "technology of glamour" that Thrift points to, the glamour magick of the witch could indeed be affective spells that the fashionista cooks up to serve their will.

The foundation of the magical perspective is to see the world as energies that flow throughout the world and the planes of manifestation. Such invisible energies can be manipulated and harnessed through the various channels and forms they take. In simple terms, energies can take higher forms, such as thoughts, or more dense forms, as in ether and life energies flowing in the body, and also charge things or crystallize into matter. Energies transform, but never go away. That is, some things seem more permanent than others. But in the end, all energies are in motion. People *participate* in these flows of energy and can *consort* to their powers by connecting to these energies of the world. Tapping into the flows of energy, and using the will with purpose and skill, the practitioner can come to be an active part in shaping the surrounding world. As *Wicca & Witchcraft for Dummies* (Smith 2005) suggests:

> The energy in the mind is not separate from the energy in the rest of the world. When a person visualizes an event (seen it as a detailed picture in the mind), he or she forms energy into patterns. A person can focus his or her

mental power to move and direct energy. By moving that energy, a person's mind can affect events or conditions in the physical world. By visualizing events in the mind, a person can direct energy and shape the physical world. That process is called *magic*. (Smith 2005, 220)

Many strands of esoteric thought put energies at the forefront of their worldview, ranging from the mystic elements in medieval alchemy, to the creative, organic, and energetic substratum of nature that appear in Mesmer's "animal magnetism," to the "Odic force" of Carl Reichenbach, Henri Bergson's "élan vital," or the "orgone" of Wilhelm Reich. These are energies in line with the Indian notion of Prana as energies flowing through the chakras of the body, or the traditional Chinese Ch'i, and its direction in space as in Feng Shui (Buckland 2018; Feldmann 2019). The magician works to participate in these flows, harnessing the energy using their spirit, directing energy with intent, and training both imagination and will. To participate means using the craft to gather energy, from within, from nature, and from divine sources, and direct this energy towards a specific purpose. As with building muscle, discipline and control are necessary to direct and enhance one's power, not unlike how compression facilitates explosive energies. With the help of the "laws of limitation," it is by knowledgeable use of constraints that the practitioner helps realize their intentions; unrestricted energies fizzle out and disintegrate, losing their intensity.

Energies attract and repel and act in love and strife. They can be directed and sent out with specific purposes, but they also return and may strike back in a new form. As is often underlined, if the practitioner sends out negativity, it may return as such. Working from negative energies may attract more of such. But this "negativity" avoids the trap of moralization, as eroticism and sexuality have been objects of censorship, suppression, concealment, and silencing, or have been reduced to shaming. As something dark and dirty, if not demonic, the taboo of the esoteric and erotic is not only tempting but a powerful force for empowerment and self-discovery (Hanegraaff and Kripal 2011). Erotic motifs and sexual energies are not merely carnal but also a pathway linked to a transcendent cosmological realm, primordial energy connecting cosmos and flesh (Hakl 2011). For practitioners of magick, tapping into and conjuring sexual energies are thus powerful means for charging spells and directing and empowering one's will. In the depths of the subconscious, strong forces await, and rather than deny or shy away from them, the magician should learn to harness them under their will, for example, by using seduction or masturbation to charge projections and visions: a practice common, for example, under the umbrella expression of "Chaos magic" (Carroll 1987).

However, this does not mean that energies of the subconscious should be avoided; rather, these are also put in use, for instance, in LaVeyan satanism. Scholar of esotericism Per Faxneld points to the commonalities across esoteric traditions in this sense, drawing parallels to Wilhelm Reich's organic life energy, which he called "orgone":

> Like Wilhelm Reich, in his theory about so-called orgone energy, LaVey views sexuality as a form of physical energy. [...] In *The Satanic Witch* [LaVey] elaborates on *The Satanic Bible's* ritual masturbation and combines it with the affirmation of sexual attractiveness also familiar from that book. After climaxing, the witch is to proclaim, "I am a witch; I have power over men!" over and over again. (Faxneld 2014, 174)

As Faxneld points out, the purpose of such ritual play is to acknowledge the power of sexual energy and put these sexual energies under the will of the witch. The goal is to reflect the male gaze of desire back at its source, becoming a power to be wielded under the will of the witch to manipulate the world. Cosmetic manipulation of appearances and seductive styles come to mind, as they are means to ensnare the attention, emotions, and physical affects of a specific audience. In the world of magick, fashion is less an image or sign and more Morgan la Fey's robes of fire.

Glamour Witches and the Magick of Fashion

The image of the witch is a recurring figure in the narratives of the hero's journey towards self-transformation. In one classic case, two women appear as central characters in Odysseus' travels. One is his wife, Penelope, waiting at home, bound by customs, and accosted by suitors. With nightly ingenuity, she reverse-engineers her weaving to subvert the societal rituals under which she is bound, effectively hacking into social protocol to carve out room for her own agency. On the other hand, the witch Circe seduced Odysseus, waits for no one, and refuses to bow to men (which she turns into swine). The hints are clear; the witch's agency is that of cunning and seduction, craft, and transformation, always with the possibility of undermining society and the rule of men. Also, fashion can subvert the delineations of social affairs. Across time, various sumptuary laws have forbidden people of lower classes from wearing certain types of attire, especially women, reserving these items for the persons with greater estates or class (Robson 2013). Garments have appeared as proof of seditious intent by the wearers and also shown up in witch trials, such as the infamous ones in Salem, where dress was used as proof against the accused, exposing how women were also persecuted for wearing finery above their status (Sollee 2017, 104). This was not an exception; as in other Massachusetts colonies in the seventeenth century, laws proclaimed that women wearing high-heeled shoe styles from France used to seduce a man into marriage would be tried as witches (Brennan 2019, 110).

The shapeshifting elements of fashion can spell liberation and danger, appearing in both historical and contemporary examples. As noted by Kristen Sollee (2022, 176), "through the ritualized use of clothing and cosmetics, contemporary witchcraft practitioners are fashioning their bodies as sites of resistance, liberation, and magic-making. By harnessing glamour spells to hex, heal, conjure, and banish—to shape-shift their inner and outer worlds." With its seasoned sensuality, "witch fashion" connotes an "all-encompassing moniker for revealing or concealing, retro or contemporary, ornate or austere—but always engaged with conceptions of feminine power" (Sollee 2022, 178) (Fig. 12.1).

Fig. 12.1 Gabriela Herstik (2022), photo by Alexandra Herstik

Building on the shapeshifting and empowering possibilities of magick, author and self-proclaimed witch Gabriela Herstik sees witchcraft in fashion in the surrealist and pagan motifs of Elsa Schiaparelli, and today in the recurring witch iconography in the collections of Alexander McQueen, Rick Owens, Rei Kawakubo, and Hedi Slimane. The fascination with the witch in fashion design is no accident, and Herstik notes that:

> The witch has always woven an enchanting glamour, subverting the gaze of society with her cloak of magick. She wields the whip of her aesthetic with precision and clarity, both threatening and enticing in her strangeness. Perhaps one of the witch's most iconic qualities is her ability to shape-shift, to bend the energy of the universe around her to contort to her will. (Herstik 2021, 470)

Herstik practises glamour magick herself and has been a writer on astrology, magic, and witchcraft for a variety of fashion media, such as *Vogue*, *NYLON*, *Allure*, and fittingly, *Glamour*. In her practice and writings, witchcraft emerges as something more than symbolic play or lifestyle:

> After claiming the word 'witch' at the tender age of twelve, I never looked back. Ever since then, I have explored what it means to be a modern witch, combining my love for clothing and fashion with a passion for magick and energy work. My belief is that by channeling ancient wisdom into the modern age, you are able to access the powerful, all-knowing, intuitive part of yourself regularly and easily. [...] Being a witch means living in this world consciously, powerfully and unapologetically. (2018, 3–4)

Using magick means to engage "energies on this plane, even those that we may not be able to see with the naked eye" (2018, 5). Herstik defines magick as "energy plus intention; it's a way to manifest a desired outcome of effect. Symbols, stories and ritual are the language of the subconscious, helping us access our unconscious mind, the part that manifests magick" (2018, 9). Furthermore,

> Everything is energy, and to work magick is to recognize this and the interplay between different things. In magick, things that have an energetic resonance are said to have a correspondence. The planets, zodiac signs, elements, seasons, herbs, plants, animals, colors, scents, and stones (to name a few), all have different correspondences and relationships to one another. Not every system will agree on what corresponds to what, but this truth still holds.

When we are able to see clothing as an aspect of this, or something we can use as a canvas for our intentions by way of correspondences, then we can use the flesh as a vessel for the energy we want to embody. (Herstik 2022)

The spell is central to the execution of magick. Herstik notes, "a spell shifts energy to change things and is equal parts intention, preparation, how you feel and the tools you have at hand" (2018, 12). Clothes and appearance can be part of such spells, and a practitioner can use energies to charge clothing, for example, by laying them out on the altar and placing crystals on top of the pieces (2018, 56). Casting a glamour spell is a way to harness the energies that appear in one's aura. The aura connects us to different planes of energy, drawing from the physical and ethereal levels and the chakras, the body's energy centres. This makes the aura our personal energetic field, the most intimate one. When we feel healthy, the aura extends around us, while the aura shrinks and loses vibrancy when sick (2018, 85).

Working with sexual energies is a powerful means to modulate the body's energies. As Herstik (2019) notes in an article she published in *Vogue*:

> My personal practice means being devoted to the Divine Feminine; working with sex magick by using orgasms to raise energy for a desired intention; working with the cycles of the moon and seasons; and using a daily meditation practice alongside tarot, breathwork, therapy, energy healing and ritual to find empowerment in the everyday. It also means seeing myself—and my power to heal—as part of the collective consciousness.

In this work, appearances, seduction, eroticism, and the multitude of modalities of sexuality are potent means to modulate the most profound life energies, working from inside-out and, the opposite, outside-in.

> In magick, we start with this inner vision, transformation that happens through the inner self first, as a means of changing the outer realm. In glamour, or the magickal application of fashion and adornment, we work the opposite formula; we use our will and imagination to transform our physical self as a means of then changing our inner self. Magick transforms us from the inside-out, glamour transforms us from the outside-in. When the two overlap it's incredibly powerful. When you use your creativity and the occult maxim of "knowing thyself" to dress and adorn the physical vehicle, the gift of the body becomes another piece of magick. Glamour becomes another

means of transforming how you move through and interact with the world. Fashion and magick are both creative acts, and we can use our self-expression as a means of interweaving the two, by creating what we want and who we want to be by adorning ourselves as such. (Herstik 2022)

Herstik emphasizes the connection between fashion and magic, as it is integrated into our lives and is intimately connected to the world around us:

Much like magick, fashion has to evolve to stay relevant. Even if we're not into fashion, even if we don't care much about style or the happenings in the fashion industry, we're still surrounded by it and exposed to it by our peers, social media, the internet and so on. Magick is similar. When it doesn't evolve with the time and its people, it ceases to be relevant, necessary and as impactful as it can be. (138)

This leads Herstik to argue for a form of "fashion magick" at the intersection of style, beauty, and glamour, the intentional infusion of energy with what we wear (139). Here, the glamour works as a magickal veil, modifying the appearance of things. "By curating how others see me, by *deciding* how I want others to see me, I'm casting a glamour" (140). This brings Herstik back to the energies and the "fashion chakra," the aura that is lying closest to the skin. It isn't about money or designer labels; the fashion chakra is "fed when she's dressed and loved intentionally; when the perfect piece finds her at the thrift store, or when a gift finds its way to her (142) (Fig. 12.2).

MINDING AND EMBODYING OCCULT FASHION-ABILITIES

At the heart of fashion lies the cruel reality that we do not choose fashion, but fashion is *inflicted upon us* (von Busch 2020). As Susan Kaiser (2012, 30) points out, "we are forced to appear." Cultivating intention and working with the energies of manifestation, the magick works of the glamour witch rip through convention and have the practitioner take an active role in shaping appearance. Using the mask of appearances to their advantage becomes a critical element of the witch's use of the magic, reclaiming facets of self beyond the approved or sanctioned hierarchies of signification.

Being forced to appear forms the foundation for how the affects of fashion come to shape perception; that is, for being receptive to fashion, one has to become primed to *mind* clothing, that is, care enough about it

Fig. 12.2 Gabriela Herstik (2020), photo by Alexandra Herstik

to notice it. As Susan Kaiser argues, "[t]he process of minding appearances is both embodied and material. The body itself, of course, is material (biological) and symbolic; indeed, it marks the intersections between the two, and can be described as the threshold of subjectivity" (Kaiser 2001, 79) Kaiser continues:

> Minding appearances enables the visual, embodied representation of who I am and who I am becoming along with ideas, possibilities, ambivalences and anxieties with which I may find it difficult to grapple, much less resolve, in a verbal, linear, conscious manner. In this sense, appearance style becomes a

working model or a tentative truth claim about identity (i.e. who I am, who I am not, who I may be becoming). The process of minding appearance enables the construction of looks, as well as tentative understandings about the self in relation to others and consumer and media cultures, at a specific time and place. (Kaiser 2001, 80)

"Minding" means turning affective imagination into reality, a reality especially prominent in the worlding processes of social relations. In such settings, as Mike Featherstone (2010) points out, a consumer gains agency through modifying appearances that animate a new sense of self; he writes, "This is the made-up person, living out, or actualizing a particular temporary fiction, or moving through the life course to realize a particular larger narrative" (Featherstone 2010, 198). What Featherstone points to as a desire to live out and actualizing the fiction of a self, the magician would call a "visualization of the will," where imagination, intention, and intuition merge into magical transformation. But the magical perspective points towards a powerful and intentional embodiment of affect. Mobilizing the emotive depths of the chakras and affective use of sexual energies and orgasms points towards a more potent use of embodiment in magick than using attire for attention and communication. Under the guise of fashion, something more is going on, beyond signalling: a total engagement with the affects of dress (and undress) to bolster intention, independence, and sovereignty.

To Herstik, the central component of witchcraft is to cultivate power and agency. Using glamour is one component in embodying one's magick: "We can turn our body into a spell by intentionally cloaking ourselves in something that makes us feel confident, protected, and centered in ourselves" (Herstik 2020, 8). As pointed out earlier, it is not about buying new things or following trends but using intent to make conscious decisions, as much as energizing one's look to build self-confidence and aesthetic intuition. It is not about fashionable stuff but about cultivating an affective capacity and capability to be fashion-*able* (von Busch 2008). This takes Herstik's "fashion magick" very close to an *esoteric* fashion-ability, namely an affective invocation of imagination, intention, and intuition for building aesthetic skills and boosting self-confidence in one's style, while charging it with embodied energies of seduction under a sovereign sense of sexuality. Herstik sees witchcraft as a form of empowerment beyond symbolic rebellion; it is a:

direct path to harnessing your power. For women (myself included) raised in environments that attempt to take away our bodily integrity and personal autonomy, witchcraft is a form of direct personal resistance. It's like playing by another set of rules that no one else knows about. It's a way to take back power while connecting to something larger than ourselves. (2018, 24)

The affective aesthetic of the witch oscillates between the hideous abject crone of horror and the dangerous grace of the enchantress. Herstik's glamour magick points to how the inclusive and experimental DIY perspective of witchcraft binds the users to a more meaningful play between masking and minding, using the esoteric mystique of glamour for affective shape-shifting. With a radical embrace of esoteric imagination, intention, and intuition, glamour seeks affects beyond representation and signification to work with energies and embodiment. Here, glamour magick becomes an avenue of subversive action and an articulation of dissenting knowledges of the flesh. That is, of how to conjure affects that tap into deeper layers of the body, the unconscious realm of desires. This means glamour magick is a conscious play with affective, embodied, and universal energies, where the witch is empowered beyond the realm of cosmetics to fully manifest more profound occult fashion-abilities. The modulation of energies and affects through imagination and will means expanding the user's spellbook of expressions and enchantments, leading to increased affective agency and a real sense of empowerment. As Herstik notes:

> Your appearance is innately vulnerable because it's how others perceive you. But you can work with glamour to create a self that represents who you want to be, who you are becoming, the self you do your best to inhabit every day. Sexuality can be a part of this. Seduction is the act of leading someone through tension and desire, and the way we veil our bodies as erotic vessels—what we choose to show and not show—is a part of this. (Herstik 2022)

Shapeshifting and fashion are both magical practices. Fashion designers tap into the realms of magick, using the witch or warlock as icons of free spirits for their spectacle. But it goes both ways; users of magick turn to the use of appearances as part of their alluring spectacle, and a means to step beyond the limits of convention also requires a shedding of the skins of habit (Buckland 2004, 2018). Famous photographs of iconic practitioners of magic often show them in their ritual attire: Aleister Crowley in ceremonial robes, Dion Fortune in elaborate raiments, and not least the spectacular impresario Anton LaVey in nemesis-like attire, surrounded by less clad witches, conjuring the erotic energies of both the universe and authoritarian nihilism. Together with the fashion designers calling upon the symbolism of the witch to tap into the esoteric affects of magick, it is as if these figureheads of twentieth-century magick want to point out not only their *outré* personalities and rejection of societal norms but also how appearances are not what they seem. As Pam Grossman (2021, 110) notes, the witch is a shapeshifter, "a protean canvas onto which humanity projects its fears and fantasies about feminine power." Fashion is just one expression of her abilities to evoke and conjure affective powers, modulating the energies of the universe and self in accordance with her will. "The fashion witch is self-possessed, first and foremost," Grossman posits, "She controls how much of herself she shows and shares. Whether others consider her anatomy a monstrosity, or a thing of majesty is of little concern. She knows her body is her own. And that is true power" (Grossman 2019, 119).

For the glamour witch, the cosmology of appearances is not dictated by the visible realm of celebrities and branded desire but evokes and guides the submerged energies of esoteric worlds. Using the will and occult fashion-abilities, the witch claims affective agency beyond that offered under consumerism. The fires of Morgan la Fey's robes defy the authority of King Arthur, challenging while simultaneously ensnaring the king through their allure.

References

Brennan, Summer. 2019. *High Heels*. New York: Bloomsbury.
Brown, Elspeth H. 2017. Queering Glamour in Interwar Fashion Photography: The 'Amorous Regard' of George Platt Lynes. *GLQ: A Journal of Lesbian and Gay Studies* 23 (3): 289–326.
Buckland, Raymond. 2004. *Wicca for one: The path of solitary witchcraft*. New York: Citadel.
———. 2018. *Wicca for Life: The Way of the Craft—From Birth to Summerland*. New York: Citadel.
von Busch, Otto. 2020. *The Psychopolitics of Fashion: Conflict and Courage Under the Current State of Fashion*. London: Bloomsbury.
Bussi, Gail. 2022. *Enchanted Kitchen: Connect to Spirit with Recipes and Rituals Through the Year*. Woodbury: Llewellyn.
Carroll, Peter. 1987. *Liber null & Psychonaut: An Introduction to Chaos Magic*. San Francisco: Weiser.

Ezzy, Douglas, and Helen Berger. 2007. Becoming a Witch: Changing Paths of Conversion in Contemporary Witchcraft. In *The New Generation Witches: Teenage Witchcraft in Contemporary Culture*, ed. Peg Aloi and Hannah Johnston, 41–56. London: Routledge.

Faxneld, Per. 2014. Cult of Carnality: Sexuality, Eroticism, and Gender in Contemporary Satanism. In *Sexuality and New Religious Movements*, ed. Henrik Bogdan and James Lewis, 165–181. New York: Palgrave Macmillan.

Featherstone, Mike. 2010. Body, Image and Affect in Consumer Culture. *Body & Society* 16 (1): 193–221.

Feldmann, Erica. 2019. *HausMagick: Transform Your Home with Witchcraft*. San Francisco: HarperOne.

Friedan, Betty. 1963. *The Feminine Mystique*. New York: Norton.

Greenwood, Susan. 2000. *Magic, Witchcraft and the Otherworld*. Oxford: Berg.

Grossman, Pam. 2019. *Waking the Witch: Reflections on Women, Magic, and Power*. New York: Gallery Books.

———. 2021. Shape-shifter: The Many Faces of the Witch. In *Witchcraft*, ed. Jessica Hundley and Pam Grossman, 110–122. Koln: Taschen.

Hakl, Hans Thomas. 2011. The Theory and Practice of Sexual Magic, Exemplified by Four Magical Groups in the Early Twentieth Century. In *Hidden Intercourse: Eros and Sexuality in the History of Western Esotericism*, ed. Wouter Hanegraaff and Jeffrey Kripal, 445–478. New York: Fordham University Press.

Hanegraaff, Wouter, and Jeffrey Kripal. 2011. *Hidden Intercourse: Eros and Sexuality in the History of Western Esotericism*. New York: Fordham University Press.

Henderson, Raechel. 2019. *Sew Witchy: Tools, Techniques & Projects for Sewing Magick*. Woodbury: Llewellyn.

Herstik, Gabriela. 2018. *Inner Witch: A Modern Guide to the Ancient Craft*. New York: TarcherPerigee.

———. 2019. Practical Magick: Women from Around the World Talk Witchcraft. *Vogue*, October 30. https://www.vogue.fr/fashion-culture/article/what-does-it-mean-to-be-a-modern-witch-3-witches-share-their-experience-of-the-craft.

———. 2020. *Embody Your Magick: A Guided Journal for the Modern Witch*. New York: TarcherPerigee.

———. 2021. Haute Macabre, Haute Couture: Witchcraft in Fashion. In *Witchcraft*, ed. Jessica Hundley and Pam Grossman, 470–476. Koln: Taschen.

———. 2022. Interview by the Author Per Email, April 14 and 22.

Hume, Lynne, and Nevill Drury. 2013. *The Varieties of Magical Experience: Indigenous, Medieval, and Modern Magic*. Santa Barbara: Praeger.

Johnson, Christi. 2021. *Mystical Stitches: Embroidery for Personal Empowerment and Magical Embellishment*. North Adams: Storey.

Kaiser, Susan. 2001. Minding Appearances: Style, Truth, Subjectivity. In *Body Dressing*, ed. Joanne Entwistle and Elizabeth Wilson, 79–102. Oxford: Berg.
———. 2012. *Fashion and Cultural Studies*. London: Bloomsbury.
MacLir, Alferian Gwydion. 2015. *The Witch's Wand: The Craft, Lore and Magic of Wands and Staffs*. Woodbury: Llewellyn.
Mueller, Mickie. 2016. *The Witch's Mirror: The Craft, Lore and Magic of the Looking Glass*. Woodbury: Llewellyn.
Robson, Ruthann. 2013. *Dressing Constitutionally: Hierarchy, Sexuality, and Democracy from Our Hairstyles to Our Shoes*. Cambridge: Cambridge University Press.
Smith, Diane. 2005. *Wicca & Witchcraft for Dummies*. Hoboken: Wiley.
Sollee, Kristen. 2017. *Witches, Sluts, Feminists: Conjuring the Sex Positive*. Berkeley: ThreeL Media.
———. 2022. Fashioning a Glamour: Magical Embodiment in Contemporary Witchcraft. In *Silhouettes of the Soul: Meditations on Fashion, Religion, and Subjectivity*, ed. Otto von Busch and Jeanine Viau, 176–187. London: Bloomsbury.
Thompson, C.J.S. 1995. *Mysteries and Secrets of Magic*. Teddington: Senate.
Thrift, Nigel. 2010. Understanding the Material Practices of Glamour. In *The Affect Theory Reader*, ed. Melissa Gregg and Gregory Seigworth, 289–308. Durham: Duke University Press.
Vestoj. 2011. Issue 2: On Fashion and Magic, ed. Anja Aronowsky Cronberg. Paris, January.
von Busch, Otto. 2008. *Fashion-able: Hacktivism and Engaged Fashion Design*. Gothenburg: ArtMonitor.
Williams, Brandy. 2021. *Cord Magic: String, Yarn, Twists and Knots*. Woodbury: Llewellyn.
Wilson, Elizabeth. 2004. Magical Fashion. *Fashion Theory* 8 (4): 375–386.
———. 2007. A Note on Glamour. *Fashion Theory* 11 (1): 95–108.
Wissinger, Elizabeth. 2015. *This Year's Model: Fashion, Media, and the Making of Glamour*. New York: New York University Press.

CHAPTER 13

Fashion Studies at a Turning Point

Lucia Ruggerone

The recent literature on fashion studies features frequent attempts by a variety of scholars to extend fashion studies beyond the representational paradigm that has dominated the field for many years. The claim is that seeing garments as mere tools to express real or ideal Egos or as techniques individuals use to shape their personality leaves out other important aspects of our relationship with clothes, namely the affective aspects of being dressed emerging from the materiality of both our bodies and the clothes we wear, as well as the atmosphere in which the clothed body is

---

This chapter develops ideas and concepts previously discussed in Ruggerone (2017) and Ruggerone and Stauss (2022). Although it aims at extending the arguments previously presented, some materials are drawn from those sources, properly referenced. However, the context in which the materials are used here is novel. I wish to thank my co-author, Renate Stauss, for granting me permission to retrace some of the ideas we developed together when writing the 2022 article.

Lv. Ruggerone (✉)
Robert Gordon University, Aberdeen, UK
e-mail: l.ruggerone@rgu.ac.uk

© The Author(s), under exclusive license to Springer Nature Switzerland AG 2023
R. Filippello, I. Parkins (eds.), *Fashion and Feeling*, Palgrave Studies in Fashion and the Body,
https://doi.org/10.1007/978-3-031-19100-8_13

immersed (see Findlay 2016; Sampson 2018, 2020; Parkins 2008; Eckersley 2008; Eckersley and Duff 2020). While authors, mostly contributing to affect theories, have proposed different ways of tackling this complexity, I want to focus here on one possible approach, which in my view constitutes a promising direction to develop an affective politics of dress. It is the invitation to further develop a dialogue between fashion studies and body studies (Eckersley and Duff 2020) to explore their interconnections and finally uncover the affective aspects of being dressed that have for long eluded the attention of fashion scholars as well as designers and consumers.

Body studies is a broad interdisciplinary area where inputs from different sources converge to create a complex network of ideas and concepts. However, to a sociologist's eye, one crucial point soon emerges from this ample literature: namely the idea that the body can never be thought of as a purely material 'thing', but is always, in all our apperceptions, already a 'cultural object'. In other words, and contrary to common belief, we cannot conceive of the body as an entity separate from culture—a 'natural element' prior to social involvement—because the very ways in which we can experience and attend to it (either our own body or the other bodies) are always already embedded in culture. This view notably implies that the human body can only be apperceived in relation to a set of formal and informal norms or rules that circulate in a given social context. The idea of the cultural body, which, in the 1980s, the then new sociology of the body quickly embraced, was by no means novel nor original. Decades before sociologists started considering social actors' bodies as worthy objects of study, in the 1930s, the anthropologist Marcel Mauss ([1934] 1979) had introduced the notion of *body techniques* to refer to those apparently instinctive bodily practices and gestures that, he argued, are the results of learnt and embodied dispositions. A few years after Mauss, albeit in a less explicit form, the importance of bodily language underpinned Erving Goffman's nearly ethological descriptions of how bodily behaviours (our deference and demeanour, but also our stigmatised traits) inform and shape the ways in which we communicate with others in interactions (Goffman 1959, 1963, 1972). The idea that culture is firmly embodied in our conduct, comportment and allure also famously inspired Bourdieu's (1984) notion of *habitus*: that set of pre-conscious or semi-conscious dispositions that make up one's identity and shape one's relation to the world. Moreover, it is at least since the 1960s that feminist analyses have continued to show the multiple ways in which a sexist culture gets inscribed onto women's bodies, both in the ways that women come to hold themselves in public and in the various forms of symbolic or material violence perpetrated on them (Conboy et al. 1997; Bartky 1991, Bordo 1993; Marsden 2004). In all these contributions it is already clear that the norms pertaining to bodily practices are not separate from, but on the contrary partake to, the processes of identity construction, deeply influencing the ways people think of themselves and relate to the world.

DIGGING DEEPER INTO SUBJECTIVITY

Although all these ideas (and others that I didn't mention) are crucial to understand the role of the body in social life and in the formation of selves, I contend that we can dig even deeper to show that the contemporary notion of the body is linked to our sense of self in ways that transcend body techniques and pertain directly to the individuals' inner sense of identity. Interestingly, in the current debate across social and psychological sciences, the body has taken centre stage: bodily (and neurological) functions are increasingly examined, when trying to explain people's behaviours, beliefs and even feelings. As some experimental psychologists remark, the body is now commonly treated as the starting point for a science of the self (Tsakiris 2017; Caldwell 2016). Although many factors contribute to create this line of approach, I propose that an important role is played by the long-standing ocularcentrism of Western culture with its prioritisation of the sense of sight to accrue knowledge and attain truth. In the last decade the importance of vision has been further magnified by the unstoppable proliferation of screens and images that punctuate not only medical practices and investigations, but also, more prosaically, the daily experience of many of us. Modern technological devices, commonly used by virtually everybody, are now capable of producing an almost infinite flow of images and mirror reflections of ourselves that ultimately impinge on our notion of selfhood and strengthen the definition of a vision-based subjectivity. It is perhaps not surprising that some authors have coined the label 'somatic individual' to indicate the form of individuality that seems prevalent in the contemporary socio-cultural context. Although the definition of somatic individual initially proposed by Rose (2001) refers mainly to the ongoing trend, in the health and human sciences, of regarding neurological processes and neurochemical reactions as the bases of selfhood, thereby transforming the psychological and mentalistic notion of personhood, I wish here to adopt the modified, 'softer' version of the term proposed by Heyes (2007), to characterise the current tendency towards an identification (or perfect fit) of self with body.

As Heyes (2007) has argued, for the somatic individual, selfhood still relates to the body in an inner/outer mode; however, this split cannot, in my view, be assimilated with a straightforward revival of a dualistic perspective, according to which mind and body are completely separate entities, with human value only residing in the mind. On the contrary, I contend that, in the contemporary regime, the self is conceived as a site of authenticity and truth (this corresponding to its value) that can only exist if/when it is made visible in the flesh. In this context, the body, far from being disparaged as a prison to be evaded in order to free the true spirit, becomes the only terrain on which we can/must operate to express our inner self and enact our plans of self-optimisation. The care of the body is thus assimilated to the care of the self and takes on a moral value: if, in order to lead the 'good life', we are to implement the correspondence between the inner and the outer, we then need to make sure that our selfhood visibly shines on the surface of our flesh. In this sense, somatic culture is a culture of total visibility, where self and appearance coincide and profoundly shape subjective experiences (Ortega 2013, 86).

To uncover how this regime was brought about and how it affects our understanding of the body in terms of its relationship with clothes and fashion, I here propose to use an approach inspired by Foucault's genealogy. Writing in the 1960s Foucault (1966) described the emphasis on the body as a trait typical of modernity, concomitant with the emergence of a certain kind of individuality, a modern idea of the self as a unique and somehow sacred individual who needs to take priority on the collective. In sociology, and approximately at the same time, Goffman (1967, 47) too underlined the process of sacralisation of the individual as a characteristic of modern secular society. Commenting on Goffman's position on subjectivity, Collins (1986, 107) argues that the self "is the archetypal modern myth. We are compelled to have an individual self not because we actually have one but because social interaction requires us to act as if we do".

According to Foucault, the process of formation and sacralisation of the individual, as we conceive of it today, finds its origin in a more distant past and starts with a new conception of the body emerging around the end of the eighteenth century. In *Discipline and Punish* (1977), while examining the transformation of power from the *Ancien Régime* to the Enlightenment era, Foucault *de facto* reverses the platonic idea of the body as the prison of the soul by arguing that modernity is on the contrary an age of "docile bodies", an era in which "the soul (has become) the prison of the body". Here, he alludes to the idea that personality is not an innate endowment of human beings (and Goffman concurs) and a mark of each individual's subjectivity, but on the contrary it is a modern invention. More specifically, he argues, it is an effect of processes of subjectification enacted on the body and in the course of people's lives through discursive formations mobilised by (disciplinary) power. On this crucial point it is worth quoting Foucault directly (2006, 55):

> We can say that disciplinary power (...) fabricates subjected bodies; it pins the subject-function exactly to the body (...) Disciplinary power is individualising because it fastens the subject-function to the somatic singularity by means of a system of supervision (...) which projects a core of virtualities, a psyche.

In Foucault's view, this process of subjectification is interestingly linked to a reversal of visibility and invisibility characterising the transition from sovereign to disciplinary power; in the new regime, those who were once invisible spectators of a visible power are turned into visible, self-contained individualities because, and in as much as, they are subjected to a (now invisible) power. To use Crossley's poignant remark: "Power functions, in part, by making people visible" (1993, 401). The notion of persons as self-contained subjects, each endowed with their own self is, in this paradigm, an effect of a complex set of technologies which constitute persons as individuals within a specific field of visibility. In this chapter, I wish to suggest that the mirror is one of such technologies and that an exploration of its effects is important to understand how we tend to formulate and study our relationship with clothes. Furthermore, I wish to draw attention to the subjectifying role of fashion and clothes. For a long time, fashion has functioned as a marker of gender and class affiliation, while more recently (and since the appearance of the somatic individual) it has become a way of expressing the presupposed 'inner self', whose character must be converted and made explicit in the mirror image while getting dressed.

THE MIRROR AND THE VISUAL CONSTRUCTION OF SUBJECTIVITY

Mirror images are commonly understood as neutral reflections (Coleman 2013a, b) of bare facts, and yet, as I will show, they are implicated in many of the theories that modern Western thought has produced to explain the construction of selfhood and subjectivity. Indeed, I would suggest that in our culture, the idea of subjectivity is mostly theorised as an effect of the ability to see ourselves as reflections of our bodies. This ability, which apparently is typical of human beings and only shared with very few other mammals (highly evolved apes and dolphins), allows us to look at ourselves in the same way we look at others. As philosophers have repeatedly remarked, this is the very skill that provides the basis for the formation of a mind (the human) capable of developing objective thought. Indeed, particularly after Descartes, Western thought has been marked by an ocularcentric bias implying a split between a subjective (human) self, looking (down) on an objective world exterior to it, as from a vantage point and "outside time" (Jay 1994, 263).[1] When in the twentieth century, psychoanalysis emerged as the science of human behaviour, one of its main tasks was indeed to explain how human selfhood is formed. Perhaps not surprisingly, both Freud and Lacan brought to the fore the perils of a vision-based subjectivity. Freud's renowned theory of narcissism ([1914] 2014) characterises it as the absorption of the self in its mirror image, while his definition of the "uncanny" is "the name for everything that ought to have remained secret and hidden but has come to light" ([1919] 1990). The importance of the mirror in forging our individuality and, at the same time, the alienating potential of the mirror image are epitomised in the work of Jacques Lacan. In his influential lecture on the "Mirror Stage", Lacan ([1949] 1977) explains that when, between 6 and 18 months, the infant begins to recognise and identify with their image in the mirror, they derive from it an illusory sense of totality and, importantly, of *self-containment*. Some commentators have emphasised the fragility of this sense of self, calling Lacan's subject "decentred" (Evans 1999) and always on the brink of dissolution, or "a hoax by which we normalize an incoherent inner reality" (Wiley 2003, 504), which we cannot make sense of and

---

[1] Reflecting on this ocularcentric tradition Heidegger (1977, 134) describes it as "the conquest of the world as picture", which he regards as "[t]he fundamental event of the modern age".

cannot be symbolised nor represented. However, although critical of the illusionary representation of the ego, which they see as founded on a misapprehension,[2] both psychoanalysts describe modern identity as "rooted in the visual—the image of the self as other" (Evans 1999, 18). The distrust of the mirror was echoed in mid-twentieth-century France by phenomenologists Sartre and Merleau-Ponty, both drawing attention in their works to the alienating potential of the mirror reflection and to the fallouts of a vision-based notion of subjectivity. More specifically, Sartre ([1943] 2003) linked the objectification caused by the mirror to the experience of shame and its power to supress the individual's freedom by turning the subject into an object of an Other's gaze. On the other hand, Merleau-Ponty (1968) held the mirror responsible for the split between "bodiliness" and "corporeality", the objectifying transition from the body schema to the body-image, and showed how the transition hinders the automatic coherence of the subject with the surrounding world by prioritising vision as our relationship to an objective world. However, as Merleau-Ponty indicates, the appearance of our body is never just an object in the world, but our means of communicating with it and, as such, relates to it with all our senses. For Merleau-Ponty the awareness we have of our bodies is never just visual but fundamentally determined by the kinaesthetic sense deriving from our immersion in the world.[3] In this context phenomenologists argue in favour of a recovery of the multisensoriality of our being in the world. In the field of sociology, Nick Crossley (1995) attempts to develop a carnal approach to shift the attention from the analysis of body techniques as inscribed on the body, towards an emphasis of the body as an active agent in implementing these techniques. In the area of feminist studies, and talking specifically about the relationship between women and their clothes, Iris M. Young (2005, 69) suggests that: "we might conceive a mode of vision, [...], that is less a gaze,

---

[2] Talking about the self, Kaja Silverman argues: "This object (the self) is able to masquerade as a subject because it is what provides us with our sense of identity, and for most of us identity equals subjectivity. But identity is foundationally fictive: it is predicated on our (mis) recognition of ourselves first within our mirror reflection, and then within countless other human and representational '*imagoes*'" (2006, 36).

[3] It is worth noting that, at the core of the phenomenological perspectives there is an interest for the dynamic body–self–world relationship where subjectivity is understood from and as a first-person perspective of oneself as a self, and this includes the level of sensing one's body—one's heartbeat or breathing—as embodied, and as 'above all a relation to the world' (Zahavi 2001, 163) which must involve all senses.

distanced from and mastering its object, but an immersion in light and color". What Young proposes is a notion of perception that involves the use of all senses alongside the mere sense of sight and that entails the immersion of our body into the world, by erasing the distance between the origin of the gaze and the field with which the body is mingled.

While taking on board these insights about the 'dangers' of a vision-based notion of identity, I here want to draw attention on another consequence of the prioritisation of sight: seeing the reflection of our body in the mirror not only carries with it an objectifying effect but also clearly returns to us the image of the body as a bounded entity separate from its surroundings. In other words, when we see ourselves in the mirror, we see the contours of our body as boundaries of the self. Thus, our personal identity emerges as a "skin ego",[4] where the skin is perceived much more as a barrier between the inside and the outside than a permeable surface facilitating the flow of energies between human bodies and other human and non-human ones. This idea underpins the modern myths of autonomy and independence of the individual and constitutes the unacknowledged assumption of many forms of knowledge: that human beings are self-contained, clearly bounded subjects, whose bodily outline coincides with the territory of the self. Indeed, the notion of the somatic individual explicitly traces this correspondence, whereby body and self are like the two sides of a coin; if I mould one side, the other changes in a corresponding way. With these premises, although individuals are theorised as 'embodied', the transcendental subject in the world still remains intact, as does its 'window' on the outside: the body boundaries as the borders of the ego.[5]

---

[4] I am indebted to Renate Stauss for introducing me to this expression through her mentioning the work of Didier Anzieu (1989) during our discussions.

[5] The whole of phenomenology is permeated by the notion of subjectivity and subjective meanings, which are repeatedly described as unknowable by other human beings. For example, when exploring the conditions of intersubjectivity, another phenomenologist, Alfred Schutz (1967), recurrently argues that, while it is impossible to share the exact experience of another, the best we can do is to find overlaps between our individual experiences of the world. All this contributes to solidify a notion of the individual as a self-contained subject endowed with a consciousness, that is, an ability to make sense of their engagements with the world.

Clothing the Body/Self

By applying a genealogical approach inspired by Foucault, I have above tried to explain how modern subjectivity (in the form of the 'somatic individual') is a function of a power regime that shapes our selves through disciplining our bodies in various, culture-dependent ways. I have also proposed that the prominence of the body-image, as the exemplar type of contemporary subjectivity, not only endorses an objectified concept of selfhood, but also stresses its separateness from (and its ability to control) the world outside. This approach draws attention almost exclusively to the humans' ability for conscious deliberation, as rational (albeit) embodied subjects making (discursive/rational) sense of their experience. I now want to examine the impact that such notion of the body and self has had on the ways in which fashion studies have traditionally conceptualised the relationship between people and clothes. Broadly speaking, I suggest that because of the way subjectivity is defined, mainly through vision and therefore foregrounding the idea of the body as pre-eminently a body-image, scholars of fashion have traditionally been led to examine clothes and fashion as props in a representation of subjects' (supposedly) authentic identities.

Limiting the scope here just to contributions dating from the late twentieth century onwards, I note that scholars tend to focus their attention on the ways in which clothes might assist people in representing themselves in everyday life. For example, Fred Davis (1992) is interested in fashion and identity ambivalence and argues that, when selecting the clothes to wear, individuals are mostly attempting a synthesis between contradictory pulls concerning their gender identification, their membership in a social class or group, and the more or less overt expression of their sexuality. Fascinated by Goffman's dramaturgical approach, Finkelstein (1996, 1998, 2007) describes clothes and fashion as a way of enhancing our social persona, by attracting the attention and the admiration of others; in her analysis, clothes are ways of self-promoting, aimed at representing to the world "a more complex ego" (Finkelstein 1996, 40). In her view, fashion and clothes serve people in the processes of self-invention they constantly need to carry out in the various situations in which they engage. Other scholars prefer to take a semantic approach and consider fashion and clothes as a kind of language (Lurie, 1981) or at least a form of non-verbal communication expressing social identities and cultural affiliations (Barnard 1996; Hebdige 1979; Polhemus 1994). It was not until the dawn of the new millennium that fashion studies started opening up to a consideration of the body, with Entwistle's (2000) analysis of clothes as situated embodied practices and a flurry of anthropological studies aimed at recuperating the materiality of clothes when encountering human bodies (Woodward 2007; Guy and Banim 2000; Miller and Woodward 2010; Woodward and Fisher 2014). Indeed, these more recent studies do focus on the body as culturally shaped by its adornments (in the form of garments, accessories, etc.); however, many are still predicated on a dualistic view of the inner/outer duet and implicitly accept the notion of selfhood as the authentic core of a person that needs to be 'worn' on the body.

Some other recent 'waves' of fashion studies include scholars equally interested in recuperating the materiality of fashion by drawing attention to the multisensoriality of being dressed that, they argue (and I agree), has been completely disregarded in the dominant representational paradigm. These contributions mainly draw their inspiration from feminist phenomenologists such as Iris Young (2005) and Sandra Bartky (1991), who extensively applied Merleau-Ponty's and Sartre's insights to the study of women's bodies in the world. Echoing Entwistle's call for a paradigm shift in fashion studies, Llewellyn Negrin (2016) proposes the adoption of a framework that enables researchers to explore those aspects of dress that elude the visual and urges researchers to follow the path opened by Young and Entwistle. Rosie Findlay (2016, 81) also evokes phenomenology and Merleau-Ponty in her exploration of getting dressed as an "imaginative act" in which "the selection and wearing of clothes mediates one's being in the world (…) by affecting one's sense of who one is as clothed". Again, using the phenomenological notion of "lived body", Ellen Sampson (2018) explores how selves and garments become entwined and at the same time cleaved, when they encounter. Finally, Danielle Bruggeman (2017) shows, in a more applied way, how the emphasis on images, paralleled by a disregard for the embodied dimension of dressing and for the materiality of making and wearing clothes, has helped to make fashion and textile one of the most exploitative and ecologically unsustainable industries in the world.

Despite all these attempts to extend the scope of fashion studies by problematising the experience of the dressed body, it is worth pointing out that outside the academic debate, in the popular culture of fashion media, in the domains of digital platforms (such as Instagram and TikTok) populated by bloggers and influencers and constantly accessed all over the world by the public of fashion, the narrative of the outfit as an expression of the authentic self is still pervasive, with very few exceptions. The tale of the inner, deep, authentic self that needs to be put into existence through an adequately adorned body has never been stronger in a culture like ours, where identity politics keeps morphing into new demands (around the issues of gender, race, sex, sexuality, neurodiversity) to affirm the rights of the individual and their inner, unique core. Here I want to propose that, to a certain extent, this turmoil could be read in a significantly different key. I think that the pluralisation of claims in identity politics, rather than pointing to the uniqueness of the individual, may actually be revealing the precariousness of the subject and its susceptibility to change. Somehow, and perhaps subliminally, it speaks of people's frustration with the forms of subjectification that an invisible power imposes on their visibility and their (in the somatic individual) identity, and it shouts out their urge to escape from the (cultural) cages, those inflexible pillars of identity that box them into docile beings. Sensing the precariousness of all identification *dispositifs* in a world continually producing different versions of reality, more people feel an urge to resist subjectification in an attempt to embrace the chance of *being* less and *becoming* more. It is my contention that, when examined in its affective potential, the encounter of dress and fashion with our bodies can be explored as a way of transmitting affects (Brennan 2004), which can activate processes of transformation into different, albeit continuously flowing, forms of life. In the following section I try to explain how.

Through Multisensoriality into the Affects

The recovery of the multisensorial aspect of being dressed is undoubtedly a huge step forward in the uncovering of the traits of that experience, which a predominantly visual and representational perspective had long left out of focus. When we are putting on an outfit, although we are probably doing this while staring at a mirror and judging the emerging image as an object of the generalised Other (the gaze), at the same time we perceive a whole set of other sensations (tactile, olfactory, acoustic and sometimes even gustatory) that indeed complete our experience.[6] However, this approach remains statically focused on the body subject and falls short

---

[6] Interestingly scholars of fashion have underlined how these sensations often can and do connect to embodied habits and memory of past events and have shown that these connections give rise to specific subjects of fashion (Eckersley and Duff 2020, 1).

of accounting for the affective flows that take place between human bodies, their clothes and the environment. Therefore, I want to suggest here that there might be a more radical way to capture a fuller sense of the affective motions involved in the event of being dressed, which exceeds the multisensorial character of the experience and provides a chance for transformations of the body/self.

To outline this approach, I need to borrow, and partially 'misread', some concepts derived from Deleuze and Guattari's work: namely the notion of the body without organs and the related assemblage, the notion of territory and territorialisation, as well as lines of flight. As elsewhere discussed (Ruggerone 2017; Ruggerone and Stauss 2022) Deleuze and Guattari's notions of the Body without Organs (BwO) and that of assemblage[7] can assist in exploring a new dimension of our relationship with clothes: in particular, in the context of fashion theory, these concepts foreground the opportunity clothes afford us to start a process of becoming that leads to unforeseeable outputs. This conceptualisation ties into the reflections on subjectivity and the role of the mirror as an agent of subjectification epitomised in the act of dressing.

Influenced by Spinoza (2002), who invoked an attention on what the body can do as opposed to what the body is, Deleuze and Guattari (1987) discuss the notion of BwO as one term of a conceptual pair, where the body organism stands as the second term of the dyad.[8] In contrast to the organicist perspective of the human body, defined as an organised ensemble of organs with complementary functions, the BwO consists of pure desire and affective capabilities. It is a body that has been freed from the conventional organisation and standardised classification of the corporeal, it is what remains after the "phantasies, and significances and subjectifications" (Deleuze and Guattari 1987, 168) have been taken away; in Foucault's terms, it is a chance to break out from the categorical grid of the docile body. Furthermore, the BwO is not something we 'have'; rather it consists of the intensities liberated by taking it away from the organisation in systems and functions so that it becomes a site of virtual possibilities, an affective assemblage open to connect with other intensities in the

[7] For a broader discussion of these notions, see Buchanan (1997).
[8] Deleuze and Guattari's theorising often makes use of conceptual pairs; other examples drawn from their work include 'the smooth and the striated', 'the molar and the molecular', 'the minoritarian and the majoritarian', just to name a few. Although related to different purposes, each pair includes a force that organises and a second one that breaks out and away from this organisation, to be eventually re-organised.

surroundings. Against this background, the traditional notion of the stable (even though multisensorial) body emerges only as a "momentary sedimentation of [a] dynamic process of oscillating connections" (Stark 2016, 71). In *A Thousand Plateaus* (Deleuze and Guattari 1987), the theme of the organism is discussed in parallel with two other themes, or strata (namely significance and subjectification), where all three are seen as devices intent on tying us down to functions of meaning and subjective identity. In the context of this discussion, individual identity, materialised in the body organism and recognised in the mirror image, emerges as a *territory*, an ordered domain of being, functioning on the basis of an inclusion-exclusion mechanism. The body organism is a territory that generates selfhoods and defines subjects supposedly capable of dominating an object-world through science and language.[9]

As elsewhere proposed (Ruggerone and Stauss 2022), I contend that the mirror, commonly perceived as a neutral reflective surface, plays a crucial role in performing this territorialisation: it carves a frozen image of an integrated body out of a fluid composition of dispersive energies, thereby channelling the affective drives of the body into normalised directions. The mirror effectively turns the awareness of our body into a consciousness: a perspective on the body informed by the other's (social) gaze that enters the body into a power-regulated territory where norms and rules about how to manage and handle it are in force. In terms of the approach that informs mainstream studies of fashion and dress, I would suggest that it is this fixation of the flux of becoming into a solid notion of self-contained identity that influences the interpretation of the clothed body as a sign of a person's identity, a manufactured representation of their inner personality.[10]

Following on from these premises, the attempt to make oneself a BwO emerges as a form of resistance aimed at exploring the bodily capacities

---

[9] Modern science has an iconic basis that can be traced back to the ancient Greeks (Plato's cave), through medieval science of optics and Renaissance perspective, to eighteenth-century empiricism (Jay 1994, 38–40). In Lacan the acquisition of language marks the entrance into the Symbolic with the overcoming of the narcissistic mirror stage and the production of the 'healthy subject', emerging from the resolution of the Oedipal phase and the formation of the Super-ego (Jay 1994, 351–2).

[10] BwO is not the sensorial body of phenomenology. The latter is a body organism where different organs are predisposed to experience different sensations and a body subject that makes sense of them. On the contrary, the BwO is a variable composition of molecules, neurons, cells but also ideas, signs, cultural symbols and so on.

before the territory of the body organism is formed (before Foucault's *dispositifs* of subjectification are enacted) and outside the paradigm of the body subject; it is also a project that, when applied to the relationship with clothes, can open up a different way of exploring the phenomenon of being dressed as well as the becomings that clothes and fashion could trigger when donned on human bodies.

The possibility to capture the affective dimension of dress is premised on a process of, in Deleuze and Guattari's language, *deterritorialization*. Through attempting to depersonalise oneself and renouncing the notion of body/selfhood as a linear identity for which experiences are related as to a subject that precedes and perceives them (the body subject of phenomenology), one may grasp the affects that ensure continuous becoming (Breuer 2015, 135). In the sphere of becoming, "the self that contemplates is nothing other than the singularities it perceives" (Colebrook 2002, 155), where each singularity alludes to the temporary positioning of a body which will immediately transform again, when relations with other bodies occur. From this standpoint a new perspective can be developed that focuses on clothes' capacity to intercept the affects that precede the formation of subjectivity and are created by the flows of intensities among all the bodies involved in an event. For fashion studies such a perspective would entail capturing what happens between human bodies, clothing and the environment and eventually being able to grasp, albeit momentarily, the many subjects of fashion forming and re-forming in a given scene. When this approach is adopted, what stands out to the scholar's attention is not the looks, nor the sensorial feedback the subject experiences, but the new modes of existing spinning off the encounter along lines which cannot be predicted. What I want to ultimately suggest is that when clothes are donned on a body, they have the potential to function as Deleuzian lines of flight, thereby dragging the human body out of the conventional and power-infused body-image into unpredictable lines of becoming. As Deleuze and Guattari (1987, 239) put it: "lines of flight [...] never consist in running away from the world but rather in causing runoffs, as when you drill a hole in a pipe". When we put on our clothes and wear them in a live event, we open up the possibility of becoming by letting ourselves susceptible to what Teresa Brennan (2004) has called "the transmission of affects".

Concluding Remarks

In this chapter I have tried to interweave philosophical and cultural theories of the body with perspectives in fashion studies, in an attempt to create a productive conversation between the two. It is my firm belief that fashion studies can only evolve towards an appreciation of the non-representational aspects of clothes if they interconnect and cross-fertilise with body studies, their conceptualisations of subjectivities and their explorations of the place that human bodies occupy in a world where the boundaries between nature and culture are rapidly shifting. Conversely, I believe that, due to the fast-paced progress in the sciences of life and in the technologies supporting them, the human sciences of the body must continue to develop and deepen the study of the relationship between human and non-human bodies, exploring objects and their agency, including clothes. More than ever before, well-being is now emerging as a disposition created at the intersection of (and striking a positive affective balance between) biological, psychological and social/collective factors. Interestingly many scholars are now actively re-engaging with some minoritarian strands of nineteenth/early-twentieth-century philosophy and sociology interested in exploring experiences that are ephemeral, invisible and have to do with extra-conscious dimensions and with collective contagion (Blackman 2008). Authors such as William James, Henri Bergson and Gabriel Tarde are being revisited, and their work reconsidered by scholars investigating affects and mood (Brennan 2004; Despret 2004; Silver 2011; Ringmar 2017; Colombetti 2017), the body as a process (Deleuze and Guattari 1987; Blackman 2020), the agency of objects and the limits of science to theorise affects (Latour 2007; Schiermer 2011; Massumi 2002; Stengers 1997). I believe that keeping in conversation with these developments is crucial for fashion scholars wishing to uncover and explore the affective dimension that fashion, clothes and all bodily apparel release, when encountering the human body in the lifeworld.

Of course, in this novel, interdisciplinary field, the issue of identity and subjectivity remains the elephant in the room. While most of these philosophical perspectives tend to hollow out the notion of the autonomous, unique subject, on the other hand, the attachment to the idea of the independent, unrepeatable, authentic individual has never been stronger, spreading from the neoliberal culture of Western countries to gain popularity all other the world. In an unstoppable process and almost virally, the myth of personalisation has evolved from a market slogan to lure consumers in, to an all-pervasive mantra that shapes the approach to a whole set of practices, from the selection of everyday commodities through to educational methods, organisational systems and even medical and therapeutic treatments. In this context, I think the need for a strand of fashion studies geared to address the affective dimension of being dressed will grow much stronger. The ability to explore the events of dress unburdened by the assumption of a fixed, self-contained personal identity will prove effective to overcome the neoliberal rhetoric of the exceptional individual, bursting to express their unique personality in (paradoxically) ever more standardised lines of clothing. Instead, it will help to shape an approach able to capture the incessant becoming of matter, ideas and practices in which clothed bodies take part. As Deleuze explained, the dynamics of life proceeds through reiterated creation of territories (order) and deterritorialisations (temporary disorder), and this pertains to all aspects of life. In terms of identity, it seems clear to me that many thrusts towards deterritorialisation are currently ongoing, and fashion studies are constantly called upon to refine their tools to be able to make sense of them.

REFERENCES

Anzieu, Didier. 1989. *The Skin Ego: A Psychoanalytic Approach to the Self.* Translated by Chris Turner. New Haven, CT; London, UK: Yale University Press.
Barnard, Malcolm. 1996. *Fashion as Communication.* London: Routledge.
Bartky, Sandra. 1991. *Femininity and Domination: Studies in the Phenomenology of Oppression.* London, UK: Routledge.
Blackman, Lisa. 2008. Affect, Relationality and the Problem of Personality. *Theory, Culture & Society* 25 (1): 23–47.
———. 2020. *The Body: The Key Concepts.* London: Routledge.
Bordo, Susan. 1993. *Unbearable Weight: Feminism, Western Culture, and the Body.* University of California Press.
Bourdieu, Pierre. 1984. *Distinction: A Social Critique of the Judgement of Taste.* Cambridge, MA: Harvard University Press.
Brennan, Teresa. 2004. *The Transmission of Affect.* Ithaca and London: Cornell University Press.
Breuer, Rebecca Louise. 2015. *Fashion Beyond Identity: The Three Ecologies of Dress.* Amsterdam: University of Amsterdam Press.
Bruggeman, Danielle. 2017. *Dissolving the Ego of Fashion: Engaging with Human Matters.* Arnhem: Artez Press.
Buchanan, Ian. 1997. The Problem of the Body in Deleuze and Guattari, Or, What Can a Body Do? *Body & Society* 3 (3): 73–91.

Caldwell, Christine. 2016. Body Identity Development: Definitions and Discussions. *Body, Movement and Dance in Psychotherapy* 11 (4): 220–234.
Colebrook, Claire. 2002. *Gilles Deleuze*. London; New York: Routledge.
Coleman, Rebecca. 2013a. Sociology and the Virtual: Interactive Mirrors, Representational Thinking and Intensive Power. *The Sociological Review* 61 (1): 1–20.
———. 2013b. *Transforming Images: Screens, Affects, Futures*. Abingdon: Routledge.
Collins, Randall. 1986. The Passing of Intellectual Generations: Reflections on the Death of Erving Goffman. *Sociological Theory* 4 (1): 106–113.
Colombetti, Giovanna. 2017. The Embodied and Situated Nature of Goods. *Philosophia* 45 (4): 1437–1451.
Conboy, Katie, Nadia Medina, and Sarah Stanbury, eds. 1997. *Writing on the Body. Female Embodiment and Feminist Theory*. New York: Columbia University Press.
Crossley, Nick. 1993. The Politics of the Gaze: Between Foucault and Merleau-Ponty. *Human Studies* 16 (4): 399–419.
———. 1995. Merleau-Ponty, the Elusive Body and Carnal Sociology. *Body & Society* 1 (1): 43–63.
Davis, Fred. 1992. *Fashion, Culture and Identity*. Chicago: The University of Chicago Press.
Deleuze, Gilles, and Felix Guattari. 1987. *A Thousand Plateaus: Capitalism and Schizophrenia*. Translated by Brian Massumi. Minneapolis, MN: University of Minnesota Press.
Despret, Vinciane. 2004. The Body We Care For: Figures of Anthropo-zoo-genesis. *Body & Society* 10 (2): 111–134.
Eckersley, Andrea. 2008. A Non-representational Approach to Fashion. IFFTI 2008—10th Annual Conference of International Foundation of Fashion Technology Institutes. Accessed 6 June 2016. http://iffti.org/downloads/papers-presented/x-RMIT,%202008/papers/p198.pdf.
Eckersley, Andrea, and Cameron Duff. 2020. Bodies of Fashion and the Fashioning of Subjectivity. *Body and Society* 22 (10): 1–27.
Entwistle, Joanne. 2000. *The Fashioned Body: Fashion, Dress and Modern Social Theory*. Cambridge: Polity Press.
Evans, Caroline. 1999. Masks, Mirrors and Mannequins: Elsa Schiaparelli and the Decentered Subject. *Fashion Theory* 3 (1): 3–32.
Findlay, Rosie. 2016. 'Such Stuff as Dreams Are Made On' Encountering Clothes, Imagining Selves. *Cultural Studies Review* 22 (1): 78–94.
Finkelstein, Joanne. 1996. *After a Fashion*. Melbourne: Melbourne University Press.
———. 1998. *Fashion: An Introduction*. New York: New York University Press.
———. 2007. *The Art of Self Invention: Image and Identity in Popular Visual Culture*. London: I.B. Tauris.

Foucault, Michel. 1977. *Discipline and Punish*. Translated by Alan Sheridan. New York: Pantheon.
———. 2006. *Psychiatric Power. Lectures at the College de France 1973–1974*. Translated by Graham Burchell. New York: Picador
Freud, Sigmund. [1914] 2014. *On Narcissism: An Introduction*. England: Read Books Ltd.
———. [1919] 1990. *The Uncanny* The Penguin Freud Library Vol 14: Art and Literature, trans. James Strachey, London: Penguin.
Goffman, Erving. 1959. *The Presentation of the Self in Everyday Life*. New York: Doubleday Anchor Books.
———. 1963. *Behaviour in Public Places: Notes on the Social Organisation of Gatherings*. New York: Free Press.
———. 1966. *Les mots et les choses [The order of things]*. Paris: Éditions Gallimard.
———. 1967. *Interaction Ritual: Essays on Face-to-Face Interaction*. New York: Doubleday Anchor Books.
———. 1972. *Relations in Public: Microstudies of the Public Order*. New York: Harper and Row.
Guy, Ali, and Maura Banim. 2000. Personal Collections: Women's Clothing Use and Identity. *Journal of Gender Studies* 9: 313–327.
Hebdige, Dick. 1979. *The Meaning of Style*. London: Routledge.
Heidegger, Martin. 1977. The Age of the World Picture. In *The Questions Concerning Technology and Other Essays*, 115–154. New York, NY: Harper & Row.
Heyes, Cressida. 2007. *Self-Transformations: Foucault, Ethics, and Normalized Bodies*. New York: Oxford University Press.
Jay, Martin. 1994. *Downcast Eyes: The Denigration of Vision in Twentieth Century French Thought*. Berkeley, CA: University of California Press.
Lacan, Jacques. [1949] 1977. The Mirror Stage as Formative of the Function of the I as Revealed in Psychoanalytic Experience. In *Ecrits: A Selection*, trans. Alan Sheridan, 1–7. London: Routledge.
Latour, Bruno. 2007. *Reassembling the Social: An Introduction to Actor-Network-Theory*. Oxford: Oxford University Press.
Lurie, Alison. 1981. *The Language of Clothes*. New York: Random House.
Marsden, Jill. 2004. Deleuzian Bodies, Feminist Tactics. *Women: A Cultural Review* 15 (3): 308–319.
Massumi, Brian. 2002. *Parables for the Virtual: Movement, Affect, Sensation*. Durham, NC: Duke University Press.
Mauss, Marcel, [1934] 1979. Body Techniques. In *Sociology and Psychology: Essays*, 95–123. London: Routledge and Kegan Paul.
Merleau-Ponty, Maurice. 1968. *The Visible and the Invisible*. Evanston, IL: Northwestern University Press.

Miller, Daniel, and Sophie Woodward, eds. 2010. *Global Denim*. London: Bloomsbury.
Negrin, Llewellyn. 2016. Maurice Merleau-Ponty: The Corporeal Experience of Fashion. In *Thinking through Fashion: A Guide to Key Theorists*, ed. Agnès Rocamora and Anneke Smelik, 115–131. London, UK; New York, NY: I.B. Tauris.
Ortega, Francisco. 2013. *Corporeality, Medical Technologies and Contemporary Culture*. London: Birkbeck Law Press.
Parkins, Ilya. 2008. Building a Feminist Theory of Fashion: Karen Barad's Agential Realism. *Australian Feminist Studies* 23 (58): 501–515.
Polhemus, Ted. 1994. *Streetstyle: From Sidewalk to Catwalk*. London: Thames & Hudson.
Ringmar, Erik. 2017. Outline of a Non-deliberative, Mood-based Theory of Action. *Philosophia* 45 (4): 1527–1539.
Rose, Nikolas. 2001. The Politics of Life Itself. *Theory, Culture & Society* 18 (6): 1–30.
Ruggerone, Lucia. 2017. The Feeling of Being Dressed: Affect Studies and the Clothed Body. *Fashion Theory* 21 (5): 573–593.
Ruggerone, Lucia, and Renate Stauss. 2022. The Deceptive Mirror: The Dressed Body Beyond Reflection. *Fashion Theory* 26 (2): 211–235.
Sampson, Ellen. 2018. The Cleaved Garment: The Maker, the Wearer and the 'Me and Not Me' of Fashion Practice. *Fashion Theory* 22 (3): 341–360.
———. 2020. *Worn: Footwear, Attachment and the Affects of Wear*. Bloomsbury Publishing.
Sartre, Jean Paul. [1943] 2003. *Being and Nothingness: An Essay on Phenomenological Ontology*. London, UK: Routledge.
Schiermer, Bjorn. 2011. Quasi-objects, Cult Objects and Fashion Objects: On Two Kinds of Fetishism on Display in Modern Culture. *Theory, Culture & Society* 28 (1): 81–102.
Schutz, Alfred. 1967. *The Phenomenology of the Social World*. Evanston: Northwestern University Press.
Silver, Daniel. 2011. The Moodiness of Action. *Sociological Theory* 29 (3): 199–222.
Silverman, Kaja. 2006. The World Wants Your Desire. *Subjectivity and Identity* 19: 31–41.
Spinoza, Baruch. 2002. *Spinoza: Complete Works*. Cambridge, MA: Hackett Publishing.
Stark, Hannah. 2016. *Feminism after Deleuze*. London, UK: Bloomsbury Academic.
Stengers, Isabelle. 1997. *Power and Invention: Situating Science*. Minneapolis: University of Minnesota Press.
Tsakiris, Manos. 2017. The Multisensory Basis of the Self: From Body to Identity to Others. *The Quarterly Journal of Experimental Psychology* 70 (4): 597–609.

Wiley, Norbert. 2003. The Self as Self-fulfilling Prophecy. *Symbolic Interaction* 26 (4): 501–513.
Woodward, Sophie. 2007. *Why Women Wear What They Wear*. Oxford: Berg.
Woodward, Sophie, and Tom Fisher. 2014. Fashioning through Materials: Material Culture, Materiality and Processes of Materialization. *Critical Studies in Fashion & Beauty* 5 (1): 3–22.
Young, Iris. 2005. *On Female Body Experience*. Oxford: Oxford University Press.
Zahavi, Dan. 2001. Beyond Empathy: Phenomenological Approaches to Intersubjectivity. *Journal of Consciousness Studies* 8 (5–6): 151–167.

PART IV

Affective Embodiment in Media

CHAPTER 14

Melancholy Fashion Moods in Aotearoa New Zealand

Harriette Richards

In 2016, fashion journalist Sonia Sly visited the Auckland studio of designer James Dobson of Jimmy D as part of her 'My Heels Are Killing Me' series for Radio New Zealand. Talking about the appeal of his work, Sly suggested that Jimmy D offers something different in the New Zealand market, something akin to the dark 'vibe' of Nom*d, the iconic brand established by designer Margi Robertson in 1986. Dobson, who established his brand in 2004, agreed, recalling that, in the early years of his career, he was often compared to Nom*d. 'Did you hate that?' Sly asked. Dobson responded:

> God! No! Margi from Nom*d has been such a huge supporter of my label from the very beginning... There hadn't really been like a second wave come through. So, I did get compared to them a lot because there weren't any other references in New Zealand... But I think I've definitely forged my own way... I always try and bring in a sense of humour to what I do. I love

H. Richards (✉)
RMIT University, Melbourne, VIC, Australia
e-mail: harriette.richards@rmit.edu.au

© The Author(s), under exclusive license to Springer Nature Switzerland AG 2023
R. Filippello, I. Parkins (eds.), *Fashion and Feeling*, Palgrave Studies in Fashion and the Body,
https://doi.org/10.1007/978-3-031-19100-8_14

dark. I love the dark side of things but I also like to have a sense of humour with what I do… I have kind of a dark sense of humour. (Sly 2016)

What was interesting about this part of the conversation was that Sly was evoking familiar comparisons between Jimmy D and Nom*d based on their shared 'vibe' or mood. She was drawing connections between Dobson's and Robertson's shared use of black and penchant for dark wit. As I was exploring the fashion moods (Findlay 2022; Parkins 2021; Sheehan 2018) of Jimmy D, I came across an interview in the University of Otago student magazine *Critic* with the designer Lela Jacobs (Averis 2011). Wellington-based Jacobs launched her eponymous label in 2010 and, like Dobson, has become known for her avant-garde approach to design and her evocative, darkly moody collections. In the interview, journalist Grace Averis asked Jacobs to describe the mood of her new collection, 'This Crooked Way.' Jacobs responded simply: 'Everything is quite dark, always monochrome.'

This recurrent reference to darkness of mood struck me. It echoed earlier descriptions of New Zealand fashion at the turn of the millennium as 'dark, edgy and intellectual' (Molloy 2004), referring in large part to the work of heritage brands such as Nom*d and Zambesi, established by Robertson's sister Elisabeth Findlay and her husband Neville in 1979.[1] Much has been written about this moment in New Zealand fashion history, and about the work of Nom*d and Zambesi in particular (Molloy and Larner 2013; Hammonds and Regnault 2010; Molloy 2004). In contrast, despite the fact that Dobson has been credited with establishing the 'second-generation New Zealand look, bringing a fresh approach to the "dark and intellectual" characteristics that remain part of local fashion culture' (Hammonds and Regnault 2010, 379), there is a dearth of scholarship investigating how these dark moods shape—and are shaped by—the work of younger designers such as Dobson or Jacobs. The similarity in the feelings evoked by these designers interests me precisely because it speaks

---

[1] As Lucy Hammonds (2010, 330) has pointed out, the New Zealand brands of the 1990s 'were not uniformly bound by the dark and moody personality that was fast attaching itself to local fashion. Helen Cherry collections [for example] were more aptly described as celebratory rather than cerebral.' Similarly, Doris de Pont (2012, 34) has noted the way the idea of New Zealand fashion as 'dark, edgy and intellectual' was seized upon and picked up by the media as actuality following the showing of the 'New Zealand Four' (Zambesi, WORLD, Karen Walker and Nom*d) at London Fashion Week in 1999 'despite the obvious disjunct between that description and the reality of, for example, the WORLD collection.'

to something lasting in the resonance of this dark mood in Aotearoa New Zealand, not only in fashion but in art, film, literature and poetry. There is no shortage of scholarship on the so-called darker side of New Zealand culture, the sense of unease and the preponderant prevalence of ghosts (Conrich 2012; Kavka et al. 2006; Schafer 1998; Neill 1995). Much of this work, identifying the presence of darkness, a feeling of profound loss and a deep sense of ambivalence, defines this uneasiness in reference to gothic traditions. This is understandable, given that much of this cultural production fits the description of the gothic mode as 'a slapstick style progressively undercut by a growing sense of desperation and a heightened sense of threat' (Perry 1994, 76). However, for me, reference to the gothic does not fully account for the complexity of this evocative feeling, especially in New Zealand fashion. Instead, I suggest that we would do better to understand this mood in relation to melancholia, characterised by a sense of loss 'that is blurred and impossible to locate' (Ferber 2013, 22) and a 'spirit of contradictions' that endows such work simultaneously with dark disquiet and sublime beauty (Benjamin 2009, 149).

In order to think through the connections between place and melancholy mood in the fashion of Aotearoa New Zealand, I draw on the work of Jonathan Flatley (2008, 5), who suggests that 'to be in the world is to be in a mood,' and Ben Highmore (2016), who writes about the 'structures of feeling' that shape the cultural worlds we find ourselves in. These moods are shaped by the world around us, yet we also shape or put into circulation certain moods. Accordingly, those moods are in place and time and in the material of our lives. When we remind ourselves, as Highmore (2016, 145) writes, 'that 'feeling' is related to a world of touch, to a sensual world that is fabricated out of wood, steel, denim, crushed-velvet and tarmac' we can pay closer 'attention to the changes in the hum-drum material world of carpets and curries, beanbags and beansprouts'—or, indeed, hemlines and shirt cuffs. Certainly, when we pay attention to the feelings of the material world, we become attuned to the social, cultural and political dimensions of our everyday lives. It is worth noting here, however, that I am not interested so much in the structures of feeling embedded in what Highmore (2016, 145) calls the 'accoutrements of domestic, habitual life'—in other words, the clothes we wear every day. There are plenty of other scholars, many of whom are featured within these pages, whose work engages in fashion in this form. Rather, I am interested here in the way fashion designers both *produce* moods and *reflect* the moods of place and time. Focusing on two images—one from

Jimmy D's 'Portrait of a Reputation' Spring/Summer 2019 (SS19) collection and one from Lela Jacobs' A-E-I-O-U-Y 2019/2020 collection—I ask: How do fashion designers use the sensual, fabricated world to produce feelings, conjure vibes, evoke moods? And what do these moods, vibes or feelings tell us about the cultural context in which that fashion is produced? I argue that the 'anxieties of belonging' (Slater 2019), which characterise settler existence within Aotearoa New Zealand, contribute to and reinforce the sense of unease, loss and ambivalence that informs the melancholy mood of much New Zealand fashion.

INHERITED MOOD-WORLDS

Fashion has an intimate relationship with cultural feelings, involved in the shaping and reshaping of the world around us and how we perceive our place within it. According to Highmore (2016, 146) attending to 'structures of feeling'—Raymond Williams' term relating, broadly, to the affective resonance of an age or period in time—'allows us access to the way feelings and tastes are an activity of "worlding" that renders life *this* life and not another, and renders time as *this* time and not another' (original emphasis). The structures of feeling that shape our cultural worlds provide us a means to better understand the specificity of time and place. It must be noted, however, that these sensorial 'worlds' are inhabited subjectively: particular sets of 'feelings' are 'felt' differently by different people. The mood-world I inhabit may be different from that inhabited by my neighbour; the cultural feelings I experience are based on my experience, social background, gender and racial identity.[2] Nevertheless, moods are not only personal. As Clare Hemmings (2012, 528) puts it, mood 'is experienced at the individual level, but does not originate in the individual's body.' Mood is public as much as it is private; moods are infectious or 'catching,' meaning that we share mood together. As such, a mood-world is cultural, resonant with the feelings of the age, both time and place.

Mood permeates the cultural products and artefacts of that time and place, which not only reflect that mood but also contribute to its

---

[2] For Hemmings (2012, 527) 'any theory of mood needs to take gender into account' in order to counter the sense that mood is neutral and to challenge the otherwise easy distinction between mood (as sustained) and affect (as transitory). Attending to the gendered character of mood, Hemmings (2012, 529–31) argues, allows us to see the ways in which mood functions as a 'regulatory regime' that 'keeps the public/private divide intact,' yet also to acknowledge the 'permeability' of this divide.

production and perpetuation. For Highmore (2017, 13), 'moods are like weather, they have their own pressure systems, there is never a possibility of having "no weather," and they exist as atmosphere.' The cultural mood of time and place circulates atmospherically; we are in it, regardless of or even despite our personal feelings. Yet we are not simply *in* a mood. The typography of our surroundings (if we continue this metaphor) alters and informs the atmospheric vibe. In other words, not only are we affected by mood, but we can also inform or produce the emergence of new or changed moods. The world, and our existence in it, is filtered through mood. And, as Flatley (2008, 5), following Martin Heidegger, writes, 'because we never find ourselves nowhere, because we always already find ourselves somewhere specific, we are never not in a mood.' Not only are we always in a mood, but we also 'find ourselves in moods that have already been inhabited by others, that have already been shaped or put into circulation, and that are already there around us' (Flatley 2008, 5). We live, Highmore (2017, 13) notes, in the 'mood-worlds we've inherited. But our mood-worlds are also determined by the force fields currently as work in society.' Moods and the worlds they shape are not static. As time changes, history shifts and so too do the cultural moods we live amongst. At the same time, the mood-worlds we inherit remain resonant, reverberating across time and space. For the dress cultures of Aotearoa New Zealand, this inheritance is crucial to the cultural feelings produced by contemporary designers.

One of the first times that a remarkably melancholy mood was identified in New Zealand fashion was in 1997, when four New Zealand designers (Wallace Rose, Zambesi, WORLD and swimwear company Moontide) showed at Australian Fashion Week for the first time. The Zambesi collection in particular made a big impression, with New Zealand fashion historian Claire Regnault (2012, 204) noting that their 'dark and moody combinations of wool pinstripe and guipure lace and dazzling ivory and white layers won plaudits, and sparked intrigue among the international contingent.' *Elle* magazine's Lee Tulloch praised the distinctive fashion shown by the New Zealand designers, writing: 'Although much more somber than any of the other shows, Zambesi's fantastically rich and inventive collection... makes me wonder about New Zealand and the depth of [artistic] talent there' (quoted in Regnault 2012, 204). Comparing the New Zealand designers to their Australian counterparts, journalists suggested that 'the New Zealand look seems a lot darker than Australia's. More intellectual' (Molloy and Larner 2013, 129). The shows presented by New Zealand designers did not just *look* different, but they *felt* different. In attempting to put into words the differences between the cultural moods of the fashion produced by New Zealand and Australian designers, journalists wrote that it 'seemed' darker, it *felt* 'more somber.'

The idea that New Zealand fashion was characterised by a darkly beautiful, melancholy mood was reiterated in press articles both overseas and at home—regardless of its relevance. The perception was so far-reaching that in 2001 Australian fashion historian Margaret Maynard (2001, 186) wrote:

> New Zealand women's fashion has shown itself to have a clearly defined, though darkly romantic, even gothic style… featuring seriously minded, neutrally dark and moody styles which seemed to capture some of the fin de siècle or millennial anxieties. There is an inward-looking quality to their work… a characteristic brooding quality.

Despite the fact that these descriptors did not (and do not) represent the entirety of New Zealand fashion, they became understood as representative of a unique New Zealand fashion identity. The idea that New Zealand fashion was characterised by this seriousness, this delicate beauty, this brooding quality, was taken up by the media and the government, who were in the process of producing a new image of contemporary New Zealand that promoted global urbanity rather than bucolic rurality. For Trade New Zealand (TNZ), the international acclaim afforded New Zealand fashion designers at the turn of the millennium was seen as an avenue through which they could 'add sophisticated, creative and cosmopolitan nuances to the indigenous, rural and green "New Zealand Way," images by then being routinely used to promote the country's export industries' (Molloy and Larner 2013, 53). The adoption of this sense of melancholy into the official national character has had profound implications for how New Zealand fashion has evolved into the twenty-first century.

The promotion, by the media and via TNZ marketing, of this dark moodiness—at the expense of other, lighter, more joyous fashion in New Zealand—at the turn of the millennium effectively shaped the fashion atmosphere in this country. Indeed, the melancholy moods taken up with such fervour by designers such as Dobson and Jacobs have been directly informed by the moods already in circulation, the moods that we inherit.[3] However, these cultural feelings are more than simply a matter of inherited atmospheric feeling. In a 2011 article for the *New Zealand Herald*, fashion journalist Zoe Walker asked whether the 'dark and moody' definition of New Zealand fashion was still relevant. She suggested that the 'darker mood' that had long lain beneath New Zealand fashion—'whether it be Karen Walker's angsty outsider tendencies, Kate Sylvester's smartypants muse, or Nom*D's long-lasting penchant for black'—had started to shift. A new wave of young designers was reshaping understandings of what constitutes New Zealand fashion. And yet, that darker mood remained. Walker wrote:

> Some would be hard pressed to find the darkness in some of the young labels who now form the strength and future of the local industry—think of Juliette Hogan's floaty pleated skirts, Stolen Girlfriends Club's cheeky irreverence or Ruby's girlish, youthful spirit. But look deeper and you'll see that even today there is an underlying *moodiness*. Those dark and intellectual ideas are there, hidden within the quirks—the angst-trimmed nostalgia of Twenty-Seven Names, Lonely Hearts' love affair with the outsider, Salasai's unassuming androgyny. Then there are those where the moodiness and intellectualism is obvious; labels like Cybèle, Jimmy D, Maaike and Company of Strangers. (Walker 2011; emphasis added)

If mood is about more than simple inheritance, why does this 'underlying moodiness' persist? What is it about the culture of Aotearoa New Zealand that makes this mood resonate across time and different artistic mediums? While Jimmy D and Lela Jacobs are certainly not the only designers to inhabit this inherited mood-world, they are two of the most prominent. Their work stands out in the perpetuation of this feeling in New Zealand fashion; they demonstrate the ongoing relevance of, even need for, expressions of melancholy mood.

---

[3] This is not to say, however, that the mood-worlds we inherit are the *only* ones we can inhabit. There are many New Zealand designers, including Trelise Cooper and WORLD, who push back against this cultural feeling of melancholy, instead producing bright, vibrant fashion brimming with optimism.

Underlying Moodiness

The darkness of mood and abundant use of black recognised in the work of these New Zealand designers have been framed as uniquely characteristic of New Zealand fashion. However, these designers both explicitly and implicitly refer to and rely on the work of numerous international fashion designers for inspiration. Both Zambesi's Liz Findlay and Nom*d's Margi Robertson cite Rei Kawakubo of Comme des Garçons and Yohji Yamamoto—avant-garde Japanese designers who work with black, asymmetry and deconstruction—as direct inspirations. Black is used widely in fashion for a multitude of reasons, not least of all in the pursuit of an edgy and intellectual style. The appeal of black stems from the nuance implied in its depths. Far from being a flat and empty colour, devoid of life, black is multiple, reflective and absorbing (Pastoureau 2008). Black can be cold, blue-based, yet it can also be warm. Black can be sharp, strong and dark, yet it can also be soft, textured and light. For a designer like Jacobs, black allows for the exploration of texture. As she explained to Regnault in 2012: 'The fabric comes first and design second with most of my work… If you were to take this same process and do it in colour it would be about the colour and the textures and true fibres would not get the attention they deserve' (208). For Dobson, black is appealing because it allows him to explore volume: 'As a designer that's so focused on volume and the sculptural aspects of a garment, I can only visualise these shapes in black—there is no distraction, it's the quintessential anti-colour colour' (cited in Regnault 2012, 210). These descriptions of the creative use of black echo John Harvey's (1995, 10–14) definition of black as the 'colour that is without colour, without light, the colour of grief, of loss, of humility, of guilt, of shame' the paradox-colour, the colour that is no-colour.[4] The way these designers employ black is fascinating, and yet the use of black alone does not produce a feeling of brooding moodiness or melancholy.

While both Dobson and Jacobs undoubtedly use plenty of black, they also frequently use colour and fun prints in their collections. So, what makes (much of) their work melancholy? I argue that, for these designers, melancholy mood is about more than colour, or tone or even the garments themselves; it is produced through an amalgam of details, including

---

[4] It is important to note that black is also embedded in the cultural identity of Aotearoa New Zealand, perhaps most iconically in the All Blacks and their internationally recognisable black rugby uniform. Thanks to the All Blacks, Ron Palenski (2012, 105) writes, 'Black has been beautiful in New Zealand since the last quarter of the nineteenth century.'

the garments, the model, the setting, the show, the photography of the collection. Together, these elements produce an affective atmosphere. As the fashion journalist Robin Givhan (2015) writes about fashion shows: 'Telling a story through fashion only begins with the clothes. A fashion show is a symphony of graphics, models, makeup, props, lighting and a host of other details, most notably, the music. It sets the mood. Because after the designers make the frocks, to sell them, they have to create a little magic.' The magic of mood-making is crucial to producing desire, inducing customers to buy; it is also fundamental to the development of brand identity and recognition. How this mood is conjured in images differs somewhat from that in a live show (at the very least, there is no music in an image), and yet both elicit what Eugenie Shinkle (2008, 216), drawing from affect theory, calls an 'affective response' in the viewer.[5] Just as being in the presence of a catwalk show has a physical impact on the bodies of the audience members, so too does being in the presence of a fashion image. As Roberto Filippello (2018, 136) describes it, when looking at an image we become 'caught in the dynamics of affective exchange between our body and the bodies in the pictures, both of which are situated in a social and material environment.' We feel ourselves in space and time, understanding the body in the image in an alternative environment yet feeling the exchange between our body and theirs.

The first of the two images I want to discuss is from Dobson's Spring/Summer 2019 collection 'Portrait of a Reputation' (Fig. 14.1). Images of this collection take two forms. First, there are the Lookbook shots, taken for the Jimmy D online store. Two slender models stand on an old Persian rug, posing in front of a grey cast concrete wall, the only other props are a glass coffee table and a single arum lily. The models are draped in pale grey or green silk, sheer black georgette or oversized cotton shirting. Of the 64 images, only 11 show a model looking directly at the camera; their heads are turned away, or their eyes are downcast. The images are shadowy, cold. They embody a loneliness and humourlessness that is characteristic of much fashion photography: the models alone and unsmiling, mere bodies on which garments hang. In addition to the Lookbook images, there is a

---

[5] The affective response experienced from viewing or witnessing the wearing of clothes on other bodies is different from how we feel when getting dressed or wearing clothes on our own body (Ruggerone 2016). However, what both experiences have in common is the connection between body and cloth and the affect that this connection entails, both personally and socially.

Fig. 14.1 *Jimmy D, Unfinished Sympathy Dress, 'Portrait of a Reputation' SS19*

small series of 16 campaign photographs. The same two models are now afforded a larger selection of backdrops. Some are shot in front of the cast concrete wall, the glass coffee table reflecting the light and the single lily now in a bunch. Others are shot against a white drop sheet or leopard print shawl. The Persian rug hangs on the wall or is wrapped around the models' shoulders. In these images the models make eye contact more frequently, their faces pale in the glare of the camera flash. Unlike the Lookbook photographs, this series is grainy, out of focus, perhaps shot on film. They are otherworldly. The models wear the same garments, yet the mood is different. The photographs shimmer with a feeling of unease. They are knowing, yet naïve; beautiful, yet sad. The images are striking, aloof and intriguing. It is this collection of images, the atmospheric constellation of material elements within the photographs, that attunes us to the mood of the collection. Like a catwalk show, the campaign photographs are an opportunity for the designer to produce a narrative and evoke a feeling in their audience.

Of the campaign images, there is one that stands out to me, eliciting perhaps the most visceral affective response. The model stands with her back to the camera, one hand against that hard, grey concrete wall, and the other like a floating apparition across her back. The funeral, poisonous arum lilies hover white in the foreground. She wears the black Unfinished Sympathy Dress, the low-cut back exposing her pale skin and the line of her spine.[6] Her face, in the flash, is ghostly, indistinct. The dress (which also came in a 'Wallpaper' floral print) is reversible, bias cut in silk georgette. Its hem and the cuffs of the long sleeves are raw, and an internal tie allows the dress to be worn asymmetrically. The cold light of the room renders the model spectral, the dress dark against her white skin. The image makes the hairs on my skin bristle. I feel cold, lonely. Yet I am enraptured by the ambiguous beauty of the image. I want to know what she is thinking and how she feels. I want to touch the fabric of the dress, the rough concrete of the wall. It is a melancholy image, attracting and repelling me in equal measure.

The second image is from Jacobs' 2019/2020 collection A-E-I-O-U-Y (Fig. 14.2). Released for the same season as Dobson's 'Portrait of a Reputation,' the collection is accompanied by 51 Lookbook images in which the model stands against a blank wall, arms loose or raised to better demonstrate the movement of the garments. These Lookbook images are punctuated by six campaign photographs introducing the name and the key features of the collection: 'A is for black silk velvet/E is for linen in it/I is for silk with cotton/O is for hand knitted linen and cotton/U is for

---

[6] The dress is named after the iconic Massive Attack single released in 1991. Recalling the song's emotionally resonant vocals, trance beat and poignant, single continuous shot video clip depicting vocalist Shara Nelson walking through downtown Los Angeles, the dress—and this image of the dress—becomes part of a longer lineage of melancholic cultural artefacts.

Fig. 14.2 *Lela Jacobs, A-E-I-O-U-Y 2019/2020*

air silk/Y is for neckwear of horse and stingray tail.' Accompanying the Lookbook are 13 additional campaign images. Whilst the images are, in many ways, very different to those of Dobson's SS19 collection, they nevertheless conjure a strikingly similar mood. The garments in this collection are in natural fibres, rough linen, fine silk georgette and cotton shirting, heavy woollen knitwear. An androgynous model with a blunt, black fringe and trailing braids poses against a blank wall, with light coming from an unseen window. This same model, their face powdered white, stretches out their arms to the light, crouching as if preparing to dive; they sit by the window, the yellow sunshine bathing their face and arms, luminous. In another image, in which the model wears a pale pink dress and large necklace made with heavy strands of horse hair, they lean against a ladder propped against the wall, now cast a shade of blue. In yet another, they lie on the concrete floor, reaching up to the camera, the horse hair necklace ornamenting their bare chest. The face of the model looks square at the camera, their dark eyes piercing, beseeching, questioning. In others, the image is cropped at the neck, rendering the model headless, bent over as if in pain. These photographs, like all of Jacobs' campaign images, tell an ambiguous story. We are drawn in, yet somehow excluded. The image that strikes me here is number nine in the campaign series. The model looks out to the middle distance, perhaps through that window, the source of light. Their arms are raised in gesture. Their hooded eyes cast shadows onto their cheeks, powdered eyebrows invisible. The white blouse buttoned up under a black knit.

What is it about these images that evoke such a mood of melancholy? Is it that they are shot in black and white? Is it the facial expression of the model, the sad eyes entreating? The affective resonance I feel, the mood produced, relies on the 'symphony' of these elements. There are other images in the series that are shot in colour yet produce the same feeling of unease, discomfort, alluring beauty cast with a mournful sense of sorrow. Certainly, the model is key to the evocation of this feeling. Their expression and the gestures of their body build the mood and carry the garments in a particular narrative direction. Like the magic produced in a fashion show, it is all the dimensions combined that conjure mood in fashion photography. But the feelings these images produce are not simply individual. I am not only interested in the subjective mood they evoke. What is more interesting to me is how these feelings resonate socially, how they circulate culturally and what they translate about the place, the moment in which the fashion was produced.

Fashioning Cultural Moods

Far from merely *reflecting* the moods of place and time, fashion contributes to the *production* of cultural structures of feeling. As preeminent New Zealand fashion designers, both Dobson and Jacobs therefore participate in shaping the cultural mood of the place. Like film makers, authors and artists, fashion designers set cultural moods in motion. However, as fashion designers, producing garments to be worn on bodies, Dobson and Jacobs perhaps have a more significant role to play in contributing to the atmospheric mood than do film makers or poets. Fashion is an 'embodied practice' (Entwistle 2015). Unlike other cultural artefacts, which we encounter by simply looking or listening, fashion is sensorial, intimate, felt in connection to the body. Lucia Ruggerone (2016, 580) describes the wearing of clothes as part of 'the fleshy experience of life we sense but cannot fully describe.' Even when experiencing images of fashion, as noted earlier, these experiences are filtered through a similarly *affective exchange*. We sense our bodies in the engagement with images of other bodies in clothes. The affective quality of dress, as defined in this way, is precisely what makes fashion such a potent contributor to the cultural moods of place.

For Highmore (2017, 11), 'while there might not be a 'national mood' in any hard and fast way, there are clearly levels of optimism and hope, of fear and anxiety, of joyousness and pessimism, that are more or less available at particular times for particular constituents of the population.' I am not arguing here that there is a 'hard and fast' melancholy national mood in Aotearoa New Zealand. Rather, I want to suggest that a mood of melancholy resonates within much cultural production in Aotearoa New Zealand, informed in large part by the 'anxieties of belonging' that Lisa Slater (2019) argues are characteristic in settler colonial states. While outward depictions of Aotearoa New Zealand rely on accounts of the country as a place of bucolic beauty, there is an unsettling undercurrent beneath the surface. As Ian Conrich (2012, 394) has noted: 'New Zealand fiction, its literature and film, has repeatedly portrayed spaces of isolation, loss and despair, of a rugged, wild, and treacherous land that can assail and entrap.' These feelings of loss and despair are no less present in New Zealand fashion, which has absorbed the inherited mood-worlds produced by these texts. Founded on histories of violence and unsettlement—in the case of Aotearoa New Zealand, both the brutal displacement of Indigenous Māori from their land and the sense of dislocation experienced by settlers in the process of migration—the settler colonial state is experienced by many settlers, especially those 'well-intentioned' (Slater 2019), as a place wrought with anxiety. Yet it is also, undeniably, a place of joy. Reconciling these feelings is an ongoing process, one that informs the melancholy mood in New Zealand art and fashion. For Pākehā New Zealanders, of which both James Dobson and Lela Jacobs (and their predecessors Liz Findlay and Margi Robertson) are, the experience of settler colonialism undoubtedly informs their work.[7] We might expect then that *all* fashion produced by

---

[7] It is worth noting that while the designers I discuss here are all Pākehā designers, in other work I have identified a similar mood in the work of contemporary Māori designers. Bobby Campbell Luke (Ngāti Ruanui), for example, conjures a profound feeling of nostalgic melancholy in his work through engagement with the losses of the past and grappling with what it means to be Māori in a settler colonial present (Richards 2021).

settler designers be shaped by these anxieties, informed by a melancholy mood that speaks of both the losses (of life and land) inherent in colonial settlement and the sense of ambivalence upon which settler existence rests. And yet, this is not the case. Much New Zealand fashion, as in other settler colonial states, is far from melancholy. So, what is it that informs the melancholy mood these designers reflect, the melancholy cultural feelings they induce?

Dobson and Jacobs design in different cities, Auckland and Wellington respectively. Different places with different weather patterns, different micro-cultures. All of these elements, the atmospheric differences in air pressure and light, the environmental variations in landscape and lifestyle, factor into their work. While, broadly, their collections are very different, recalling different aesthetic heritages and traditions, they share the sense of melancholia that we can also feel in the work of earlier designers and in the work of multiple other cultural producers. Certainly, my reading of the moods they produce is connected with my own settler identity: a Pākehā New Zealander looking in from abroad. The sense of unsettlement and anxiety I read in these designs and their imagery is refracted through my cultural identity, my experiences of time and place. However, I am not the only one who perceives this mood; I am not the only one who feels it. It might be the mood I experience individually, but this mood is also social (Ahmed 2004, 2014); in being shared it becomes cultural. I suggest that the histories of place have more influence than we might think; the unfinished business of colonisation continues to trouble progressive settlers who acknowledge the histories of dismissal and forgetting yet remain bound to the outcomes of the colonial project. The work produced by designers in these places therefore frequently reflects these feelings of loss, anxiety, distress, unease—even when these are not explicitly referenced. The work presents ghostly landscapes, spectral figures and simmering threat.[8] Undoubtedly this feeling of melancholy is bound to this place and the experiences of its people, both Māori and Pākehā.

---

[8] Avery Gordon (2008, 7) argues that haunting is a key component of modern life and that, in order to study and understand this social life, we must 'confront the ghostly aspects of it.'

Conclusion

In the radio interview with Sly, Dobson talked about his love of slogans, how he uses text to weave wit and dark humour into his work. In one of his early collections, he printed the words 'It's Hard to be Avant Garde' across the designs. Emblazoning this text on black fabric, Dobson was making a self-conscious statement about place and fashion in Aotearoa New Zealand. In an attempt to do things differently, to stand out and be avant-garde in a small domestic industry, he, like Findlay and Robertson before him, had adopted the well-worn tropes of what is perceived as intellectual, cutting-edge design. Yet, at the same time, he was vociferous in his appeals to humour, citing his own love of black comedy, anxious not to be perceived as taking himself or his work 'too seriously.' Certainly, the elements of Dobson's work are familiar, yet how they are rendered is particular. This darkness of mood can be identified elsewhere and at other historical moments. However, the fact that it is identifiable in so much of the creative production of Aotearoa New Zealand, not least of all the fashion, is significant. It speaks to a mood of place that draws on the landscape, the cultural myths, the people and their experiences of history.

In this chapter, I have argued that by reading fashion *through* the moods it evokes, and the moods that are embedded in the material objects and their imagery, we can learn something about the time and place in which that fashion was produced. For Pākehā designers attuned to the unsettling history of colonialism, the inherited mood-worlds of melancholy resonate. Contemporary designers such as Dobson and Jacobs continue to reckon with the anxieties of belonging that circulate within the settler colonial state. Their work, in perpetuating the melancholy moods of their predecessors, speaks of this unease, the realities of settler existence on these South Pacific islands. The ambiguous stories they tell in their collections, especially those I have examined closely here, speak of the moment and the place in which they were produced, 2019/2020: Aotearoa New Zealand. They may reference ancient lore and far-away lands, yet they remain grounded in place, in time, absorbing, reflecting and continuing to shape the cultural moods that circulate. The work responds to the history of unsettlement and the losses this history has wrought. What Flatley (2008, 5) calls 'counter-moods' do circulate. And yet, the dark vibes of melancholy so long recognised in New Zealand cultural production continue to persist, responding to a continued sense of unease. Feeling this cultural affect tells us about this place, alerts us to sides of New Zealand culture not visible in imagery of bucolic pastoral paradise.

REFERENCES

Ahmed, Sara. 2004. *The Cultural Politics of Emotion.* Edinburgh: Edinburgh University Press.
———. 2014. Not in the Mood. *New Formations: A Journal of culture/Theory/Politics* 82: 13–28.
Averis, Grace. 2011. Lela Jacobs of Lela Jacobs. *Critic*, April 26. https://www.critic.co.nz/features/article/912/lela-jacobs-of-lela-jacobs. Accessed 25 July 2021.
Benjamin, Walter. 2009. *The Origin of German Tragic Drama.* London: Verso.
Conrich, Ian. 2012. New Zealand Gothic. In *The New Companion to The Gothic*, ed. D. Punter, 393–408. London: Wiley-Blackwell.
De Pont, Doris. 2012. Why Do We Wear Black? An Exploration of Its History and Context. In *Black: The History of Black in Fashion, Society and Culture in New Zealand*, ed. D. de Pont, 6–37. Auckland: Penguin Books.
Entwistle, Joanne. 2015. *The Fashioned Body: Fashion, Dress and Social Theory.* 2nd ed. Cambridge: Polity Press.
Ferber, Ilit. 2013. *Philosophy and Melancholy: Benjamin's Early Reflections on Theater and Language.* California: Stanford University Press.
Filippello, Roberto. 2018. Thinking Fashion Photographs Through Queer Affect Theory. *International Journal of Fashion Studies* 5 (1): 129–145.
Findlay, Rosie. 2022. Fashion as Mood, Style as Atmosphere: Literary Non-Fiction Fashion Writing on SSENSE and in *London Review of Looks*. In *Insights on Fashion Journalism*, ed. R. Findlay and J. Reponen, 146–159. London: Routledge.
Flatley, Jonathan. 2008. *Affective Mapping: Melancholia and the Politics of Modernism.* Cambridge, MA and London: Harvard University Press.
Givhan, Robin. 2015. The Art of the Fashion Show: How Designers Set a Mood for You to Fall in Love with Their Frocks. *The Washington Post*, September 16. https://www.washingtonpost.com/news/arts-and-entertainment/wp/2015/09/16/the-art-of-the-fashion-show-how-designers-set-a-mood-to-make-you-fall-for-their-frocks/. Accessed 5 Dec 2021.
Gordon, Avery. [1997] 2008. *Ghostly Matters: Haunting and the Sociological Imagination.* Minneapolis and London: University of Minnesota Press.
Hammonds, Lucy. 2010. The Nineteen Nineties: Search for a Style. In *The Dress Circle: New Zealand Fashion Design since 1940*, ed. L. Hammonds, D.L. Jenkins, and C. Regnault. Auckland: Random House New Zealand.

Hammonds, Lucy, and Claire Regnault. 2010. The Two Thousands: Our Fashion Moment. In *The Dress Circle: New Zealand Fashion Design since 1940*, ed. L. Hammonds, D.L. Jenkins, and C. Regnault, 340–391. Auckland: Random House New Zealand.
Harvey, John. 1995. *Men in Black*. London: Reaktion Books Ltd.
Hemmings, Clare. 2012. In the Mood for Revolution: Emma Goldman's Passion. *New Literary History* 43 (3): 527–545.
Highmore, Ben. 2016. Formations of Feelings, Constellations of Things. *Cultural Studies Review* 22 (1): 144–167.
———. 2017. *Cultural Feelings: Mood, Mediation and Cultural Politics*. London and New York: Routledge.
Kavka, Misha, Jennifer Lawn, and Mary Paul, eds. 2006. *Gothic NZ: The Darker Side of Kiwi Culture*. Dunedin: Otago University Press.
Maynard, Margaret. 2001. *Out of Line: Australian Women and Style*. Sydney: University of New South Wales Press.
Molloy, Maureen. 2004. Cutting-edge Nostalgia: New Zealand Fashion Design at the New Millennium. *Fashion Theory* 8 (4): 477–490.
Molloy, Maureen, and Wendy Larner. 2013. *Fashioning Globalisation: New Zealand Design, Working Women and the Cultural Economy*. London: Wiley-Blackwell.
Neill, Sam. 1995. *Cinema of Unease: A Personal Journey by Sam Neill*. NZ on Screen.
Palenski, Ron. 2012. Black Heroes: New Zealand Sport. In *Black: The History of Black in Fashion, Society and Culture in New Zealand*, ed. D. de Pont, 104–117. New Zealand: Penguin Books.
Parkins, Ilya. 2021. 'You'll Never Regret Going Bold': The Moods of Wedding Apparel on *A Practical Wedding*. *Fashion Theory* 25 (6): 799–817.
Pastoureau, Michel. 2008. *Black: The History of a Color*. Princeton and Oxford: Princeton University Press.
Perry, Nick. 1994. *Dominion of Signs: Television, Advertising and Other New Zealand Fictions*. Auckland: Auckland University Press.
Regnault, Claire. 2012. A Culture of Ease: Black in New Zealand Fashion in the New Millennium. In *Black: The History of Black in Fashion, Society and Culture in New Zealand*, ed. D. de Pont, 200–219. New Zealand: Penguin Books.
Richards, Harriette. 2021. Practices of cultural collectivity: Style activism, Miromoda and Māori fashion in Aotearoa New Zealand. *Critical Studies in Fashion & Beauty* 12 (1): 131–149.
Ruggerone, Lucia. 2016. The Feeling of Being Dressed: Affect Studies and the Clothed Body. *Fashion Theory* 21 (5): 573–593.
Schafer, William J. 1998. *Mapping the Godzone: A Primer on New Zealand Literature and Culture*. Honolulu: University of Hawai'i Press.

Sheehan, Elizabeth M. 2018. *Modernism à la Mode: Fashion and the Ends of Literature*. Ithaca and London: Cornell University Press.

Shinkle, Eugénie. 2008. The Line Between the Wall and the Floor: Reality and Affect in Contemporary Fashion Photography. In *Fashion as Photograph: Viewing and Reviewing Images of Fashion*, ed. E. Shinkle, 214–226. London: I.B. Tauris.

Slater, Lisa. 2019. *Anxieties of Belonging in Settler Colonialism: Australia, Race and Place*. New York: Routledge.

Sly, Sonia. 2016. Jimmy D: There's More to Life Than Fashion. *My Heels are Killing Me*, RNZ, November 2. https://www.rnz.co.nz/programmes/my-heels-are-killing-me/story/201820381/jimmy-d-there's-more-to-life-than-fashion. Accessed 22 July 2021.

Walker, Zoe. 2011. What is New Zealand's Fashion Identity? *New Zealand Herald*, September 1. https://www.nzherald.co.nz/lifestyle/what-is-new-zealands-fashion-identity/FBUZOWMOKX7W3JBRI3GLEB3WMM/. Accessed 30 July 2021.

CHAPTER 15

On Boredom and Contemporary Fashion Photography

Eugenie Shinkle

Several years ago, following a decade spent thinking and writing about fashion photography, I found myself unable to find satisfaction in looking at it any more. It's not that fashion photographs themselves are boring. Indeed, the past ten years have witnessed a kind of renaissance in the genre: conventional definitions of beauty have expanded to include a wider range of body shapes and racialised subjects; photographers regularly cross over with painting, sculpture, illustration and installation art. Beneath the diversity, though, all I could see was an endless procession of variations on the same narrow range of themes, the same minor transgressions of aesthetic norms: symmetrical faces, proportional limbs, unlined skin. How could there be so much sameness in such variety?

It's not that sameness and repetition isn't a problem in other photographic genres. But it was especially disappointing to find myself bored of fashion photography. From the 1990s up to the turn of the millennium, fashion photography had seemed poised to tear itself free from the banal

E. Shinkle (✉)
University of Westminster, London, UK
e-mail: E.B.Shinkle@westminster.ac.uk

© The Author(s), under exclusive license to Springer Nature Switzerland AG 2023
R. Filippello, I. Parkins (eds.), *Fashion and Feeling*, Palgrave Studies in Fashion and the Body,
https://doi.org/10.1007/978-3-031-19100-8_15

imperatives of commerce and reinvent itself as a form of critical discourse. In a 2002 essay, Gilles Lipovetsky singled out contemporary fashion photography as a form rich in political potentiality. 'The fashion photograph is becoming independent of the logic of clothing,' (T8) he remarked, and was now free to explore existential, social and cultural themes of its own, replacing the 'scenography of elegance' with a 'theatricality of meaning' (T9). But this promise was short-lived. As we entered the second decade of the new millennium, with market forces moving swiftly to incorporate non-market actors, there was not much evidence that fashion photography had accomplished anything significant in the way of cultural critique.

In this chapter I use my own disinterest in fashion photography as a springboard for thinking through the relationship between fashion, boredom and politics. Boredom, as I'll show, has a *structural*—rather than a merely subjective or incidental—relationship with fashion photography. To speak of boredom as structural is to move the discussion beyond judgements around the merit of individual photographers or the content of specific images, and to open up a new space for discussing the complex phenomenology of boredom: its timeframe, its relationship to desire and the constellation of other affects that come bundled with it. Boredom, as I'll show, cannot be understood apart from the affective and cognitive states of dissatisfaction and emptiness—states that are also characteristic of desire itself.

The fashion image departs from conventional definitions of boredom that frame the latter predominately in terms of unfilled time. Following the logic of fashion itself, contemporary fashion photographs are destined (if not specifically designed or intended) to be almost immediately *out* of style. Helped along in recent years, by technologies that are optimised for the instantaneous transmission and consumption of images, fashion photography's accelerated timeframe permits little time or space for reflection. The temporal register of the fashion photograph is one of rapid change: a continuous stream of novelty closely followed by disinterest. The structural boredom of the fashion image, in other words, is a consequence of the perceptual habits that it invites and encourages.

Lipovetsky's confidence in the transformative potential of the fashion image seems misplaced here. But perhaps he was looking for transformation in the wrong place, and in the wrong way, expecting fashion photography to somehow step into the role of the documentary or journalistic photograph. But the political potential of fashion photography is not *in* the image itself; it is not linked specifically to its subject matter. Fashion images may not have the transformative power that they were expected to deliver at the turn of the millennium, but, as I'll suggest, this refusal of meaning can be understood as productive in and of itself. Unlike more persistent forms of boredom such as *ennui*, the boredom linked to fashion photography doesn't necessarily constitute an existential challenge to the subject, but it can be understood nonetheless as existentially revealing. It is in the fashion photograph's tendency to resist reflective engagement—to invite and incite boredom—that the promise of real political transformation lies. The final sections of the chapter reflect on this possibility, setting the passivity of boredom as something to be avoided against a more active will to embrace it. Here, the subject's encounter with meaninglessness is not 'an absolute end in-itself but ... a prelude to creating meaning' (Haladyn 2015, 92).

* * *

Acedia—a hybrid state of idleness and indifference towards the world—has been part of the human condition since antiquity. Originally, *acedia* was considered a moral failing—a rejection of the beauty of God's creation and a sin to be repented. Prior to the industrial revolution and the consequent democratisation of free time, it was a condition suffered by the few rather than the many.

As a condition affecting the masses, boredom is a specifically modern invention. Set in the context of an industrialised world, boredom is 'a consequence of the increasingly mechanised, standardised and alienated structures of work, technology and urban living conditions and, by extension, the dictatorial patterning of habitual behaviour, mundane routines and cultural life' (Sandywell 2019, 40). Boredom is a side effect of lives lived according to abstract timescales of work and leisure, alienated routines and pointless rituals—a standardised existence, exacerbated by the novel burden of unfilled time. Definitions of boredom are also linked to the void that is left behind when traditionally meaningful aspects of life disappear. Enlightenment ideals that emerged in the late eighteenth and early nineteenth centuries placed new expectations on the individual to find their own place within a society that no longer relied on a higher power to guarantee the meaning of existence. With growing self-determination came an equally urgent requirement that life should consist of more than just being alive—it also needed to have a purpose and be *interesting*. For those who failed (on their own terms or the terms of others) to live a sufficiently full and purposeful life, existence became little more than a quest to satisfy an endless procession of desires.

Consumer culture is the primary playground for these desires, providing an endless stream of goods and entertainments and a multitude of distractions to paper over existential malaise. Rather than doing the inner work of self-realisation, the modern subject is encouraged to accumulate external markers of value. But an excess of things and pastimes can never fully compensate for a life that is empty of meaning. In nineteenth-century literature, dramatisations of boredom are often framed as 'an *effect* of the surfeit of well-being, prefiguring the many contemporary psychopathologies of affluence' (Sandywell 2019, 40). For the modern subject, boredom is not just a matter of too much time, it is also a side effect of *too much stuff*.

Fashion, for its part, is not simply a subset of contemporary consumer culture, but its primary motivating force, extending its reach and its processes into every part of society (Lipovetsky 1994; Lehmann 2000). Its effect on the self is both destructive and compensatory. On the one hand, fashion's obsession with the ephemeral can be understood as a response to the deadening effect of unfilled time—the boredom of simply *being* in an attention economy characterised by distraction. On the other hand, fashion is the structural principle behind the 'splintering of the "I" into multiple identity positions' (Stahel 2002, 21), draining substance from the self and replacing it with a succession of images. Fashion, then, occupies a curious position. Superficially, it appears both to alleviate boredom and, as Lipovetsky (1994) has argued, to enable self-expression, functioning as the supreme agent of modern democracy. But it is also wholly reliant on the modern subject's propensity for boredom and existential emptiness. We're accustomed to thinking of desire as the affective engine that drives the economy of fashion. But boredom, too, has a vital role to play.

It's useful here to distinguish between the three types of boredom that the philosopher Martin Heidegger identified in his 1930 lecture series *The Fundamental Concepts of Metaphysics: World, Finitude, Solitude*. For Heidegger—and for many theorists of boredom who follow in his footsteps—boredom can be parsed into three distinct forms. The first of these, situational boredom, is the temporary state of being bored *by* something—waiting in an airport, for instance. Being bored *with* something is a more complex condition in which the subject is not always aware of being bored in the moment. In this situation, the subject comes to understand, often retrospectively, that the activity itself (Heidegger gives the example of a dinner party) holds no meaning for them and plays no part in their self-realisation.

The third form, profound boredom, is an extreme existential condition where everything, even life itself, seems stripped of meaning. This type of boredom, Heidegger writes, is a 'form of attunement', a 'moment of vision' that compels the subject to reflect on the nature of being itself (1995, 139). Paradoxically, Heidegger regards profound boredom as the form with the most political potential:

> In that moment of totalizing boredom, we can come to understand what projects carry proper significance to us—that is, we can discern the projects that are related to our past and that define us, both in the present and in the future. In doing so, we come to understand not only that we are the type of being for whom existence is an issue, but also that we can take up and appropriate (at least to a certain extent) our own existence. (Elpidorou and Freeman 2019, 8)

Profound boredom, in other words, can be an enticement to actualise the world subjectively, on our own terms—to *create* meaning rather than simply accepting the shallow and ephemeral satisfaction provided by a procession of commodities. All these forms of boredom share two key affective moments: a sense of dissatisfaction (being 'left empty', as Heidegger describes it) and meaninglessness (being left 'in limbo' (1995, 87), with no possibility of taking meaningful action). For Heidegger, only profound boredom can bring about self-realisation. More recent readings of his work suggest that the difference between the three forms is not necessarily as pronounced as Heidegger insists, and that all three can be transformative (Elpidorou and Freeman 2019, 21–22; Haladyn 2015, 94). It is the second of these—boredom *with*—that is aligned most closely with the temporal and affective landscape of contemporary fashion photography.

* * *

Our normal experience of time is multidirectional: along with the present moment, it also comprises retention (an orientation towards the past) and pretension (an orientation towards the future). The timeframe of boredom, on the other hand, is generally said to be protracted and without direction: the endless present of a world that *should* be filled with diversity and significance but that is bogged down instead in monotony. Against the continuous flux of doing, being and meaning, boredom's temporal dimension is typically linked to the inertia of nothing-to-do. The accelerated time and constant change characteristic of fashion would seem superficially to work as a hedge against boredom. But the logic of fashion also requires that the new quickly and predictably becomes routine and is replaced by something *newer*—distinct enough to be stimulating, but rarely so radical that it challenges expectations. Here again, boredom shows itself in/as a kind of paradox: an endless stream of apparent novelty cloaking a procession of marginal difference and a resistance to significant change. The resulting affective landscape is characteristic of fashion's logic: a continuous cycle of anticipation, arousal and disinterest.

The fashion photograph is an embodiment of this logic, playing it out in a surfeit of images. Its temporality is that of an endlessly repeated now, oriented towards a future that vanishes just as quickly. Olivier Zahm, editor and co-founder of *Purple* magazine, writes that unlike its twentieth-century precursors, contemporary fashion photography 'no longer has any specifically artistic or sociological referent' (2002, 30), behaving instead as a sort of restless vampire, feeding on a broad spectrum of social, aesthetic historical and political tropes. It is hybrid in essence, unstable and lacking any secure aesthetic or generic foundation. Its orientation to the past is, for the most part, superficial, accumulating historical and cultural references on the basis of their appearance and transforming them into visual content.[1] Its function is not to document, to analyse or to predict, but to define novelty in the moment of its existence and to consign it at once to the past. The only certainty that a fashion image provides is that the future will be filled by an item that is better or different than the one we are looking at in the present moment. Alongside the latest styles and trends, in other words, the subtext of every fashion photograph is its own imminent obsolescence.

* * *

The persistent dissatisfaction and endless deferral of meaning associated with boredom is not much different from that of a psychic marker to which fashion photography has persistently been linked: that of desire.

---

[1] Fashion photography is a collection, as Stahel remarks, 'of small theatrical stages on which any number of different scenes are underway, each seismically connected, with just a few nerves, to the basic mood of reality' (Stahel 2002, 21).

Along with identification, desire is one of the psychic processes responsible for constituting the self. Under the Lacanian model, desire emerges when the subject first enters the symbolic order. Learning to function within language comes at a price, however: it cuts the subject off from the fullness of being. Desire, as Kaja Silverman frames it, 'is the product of the divisions by means of which the subject is constituted, divisions which inspire in the subject a profound sense of lack' (1983, 176). Desire has no specific object; instead, it plays out as an endless process of trying to compensate for this lack. To desire something, in other words, 'is to be in a state of perpetual dissatisfaction' (Bancroft 2012, 60).

Desire is directed towards ideal representations—many of them supplied by visual culture—which always remain beyond the subject's reach. Fashion photography is known to be complicit in the production of desire; indeed, the fashion system thrives on it. Within this system, the task of the fashion image is to create and perpetuate desire, to treat it as something that can be temporarily addressed by a stream of novelty but never satisfied. This suggests that we need to rewrite the narratives that set out the fashion image as nothing more than a kind of high-end advertisement. Rather than the specific goal of selling clothes, I want to suggest that the fashion photograph is driven by a more general imperative *not to be trivial* in the moment of its consumption. In other words, it is the need to stimulate—rather than to document, advertise or sell specific garments—that is fashion photography's primary aim. And, to continue the analogy, the commodity that is offered to the consumer of fashion photography is not an image of a garment or accessory—nor is it even fashion itself—but a sense of temporary and shallow self-realisation; a promise that can never be delivered.

The problem of being bored with fashion photography, then, is not one of unfilled time or unengaging content, but of time that is filled *too quickly*, with an image that is not intended to provoke a response beyond an unfocused desire for the next one. It's not that fashion photographs are boring in and of themselves, but that they treat desire in a way that mimics the very mechanisms of contemporary boredom. We could say, then, that the fashion image performs a kind of affective labour,[2] one that marries

---

[2] Affective labour is the outcome of a shift in capitalist economies in which the primary products are not durable goods, but information, knowledge and affects. The products of affective labour are intangible in and of themselves, but they are linked in vital ways to the production and consumption of commodities. See, for instance, Oksala 2016.

perfectly with the logic of fashion, but which plays out for the subject as a set of negative affects—emptiness and dissatisfaction—that are characteristic of both desire and boredom. Desire is, by its very nature, destined never to be fulfilled, and this is precisely the energy that the fashion photograph thrives on. By tapping into the frustration that is characteristic of desire, fashion photography furnishes the impetus for an unending stream of images. In doing so, it ensures that boredom and desire march in lockstep, the one almost indistinguishable from the other.

* * *

This impetus to a constant flow of stimulus is enabled by the new, instantaneous technologies on which fashion photography has grown to depend. Though the magazine remains (in the face of numerous predictions to the contrary) a key form for the dissemination of fashion photography, it has also found a new home on digital platforms such as Instagram, which are designed for a continuous flow of engagement and affective feedback (Davies 2017). Here, images are destined for such rapid consumption that they make the magazine form look positively contemplative. As journalist Ian Brown remarked in 2013, the volume of photographs made today 'guarantees that most of them are forgettable'. We take photographs, he claims, '[for] the same reason addicts are addicted to anything: to kill the pain of awareness, the uncomfortable difficulty of actually seeing' (np). Created and circulated almost instantly and just as quickly forgotten, most photographs are no longer made in the expectation that they will be meaningful. As Annebella Pollen (2016) observes, laments for the loss of photographic meaning are often implicit indictments of the lack of expertise and quality associated with 'mass' photography—it's not that there are too many photographs, she writes, but that there are 'too many photographs *of the wrong kind*' (4).

Fashion photography, however, thrives under these conditions. Digital fashion images, in particular, are not designed to be lingered over—tiny in size, rapidly proliferating, just as rapidly forgotten. They are intended to operate within a different microtemporal scale, keeping the viewer perpetually engaged, but diffusing that engagement across a constant flux of images without giving it the opportunity to settle. Fashion photographs are fully keyed into an information ecosystem that preys on our attention, appealing to it with notifications, alerts, badges and rewards, along with the superficial serotonin hit of the 'like'. Regardless of the use we may ultimately make of them (collecting, analysing, etc.) on an ontological level, contemporary fashion photographs deliberately manipulate attentional limits without, for the most part, specifically engaging with boredom as their subject matter.

* * *

If interest is the most positive kind of sensorial engagement that the modern subject can have with the world, boredom ostensibly represents the loss of this possibility. Boredom, then, might be seen as a form of withdrawal, or following cultural theorist Sianne Ngai's discussion of negative affects, as a kind of 'suspended agency' (2005, 1).

Lipovetsky was not the only commentator who was confident that fashion photography could transcend boredom. Writing in the same 2002 volume, Zahm alleged that certain photographers were able to actively distance themselves from the spectacle in search of something more authentic. Such photographers, he believed, could carry out a 'conscious poetic form of subjective resistance' in order to 'get behind the glorious mask of the spectacular body to restore the fragile, singular human body in its precarious existence and refusal to be dispossessed, isolated and subjected to the alienation of the market' (33). His formula for resisting 'the rules of spectacular domination' hinged on the belief that fashion images could be detached from the world of consumerism to offer a less alienated, less conventionally beautiful kind of imagery.

Zahm's essay hinted presciently at work that would gain prominence in the early years of the new millennium, and that favoured (often negative) affect over signification. Over the course of the next decade or so, fashion photography exhibited a growing fascination with the grotesque, the awkward and the deliberately strange. I've written elsewhere that such work 'disrupts, even if only temporarily, the standard trajectory of desire—the constant striving towards a state of perfection that is destined never to be reached—and grounds subjectivity in the here and now, in the materiality of bodies …' (2017, 216). If perfection, as Lucy Alford writes, 'slackens the line of interest' (2021, 248) and fails to fully hold our attention, then fashion photography's engagement with uncomfortable bodies and unusual faces seemed like a way of mitigating the boredom of the too-perfect.

These days, I'm less convinced that increasingly novel and transgressive forms of imagery are able to fully sidestep the structural logic of fashion photography. Rod Metts (2001) describes the effect of such images as 'monologic' (35), their power of estrangement limited and commercially captive. Watching a parade of ostensibly transgressive bodies flow past on a phone screen allows viewers to 'fetishize the new exotic Other vicariously and at a safe distance' (36). Transgressive only in the most narrow and superficial sense, images such as these remain anchored within established power relations, 'conservative artifacts masquerading as radical images ... caught up in a capitalistic logic where market values supercede human values and human agency. ... there is little beneath the surface to suggest anything other than what already exists' (42).

So we're left to ponder yet another paradox: such images may, on the one hand, draw attention to the body as the root of all political action, but, on the other, they continue to function as superficial signs that do little more than negate conventional norms, deploying 'transgression' in the service of consumption. More to the point, if *boredom-with* the fashion image is, as I've suggested above, independent of content, then such imagery is no less apt to bore the viewer than any other. We can make the content as radical as we like; if the structure remains the same nothing will change. The final sections of this chapter ask how we might turn fashion photography's propensity for boredom back on itself.

* * *

The period around the turn of the millennium was a key moment not just for fashion photography, but for political theory. While Lipovetsky and Zahm were reflecting on the critical possibilities of fashion photography, scholars and thinkers in other fields were challenging classical and modern notions of politics as a discursive formation, and political decision-making as a matter of choices governed by social and ideological codes. According to political theorists like Brian Massumi, affect forms the very foundation of meaning and of political expression. Political attitudes, he writes, are shaped not just by shared ideologies, but by affective intensities that arise in, and circulate between, individual bodies. Political statements and decisions are now understood to be bound up with affective intensities—with styles of rhetoric and presentation 'by which forms of morality and images of subjectivity are produced at particular historical moments' (Spinks 2001, 24).

What if we were to consider boredom not as something that must necessarily be overcome in order to effect change, but as an affect that can show us a different image of subjectivity? More than one writer on the subject has framed boredom as potentially transformative. Barry Sandywell, for instance, sets conventional definitions of boredom against what he terms *lassitude*. He suggests that while boredom 'freezes *becoming*, lassitude precipitates *change* and *self-transformation*. ... [It is] a necessary, if not sufficient, precondition of counter-factual reflection and imagination' (2019, 45). Rather than the passivity of boredom, lassitude rejects the taken-for-granted character of the status quo, filling surplus time with curiosity, with ideas, with the seeds of creativity. It is a potentially subversive phenomenon, emerging from a desire to escape from social norms and normal expectation. In this way, he writes, boredom can become 'a subversive and transformative source of creative selfhood and communality ...' (2019, 39). Lassitude, in other words, is a space for imagining alternatives—a space of play, fantasy, dreaming and utopic transgression.

Here, boredom is posed as a challenge to the constant distractions presented to us by the attention economy, its political potential linked to the suggestion that we are not allowed, in contemporary society, to get bored *enough*. Other writers, such as Jenny Odell, have made similar calls for a return to 'deeper, hardier, more nuanced forms of attention [that] are less susceptible to appropriation' (2019, 118). The ability to take pleasure in boredom, as Sandywell suggests, might allow us to sidestep the desire that the fashion photograph attempts to incite. Here, boredom becomes an affective lens through which we can encounter fashion images not as passive consumers, but as active antagonists of capitalist systems. There is an attachment at play in this kind of slowed-down looking that could be described as erotic[3]—the latter term understood here not in a sexual sense, but as 'a power that can be drawn upon to resist oppression, pursue change, and build liberatory communities' (Johnson 2019).

* * *

Of course, it is possible to be bored by anything at all, but fashion photography's structural dependence on boredom gives it a strategic advantage in encouraging the viewer towards a more agential form of resistance. Haladyn argues that boredom is more than a passive position of retreat; it is a 'coactive position of (aesthetic) refusal' (2015, 4) with the potential to challenge not just the perceived meaninglessness of the image, but of

[3] I'm indebted to Roberto Filippello for these observations on the erotics of boredom.

existence itself. His argument allows us to see precisely how fashion photography's structural logic can be made to work against itself, leading the viewer towards a more active mode of affective and political engagement.

In mainstream aesthetics (in which fashion photography participates on the level of the content of the image), meaning is typically understood as something given, which the individual is expected to recognise or find. This 'given' perspective, as Julian Haladyn notes, is 'an aesthetic of mainstream consumerism in which the modern subject, like the commodity objects it perpetually desires, is identified with a repeatable and interchangeable position that individuals are expected to take on by choosing between ready-made standpoints that appear to be *complete without them*' (2015, 90). If the subject is unable to find or identify this given meaning, they experience a feeling that the world is not sufficiently engaging—in other words, they experience boredom.

This is exactly the sort of encounter that the fashion photograph encourages. It's not that individual images are necessarily perceived as dull in the moment of viewing; often they are quite the opposite. But the fashion photograph is structurally *obliged* to be unsatisfactory in the longer term—to leave the individual empty and in limbo—to leave them in the grip of a boredom which is easily mistaken for desire. By forcing an encounter with boredom, the fashion photograph pushes the viewer towards a potentially transformative experience. Haladyn's argument is so closely aligned with the logic of the fashion image that it's worth quoting at length here. Capitalist society, he remarks, co-opts the creative drive of the subject as a motivating force for consuming, rather than being and doing:

> In capitalist culture ... the subject's creative drive is used as a means of fuelling the need for a goal even without the possibility of achieving it—except temporarily, through the superficial engagements provided by ready-made commodified object-events that stage creativity as acts of choice. Such choices represent limitations that make us both the same and different, with our repeated experiences being marked by *fascinations that are also boredoms*. (2015, 95; italics mine)

The logic of fashion aims to keep the subject in a perpetual state of desire without resolution—a desire that is experienced as boredom (and vice versa). And this boredom, for its part, is an essentially passive state in which the subject is resigned to accepting a stream of novel experiences as a substitute for true meaning.

But boredom can also be actively linked to a deeper form of desire, which is the modern subject's wish to live a meaningful life. Here, the subject perceives meaninglessness 'not as an absolute end in-itself but in the possibility of the end being a prelude to creating meaning' (Haladyn 2015, 92). Haladyn uses as an example Manet's painting *The Railway*, which had, in its time, no clear meaning or interpretation in the conventional sense. In aesthetic encounters that seem to demand boredom as an outcome, it is possible to embrace boredom as a form of aesthetic judgement, an enticement to find or create meaning where none exists. By tackling the absence of meaning head-on—rather than, as Sandywell suggests, using unfilled time as a space for imagining alternatives—the subject reframes it 'as a challenge to create meaning through the meaninglessness of the encounter' (2015, 93). In other words, boredom becomes the basis for questioning what we are looking at, why and perhaps most importantly, *how*.

In other words, it is by lingering in boredom, refusing the restless movement of the attention economy, that we might begin to find a way beyond it. This has significant implications in terms of the critical potential of fashion photography. To be actively bored of fashion photography, rather than captivated by it, is to destabilise the channels of endless novelty, desire and lack, through which it usually operates. To embrace the boredom that it produces—to encounter boredom critically, to question it not just on the level of meaning, but on the level of ontology—interferes with its temporality; as such it is the most transgressive, transformative response that we can have to it. Embracing boredom as a form of aesthetic judgement linked to the subject's will to meaning can help us to understand the fashion image not as a corollary of consumerism but as a subtle form of political discourse. To be bored of fashion photography, in other words, may well be a pathway into a more critical engagement with it.

References

Alford, Lucy. 2021. *Forms of Poetic Attention*. New York: Columbia University Press.
Bancroft, Alison. 2012. *Fashion and Psychoanalysis: Styling the Self*. London: I B Tauris.
Brown, Ian. 2013. Six Billion Photos and Nothing to See. *The Globe and Mail*, June 22.

Davies, William. 2017. How are we now? Real-time mood-monitoring as valuation. *Journal of Cultural Economy* 10 (1): 34–48.
Elpidorou, Andreas, and Lauren Freeman. 2019. Is Profound Boredom? In *Heidegger on Affect*, ed. Christos Hadjioannou, 177–203. New York: Palgrave Macmillan.
Haladyn, Julian Jason. 2015. *Boredom and Art: Passions of the Will to Boredom*. London: Zero Books.
Heidegger, Martin. 1995. *The Fundamental Concepts of Metaphysics: World, Finitude, Solitude*. Trans. William McNeill and Nicholas Walker. Bloomington IN: Indiana University Press.
Johnson, Brooke. 2019. The Erotic as Resistance: Queer Resistance at a Militarized Charter School. *Critical Military Studies* 5 (3): 195–212.
Lehmann, Ulrich. 2000. *Tigersprung: Fashion in Modernity*. Cambridge, MA: MIT Press.
Lipovetsky, Gilles. 1994. *The Empire of Fashion: Dressing Modern Democracy*. Trans. Catherine Porter. Princeton and Oxford: Princeton University Press.
———. 2002. More Than Fashion. *Chic Clicks: Creativity and Commerce in Contemporary Fashion Photography*, 8–11. Ed. Hatje Cantz.
Metts, Rod. 2001. Fetishizing the grotesque body: The images of Calvin Klein. *Visual Anthropology* 14 (1): 33–48.
Ngai, Sianne. 2005. *Ugly Feelings*. Cambridge, MA: Harvard University Press.
Odell, Jenny. 2019. *How to do Nothing: Resisting the Attention Economy*. New York & London: Melville House Publishing.
Oksala, Johanna. 2016. Affective Labor and Feminist Politics. *Signs* 41 (2): 281–303.
Pollen, Annebella. 2016. The Rising Tide of Photographs: Not Drowning But Waving? *Captures* 1 (1).
Sandywell, Barry. 2019. The Dialectic of Lassitude: A Reflexive Investigation. In *Boredom Studies Reader: Frameworks and Perspectives*, ed. Michael Gardiner and Julian Jason Haladyn, 38–52. London: Routledge.
Shinkle, Eugenie. 2017. The Feminine Awkward: Graceless Bodies and the Performance of Femininity in Fashion Photographs. *Fashion Theory* 21 (2): 201–217.
Silverman, Kaja. 1983. *The Subject of Semiotics*. New York & London: Oxford University Press.
Spinks, Lee. 2001. Thinking the Post-Human: Literature, Affect and the Politics of Style. *Textual Practice* 15 (1): 23–46.
Stahel, Urs. 2002. Absolut Fashion. In *Chic Clicks: Creativity and Commerce in Contemporary Fashion Photography*, 19–21. Berlin: Hatje Cantz Verlag.
Zahm, Olivier. 2002. On the Marked Change in Fashion Photography. In *Chic Clicks: Creativity and Commerce in Contemporary Fashion Photography*, 28–35. Berlin: Hatje Cantz Verlag.

CHAPTER 16

Hair Dressing: Fetish, School Uniforms and *Shōjo* in *Cocoon, Entwined*

Masafumi Monden

> For the dresses no one except the women themselves can touch, the women made them by using their hair. Those dresses were so beautiful, and the women who wore them, word has it, all said that "it feels as if the dress breathes …" Yuriko Hara, *Cocoon, Entwined* (2018), vol. 1, pp. 25–26.

Hair is often perceived as one of the most intimate forms of physical ornament for humans, closely followed by dress. Manga—Japanese comics—use both clothes and hair as fundamental aspects of identity, providing a way to clearly define characters in a two-dimensional medium operating without the benefit of audio or, in many cases, colour. Importantly, hair and dress also carry conceptual and symbolic meanings that are deeply intertwined with the narrative themes. This chapter examines Yuriko Hara's popular manga series *Cocoon, Entwined* (2018–present). Set in modern Japan, *Cocoon, Entwined* is a tale of schoolgirls who attend an exclusive girls' academy. Often regarded as beautiful, romantic and yet

---

M. Monden (✉)
The University of Sydney, Camperdown, NSW, Australia
e-mail: masafumi.monden@sydney.edu.au

© The Author(s), under exclusive license to Springer Nature Switzerland AG 2023
R. Filippello, I. Parkins (eds.), *Fashion and Feeling*, Palgrave Studies in Fashion and the Body, https://doi.org/10.1007/978-3-031-19100-8_16

passive, the state of ideal girlhood—which is known as *shōjo* in Japanese—is depicted in binary terms. While using the ideal perception of *shōjo* as a framework, I believe what is significant about this manga is the idealization and de-romanticization of this cultural imagination of ideal girlhood via playing with, inverting and sometimes even subverting it.

The school uniform of the academy worn by the first-year students is, unusually and perhaps alarmingly, made from the long hair of girls in their final year. The school uniform, therefore, as the manga starts with a narrative, says, "Makes sound as it breathes." The medium of manga allows such creative expressions of fashion, which would be impossible or impractical in the real world. As this chapter unfolds, the school uniform made of girls' hair serves as a metaphor for the intimacy between the principal girl characters, and critiques a rigid demarcation of *shōjo* that is often based on age and (non-)productivity. Instead, this manga offers a more fluid perception of *shōjo*, where women, even when they "leave" the *shōjo*-scape and mature, also leave a trace of their *shōjo*-hood. Together with its unique imagining of the school uniform—the ultimate symbol of adolescent femininity in Japan—the school uniform in *Cocoon, Entwined* has become a memory object that allows us to see this iconic representation of femininity and girlhood in a more complex way. The mature woman's link to *shōjo* is never really severed; they are separate but connected to parts of the woman's psyche.

The Meanings of Dress in Manga

In the socio-anthropology of fashion, dress is defined as what "embellishes the body, the materials commonly used, adding a whole array of meanings to the body that would otherwise not be there" (Entwistle 2001, 34). In this view, dress carries symbolic meanings and is a form of communication (Davis 1992). However, the meanings communicated via clothing are often "highly differentiated in terms of taste, social identity, and a person's access to the symbolic wares of a society" (Davis 1992, 8). We therefore need a degree of caution for the meanings dress carries can be subtle and complex. As Valerie Steele (1989, 6) articulates, meanings are more like music than prose:

> [T]hey are expressive in an indirect and allusive way. There is rarely a single meaning attached to each article of clothing. Instead, its meanings depend on the context—who wears it? When? Along with what other clothes? What was the history of the garment?

Fictional texts often use dress as a deliberate device to convey meaning. Clair Hughes argues that "[t]raditionally, aspects of dress have been used to portray aspects of personality, particularly when a character first enters the story" (Hughes 2006, 7). Japanese manga use dress frequently in this way, particularly *shōjo* manga (literally girls' comics), whose primary target audience are girls and young women.

Technically, dress in manga is important because characters in manga are drawn in two dimensions, through line and tone, and are usually stylized. Manga artists usually have a style upon which all their graphic depictions of characters are based. This means characters drawn by the same manga artist generally look alike. As a result, characters are often distinguished through what manga critic and scholar Hōsei Iwashita (2013, 256–7) calls "character imageries," to signify their different personalities. Building upon manga theorist Go Itō's theory of manga characters, Iwashita describes the way a character is crafted in manga from what he terms "character imagery": visual symbols which are combined to establish a "character personality." In semiotic terms the elements of "character imagery" are signifiers, and "character personality" is the signified, linking images in different panels and pages to one character (Iwashita 2013, 256–7). Hairstyles and especially clothes are considered to be a fundamental aspect of character imagery to graphically indicate character personality in different panels. In other words, it is crucial for the manga reader to be able to understand something of the character with a single glance, and often dress and hairstyles serve this purpose (Takemura 2012, 16). Many *shōjo* manga artists, both established and contemporary like Yukari Ichijō (b. 1949), A-ko Mutsu (b. 1954), Ryo Ikuemi (b. 1964) and Setona Mizushiro (b. 1971), base their characterizations on dress, including personality, financial and social status, by using hand-sewn clothes, ready-to-wear, high fashion or second-hand clothes (see Takemura 2012).

On the subject of clothing in fiction, Anne Hollander contends that "the most sophisticated writers have always kept strict control over visual material; but it has a rather special application in the case of clothes, since characters cannot do without them" (1978, 420). Hollander also writes: "Dress is a form of visual art, a creation of images with the visible self as its medium. The most important aspect of clothing is the way it looks; all other considerations are occasional and conditional" (1978, 311). While this point perpetuates the separation of aesthetics from the body and from the other spheres of social life in our real three-dimensional world (Negrin 2012, 48), it is certainly applicable to dress in manga. This is because characters in manga, as previously mentioned, inhabit a two-dimensional graphic medium where the audience reads images and graphics as part of the narrative along with text (Berndt 2003, xi). Like manga, dress "involves images as well as objects," and it is constituted of "visual culture, involving form, colour, and texture" (Steele 2012, 24).

In addition to functional importance, dress may carry a symbolic function in manga that is central to the narrative. In Riyoko Ikeda's famous *shōjo* manga *The Rose of Versailles* (berusaiyu no bara 1972–1973), the militant heroine Oscar François de Jarjayes dresses in a woman's robe (the *robe l'odalisque*) at a ball, signifying her oscillation between male (militant) and female (romantic) roles (King 2021). In Mariko Iwadate's *White Satin Ribbon* (shiroi saten no ribon, 1993), dress also plays a central role—this time a grandmother's white lace dress with a big satin ribbon, symbolic of familial affection, that the heroine Namiko desires (Monden 2020).

Cocoon, Entwined

Cocoon, Entwined (mayu, matou 2018–present) follows the lead of these earlier works in making dress central to the narrative. The artist, Yuriko Hara, made her manga debut in 2015 while studying manga at Kyoto Seika University. In 2018, she started serializing *Cocoon, Entwined* in the monthly manga magazine *Comic Beam*. Launched in 1995 by major publishing company Kadokawa Shoten, this monthly manga magazine is known for featuring works in wide-ranging genres with much less editorial restriction than more mainstream, commercial manga magazines.

The story is set in Japan in the contemporary period, with a few added fantasy elements. Most of the scenes in *Cocoon, Entwined* take place in an exclusive girls' academy where the students in the final year of senior high school cut their long hair in a ritualistic way, which is then used to weave school uniforms for first-year students. The protagonist in the manga is Hoshimiya, the granddaughter of the school principal. Hoshimiya's facial features are deliberately hidden and left blank—as if she had no facial features—whereas the face is normally important for reader identification in manga culture (Itō 2012). The superficially peaceful academy is thrown into confusion when Hoshimiya's celebrated, beautiful hair flies out of the window of her dorm room; she has shed her precious hair before donating it for the school uniforms, thus wasting it. The story is threaded together from the perspectives of multiple narrators, most of them students of the academy, including Yōko Yokozawa and Hana Saeki. Yōko has a crush on

16 HAIR DRESSING: FETISH, SCHOOL UNIFORMS AND SHŌJO... 289

tall and boyish Hana, who plays a "princely" role in the all-girls academy, whereas Hana is infatuated with enigmatic Hoshimiya. As the next section discusses in more detail, the manga's focus on the homosocial relationship between adolescent girls as well as its settings, motifs, clothes and graphic styles, all strongly reference the idea of *shōjo*. While the literal translation of *shōjo* simply means "girls," in Japanese culture the term references a specific and iconic representation of femininity and girlhood.

SHŌJO AND EMOTION

According to Masuko Honda, a pioneer figure in childhood studies in Japan and an exponent of *shōjo* theory, the state of *shōjo* is a temporary one, a liminal state in between that of child and adult. In this conceptual, suspended time-space, the girl is spared from being too mature and responsible, and is allowed to direct her main concerns towards her inner-world (Honda 1992 [1980]). Honda terms this in-between space *hirahira* due to the fluttering qualities of items like flowers, ribbons and frills that visually define it, and the textual equivalent of poetic, fragmentary language (Honda 1992, 150). In contrast to *shōjo*, the *shōnen*—adolescent boys— have traditionally been understood in modern Japanese culture as being bound to duties, responsibilities, future goals and ambitions, being instructed to prioritize functionality over aesthetics (Yagawa 2006 [1990], 220; Takahara 1999, 8). Moreover, Honda has argued that the idea of *shōjo* was originally conceptualized by denying all things masculine or *shōnen*-like. Poetic, romantic, lyrical, spiritual and sentimental have come to characterize *shōjo*/girls' culture and the aesthetics associated with it (Honda 1990, 23). In other words, *shōjo* and *shōnen* have conventionally been treated quite separately. However, there is a kind of *shōnen* image that is very similar to *shōjo*, that is seen as a recipient of "feminine" beauty. The *bishōnen* (literally beautiful boy) type refers to a beautiful boy with melancholic sentiments like the *shōjo* girl (Monden 2018).

Shōjo manga, or comics whose primary readers are young women, are known for their prioritization of emotion, love, human relationships and highly defined aesthetic sensitivities, which reflect the characteristics of the world of *shōjo* (Takahashi 2008, 128–9; Fraser and Monden 2017, 550). While the narrative themes it encompasses can differ widely, *shōjo* manga has become a collective genre that alludes to certain established aesthetic styles and techniques of representation (Prough 2010, 94). This includes girls with flowing locks, slender limbs, elongated necks and large eyes adorned by feminized eyelashes, cast downwards in a dreamy gaze, and a scattering of flowers in the background, all drawn with a sensitive and graceful pen (Ishida 1992, 79). While not a *shōjo* manga in its strict sense, the theme of *Cocoon, Entwined* (*shōjo* characters and their relationship in a school—a *shōjo*-scape) and its graphics give the manga an aesthetic typical of the *shōjo* manga genre.

The exclusive girls' academy that is surrounded and hidden by a grove of silver birch, echoes the idea of girls' school as a privileged and private *shōjo*-scape in Japan (Yoshimi 2015, 23). It alludes to pre-war *shōjo* culture such as the *shōjo* fictions (*shōjo shōsetsu*) of famous writer Nobuko Yoshiya (1896–1973), which have become a paragon of *shōjo* culture and aesthetics (Dollase 2003, 744; Frederick 2005). This is expressed both graphically and conceptually. The boarding house at the academy—where only wealthy and chosen girls can enrol—features chandeliers, antique furniture and a highly decorative gazebo where lavish tea parties with confectioneries and flowers are held, providing a nostalgic, rarified environment. This clearly signals the girls at Hoshimiya Academy as *shōjo*.

Another aspect that draws parallel between *Cocoon, Entwined* and pre-Pacific War *shōjo* fiction is a homoerotic relationship between girls. The romantic friendship between girls is an ongoing theme in Japanese girls' culture. A degree of homoeroticism is allowed in, and even characterizes, the *shōjo*-scape (e.g. Kawasaki 1990; Frederick 2005). Such relationships have been most obviously associated with *shōjo* fiction in the early 1900s, with Yoshiya, who publicly had a female partner, as the main exponent of the genre, but they continue to be part of Japanese *shōjo* manga culture even today. These romantic relationships often involve two girls—one of them being tall, active, independent and handsome, while the other is petite, girlish, sweet and innocent (Fraser and Monden 2017, 556). Until the 1990s, such relationships were depicted as short-lived, for these girls were soon integrated into heterosexual romance or, if the story ended tragically, the former girl died for the latter girl. This changed after the 1990s, as more positive endings have been introduced to the romantic girl-girl relationships.

The homoerotic atmosphere of the academy—such as when the school uniform is depicted in the girl's form and holds Yōko (vol 2. 9–11) and when the junior student combs her senior's long hair after bathing (vol. 2, 47–50)—also alludes to the concept of the "S" relationship (S stands for sisters, referring to an older and younger girls' homosocial ties in pre-war girls' schools) in Yoshiya's pre-war fictions. It also references the subgenre of *Yuri* (literary "lilies" in Japanese), a metaphorical term for female homosexuality in post-war Japanese culture (Kawasaki 2014, 45).[1] Hara herself refers to this work as "Yuri" manga, inspired by Akio Yoshida's now classic manga *Cherry Blossom Garden* (Sakura no sono 1985–1986) (Village Vanguard 2020). Yoshida's manga is considered as offering an affirmative depiction of alternative gender possibilities and same-sex affection, and as James Welker argues, "its critique of the heteropatriarchal limits imposed on women, mark it as a lesbian text" (2009, 163). The affirmative portrayal of same-sex affection and complex perception of gender is also evident in Hara's *Cocoon, Entwined*. Each cover of its paperback (*tankōbon*) editions (upon which this chapter is based) depicts the two girls in each other's arms, or even exchanging a kiss (vol 4), with their long hair surrounding the bodies of the two girls as if they are attached by strings, graphically conveying to readers that this manga is about a romantic relationship between two girls. By cementing its ties to the *shōjo*-scape further, Hara's manga uses another obvious reference to pre-war *shōjo* culture: the school uniform.

Shōjo and the School Uniform

Japanese girls' school uniforms are a primary sartorial symbol of girlish femininity, particularly the "sailor" school uniforms which had become standardized by the 1950s. "Sailor" styles are strongly associated with purity, ephemerality, innocence, vulnerability and sexuality (McVeigh 2000; Sugawa-Shimada 2019, 57). These uniforms are quite dissimilar to the clothes girls wear in adulthood (Craik 2005, 64–66), unlike boys' school uniforms, which are more representative of adult male dress codes. Girls' school uniforms therefore signify a very specific period in a woman's life, up until the ages of seventeen or eighteen: neither a child nor fully socially mature as a woman.

The school uniform of Hoshimiya Academy, the story tells us, is one of the main attractions of the academy for girls (and their mothers, e.g. vol. 2, 130). A classic dress type with puffed long sleeves, sailor-collar and a princess-line silhouette, the design of the uniform is an obvious reference to pre-Pacific War *shōjo* culture. Rather than a modern sailor-style school uniform, the one in *Cocoon, Entwined* resembles the first western-style

---

[1] For more on Yuri subgenre, see the works of James Welker (2009) and Erica Friedman (2022).

uniform that was introduced in 1920 and spread across Japan by the 1930s, the era when *shōjo* fiction like Yoshiya's and illustrations by the famous illustrator and designer Jun'ichi Nakahara were creating the foundations of Japan's *shōjo* culture (Heian Jogakuin Official Website n.d.). The dress style of the sailor uniform has become increasingly anachronistic, with a blazer and skirt now being the dominant school uniform for girls (the ratio of blazer and skirt vs. sailor outfit is 56.3% to 14.3% according to one survey), indicating the manga's use of a classic *shōjo*-scape (*PR Times* 2021).

However, rather than being a simple homage to this romantic and melancholic *shōjo* romanticism, I would argue that *Cocoon, Entwined* plays with traditional *shōjo* concepts by inverting, and sometimes even subverting, the very concepts. In Honda's idea of *shōjo*, such as Yoshiya's pre-Pacific War *shōjo* fiction, what characterized *shōjo* was the girl's attention, which is directed away from outward concerns and towards her inner self (Miyasako 1989 [1984]). Placing the *shōjo* like pupae in their own small rooms until maturity means depriving them of independence and an opportunity to broaden their interests to "outside," rendering them as dolls filled only with self-interest, according to Chizuru Miyasako (1989, 205) in her criticism of Honda's *shōjo* theory. Consciously playing with this idea (as the title *Cocoon* itself suggests), the main *shōjo* girls in the manga look outside of this *shōjo*-scape. The manga does not deny *shōjo* aesthetics—one of its appeals is undoubtedly the embrace of emphatically, often hyperbolically, romantic *shōjo* graphic and narrative norms. But this is skilfully combined with the rather worldly characters of Yōko and Hana, who while physically *shōjo* are perhaps psychologically situated on the boundary of the *shōjo*-scape. As the later sections of this chapter reveal, *Cocoon, Entwined* imitates, plays with, but also inverts and twists the styles and expectations of *shōjo* culture, and in so doing the reader is exposed to both the idealized and more complex aspects of *shōjo*-scape.

Weaving Hair, Dress and the Body

The most striking aspect of the *shōjo*-scape in *Cocoon, Entwined* is the human hair used to make the girls' school uniform. Separately, both clothes and hair are intimate expressions. As Vera Mackie (2009, n.p.) says, clothes are "the boundary between body, self and society" and they can be used to show acceptance and conformity to, or refusal of, social expectations, including those of gender. Clothes, school uniforms included, are a layer positioned between the body and society. Making those clothes from the hair of another person creates another level of intimacy and complexity. Long hair has been a sign of beauty in Japanese culture; as Emerald King writes, "since at least the Heian period when Japan started to form its own beauty ideals instead of following Chinese court tradition" (2019, 203).[2] Long black hair has become a symbol that amalgamates contradictions of attraction and flight, desirability and danger (Ebersole 1998, 8; King 2019, 203). Long hair that is longer than the shoulder in contemporary Japan is considered "kawaii" or cute, and is often associated with younger women and girls.

Hair is considered as part of dress and fashion, because it can easily be manipulated, be changed as well as connote meanings such as social classes and identities (Synnott 1987, 387; Weitz 2004). Hair is both physiological and cultural, and the symbolic meaning of hair is enhanced by its personal quality (Synnott 1987, 404). This is because hair, unlike other fashion items and accessories, grows from and is part of the physical human body, and thus it not only symbolizes the self, but it is also an integral part of the self. Hair is the "most powerful symbol of individual and group identity," writes sociologist Anthony Synnott (1987, 381), "powerful first because it is physical and therefore extremely personal, and second because, although personal, it is also public rather than private." The human face is an important factor in the perception of attractiveness, with the head being the most looked at part of the human anatomy (Ribeiro 2011, 2). Hair is a major site of self-definition on personal, gender and socio-political levels because it is read as profoundly linked to identity. As sociologist and gender studies scholar Rose Weitz (2004, vxi) puts it, hair is "part of a broader language of appearance, which, whether or not we intend it, tells others about ourselves."

Sociological studies of hair indicate that it carries a vast and complex range of associations, meanings and connotations. This means that there is no intrinsic meaning of a specific hairstyle, as the same hair may symbolize different realities and express different, or even opposite, values or messages in different contexts (Synnott 1987, 407; Weitz 2004, xvi). On the other hand, as Galia Ofek (2009, 2) writes in relation to Thorstein Veblen's idea of conspicuous leisure, hairstyles "became a dominant aspect

[2] The Heian period lasted from 794 to around 1185.

of the conspicuous leisure, wealth and waste which Veblen held to be characteristic of an acquisitive society." In this sense, maintenance of one's long hair could be both expensive and require significant effort by the wearer (Synnott 1987, 384). This also implies the exclusivity and privileges that the girls at Hoshimiya Academy enjoy.

According to Peter Stallybrass (1997 [1993], 29), to think about clothes is "to think about memory, but also power and possession," and indeed, the ownership of the uniform symbolizes the power dynamic of the girls at the academy, who are seen as unique from outsiders due to their exceptionally long hair and their iconic school uniforms. Uniqueness is an important feature in *shōjo*. For example, Sumiko Yagawa, another exponent of *shōjo* theory, has argued in relation to the common narrative structure of imprisoned maidens (and hence *shōjo*) that their imprisonment is a result of being "chosen." This is crucial for *shōjo* as it is an acknowledgement of the *shōjo*'s power—be it wealth, status, knowledge or appearance—which in some cases resembles the attributes of masculine power. Yagawa's idea relates to Takahara Eiri's concept of the "consciousness of the girl." Takahara (1999, 17) argues that this subject position is about the self-satisfaction associated with narcissism, developing into the girl's feeling that she is above others around her. Indeed, in some sequences (e.g. vol. 1, 110, vol. 3, 132), Hana and Hoshimiya are identified and distinguished by women and men outside the academy as being special because of their long hair and school uniform.

While using the framework of *shōjo* narratives, *Cocoon, Entwined* also inverts some of its traditions. As mentioned earlier, the romantic relationship between the girls in *shōjo* narratives was depicted through the binaries of active and demure young women. Graphically, tall Hana and girlish Yōko fit this tradition. However, as the story proceeds, Hara problematizes this dichotomous pairing. Hana, for example, appears reasonably feminine with her long hair and wearing of the girl's school uniform, much against the almost cross-dressed depiction of these princely girls in the homosocial *shōjo* genre. She does not completely fit the conventional depiction of homosocial paring in terms of her personality, either. Hana increasingly shows her emotional fragility and thus is the one being protected and looked after by the "girly girl" Yōko, who increasingly builds her mental toughness. These "flaws" in the principal characters serve to blur the traditional "gender" separation between the *Cocoon, Entwined* characters, while outlining complex interiority and a sense of realism.

School Uniform as a Memory and Fetish Object

The senior girls cut their hair to make the uniforms in their last year of high school, just before their last term. These girls remove their hair in a symbolic and aesthetic ritual, bidding farewell to their *shōjo*-scape and hence their *shōjo* selves, before departing into the outside world. Indeed, for girls like Hana and Hoshimiya, their exceptionally long locks (and their school uniforms) are fetters that chain them to this closed world, signalling their closed *shōjo* status even in the outside world, and thus preventing them from reaching out to a future beyond the academy. On the other hand, girls like Ayane Kujō, with "the most beautiful hair," almost obsessively cling to the "present"—that of life in the academy—rejecting the outside world. While Hoshimiya's interiority is almost erased, just like her facial features, in the manga, Ayane is depicted as a complex character with several facets: a Miss Perfect in front of her juniors, a sensual "older sister" to her "young sister" in the ritual sisterhood pairing and a daughter who wishes to please her glamorous, former actress mother with her demands to have the most beautiful daughter in the academy. Ayane's almost schizophrenic characterization makes her character sink in dark obsession, to obsessively seek for the position of the most beautiful girl in the academy, the position she needs to compete with the ethereal Hoshimiya. Here, the school uniform, and hence the long hair, serves as a metaphor not only for the innocent, perfect, idealized *shōjo* identity that Ayane believes she will be imbued with by maintaining her long, luscious hair, but also a sense of identity she can only feel is intact by receiving admiration for her hair. This is because treasured clothes are associated with identity and deeply interwoven within the wearer's relationship with other people (Slater 2014, 132). By wearing the uniform, Ayane imagines that she will cement her desired place in the world.

The contrast between Ayane's dark psychological obsession and the girls like Hana and Yōko is used in the manga to create a dialectic between the idealization and de-romanticization of the *shōjo*-scape. Ayane's obsession with the *shōjo*-scape is further emphasized by her maturity, signalled both in the graphics and in the text. As mentioned earlier, Ayane's association with her "younger sister" is sensual, with emphasized physical closeness: for instance, she combs Ayane's freshly washed hair, and holds and caresses her on the sofa (vol. 4 75–84). Graphically, Ayane is the only main *shōjo* character apart from Hoshimiya who has no bangs. Long hair without bangs was a symbol of upper-class, mature femininity in 1970s *shōjo* manga, and then became closely associated with the sexy, mature style of tight-fitting bodycon in the late 1980s to early 1990s Japan (Fraser and Monden 2017). Her looks and her upper-class, ladylike locution all highlight her personality as a less girlish "other" to Yōko and Hana. This makes Ayane's attachment to the *shōjo*-scape—in contrast to Yōko and Hana's desires to move out of it—ironic, desperate and obsessive. Through the comparison of these characters, the manga offers two views on the *shōjo*-scape: an idealized view according to which girls like Ayane desperately wish to be present, and a de-romanticized one, where characters like Yōko and Hana, who fit perfectly the image of *shōjo*, struggle to leave. In addition to inverting the traditional *shōjo* concepts through complicating the characterizations of Hana and Yōko and the roles they play, Ayane's character—a mature girl who does not signal her "Otherness" to the girlish and youthful *shōjo*-scape—shows the strongest attachment to this very *shōjo*-scape, thus subverting the conceptual framework of *shōjo*.

Using human hair to weave the uniform dress effectively makes it a fetish object, in the original sense of the term, a material object imbued with a magical power which fixes desires, beliefs and narrative structures (MacGaffey 1994). According to Valerie Steele (2015, 332):

> The term fetish was ... extended to refer not only to objects allegedly possessing magic powers, but also to anything that was irrationally worshiped. Karl Marx famously coined the term "commodity fetishism" to describe the way objects produced through human labor acquired an exaggerated exchange value. Sexologists and psychiatrists traditionally described fetishism as a sexual "perversion." Today, fetishism is usually characterized as a type of variant sexuality, in which arousal is associated with a (nongenital) part of the body, such as hair, or an inanimate object, such as a shoe.

Ayane's obsessive attachment to the *shōjo*-scape, and both the maintenance of long hair and school uniform as symbolic of that realm, alludes to the concept of fetish. Moreover, the school uniform is seen as symbolic of sensuality; rather than creating a material boundary between the wearer and other girls, it binds the wearer and the girl whose hair is used to create it. This symbolic function calls into question the idea of *shōjo* as sexually innocent. This overt, literal fetishization in the *shōjo*-scape is what I argue gives an element of subversion to the manga.

The hair uniform in *Cocoon, Entwined* also reflects the homosocial link between the girls. Alison Slater argues that "'treasured' garments are associated with identity and deeply embedded in the wearer's relationship with other people" (2014, 132). This relationship is illustrated in the manga when Hana enters the Academy. Hana was too tall to wear any of the school uniforms available, but the suggestion of adding non-human hair threads to lengthen the uniform saddened her, perhaps reminding her of her "alien" status in the academy as a tall, rather idealized *bishōnen* (beautiful boy) prince, and hence being marginalized in the *shōjo*-scape (vol. 1, 90). However, Hoshimiya cut a lock of her famously beautiful hair and offered it to Hana to extend her uniform (vol. 1, 126). This act created a special attachment to Hoshimiya in Hana's mind, as if they shared a physical bond. The role of the uniform in the manga exemplifies the argument by Stallybrass (1997 [1993], 38) that "the transmission of clothes is a transmission of wealth, of genealogy, of royal connections, but also of memory and of the love of mother for daughter," although in this case, the mother is replaced by the sisterhood/*senpai*. Writing about the concept of "magic fashion," Elizabeth Wilson contends that garments "are far from being simply functional adjuncts to the body, or even a language of communication ... but take on symbolic significance in ways of which we are not always even aware," thus making garments "magical" (2004, 379). In this sense, fashion is, as Otto von Busch (2018) writes, a form of magic: abstract and romantic, yet still very real.

Juliet Ash (1996, 219) also says of clothes and memory: "clothes are *of* human beings as much as *the property of* human beings. Clothes relate to our feelings more than perhaps any other designed artefacts." And thus "memory objects," such as the school uniform "can, and do, have powerful repercussions in terms of visual and emotional affectivity" (Ash 1996, 219). Garments generate such affectivity because of a unique combination of visual, tactile and olfactory perceptions, triggering multiple pathways to emotions. This is well-documented in *Cocoon, Entwined*, where the school uniforms carry the memory and emotions of girls from whose hair they were made, and characters like Yōko feel those emotions through the breathes the uniform makes. *Cocoon, Entwined* experiments with the idea that this is even more true when the garment itself is made of an intimate part of the human body that once belonged to someone she (Hana) idolizes (Hoshimiya).

In creating the school uniform made of girls' hair, Hara was inspired by the artist Motohiko Otani's 1997 work titled "Double Edged of Thought (Dress 02)," a dress made of human hair (famitsu.com 2020). Such garments would not be functional, and their durability—one of the most important attributes for a school uniform in real life—is questionable. Although hair shirts and other garments are known, these are generally made from coarse animal hair and their function is specifically to be uncomfortable to wear. Of course, all dress in manga, including school uniforms, do not exist in a primary physical sense, but in the imagination of the designer and the reader. Dress in manga need not age in a realistic way, with the human imprint of the sweat and stains of everyday life. It does not need to exist at all because "unlike photography or film, manga do not depend on an object which has to be shot, and so, do not need to be measured by criteria of conventional realism" (Berndt 2006, 24). Indeed, Itō (2005, 85) and Iwashita (2013, 232) argue that one of the important things about the concept of reality in manga is the making of apparently unrealistic depictions to be read as realistic along with the assumption that readers will interpret it in that way. Accordingly, Hara's beautiful, sensitive graphics and spellbinding narratives make readers feel unconcerned with such unrealistic aspects.

The school uniform in *Cocoon, Entwined* instead becomes a magic or fetish object because it carries the memory of the girl from whom it was made. It is thus a form of transgenerational homosocial bonding through hair/dress that is taking place. It can be argued that in the affective economy of *Cocoon, Entwined*, hair figures as a hand-me down cloth that binds the characters into a form of felt—yet perhaps not practically experienced—homosocial girlhood. This treatment of the school uniform confirms Stallybrass's idea of clothes and memory: clothes "[tend] to be powerfully associated with memory … When a person is absent or dies, cloth can absorb their absent presence" (1997, 30) because clothes are "able to carry the absent body, memory, genealogy, as well as literal material value" (36–37). Clothes can "trigger a body image and thus a memory of the body" (Gibson 2008, 111). Garments worn over time, moreover, "age with the wearer, becoming like a second skin" (Woodward 2007, 78). The clothes, in this sense, "are preserved; they remain. It is the bodies that inhabit them which change" (Stallybrass 1997, 38). The idea of items of clothing being imbued with the attributes of their wearer is in fact widely prevalent in Japanese culture. The treatment of the uniform in *Cocoon, Entwined* has echoes of the romantic ritual in Japanese schools, where, on graduation day, a girl would ask for the second button of a *gakuran* uniform belonging to the boy she has a crush on. The *gakuran* is the traditional boy's school uniform modelled on a Prussian military jacket and in one hypothesis the significance of the second button is that it is situated closest to the heart. Thus, the sartorial button becomes a memory object and a simulacrum of the wearer. The school uniform in *Cocoon, Entwined*, as in the episode where Hoshimiya's locks are braided into Hana's school uniform, retells this logic.

Similarly, the cutting of hair to symbolize a life change is in itself unremarkable in Japan, from the ritual severing of the samurai's topknot on the resignation of his commission, to the more practical, shorter styles favoured by women as they mature today. Ofek (2009) explains that in Europe, in Victorian times, a woman's hair was often connected to female sexuality, or her hair was a sign of her sexuality. Cultural expectations required "respectable" Victorian ladies, mothers and wives to dress their hair in a neat, cultivated order, and women with dishevelled hair were associated with sexual immorality. But a young girl's dishevelled hair had a different social meaning: as she was not sexually mature it denoted innocence and virginity rather than the "disordered" sexuality of the mature female. "Hair is inextricably linked ... to sexual maturity" in Japanese culture, too (King 2019, 204). A coming-of-age ceremony for a girl in the pre-Meiji era, for example, involved coiffing her previously long hair (Ogiwara 2020, 169). Hara (Village Vanguard 2020) herself refers to the metaphorical meaning of cutting hair as the cutting of strings that confine women in their inner-world to become independent, and something that girls lose when they grow into women (*Anuigalla review* 2019). Indeed, most of the female characters who have passed the period of *shōjo* in the manga have short hair. This is especially noticeable in the young teacher and her sister (vol. 3, episode 16) both of whom were, not long ago, *shōjo* students at the Hoshimiya Academy.

Conventionally, *shōjo* has been perceived as a period when girls may be sexually mature but are not yet sexually active (Ōtsuka 1989, 105; Watanabe 2007, 17). The *shōjo* exists in opposition to the idea of "mother/maternal productivity" in a society that fetishizes the concept of productivity (Orbaugh 2003, 96). The idea of non-productivity associated with *shōjo* is expressed in Honda's highly aesthetic *shōjo* concept of *hirahira*. It is significant that the ceremony which the girls in *Cocoon, Entwined* go through as they depart from the *shōjo*-scape is to sever the long hair that they have tended to throughout their schooling in order to produce a uniform for the next generation of *shōjo*. Furthermore, *Cocoon, Entwined* frequently references the perception held by girls in their senior year that cutting their hair is synonymous with death (e.g. vol. 3, 172). This parodies the idea, common both within Japan and outside, of the cultural importance placed on women's hair (see Weitz 2004). However, the *shōjo* girls at Hoshimiya Academy believe that their spirit of *shōjo* will live on in the form of their school uniform (as is articulated in episodes 8, vol. 2, and in episode 16, vol. 3).

Whether it is intentional or not, I argue that the subversion of *shōjo* concepts is particularly evident in the episodes which are narrated from the perspective of the school uniform worn by Yōko. The uniform still shares its romantic affection, physical intimacy and nostalgic yearning for the girl whose hair it was created from, that is, the younger sister of the teacher at the academy. The girl still shares this emotional attachment with the school uniform (and occasionally with Yōko) through dreams. Now a young woman in her post-*shōjo* period, the teacher's sister refuses to grow her hair long again. Although her facial expressions indicate conflicting and complex feelings of agony, hesitation and nostalgia, the girl does not die after cutting her hair short; instead, she has left the spirit of *shōjo* within the *shōjo*-scape, embodied in the fetish object of the uniform. The melancholy associated with the *shōjo*-scape is based on ephemerality: that *shōjo* will die and becomes a woman. *Cocoon, Entwined* plays with this idea, but with a twist: the *shōjo* will leave the realm of *shōjo*, but as they leave their traces of their *shōjo*-hood at the academy, in the form of school uniform, they will never leave *shōjo* entirely. And in the clothing house, on an underground level that resembles a catacomb according to Hana (vol 1. 82), lie all of the old uniforms, the mortal remains of *shōjo*.

Conclusion

Hara's manga *Cocoon, Entwined* is a primary example of Japanese popular culture where both clothes and hair are understood as the most intimate forms of physical ornament for humans. Amalgamating hair and clothes in the form of a school uniform for girls made of hair, *Cocoon, Entwined* uses these elements to embellish a closed world of homosocial *shōjo* where flowing locks, fluttering hems of dress and blossoming flowers reign. By adding an aspect of magical realism in which the school uniform breathes, however, Hara also skilfully uses the idea that clothes are memory objects, carrying the memory and emotions of the former *shōjo* whose hair is used to create them. In so doing, Hara successfully delineates the world of *shōjo* through the subjectivities of the *shōjo* themselves, both idealizing and de-romanticizing the concept of adolescent girlhood that has so long captivated artistic imaginations in Japanese popular culture. While using the style and concepts of *shōjo* as a framework, this manga also plays with, inverts as well as subverts, some elements of this cultural imagination of ideal girlish identity in Japanese culture. This overt, literal fetishization of the *shōjo*-scape is what, I argue, lends the element of subversion to the manga. This chapter has shown that Hara's manga effectively both validates and critiques the idea of *shōjo*, the iconic representation of ideal girlhood in Japanese culture, as something both tempting and dangerous, haunting and frightful, and above all, both ethereally beautiful and realistically suppressive like a school uniform.

Acknowledgement I thank David Jellings for his tireless editing and reading of this chapter.

References

Ash, Juliet. 1996. Memory and Objects. In *The Gendered Object*, ed. Pat Kirkham, 219–224. Manchester: Manchester University Press.

Berndt, Jaqueline. 2003. Jobun [Preface]. In *Manbiken: manga no bi/gakuteki na jigen e no sekkin [Towards an Aesthetics of Comics]*, ed. Jaqueline Berndt, i–xv. Kyoto: Daigo Shobō.

———. 2006. A Manifold 'Flat Battlefield': The Critical Potential of Manga as Seen Through Okazaki Kyoko's Works. In *Raifu ten katarogu ("Life" Exhibition Catalogue)*, 23–26. Exhibition catalogue. Mito: Mito Geijutsu Gendai Bijutsu Center.

Craik, Jennifer. 2005. *Uniforms Exposed*. New York & London: Berg.

Davis, Fred. 1992. *Fashion, Culture, and Identity*. Chicago: University of Chicago Press.

Dollase, Hiromi Tsuchiya. 2003. Early Twentieth Century Japanese Girls' Magazine Stories: Examining Shōjo Voice in Hanamonogatari (Flower Tales). *Journal of Popular Culture* 36 (4): 724–755.

Ebersole, Gary L. 1998. 'Long Black Hair Like a Seat Cushion': Hair Symbolism in Japanese Popular Religion. In *Hair: Its Power and Meaning in Asian Cultures*, ed. Alf Hiltebeitel and Barbara D. Miller, 75–104. New York: State University of New York Press.

Entwistle, Joanne. 2001. The Dressed Body. In *Body Dressing*, ed. J. Entwistle and E. Wilson. Oxford: Berg.

Fraser, Lucy, and Masafumi Monden. 2017. The Maiden Switch: New Possibilities for Understanding Japanese Shōjo Manga (Girls' Comics). *Asian Studies Review* 41 (4): 544–561.

Frederick, Sarah. 2005. Not that Innocent: Yoshiya Nobuko's Good Girls. In *Bad Girls of Japan*, ed. Laura Miller and Jan Bardsley, 65–80. New York: Palgrave.
Friedman, Erica. 2022. *By Your Side: The First 100 Years of Yuri Anime and Manga*. Vista: Journey Press.
Gibson, Margaret. 2008. *Objects of the Dead: Mourning and Memory in Everyday Life*. Carlton: University of Melbourne Press.
Hara, Yuriko. 2020. 'Mayu, matou', chosha Hara Yuriko sensei o sukutta noha, masaka no BL manga deshita [What Saved Yuriko Hara, the Author of Cocoon Entwined, was Surprisingly BL Manga]. *Village Vanguard*, June 18. https://www.village-v.co.jp/news/media/6923. Accessed 18 March 2022.
Heian Jogakukuin Official Website. n.d. School's History Resources. http://jh.heian.ac.jp/school_profile/academy_history. Accessed 18 March 2022.
Hollander, Anne. 1978. *Seeing Through Clothes*. Berkeley and Los Angeles: University of California Press.
Honda, Masuko. 1990. Shōnen to shōjo [Boys and Girls]. *Panoramic Magazine IS* 47: 21–24.
———. 1992 [1980]. "Hirahira no keifu" [The Genealogy of Hirahira]. In *Ibunka to shite no kodomo [The Child As Another Culture]*, ed. Masuko Honda, 148–185. Tokyo: Chikuma shobō.
Hughes, Claire. 2006. *Dressed in Fiction*. Oxford and New York: Berg.
Ishida, Saeoko. 1992. 'Shōjo manga' no buntai to sono hōgen sei [The Drawing Styles in Girls' Comics: A Dialect of Subculture]. In *Komikku media: yawarakai jōhō sōchi to shite no manga [Media Co-mix]*, ed. Kayama Rika, 55–56. Tokyo: NTT Shuppan.
Itō, Go. 2005. *Tezuka izu deddo: hirakareta manga hyogenron e* [Tezuka is dead: postmodernist and modernist approaches to Japanese manga]. Tokyo: NTT Shuppan.
Itō, Gō. 2012. Manga nofutatsu no kao [Two Faces in Manga]. *Nihon 2.0: shisouchizuβ* 3: 436–483.
Iwashita, Hōsei. 2013. *Shōjo manga no hyōgen kikō: Hirakareta manga hyōgenshi to Tezuka Osamu [Aesthetic Mechanisms of Shōjo Manga: An Open-Minded History of Manga Aesthetics, Related to the Role of Tezuka Osamu]*. Tokyo: NTT Shuppan.
Kawasaki, Kenko. 1990. *Shōjo biyori [A Perfect Day for the Girl]*. Tokyo: Seikyusha.
———. 2014. Hankai no shinboru [The Symbol of Partial Destruction]. *Yuriika* 46 (15): 42–49.
King, Emerald. 2019. Tangled Hair and Broken Bodies: Remaking Women and Technology in Japanese Gothic Horror Tradition from *The Tale of Genji* to *Ringu*. In *Gothic Afterlives: Reincarnations of Horror in Film and Popular Media*, ed. L. Piatti-Farnell, 199–212. Lexington Books.
———. 2021. *La Robe à la Francaise et la Robe l'Odalisque*: Wearing Women's Clothing in *The Rose of Versailles*. *Studies in Costume & Performance* 6 (1): 29–47.

MacGaffey, Wyatt. 1994. African Objects and the Idea of Fetish. *RES: Anthropology and Aesthetics* 25 (Spring): 123–131.
Mackie, Vera. 2009. Transnational Bricolage: Gothic Lolita and the Political Economy of Fashion. *Intersections* 20 (April): n.p. http://intersections.anu.edu.au/issue20/mackie.htm.
McVeigh, Brian J. 2000. *Wearing Ideology.* Oxford & New York: Berg.
Miyasako, Chizuru. 1989 [1984]. *Chōshōjo e [Toward Super-/beyond-Girl].* Tokyo: Hokusosha.
Monden, Masafumi. 2018. The Beautiful Shōnen of the Deep and Moonless Night: The Boyish Aesthetic in Modern Japan. *Asien: deutsche Zeitschrift fuer Politik, Wirtschaft und Kultur* 147: 64–91.
———. 2020. Shrouded in Memory: Time, Desire and Emotions in Iwadate Mariko's *A White Satin Ribbon. U.S.—Japan Women's Journal* 57: 78–106.
Negrin, Llewellyn. 2012. Aesthetics. In *Fashion and Art*, ed. Adam Geczy and Vicki Karaminas, 43–54. London and New York: Berg.
Ofek, Galia. 2009. *Representations of Hair in Victorian Literature and Culture.* Surrey: Ashgate.
Ogiwara, Keiko. 2020. Bungaku kyōzai no kenkyū: 'Taketori monogatari' no gengo hyōgen [A Study on Japanese Language Art Education: A Verbal Expression of Teketori Monogatari]. *Bulletin of Kyushu Women's University* 57 (1): 165–172.
Orbaugh, Sharalyn. 2003. The "Shojo Fatale" in the Works of Kanai Mieko. Symposium proceedings. *Constructing Japanese Studies in Global Perspectives*: 93–97.
Ōtsuka, Eiji. 1989. *Shōjo minzokugaku [Ethnography of Shōjo].* Tokyo: Kōbunsha.
Otto von Busch. 2018. Inclusive Fashion—an Oxymoron—Or a Possibility for Sustainable Fashion? *Fashion Practice* 10 (3): 311–327.
PR Times. 2021. Press Release. December 28. https://okayama.keizai.biz/release/103834/. Accessed 18 March 2022.
Prough, Jennifer. 2010. *Straight from the Heart: Gender, Intimacy, and the Cultural Production of Shōjo Manga.* Honolulu: University of Hawai'i Press.
Ribeiro, Aileen. 2011. *Facing Beauty.* Yale and New Haven: Yale University Press.
Slater, Alison. 2014. Wearing in Memory: Materiality and Oral Histories of Dress. *Critical Studies in Fashion and Beauty* 5 (1): 125–139.
Stallybrass, Peter. 1997 [1993]. Worn Worlds: Clothes, Mourning, and the Life of Things. In *Cultural Memory and the Construction of Identity*, ed. Dan Ben-Amos and Liliane Weissberg, 27–44. Detroit: Wayne State University Press.
Steele, Valerie. 1989. Appearance and Identity. In *Men and Women Dressing the Part*, ed. C.B. Kidwell and V. Steele, 42–63. Washington: Smithsonian Institution Press.
———. 2012. Fashion. In *Fashion and Art*, ed. Adam Geczy and Vicki Karaminas, 13–28. London and New York: Berg.

———. 2015. Fetish Fashion. In *The Berg Companion to Fashion*, ed. Valerie Steele, vol. 332. London and New York: Berg.
Sugawa-Shimada, Akiko. 2019. Playing with Militarism in/with Arpeggio and Kantai Collection: Effects of Shōjo Images in War-Related Contents Tourism in Japan. *Journal of War & Culture Studies* 12 (1): 53–66.
Synnott, Anthony. 1987. Shame and Glory: A Sociology of Hair. *The British Journal of Sociology* 38 (3): 381–413.
Takahara, Eiri. 1999. *Shōjo ryōiki [The Territory of the Girl]*. Tokyo: Kokusho kankōkai.
Takahashi, Mizuki. 2008. Opening the Closed World of Shojo Manga. In *Japanese Visual Culture: Explorations in the World of Manga and Anime*, ed. Mark Wheeler Macwilliams, 114–136. New York: M. E. Sharpe.
Takemura, Mana. 2012. *Manga fasshon [Manga Fashion]*. Tokyo: Pai Intānashonaru.
Watanabe, Shūko. 2007. *Shōjo zō no tanjō –kindai nihon ni okeru "shōjo" no keisei [The Birth of the Images of Shōjo—The Construction of Shōjo in Modern Japan]*. Tokyo: Shinsen- sha.
Weitz, Rose. 2004. *Rapunzel's Daughters: What Women's Hair Tells Us About Women's Lives*. New York: Macmillan.
Welker, James. 2009. From The Cherry Orchard to Sakura no sono: Translation and the Transfiguration of Gender and Sexuality in Sho-jo Manga. In *Girl Reading Girl*, ed. Tomoko Aoyama and Barbara Hartley, 160–173. Abingdon: Routledge.
Wilson, Elizabeth. 2004. Magic Fashion. *Fashion Theory* 8 (4): 375–385.
Woodward, Sophie. 2007. *Why Women Wear What They Wear*. Oxford: Berg Publishers.
Yagawa, Sumiko. 2006 [1990]. *"Chichi no musume"-tachi: Mori Mari to Anaisu Nin [The Fathers' Daughters: Mari Mori and Anais Nin]*. Tokyo: Shin'yōsha.
Yoshimi, Shunya. 2015. Michiko-hi to kanba michiko: ten'kanki no josei zō [Princess Michiko and Michiko Kanba: The Image of Women in the Time of Changing]. In *60-nen Anpo: 1960-nen zengo*, ed. Kurihara Akira, 17–46. Tokyo: Iwanami shoten.

CHAPTER 17

"What's Getting Us Through": *Grazia* UK as Affective Intimate Public During the Coronavirus Pandemic

Rosie Findlay

During a panel on 'The State of Fashion Magazines', hosted by *The Business of Fashion* seven months into the coronavirus pandemic, Kenya Hunt, then-Deputy Editor of *Grazia* UK, reflected on how the crisis had reshaped the magazine's content:

> We have the shopping at the front of the book that has been called 'What's New Now' but we changed it in COVID to [...] 'What's Getting Us Through' [...] Those newsy pages [are] where the brands probably are like, 'can you put this launch in here, we've got this anniversary' [...] Historically, that is what those pages had been for. But with us, it's really more so about [...] those moments that will make a reader feel understood; it's less about consuming the new thing although we still have that in there as well. But it's

R. Findlay (✉)
University of Kent, Canterbury, UK
e-mail: r.findlay@kent.ac.uk

© The Author(s), under exclusive license to Springer Nature Switzerland AG 2023
R. Filippello, I. Parkins (eds.), *Fashion and Feeling*, Palgrave Studies in Fashion and the Body,
https://doi.org/10.1007/978-3-031-19100-8_17

really about acknowledging this shared experience that we're having. (BOF Team 2020)[1]

The intimacy and sense of a shared common world that Hunt gestures towards here are qualities germane to women's magazines, yet they assumed a particular resonance during the pandemic. After weeks of mixed messages from the British government about the severity of the crisis, on 23 March 2020, the UK's first national lockdown began. Overnight, everyone in the UK was required to shelter in place, working from home (WFH) or put on furlough unless they were an 'essential worker'. People were forbidden from meeting with anyone outside their household, and from entering someone else's residence, including those of family members and intimate partners, with the exception of children whose parents resided in separate households. School and university classes went online. All non-essential businesses closed. Compounding the shock of the rhythms of everyday life being stopped was the horror of watching a deadly virus, about which little was known, quickly spread through the community.

Grazia UK is a weekly "fashion-focused" women's magazine (Bradford 2019, 22), launched in 2005 in response to the speeding up of the fashion cycle, typically covering "what's on shelves that week" (103) from luxury to fast fashion.[2] Except for their fashion editorial, weeklies are typically produced within a week, and in *Grazia*'s case, this results in content with an immediate focus: key news stories, from celebrity to current affairs; new product releases in fashion, beauty, entertainment and homewares; and features couched in personal perspective. That its content "cut[s] across categories" (1987, 13) is consistent with Janice Winship's reading of women's magazines as reflective of women's lives, where leisure is mixed with work, "private time and space are precious […] and dreams and escape often feed on a modest vocabulary of everyday possibilities" (13). Understandable, then, that during the pandemic *Grazia* turned to "really explor[e] how our new reality had changed" (Hunt in BOF Team 2020): with its purpose to provide its predominantly middle-class, professional,

---

[1] The name of the section was changed to "What's keeping us going now", but the phrase 'getting us through' was frequently used in the magazine during the lockdown issues.

[2] *Grazia* moved to a fortnightly production cycle in May 2020, presumably in response to the challenges of producing an issue each week during the pandemic. While this change was initially framed as short-term, at the time of writing the magazine was still being published fortnightly.

female reader with tools to navigate the world around her, *Grazia* risked looking out of touch (at best) if it didn't respond to the cataclysmic shift the pandemic prompted in all spheres of everyday life. And yet, the magazine's tone is usually bright, upbeat and friendly, particularly when reporting on fashion, where the pleasures of consumption and fashion's capacity to realise new femininities are foregrounded. The affects that the pandemic engendered—fear, anxiety, isolation, uncertainty, grief, strain and, for some, tedium—were decidedly at odds with this optimistic tenor and remit.

This chapter is interested in the ways *Grazia* UK responded to the pandemic's "ugly feelings" (Ngai 2005). Through the close reading of five issues of *Grazia*, all produced during the UK's first lockdown (23 March–June 2020, see Institute for Government n.d.), we will see how fashion was discursively produced as a means of affective sustenance for readers through its consoling pleasures and promise of momentary escape.[3] In this content, the magazine largely remained faithful to its customary ideological commitment to neoliberal feminism: encouraging individual resourcefulness and self-transformation as a response to the challenges and ongoing project of being a woman in a particular time and place. Yet at the same time, the painful affects prompted by the pandemic opened a space for *Grazia* to critique the fashion system and—to an extent—question consumer culture, resisting the insistence on the self-sustaining subject to advocate for collective action and social investments. This possibility was predicated on the pandemic's disruption of everyday life and the structural inequalities it laid bare. In *Grazia*'s gestures towards collective politics, however partial and tentative, we see the potential of women's media to critique the capitalist systems within which it is imbricated. Lauren Berlant's concept of "intimate publics" (2008) will anchor this discussion, as will feminist literature on women's magazines.

---

[3] The issues I discuss in this chapter are Issue 770 (23 March 2020), Issue 771 (30 March 2020), Issue 772 (6 April 2020), Issue 776 (5 May 2020) and Issue 777 (18 May 2020). The UK's emergence from lockdown was conducted in stages: people who couldn't work from home returned to the workplace from 10 May, schools had a phased re-opening on 1 June and non-essential shops re-opened on 15 June.

GRAZIA AS INTIMATE PUBLIC

In their work on twentieth-century women's sentimental texts, Lauren Berlant mapped the ways in which women's culture provides spaces for affective recognition and connection between women, promising proximity to the longed-for "better good life" (2008, 270) even as it avoids mobilising political engagement to prompt structural change. The concept of intimate publics articulates the stranger relationality mediated and made possible by these texts (see also Berlant 2011, Warner 2002 and Felski 1989). The public the text addresses is presumed to "already share a worldview and emotional knowledge that they have derived from a broadly common historical experience" (2008, viii), the text functioning as a space where those individuals can feel recognised—the problems arising from their minoritised status acknowledged and framed as shared experience, their interests validated, their dreams encouraged—as it circulates affectively charged narratives to affirm a vaguely expressed collective belonging. In intimate publics "emotional contact, of a sort, is made" (2008, viii) through an individual's identification with what is represented as generally experienced phenomena. Through this open-ended representation of experience and invitation to identify, reflect and seek relief through commodity culture, intimate publics provide a "complex of consolation, confirmation, discipline and discussion about how to live as an *x*" (viii).

Importantly, while the intimate publics Berlant discusses have the capacity to make women (and other marginalised people) feel that their lives—and the specific political and social issues arising from their subjectivity—matter, by articulating and validating these experiences in a space marked for them, their "relation to the political and to politics [are] extremely uneven and complex" (2008, viii). Intimate publics render conventional the forms of collective suffering or marginalisation claimed as part and parcel of women's lives, yet they are

> juxtapolitical [… thriving] in proximity to the political, occasionally crossing over in political alliance, even more occasionally doing some politics, but most often not, acting as a critical chorus that sees the expression of emotional response and conceptual recalibration as achievement enough. (x)

The concept of intimate publics offers a valuable lens through which to evaluate *Grazia* and the work it did during the first 2020 lockdown. Many of the characteristics Berlant identifies as inherent to an intimate public are true of this publication. *Grazia* is for women, specifically those in the 25–45 age range and mostly with a professional-class socio-economic profile.[4] The concept of community is explicitly stated in *Grazia*'s Media Pack, which characterises readers as "a community of stylish, funny, ambitious, aspirational, warm, intelligent and successful women" (Bauer Media Group n.d.). The notion of readers as participants in a community is central to the magazine's discursive construction and reflected in its content, which often grounds stories in individual experience, such as the section 'Things You Only Know If …', comprising a personal essay from a contributor reflecting on a difficult circumstance. The presumed relatability of these experiences is predicated on being a woman in the UK and suggests that readers share enough of a common lifeworld to recognise themselves in the content.

A fundamental aspect of *Grazia*'s content is its coverage of issues relating to women's political and social inequality in the UK. This ranges from raising topics to inform readers (often written up in the regular one-page 'Grazia View' section) to urging political leaders to advocate for policy change. For example, in November 2019, *Grazia* joined a campaign led by two UK MPs and campaign group We Can't Consent to This to lobby the UK government to add a clause ending the 'rough sex' defence to the Domestic Abuse Bill. *Grazia* invited readers to sign a petition, resulting in 67,000 signatures and, in the run-up to the 2020 General Election, asked the leaders of the three major political parties whether they would support this amendment to the bill (see Evans 2019). It was added in June 2020 and passed into law in 2021 (see Bauer Media Group 2020). At other times, *Grazia*'s work is more juxtapolitical, gesturing towards the need for change without unpacking how such change might be realised. In these instances, coverage of women's issues is framed as "conceptual recalibration" (Berlant 2008, x), or awareness raising—for instance, the final sentences of a Grazia View on casting women in traditionally male roles read "Hollywood's gender-swaps won't solve sexism. We deserve our own thrilling stories—and our own heroes" (762, 5).

---

[4] Grazia's Media Pack identifies their target reader as having an 'AB' profile. The UK Office for National Statistics categorises UK consumers into six categories according to their socio-economic status. 'AB' is the profile that classifies "higher and intermediate managerial, administrative, professional occupations" (UK Geographics n.d.).

However, it is important to note that *Grazia* never claims to offer hard news coverage or analysis and neither does it clearly align with a partisan position. Here, as Janice Winship has argued of commercial women's magazines more generally, "the form the political takes [...] is about a commitment to certain ideologies" (1987, 21). In *Grazia*, this iterates as a commitment to neoliberal feminism, which "very clearly avows gender inequality" while "simultaneously disavow[ing] the socio-economic and cultural structures shaping [women's] lives" (Rottenberg in Banet-Weiser et al., 2020, 7). The feminist subject formed by this ideology is one, as Catherine Rottenberg has observed, "who accepts full responsibility for her own well-being and self-care" (7). Extending from this, we can understand *Grazia*'s reader as responsible for shaping the project of her life, the core constituents of which are reflected in the magazine's content: she takes an active interest in the world around her, intervening where she can but mostly just being aware of the key issues each week (current affairs content); she enjoys the pleasures of fashion and beauty, seeing her home as an extension of herself, a place to entertain and rest (lifestyle and fashion content); and she strives to achieve 'balance' through attending to her finances, her mental health and general wellbeing (advice content, occasional fitness and cooking content). This idealised disposition recalls Angela McRobbie's critique of "the perfect", a benchmark for women that, she argues, arose to modify the "patriarchal retrenchment" enacted by feminism, and which equates female success with control (of one's affairs and one's body) and individualism (2015, 4). The theme of 'balance' also arises in relation to *Grazia*'s non-partisan approach to British politics. Occasionally, MPs from one of the main political parties in the UK will contribute on issues relating to being a woman in the public eye or on political issues pertaining to gender equality. Election coverage typically includes perspectives from candidates or voters from across the political spectrum. The accommodation of different political commitments can be read in line with neoliberal feminism, which "sh[ies] away from argument and confrontation" (Rottenberg 2018, 82), also evident in the magazine's statement that their readers are "feminists who are redefining how their versions of feminism play out for them" (Bauer Media Group n.d.).

Understanding *Grazia*'s content in this way helps us appreciate the significance of the lockdown issues' shift in content and tone. Optimism fell away, as did the magazine's "positive and productive" ethos (Bauer Media Group n.d.), its discursive construction that emphasises the reader's agency and ability to succeed if she works hard and smart enough. Yet, instead of completely destabilising the publication and its editorial purpose, *Grazia* drew on its habitual conventions—including its discursive construction of fashion—to reassure readers and sometimes even indicate towards the importance of collectivity rather than individualism.

FEELGOOD FASHION

One of the effects of the outbreak and rapid global spread of COVID-19 was the rupturing of the fantasy of the 'good life' so central to women's media (see Winship 1987, Ferguson 1983, Gough-Yates 2003, Duffy 2013, McRobbie 2015). This fantasy is predicated on the investment in a future in which happiness and fulfilment is possible. It promises that the idealised feminine self, home and career found in the magazine's pages—the good life and the better you who lives it—can be realised through consumption and by investing in and regulating the self. The specific characteristics of this ideal, and its apparent proximity or distance from the reader's lifeworld, depends on the title, but the good life's dependence on self-actualisation—and the fundamental role commodities and self-work play in realising it—do not. Not only did the shock and horror of mass disease and death, and the subsequent restrictions placed on civilian populations, suspend any illusion of the good life currently being lived, but the likelihood of a better future was also temporarily cast in doubt. The affects arising from this sudden occurrence are consistent with Sianne Ngai's definition of "ugly feelings", which she argues can be conceived of as negative in three ways: they are "dysphoric", in evoking "pain or displeasure" (2005, 11); "semantically negative", in being "saturated with socially stigmatizing meanings and values" and "syntactically negative [...] organized by trajectories of repulsion rather than attraction" (2005, 11). *Grazia* could not maintain its customary "breathless and excitable and giddy and fun" tone (Polly Vernon in Bradford 2019, 136) and remain relevant to readers' lives. Instead, it drew on the lexicon of fashion consumption as pleasurable, reframing its distracting pleasures as consolatory and an anticipatory investment in a temporarily postponed future. In this way, the magazine reacted to the "politically charged predicament of suspended agency" (Ngai 2005, 12) by offering readers a route, through fashion and dress, by which dysphoric feelings could be momentarily escaped or transformed into positive feelings with the power to 'keep us going'.

Indeed, one of the dominant messages attached to fashion in these issues is its mood-boosting properties. Sometimes this was framed through the transformative promise of buying something new—for example, Gucci's chain-link pumps "promise to bring you some much-needed joy right now" (772, 57); at others, it was enough to simply get dressed. Issue 771, which appears to be the first issue wholly produced by the team working from home (WFH), hit newsstands a week after the UK went into lockdown. It includes a story titled "Working from home? There's an outfit for that now" (16). It does not directly reference depression, but much of the advice given indexes the lethargy and sadness inherent to that state: "so what should you be wearing? Well, start by wearing something. Anything. The power of getting up and getting dressed is not to be underestimated" (16). The article mildly jokes about turning into an unshowered slob before advising readers to "*feel* work-ready" (my emphasis) by dressing in "something softly-tailored" rather than "a stained tracksuit and no bra" (16). The suggestion that readers can transmute low feelings into feelings of preparedness by getting dressed is also framed as a form of self-care: "swathing yourself in softness, without forgetting style, is a fashion reminder to be kind to yourself" (17).

Clothes as a source of comfort and power elaborated in the next issue through a feature with the same name. Getting dressed becomes a "personal pact to take something out of the day and to engage with the world, even when you're behind closed doors" (772, 45). The circumstance for getting dressed here is WFH, but instead of offering a selection of specific looks for readers to adopt, the feature espouses an eclectic array of garments with different comforting properties: "the coddle of a cashmere sweater, the anarchic comfort of an elasticated waistband, the peppy energy boost of a[n] incongruously glamorous top, [which] are all a tonic in these most unsettling times" (45). These garments reveal the different comforts afforded by clothes in this context, whether sensory (feeling held by the softness of cashmere) or affective (the spirits being lifted through wearing colourful clothes). This affective interplay between wearer and clothing recalls Ilya Parkins' observation that "dress is a profoundly intimate and co-invested mediator of mood, worn as it is on the body—it helps us see that mood is circulated through a provisional articulation of living beings and non-human material" (2021, 805).

Advice took a different form in a feature by Polly Vernon in the same issue, drawing on her experience of having worked from home for years as a freelancer. She couches her guidance in the affective: "you should be prepared for how epically discombobulating [WFH] feels in the early days" because the absence of the office is "a loss" (772, 55). She advises adopting routines and avoiding a low affective state by choosing not to stay in "ratty T-shirt and battered PJ pants [… because] 'no one will know' […] *You will know*! And you will not feel good about it" (56, emphasis in original). Vernon also reframes the curtailment of agency imposed by governmental lockdowns as an opportunity (in line with *Grazia*'s customary upbeat tone): she suggests using the time saved from commuting "to work on the ever-evolving oeuvre that is your look […] (NB: this is also a realistic goal for quarantine. I know you think you're going to learn French and write a novel—but you're not. You may well, however, emerge from it better styled than you were when you went in.)" (56). Vernon's message here is galvanising—there's something you can do to meet the uncertain conditions head-on—as is the humour with which it is conveyed. She embraces the "shallowness" of her solutions because "a) shallow is all that's standing between me and madness right now (Keep Shallow and Carry On), and b) […] when we dress ourselves […w]e establish an intention for ourselves […] We remind ourselves that there is more to us than merely 'getting through' the next few days, weeks, months" (56). In this way, the mood-boosting properties attributed to clothes defied the seriousness and heaviness of the pandemic, evident too in the same issue's recommendation of "silly dressing" (772, 7). Whether taking form through a tulle Maison Cléo dress—"No such thing as De Trop in your home!"—or a pink American Vintage boilersuit—"If you don't need a pair of pink overalls now—then when?" (7)—the playfulness of clothes and the pleasures of consuming new ones were foregrounded. There seems also an implied release here from the ways that anticipation of other people's perception can curtail the possibilities of dressing. The giddy exhortation is to dress however you please, because in the enclosure of your own home, who's going to see you?

The magazine also encouraged readers to invest in the imaginative escapism afforded by buying clothes to wear in the better future. This discursive device—dressing towards the future through the accoutrements of a new season—is, of course, common to fashion magazines. Yet here, emptied of the blithe certainty of pre-lockdown issues, it assumed the keen edge of a longed-for time whose actual arrival was uncertain. Issue 776 encouraged readers to "make the beach feel closer" by buying a holiday wardrobe even though their "holiday plans might be on ice" (58), whereas Issue 777 invited them to plan a post-lockdown holiday inspired by Gucci's pre-fall 2020 campaign or Maje's new capsule collection featuring Slim Aarons' photographs. This wishful thinking bypassed the ugly feelings of lockdown using fashion and fashion imagery—that which is available now—to conjure the relief of dreaming of better days. Summer holidays not only signified escape from the familiarity and tedium of being confined to one's home but also anticipated distant, optimistic affects: release, pleasure, relaxation. Acquiring new summer clothes offered a means of materialising that hope, even if once acquired they would remain unworn indefinitely.

Without wishing to be cynical, or to discount the genuine efforts of the *Grazia* team to offer readers comfort and light relief, the magazine's neoliberal feminist ideology is resonant in these messages. Catherine Rottenberg defines neoliberalism as "a dominant political rationality that moves to and from the management of the state to the inner workings of the subject, recasting the individual as human capital and thus capital-enhancing agents" (Banet-Weiser et al., 2020, 8). The individual is idealised as a self-managed and self-sustaining economic unit, as market logics infiltrate into private space and concepts of identity and personhood. Neoliberal feminism partially resists this unchecked expansion of capital logics through the notion of "happy work-family balance" (Rottenberg 2018, 14), which functions as "normative frame and ultimate ideal" (Banet-Weiser et al. 2020, 8). The ability of the neoliberal feminist subject to achieve emancipation through her balance of home and professional commitments signals liberation from having to choose between or, crucially, sacrifice the pleasures (and profits) of either.

This striving for balance is characteristic of *Grazia*, evident in the range of topics included in the publication, yet it is particularly interesting to consider in relation to how these concerns are distributed in the lockdown issues. Coverage of the challenges of parenting and undertaking domestic labour was often published in the Hot Stories section or as a Grazia Feature, thereby framing these as issues relating to gender equality and requiring the reader's attention. When working from home was invoked, it always referenced undertaking professional paid employment from the home: 'working' in the context of the fashion coverage did not seem to include domestic labour or parenting. The challenge to be surmounted here (as remedied through the fashion content) was therefore not only the strangeness and isolation of working from home but the need to look professional while doing so—for the domestic environment to not destabilise the working woman's performance of competence. So much is evident in the language used to discursively construct the fashion items featured in a spread titled "Boss your WFH wardrobe—we've got an outfit for every home office scenario" (772, 58). The adjectives used to render the clothes meaningful mirror the dispositions they could produce in their wearer: "*hard-working* basics"; "*energising* florals"; "*smart* dresses" (59–61, my emphasis). By extension, we could read *Grazia*'s encouragement of readers to master WFH dressing, taking time to dream of a better future (and consume towards it) and embrace silly dressing as a means to both exhaust the affective incoherence prompted by the pandemic and to persevere—to be able to continue producing a capable, balanced and stylish individualised feminine subjectivity.

However, interestingly, this ideology was at times challenged within these same issues. Where *Grazia*'s ideal subject is "a savvy, affluent, confident, busy and modern woman who actively participates in the world around her" (Bauer Media Group n.d.), in these issues, the ground of her success is her ability simply to cope, ideally with a measure of humour, resilience and style. Seeing the lockdown as an opportunity to over-achieve and 'upskill' was gently critiqued, as evident in Polly Vernon's mockery of unrealistic goals, above, or in Issue 776's admonishment of Gwyneth Paltrow for treating lockdown like "a hybrid of an extended spa break and Open University degree" (23). By contrast, readers are given permission to not feel guilty "if all you're achieving is just coping. Be gentle on yourself and stay safe" (772, 23). That *Grazia* could accommodate these conflicting messages is consonant with the contradictory nature of women's magazines (see Winship 1987 and Gill 2007). Rosalind Gill reads this quality as indicative of "the fragmented nature of ideologies" (2007, 173) and the result of seeking to appeal to a diverse group while addressing them as if they all share a common lifeworld. Yet perhaps *Grazia*'s conflicting messages can be understood in this context not as the result of conflicting ideologies so much as the result of conflict between the neoliberal investment in the individual's ability to succeed if they just work hard enough and the ways in which the pandemic laid bare the futility of this ideology. A means of coping with the shock of the realisation—for *Grazia* staffers and by extension, their readers—of their limited agency was to find ways of replicating familiar behaviours (dressing for success, comforting and pleasing the self through fashion consumption) while acknowledging the overall alienation and anxiety of their circumstances.

Yet, at other times, *Grazia*'s lockdown-era issues reject this ideology entirely, moving away from the emphasis on the individual to advocate for community and question whether the pandemic might usher in systemic change. This content offers a glimpse of the political and affective affordances of women's media, a focus to which I now turn.

We're in This Together

One of the tensions inherent in women's magazines is that despite the intimacy of the discursive 'we' that presumes common female experience, the solutions to the social and political challenges of women's experiences are framed as resolvable at the level of the individual "with an emphasis on personal solutions at the expense of collective social or political struggle" (Gill 2007, 165). Berlant identifies "aloneness" as "one of the affective experiences of being collectively, structurally underprivileged" (2008, ix), so for women to encounter the fantasy of "my life [...as] an experience understood by other women" is one of the consolations offered by women's texts and their "commodified genres of intimacy" (x). The individual's ability to overcome is usually harnessed to her personal resources and consumption. As Brooke Erin Duffy argues, by harnessing a consumer ethos to idealised femininities, women's magazines "ostensibly convey the notion that women can resolve their problems within the marketplace" (2013, 34).

Yet in *Grazia*'s lockdown issues, three forms of collectivity surfaced, serving to shift the magazine's customary focus on the individual and elision of collective politics. These included acknowledging the comfort inherent in addressing the pandemic's collectively experienced ugly feelings; gesturing towards the importance of collective assumption of responsibility to address the pandemic's social exigencies; and encouraging readers to take advantage of the pandemic's interruption of 'normal life' to rethink consumption and question the fashion industry's unsustainability. These were all parsed in *Grazia*'s intimate tone and couched in the discursive construction of equivalence between magazine team and reader, framing our common experience as a way of 'getting through' to a better, kinder, more sustainable "new dawn" (777, 71).

While what is shared amongst the female readers of women's magazines tends to be vague and open-ended, the restrictions of the nationally mandated lockdown did induce a somewhat collective experience amongst the population. For *Grazia* to invoke feelings that 'we' were going through reflected a horizon of experience familiar to its readership of predominantly middle-class, professional, female readers, most of whom would have been either working from home or on furlough. While the issues did not consistently address the specificities of what readers may have found challenging, its assumption was that the lockdown was alienating and difficult for everyone, regardless of whether their particular strains related to childcare, being unpartnered, being pregnant, and so on. Readers, like *Grazia*'s editorial team, didn't know how long the lockdown would be in place or what short- and long-term effects the pandemic would have on their health, that of their loved ones, the economy or their livelihood. In this context, *Grazia*'s frequent references to the affective strain of the lockdown can be read as a continuation of the ways in which intimate publics suggest a "broadly common historical experience" and "commonly lived history" (2019, viii) but with direct resonance to the circumstances in which its predominantly professional-class readers found themselves. By addressing the multitudinous affects of the pandemic, the magazine fostered a "place of recognition and reflection" (2019, viii) and provided "anchors for realistic, critical assessment of the way things are" (2019, viii). This approach was successful for the title, which saw average issue sales increase by 65% compared with pre-pandemic sales, despite their shift in publishing from weekly to fortnightly (BOF Team 2020). There was comfort to be found in letting go—"the world feels like it's ending and you've run out of toilet roll, so why not relax and watch something nice?" (772, 77)—in letting clothes "lift your spirits" (776, 57). Everyday efforts to cope were framed as providing some ballast against the collectively experienced "strange, surreal and scary" (772, 3) "time of anxiety" (770, 10). That the *Grazia* team were in it with 'us' often came through in Editor Hattie Brett's 'Welcome to the Issue' letters, where she reflected on the disorienting speed of change and its implications for how the magazine was put together and what it focused on. "When we started planning this week's high street issue we could never have imagined that the world would be in the grips of a pandemic" (770, 3); "like a lot of you, the entire Grazia team is now working from home" (772, 3)—direct addresses that create a sense of equivalence between team and reader, further reiteration that, as Brett writes in Issue 771, "we're in this together" (3).

In such use of language, the *Grazia* team assume the role of Everywoman, a long-established rhetorical device of equivalence between magazine teams and readers. Indeed, journalists interviewed by Angela McRobbie for a study of women's magazines described the identification they felt with the readers of their publications, "making decisions and arguing their case by casting themselves as readers [... and seeing] themselves as actively assisting and thereby producing readers as fashionable young women" (1996, 179–180). While the lockdown issues still encouraged consumption, as organised by the expert eye and insider knowledge of the team, the expert orientation of the cultural intermediary was affectively reframed: the *Grazia* team discursively performed being as unmoored as their readers, thereby heightening the sense of a shared (overwhelming) experience and an open-ended sense of belonging and support. This work was supported by an audience research strategy *Grazia* implemented at the beginning of the pandemic: they "recruited 20 readers from across the country to be part of a WhatsApp group in which they discussed their changing habits, their feelings, hopes, and fears" which, according to publisher Lauren Holleyoake, offered insights on "what our audience needed from us" that then shaped *Grazia*'s content (Holleyoake in Browne-Swinburne 2021).

Fashion was also used as grounds for reflecting on how the collective nature of this experience might change one's values and perspective. Readers were invited to rethink the concept of luxury in 'The Great Rethink', a feature in Issue 777 in which a number of British fashion designers described what luxury meant for them during lockdown. Here, the common experience of having the rhythms of one's professional life interrupted and being restricted to one's domestic space—which, for many, may not have felt luxurious in any way—was framed as opportunity to re-evaluate one's perception of what is most rare and valuable. The kinds of luxuries described were predominantly relational, including "heightened appreciation for family" (Christopher Kane), "reassessing consumption" (Matty Bovan) and having time to spend with their children (Preen's Justin Thornton and Thea Bregazzi). Designers spoke about living with their parents, doing craft with their children and embracing simple pursuits such as looking at art, taking baths and reading.

The comfort of acknowledging that lockdown was a shared experience, however traumatising and disorienting, also galvanised through appeals to the reader to see their responsibility as a collective one: to act in accordance with guidance about minimising the spread of COVID-19 and to shop to save British jobs. For Issue 772, *Grazia* produced four alternate covers, each featuring an NHS worker in scrubs, briefly shot in the carpark of the hospital where she was on shift. The main coverline appealed to readers' sense of moral duty, reading, in part, "From the Frontline: 'We're putting ourselves in danger. Please help us help you'". [5] The accompanying article shared the four workers' accounts of the pain of caring for dying patients unable to say goodbye to their families, the dire need for more PPE, their fear that they'd spread the virus to loved ones and a direct appeal to readers: "I just need to know I can trust you to stay at home" (paramedic Sarah Blanchard, 15).

If these experiences offered a bracing insight into the 'frontline', at other points, the same issue offered encouragement by pointing to the ways citizens were working together as members of a community. "This pandemic is bringing out the best in us", declared the issue's Grazia View (772, 5). "It's easy to feel overwhelmed right now and spend evenings panic-scrolling [but] doom and gloom aside, this country is shaping up to be pretty incredible when it comes to handling a crisis" (5). Evidence of this included references to "community efforts to help neighbours who feel lonely or isolated and a rush of gifts being left on ambulances" (5). The invocation of a resilient national spirit and allusion to being at war with the virus paralleled comparisons being made in British media more generally at the time to Britons' 'Blitz spirit' during the Second World War. By referring to historical precedent, however applicable it may have been to the 2020 lockdown, the coronavirus pandemic was framed as a large-scale catastrophe that could be met—and eventually overcome—by communities working together and fostering a resilient spirit.

The importance of seeing one's contribution to society as a collective responsibility was framed differently in relation to the British high street. The issue that coincided with the start of lockdown happened to be a 'high street issue', devoted to covering what was new from fast fashion brands whose stores are found on the 'high street', a British term for the main street of a city or town where local shops and businesses are located (Office for National Statistics 2019). In her Welcome to the Issue, Hattie Brett wrote of her hope that "our high streets will remain [after the lockdown]; not only because they're a crucial part of our culture, but because they help connect communities" (770, 3). The next issue declared "Your shops need you!" referencing "Your country needs you" (Leete n.d.), the famous First World War propaganda campaign urging men to join the British war effort. In this story, shopping is constructed as a way of helping

---

[5] The four covers can be viewed on Bauer Media Group's website: www.bauermedia.co.uk/news/grazia-magazine-publishes-four-split-covers-featuring-four-frontline-nhs-workers-for-nhs-dedicated-issue.

by supporting the livelihood of fashion businesses and their employees. Focus is initially given to Italian fashion businesses, then at the "epicentre of Europe's coronavirus crisis" (770, 24) and therefore "need[ing] plenty of love right now" (24). Then readers are exhorted to prioritise shopping with small businesses and independent labels, their choices guided by the selection of clothes displayed alongside the text. Issue 777 reiterates this mindset by advising readers of the "homegrown labels [...] to be supporting now" (64), consumption conceptualised as a benevolent act. This discourse bears striking resemblance to the ways that American women were exhorted to "shop to save the country [...] and asked to do their part for the war effort" (Mayhall 2009, 34) in the wake of the 9/11 terrorist attacks. In this parallel instance, fashion consumerism was mobilised as a "key [factor] in the short-term economic and emotional recovery of the United States" (Pham 2011, 386) by politicians and prominent players within the fashion industry, effectively harnessing neoliberal concepts of individuality and self-determination to fashion (see Pham 2011).

However, the ethics of consuming anything at all is briefly questioned in Issue 776's "The Great Debate: Should you be shopping right now?" (54). The affirmative response emphasised the positive effects of shopping, perhaps best summarised by Laura Antonia Jordan's encouragement to readers to "take those reasons to smile where you can" (55). On the other hand, the negative position urges readers to take advantage of the disruption afforded by the pandemic to "reassess our relationship with our clothes" (56). The connection between responsibility and the high street shifts here, as Eco-Age founder Livia Firth, quoted in the piece, urges readers to think of the "millions of garment workers in countries such as Bangladesh or Cambodia [...] who are considered] disposable [...] abandoned by the fast-fashion brands they were producing for" (56). Firth here references the refusal of several US and European fast fashion brands to pay suppliers for orders placed before the outbreak of coronavirus, an outstanding debt estimated at £12.3bn (McNamara 2020). Yet, rather than dwell on this exploitation, the mood is re-set by Natalie Hammond, who encourages readers to look through what they already own to "unearth [...] gems that will put a spring in your step" (56). Indeed, *Grazia* only briefly gestures towards the extractive, exploitative practices of global fashion production; one other instance is in "The Great Rethink", where Kenya Hunt writes that even before the pandemic, the fashion industry "was at a crossroads, as questions about its relentless pace, enormous carbon footprint and patchy track record on diversity overshadowed the clothes" (44). Yet the possibilities afforded by the pandemic for consumers to pursue or demand more sustainable action from fashion producers were immediately foreclosed by the re-attachment of fashion to dress, to the individual. As in Hammond's piece, above, Hunt concludes that a solution lies in "get[ting] dressed in a more mindful way" (44).

By contrast, Issue 777 elaborates the notion of collective responsibility in a more directly political way in a story by British journalist Sarah Mower titled "How the fashion industry became an emergency service" (777, 13). The first sentence reads: "Who knew that an industry much-faulted for its superficiality, its feeding of narcissistic consumerism and its damage to the planet would be the very one to weigh in with pandemic emergency services much more quickly than many a Western government?" (14), immediately marking this as a very different kind of fashion feature than the magazine usually runs. From milliners in London's East End making face shields for hospital workers to Louis Vuitton making PPE in its factories, Mower praises the speedy response of "designers, mega-brands and manufacturers" and individuals—"bespoke tailors, students, citizen volunteers, drivers- people involved in fashion everywhere [...] and throughout the length and breadth of Britain"—responding to the lack of "central system in charge" (14). Indeed, Mower frames the failures of the UK government as putting "hurdles" in the way of the "extraordinary British women" leading community efforts. One example given is that of Caroline Gration, organiser of The Fashion School's sewing programme for children, whose daughter runs an ICU unit. She organised a "sanitised, socially-distanced production unit making surgical gowns from repurposed operating theatre drapes for the Royal Brompton Hospital" (14), taken as characteristic of "a kindness, a resourcefulness, and a capacity for work that could bring hope of employment all over Britain" (14). Frustration and fear are the ground from which agency is mobilised, the individual encouraged to admire—and ideally join—collective, community-based direct action. The trope of the neoliberal feminist, embodied here by Gration, is re-situated within a network of collective action, being offered as a relatable route into a collective mindset rather than as a heroine whose agency is testament to her alone. Moreover, importantly, Mower indicates here towards a better future reshaped by this collective work: "what we're learning through this time will count for the future of our country. It's taught us the power of localism, of what can be achieved even when there's no central system in charge" (14). The necessity of local, collective action to address the failures of government services is hardly a new concept, but that it is framed as such within this article demonstrates how unusual this message is within *Grazia*'s remit. Its political work, as introduced earlier, usually focuses on a single issue at a time, with a direct course of action for individual readers: sign the petition, write to your MP, be aware. What Mower outlines here is much more open-ended, inviting readers to question, "what effect this time will have on our loyalties in the future: will we want to see social responsibility literally woven into the fabric of what we buy?" (14)

Keep Shallow and Carry On

Issue 780 was released on 16 June 2020, the day after non-essential shops in the UK re-opened. Its main coverline read: "It's time to get dressed again! The best 're-entry' buys". While the issue devoted considerable space to addressing George Floyd's murder and the resulting widespread Black Lives Matter protests, the tone of the fashion content resumed a cautiously optimistic register. This is most evident in a feature by Hattie Crisell reflecting on how she lost her taste for getting dressed during the lockdown yet concluding on a hopeful note, as she anticipates what to wear to a birthday "as the first hints of movement emerge after a season of standing still. Something hopeful, something defiant, something fabulous […] We're back, after all—and fashion, our old friend, has waited for us" (47). Whatever glimpses the lockdown offered for *Grazia* to re-evaluate their commitment to promoting consumption, interrogate the practices of the fashion industry or encourage a collective mindset receded as soon as the restrictions started to ease.

What are we to make of this fascinating record, the "storehouses of information" these issues provide "about the values, social practices and behaviours of the [era] in which they [were] published" (Hunt 2012, 131)? We have seen how the timescale of *Grazia*'s production schedule resulted in content that mapped in real-time the pandemic's affective shifts, from disbelief in the first weeks of the lockdown, to the growing realisation of the scale and intensity of the crisis, to deep uncertainty of how to think about the future—indeed, of what kind of future would be waiting on the other side. One striking aspect of these issues was how their customary affective register could be suspended without destabilising their commitment to promoting consumption. By framing consuming fashion as an agentive response to the "flatness" and "ongoingness" of the pandemic's ugly feelings (Ngai 2005, 7), clothing was invested with the power to comfort, console and, at times, change the mood entirely. That this process was couched in personal experiences and laden with connotations of self-care and self-motivation demonstrated the resilience of neoliberal feminism as an ideological underpinning, even when any semblance of 'balance' between working and home life had evaporated.

At the same time, the shortening of the horizon of futurity against which *Grazia* could project opened a conditional space in which aspects the magazine rarely criticises or mentions could be voiced, however briefly and tentatively. The painful affects and disruption caused by the pandemic made this possible, just as the perception of leaving that period behind again made resonant discourses of unreserved fashion consumption. The lacuna opened by the pandemic's interruption of everyday life functioned as both prompt and space for reflecting on the ways the fashion system is predicated on unsustainable and unethical practices but that this was structured by negative affects meant that emerging from lockdown entailed a relieved escape from both the issues and the feelings.

While this case study exemplifies Berlant's argument that there is immense difficulty in "inducing structural transformation out of shifts in collective feeling" (2008, xii), it also reveals the flimsiness of neoliberal feminism's investment in consumer culture. The subtext of *Grazia*'s endorsement of clothes' capacities to boost the mood was that this capacity is ephemeral, transitory. What "power" does clothing offer beyond helping the wearer feel more able to meet the demands of their day? To what sustained end the mood-boosting? Getting dressed and consuming clothes certainly offer momentary pleasures and afford different ways of experiencing the self, but the gap between these capacities and the existential crisis posed by the pandemic revealed the need for more concerted, sustained political action to create a world in which the dignity and safety of human life could be maintained. The ephemerality of fashion's feelings showed their limits: they ameliorated but could not resolve. Framing the contents of consumer culture as some small consolation—not insignificant, but unable to truly a way forward to a better self and life—led the magazine to start exploring different ways that 'we' could project into the future. That this, too, was foreclosed by the return to discourses of fashion as integral to the realisation of a new self, ready to re-meet society, perhaps demonstrates how contingent that tentative political work was on the system being interrupted.

REFERENCES

Banet-Weiser, Sarah, Rosalind Gill, and Catherine Rottenberg. 2020. Postfeminism, Popular Feminism and Neoliberal Feminism? Sarah Banet-Weiser, Rosalind Gill and Catherine Rottenberg in Conversation. *Feminist Theory* 21 (1): 3–34. https://doi.org/10.1177/1464700119842555.

Bauer Media Group. 2020. Victory for Campaigners and Grazia Readers as Government Bans the 'Rough Sex' Defence. http://www.bauermedia.co.uk/newsroom/press-releases/victory-for-campaigners-and-grazia-readers-as-government-bans-the-rough-sex-defence. Accessed 7 March 2022.

———. n.d. Grazia Media Pack. http://www.bauermedia.co.uk/brands/grazia/. Accessed 7 March 2022.

Berlant, Lauren. 2008. *The Female Complaint: The Unfinished Business of Sentimentality in American Culture*. Durham and London: Duke University Press.

———. 2011. *Cruel Optimism*. Durham and London: Duke University Press.

BOF Team. 2020. #BoFLive: The State of Fashion Magazines. http://www.businessoffashion.com/articles/media/boflive-fashion-magazine-instyle-allure-harpers-bazaar-grazia-change-media. Accessed 20 April 2021.

Bradford, Julie. 2019. *Fashion Journalism*. 2nd ed. Milton: Taylor & Francis Group.

Browne-Swinburne, Jess. 2021. Lauren Holleyoake | Publisher | Grazia, Bauer Media. https://www.ppa.co.uk/article/lauren-holleyoake-or-publisher-or-grazia-bauer-media. Accessed 25 March 2022.

Duffy, Brooke Erin. 2013. *Remake, Remodel: Women's Magazines in the Digital Age*. Urbana and Springfield: University of Illinois.

Evans, Rhiannon. 2019. Grazia Asks Boris Johnson, Jeremy Corbyn and Jo Swinson: How Vain Are You? http://graziadaily.co.uk/life/in-the-news/boris-johnson-jeremy-corbyn/. Accessed 25 March 2022.

Felski, Rita. 1989. *Beyond Feminist Aesthetics: Feminist Literature and Social Change*. Cambridge: Harvard University Press.

Ferguson, Marjorie. 1983. *Forever Feminine: Women's Magazines and the Cult of Femininity*. London: Heinemann.

Gill, Rosalind. 2007. *Gender and the Media*. Cambridge: Polity.

Gough-Yates, Anna. 2003. *Understanding Women's Magazines: Publishing, Markets and Readerships*. London and New York: Routledge.

Hunt, Paula D. 2012. Editing Desire, Working Girl Wisdom and Cupcakeable Goodness: Helen Gurley Brown and the Triumph of Cosmopolitan. *Journalism History* 38 (3): 130–141. https://doi.org/10.1080/00947679.2012.12062882.

Institute for Government. n.d. Timeline of UK Coronavirus Lockdowns, March 2020 to March 2021. https://www.instituteforgovernment.org.uk/sites/default/files/timeline-lockdown-web.pdf. Accessed 4 May 2022.

Leete, Alfred. n.d. Your Country Needs You. http://www.iwm.org.uk/collections/item/object/16576. Accessed 14 March 2022.

Mayhall, Stacey L. 2009. Uncle Sam Wants You to Trade, Invest, and Shop! Relocating the Battlefield in the Gendered Discourses of the Pre- and Early Post-9/11 Period. *NWSA Journal* 21 (1): 29–50.

McNamara, Mei-Ling. 2020. World's Garment Workers Face Ruin as Fashion Brands Refuse to Pay $16bn. http://www.theguardian.com/global-development/2020/oct/08/worlds-garment-workers-face-ruin-as-fashion-brands-refuse-to-pay-16bn. Accessed 14 March 2022.

McRobbie, Angela. 1996. More! New Sexualities in Girls' and Women's Magazines. In *Cultural Studies and Communications*, ed. James Curran, David Morley, and Valerie Walkerdine, 172–194. London and New York: Arnold.

———. 2015. Notes on the Perfect: Competitive Femininity in Neoliberal Times. *Australian Feminist Studies* 30 (83): 3–20. https://doi.org/10.1080/08164649.2015.1011485.

Ngai, Sianne. 2005. *Ugly Feelings*. Cambridge, Mass: Harvard University Press.

Office of National Statistics. 2019. High Streets in Great Britain. https://www.ons.gov.uk/peoplepopulationandcommunity/populationandmigration/populationestimates/articles/highstreetsingreatbritain/2019-06-06#high-street-features. Accessed 9 May 2022.

Parkins, Ilya. 2021. "You'll Never Regret Going Bold": The Moods of Wedding Apparel on a Practical Wedding. *Fashion Theory* 25 (6): 799–817. https://doi.org/10.1080/1362704X.2020.1750832.

Pham, Minh-ha T. 2011. The Right to Fashion in the Age of Terrorism. *Signs* 36 (2): 385–410.

Rottenberg, Catherine. 2018. *The Rise of Neoliberal Feminism*. Oxford: Oxford University Press.

UK Geographics. n.d. Social Grade A, B, C1, C2, D, E. http://www.ukgeographics.co.uk/blog/social-grade-a-b-c1-c2-d-e. Accessed 7 March 2022.

Warner, Michael. 2002. *Publics and Counterpublics*. New York: Zone Books.

Winship, Janice. 1987. *Inside Women's Magazines*. London: Pandora Press.

CHAPTER 18

Afterword

Elspeth H. Brown

The pandemic drove me to sewing. As a queer person growing up in the 1970s, a young feminist in a Florida public high school that required a course called "Communism vs. Americanism," I refused to learn sewing. Girls learned to sew in the required home economics course; boys were required to take woodworking. I tried, and failed, to enroll in the woodworking course: it was for boys only. To me, sewing signified gender conformity and domesticity; woodworking connoted strength, expansiveness, and possibility. Years later, after university, I became a woodworker, building houses, millwork, and furniture for a series of small companies, eventually working on my own for a word-of-mouth network of friends and family. Woodworking brought together theory and praxis, head and hand, solitude and community—while at the same time enabling me to make a living. As the world shut down during the pandemic, with my woodworking years long behind me, I reconsidered sewing. I borrowed a machine from a colleague sewist and, like so many others, learned to sew courtesy of YouTube and some rescue interventions from generous, highly skilled

E. H. Brown (✉)
University of Toronto, Toronto, ON, Canada
e-mail: elspeth.brown@utoronto.ca

© The Author(s), under exclusive license to Springer Nature Switzerland AG 2023
R. Filippello, I. Parkins (eds.), *Fashion and Feeling*, Palgrave Studies in Fashion and the Body,
https://doi.org/10.1007/978-3-031-19100-8_18

friends. Sewing and woodworking, I realized, are a lot alike. They are both three-dimensional crafts that rely on plans, measuring, cutting, machines, and various forms of joinery. The main difference is that it's easier to wear clothing than it is furniture. If I had only had the advantage of reading this volume as a young person, I would have had a more complex and nuanced understanding of the relationship between fashion, feeling, materiality, and identity. Sewing clothing might have been a site of queer worldmaking, rather than the gender incarceration I perceived it to be.

As these fantastic essays show us, clothing is a technology of the self, a vibrant thing, in the Bill Brown sense; clothing collaborates with makers and wearers in the creation of new selves (Brown 2001). The essays, like fashion itself, bring together representation and materiality, mimesis and ontology. One powerful thread running throughout the collection speaks to clothing's capacity, as agential and vibrant matter, to absorb and carry feeling, from maker to wearer. Presley Mills and Justine Woods show in their lovely essay how a tiny hand-made object, a glass bead, has a "deep spiritual effect on our bodies because of the energy that was put into making it." Timo Rissanen movingly describes the practice of stitching as a site of spirituality and affective intensity, where sorrow and loss migrate from maker to material, imbuing cloth with a somber liveness. In their wonderful essay, Thuy Linh Nguyen Tu and Jessamyn Hatcher untangle the warp and woof of clothing made by WWI-era French garment workers to reveal the affective traces of their loss and fear in the midst of the Great War. In analyzing the collaboration between Stockholm's Nobel Museum and students at Stockholm's Beckmans College of Design and other institutions, Elizabeth M. Sheehan persuasively shows how peace is not only a political concept, but an affective and creative one as well. For all of these scholars, as well as several others in this volume, fashion and feeling come together as agential forces, doing things in the world.

One of the tremendous strengths of this ground-breaking volume is how several essays bring questions of representation into dialogue with fashion's material qualities. Rather than cordoning off fashion imagery from clothing's haptic and somatic dimensions, several essays chart new directions in showing how scholars bring a focus on representation into dialogue with fashion theory's engagement with affect. Sunny Xiang's brilliant essay on post-WWII leisure wear draws on both the era's Hollywood cinema and military records to explicate how imperialism and white fragility produced a militarized comfort that became an everyday fashion norm in the post-war years. In exploring the dark mood of contemporary New Zealand designers, Harriette Richards ingeniously pursues a close reading of their fashion shoots to map a melancholic, settler-colonial, structure of feeling. Bethan Bide, in expertly analyzing 1940s British comedy, explores how these films allowed audiences to navigate the complex emotional terrain of post-war life through their engagement with the clothing's materiality on screen. Masafumi Monden inventively shows how the metaphor of the school uniform in Japanese manga enables a more complex perception of ideal girlhood, what is known as shōjo. In her excellent analysis of Grazia UK's pandemic issues, Rosie Findlay argues that in response to the pandemic's "ugly feelings," the magazine discursively produced fashion as a site of sustenance for readers. Together, these essays bring the field's emphasis on representation into dialogue with affect studies, pointing the way toward new approaches with fashion studies that joins representation with material and somatic methodologies.

Indeed, the entire volume provides further evidence of what Lucia Ruggerone argues in her fine essay: the turn to affect has enabled a multiplicity of approaches to understanding fashion, including but not limited to representation. We see a range of creative and compelling methodologies in *Fashion and Feeling*. In her essay on the stain and ambivalence, Ellen Sampson uses a practice-based research methodology to understand both her own embodied experience and the stain as an "in between" object. In "Closet Feelings," Christina H. Moon draws on history, memoir, and creative non-fiction to craft a moving reflection on her own "closet archive." Eugénie Shinkle hilariously begins her essay with an autoethnographic confession, only to turn her observation on boredom into a treatise on its emancipatory potential. These essays, among others, further the field's movement toward understanding the relationship between the body, affect, and clothing in ways that account for visuality while, at the same time, offering suggestions for alternative methodologies that allow us to pose new questions.

Several essays ask us to think about not what fashion represents, but what fashion does to us or with us, in our embodied complexity. These contributions push the field toward fashion's performative potential, in the Butler sense: the capacity for clothes to make and remake subjectivity, perhaps the body itself. Renate Stauss' fascinating essay excavates the therapeutic thread of "dress therapy," exploring three iterations from 1959 San Francisco to contemporary Germany. She uses these examples of clothing's haptic dimensions to argue for scholars' engagement with fashion's materiality, to understand dress not only as a noun, but also as a technology of becoming. Ben Barry and Philippa Nesbitt, in their Cripping Masculinity fashion hacking workshops, collaborated with workshop participants to recreate personal garments to meaningfully express intersectional gender identities; their work together created a crip-centered liberated zone, a multidimensional community of love. Fashion, Otto Von Busch, shows us in his fine essay on magick, can change us: clothing is transformational, sparking metamorphosis.

Metamorphosis has long been a favored concept for trans activists, who have found the transformation from larva to butterfly a powerful metaphor for gender transition. Metamorphosis, for example, was the title of trans activist Rupert Raj's 1980s international newsletter, the period's most important resource for trans men seeking information about surgery, hormones, and other forms of support. Trans engagement with clothing and becoming suggests how two of fashion's strongest methodological approaches—representation and materiality—are mutually constitutive in the project of ontological transformation and identity confirmation. While we might see representation and materiality as separate affective pathways within fashion, they can be intertwined and reinforcing. For Raj, as well as for other transcestors such as Louise Lawrence, the project of affirming gender through dress was an ongoing process weighted with significance, stabilized or fixed through photographic representation. The selection and donning of clothing associated with a gender different from the one assigned at birth brought with it an ontological significance, confirming one's gender identity through clothing, but it was the representation of that transformation through photography that fixed the image, so to speak, for the wearer. Two examples suffice to explain my meaning. In Raj's case, one of his first acts after his parents' untimely passing when he was 16 was to "start wearing my father's tweed jacket and tie as a signifier of my male core" (Raj, 28) and to create a series of photographic self-portraits of himself wearing the jacket and tie, which he pasted into his photo album (Rupert Raj fonds). Trans activist Louise Lawrence, who collaborated with Alfred Kinsey in his late-career trans research, documented her first days of transition in a diary where dress figured prominently. On March 2, 1944, her first day, she wrote "dressed all day...so damned nervous. Can't do anything." Five days later, her first full day *en femme*, she began her diary with a reference to her clothing: "put on my red dress and black suede." For her as well, photography and representation played a key role in her transition: her archives at the Kinsey Institute include an entire folder of fashion images featuring an haute couture French model almost identical to Audrey Hepburn, as well as several boxes of color slides documenting herself and her network (Louise Lawrence Collection). For Raj and Lawrence, fashion and photography functioned as collaborative technologies of the self, working together to create new gendered ontologies.

The wonderful essays in *Fashion and Feeling* have succeeded in lighting a pathway for fashion scholarship for years to come. By bringing affect studies into dialogue with fashion studies, these contributions offer a wide array of compelling and inspiring approaches to understanding dress, clothes, and fashion in historical perspective. I will be carrying these provocations with me as I pursue my own research, and hope you do as well.

REFERENCES

Brown, Bill. 2001. Thing Theory. *Critical Inquiry* 28 (1): 1–22.
Louise Lawrence Collection. Box 5, Series IV, Folder 5, Kinsey Institute, Indiana.
Rupert Raj. 2020. *Dancing the Dialectic: True Trails of a Transgender Trailblazer*. 2nd ed. Victoria, MC: TransGender Publishing.
Rupert Raj Fonds. *The ArQuives: Canada's LGBQT2+ Archives*. Toronto ON.

INDEX[1]

A
Accountability, 115
Affective labour, 93, 277
Affective turn, 7, 12, 14
Affect theory, 1, 6, 8, 9n6, 10n7, 11, 12, 259
The Affect Theory Reader (Gregg and Seigworth), 180
Ahmed, Sara, 4, 11, 265
Aliveness, 140, 142, 144, 146, 149
Ambivalence, 186, 191, 192
Arpillera, 143
Ash, Juliet, 297
Augé, Marc, 88
Austerity, 67, 68, 71, 72, 74, 75, 78

B
Baert, Barbara, 185, 189
Barad, Karen, 181
Beadwork, 121, 127, 131, 133

Benjamin, Walter, 198
Bennett, Jane, 85, 89
Berger, John, 34
Berghan, Amie, 139, 141
Berlant, Lauren, 1, 2, 8, 10, 307–309, 311, 316, 323
Berlo, Janet Catherine, 144
Bodies of Fashion and the Fashioning of Subjectivity (Eckersley and Duff), 230
Boredom, 272, 273, 276, 277, 280
Bourdieu, Pierre, 66, 230
Brennan, Teresa, 239, 242, 243
Brown, Judith, 201
Bruno, Giuliana, 65

C
Callot Soeurs, 90, 91
Care work, 88
Celebrity, 216

[1] Note: Page numbers followed by 'n' refer to notes.

© The Author(s), under exclusive license to Springer Nature Switzerland AG 2023
R. Filippello, I. Parkins (eds.), *Fashion and Feeling*, Palgrave Studies in Fashion and the Body,
https://doi.org/10.1007/978-3-031-19100-8

Chandler, Eliza, 107, 112
Class, 69, 79
Closet, 27, 28, 31, 32
Closet archive, 33–37
Clothing industries, 84
Cold War, 42, 43
Colls, Rachel, 165, 171
Colonialism, 45, 46, 59, 264
Colonization, 122
Comfort, 43–45, 47–52, 54, 55, 58
Commodity, 93
Commodity fetishism, 90, 95
Commodity racism, 45
Community, 111, 112, 126
Corntassel, Jeff, 131
Costume, 63, 64, 67
Creativity, 197
Crip beauty, 112
Cripping, 100
Crip time, 104, 105
Crossley, Nick, 235
Cvetkovich, Ann, 11

D
Davis, Fred, 237, 286
The Deceptive Mirror: The Dressed Body Beyond Reflection (Ruggerone and Stauss), 240, 241
Decolonization, 124, 130–132
Decolonization is Not a Metaphor (Tuck and Yang), 130
Deleuze, Gilles, 6, 240–242
De Perthuis, Karen, 13
Desire, 277
Disability Justice, 99
Distress, 94
Dress therapy, 154

E
Eckersley, Andrea, 230
Embodiment, 70, 113, 115

Emotional histories, 80
Emotional improvisation, 69, 71, 79
Emotional practice, 78
Emotional regimes, 72, 79
Entanglement, 8, 179, 180
Entwistle, Joanne, 101, 111, 238, 263, 286
Eurocentricism, 133

F
Fashion atmosphere, 256
Fashion hacking, 100, 103, 109, 116
Fashioning Globalisation: New Zealand Design, Working Women and the Cultural Economy (Molloy and Larner), 252, 255, 256
Fashion photography, 276–278, 282
Fast fashion, 84
Faxneld, Per, 218
Featherstone, Mike, 224
Femininity, 159, 286, 289, 291
Ferrante, Elena, 37
Filippello, Roberto, 259
Findlay, Rosie, 252
Finkelstein, Joanne, 237
Flatley, Jonathan, 253, 255
Fleetwood, Nicole, 205
Foucault, Michel, 161, 164, 167, 232
Frantummàglia, 37
Free labour, 83, 84
Futurism, 58

G
Garment workers, 94, 96
Gaudry, Adam, 130
Gill, Rosalind, 315, 316
Girlhood, 286, 289
Glamour, 215, 225
Goffman, Erving, 160, 230, 232, 237
Grazia UK, 306
Greenwood, Susan, 212

Grief, 138, 144, 147, 150
Grunwald, Martin, 166, 167
Guattari, Félix, 6, 240–242

H
Habitus, 66
Hair, 288, 292, 293, 295, 298, 300
Haladyn, Julian, 273, 275, 281, 283
Heidegger, Martin, 274, 275
Heyes, Cressida, 232
Highmore, Ben, 253–255, 264
History of emotions, 66
Hollander, Anne, 287
Homoeroticism, 290
Honda, Masuko, 289, 292, 299
hooks, bell, 141
Hyper-realism, 78

I
Ignagni, Esther, 107
Imperialism, 42, 45, 52
Indian Act, 130
Indigenous knowledge, 122
Interdependence, 113
Intimate publics, 11
Iwashita, Hōsei, 287

J
Jangnong, 29, 30, 33

K
Kafai, Shayda, 101, 111, 114–116
Kafer, Alison, 104, 114
Kaiser, Susan, 222, 223
Kinship, 111, 112, 135
Klein, Melanie, 182, 183
Knowing through Needlework (Andrä et al), 142

L
Labour, 94, 105
Labour activism, 95
Lacan, Jacques, 234
Lakshmi Piepzna-Samarasinha, Leah, 105, 106
Law, John, 156
Leisure, 43, 44, 54, 55, 57
Lipovetsky, Gilles, 272, 274, 279
Liveliness, 86, 87, 201
Lorenz, Danielle, 130
Love, 101, 103, 105, 109

M
Magic, 211, 213, 222
Marshik, Celia, 198
Massumi, Brian, 7, 156, 280
Material experience, 63
Materiality, 64, 65, 68, 72, 75, 77–79, 84, 92, 138, 149
Material memory, 77
Mauss, Marcel, 230
McBrinn, Joseph, 144, 147
McClintock, Anne, 45
McRobbie, Angela, 310, 311, 317
Melancholy, 253, 256, 257, 263, 265
Memory, 30, 33–35, 297
Merleau-Ponty, Maurice, 235
Metts, Rod, 280
Militarism, 45, 59
Militourism, 42
Mingus, Mia, 99, 102, 110, 115, 117
Mirror, 233
Mobility, 55
Modelling, 203
Molloy, Maureen, 252
Mood, 16, 254, 255, 261, 263, 265, 266, 313

N
National identity, 79
National mood, 73
Needlework, 144, 146
Ngai, Sianne, 307, 311, 322
Nguyen Tu, Thuy Linh, 46

O
Ocularcentrism, 160, 169, 231, 234, 236
Ofek, Galia, 293, 299
O-Young, Lee, 29

P
Pandemic, 306, 317, 319, 320
Parkins, Ilya, 252, 312
Peace, 199
Postwar fashion, 53
Precarity, 2
Prete, Tiffany Dionne, 122, 123
Protection, 51, 52

R
Rabine, Leslie, 161
Racism, 49, 50, 57, 59
Regnault, Claire, 255, 258
Resurgence, 132
Rottenberg, Catherine, 310, 314
Rufo, Marcel, 162–165
Ruggerone, Lucia, 15, 154, 165, 188, 240, 264

S
Sampson, Ellen, 155, 160, 169
Sandywell, Barry, 273, 274, 281, 283
Scheer, Monique, 66
School uniform, 291, 295–301
Second skin, 45, 56, 58
Security, 168
Sedgwick, Eve Kosofsky, 9
Selvage, 91
Sexuality, 217
Shame, 184
Sheehan, Elizabeth M., 252
Shōjo, 286, 288, 289, 291, 292, 294, 296, 301
Simpson, Leanne, 126
Slater, Alison, 296
Slater, Lisa, 264
Social realism, 67
Sollee, Kristen, 212, 219
Specialization, 48
Spinoza, Baruch, 6
Stallybrass, Peter, 13, 87, 189, 294, 297, 298
Standardization, 48
Standard of living, 53, 59
Steele, Valerie, 197, 286, 288, 296
Stitching, 138
Storytelling, 124
Sullivan, Erin, 69
Sullivan, Nick, 54, 55
Surowiec, Catherine, 67
Sustainability, 200
Synnott, Anthony, 293
Synthetic fabrics, 55, 56, 58

T
Teaiwa, Teresia, 42, 57
Temporality, 76, 190, 204
Thrift, Nigel, 200, 214–216
Tomkins, Silvan, 9
Trauma, 149
Tu, Thuy Linh, 202
The Two Thousands: Our Fashion Moment (Hammonds and Regnault), 252

U
Unease, 253
Uniform, 42

V
Von Busch, Otto, 139, 140, 170, 222, 224

W
Wardrobe, 27, 28, 30
Ways of becoming, 15
Wear, 70, 73

Weitz, Rose, 293
Whiteness, 44, 45, 47, 49–51, 55, 57, 59
Wilson, Elizabeth, 215
Winship, Janice, 310, 311
Wissinger, Elizabeth, 203, 204, 206
World War II, 41

Y
Young, Iris Marion, 15, 161, 235

Z
Zahm, Olivier, 276, 279

Printed in the United States
by Baker & Taylor Publisher Services